M000032834

ARTHUR J MARDER was a meticulous researcher, teacher and writer who, born in 1910, was to become perhaps the most distinguished historian of the modern Royal Navy. He held a number of teaching posts in American universities and was to receive countless honours, as well as publish some fifteen major works on British naval history. He died in 1980.

BARRY GOUGH, the distinguished Canadian maritime and naval historian, is the author of *Historical Dreadnoughts: Arthur Marder, Stephen Roskill and the Battles for Naval History*, and contributed new introductions to Marder's five-volume history of the Royal Navy in the First World War *From the Dreadnought to Scapa Flow* and *From the Dardanelles to Oran*, all recently published by Seaforth Publishing.

Churchill with General Irwin, G.O.C. 11 Corps, on his left, and General Sir Ronald Adam, G.O.C. in C. Northern Command (far right) in East Anglia just before operation 'Menace' in 1940

OPERATION
MENACE

THE DAKAR EXPEDITION
AND THE DUDLEY NORTH AFFAIR

ARTHUR MARDER
INTRODUCTION BY BARRY GOUGH

Naval Institute Press
Annapolis

To
SAMUEL CLYDE McCULLOCH

with warm appreciation
for his steadfast friendship

Copyright © Arthur J Marder 1976
Introduction copyright @ Barry Gough 2016

First published in Great Britain in 2016 by
Seaforth Publishing,
Pen & Sword Books Ltd,
47 Church Street,
Barnsley S70 2AS

www.seaforthpublishing.com

Published and distributed in the
United States of America and Canada by the
Naval Institute Press,
291 Wood Road, Annapolis,
Maryland 21402-5034

www.nip.org

British Library Cataloguing in Publication Data
A catalogue record for this book is available from the British Library

Library of Congress Control Number: 2016934373

(UK) ISBN 978 1 84832 390 2
(US) ISBN 978 1 59114 725 1

All rights reserved. No part of this publication may be reproduced or transmitted in any form
or by any means, electronic or mechanical, including photocopying, recording, or any
information storage and retrieval system, without prior permission in writing of both the
copyright owner and the above publisher.

Printed and bound in Great Britain by CPI Group (UK) Ltd, Croydon, CR0 4YY

Introduction

THE GERMAN INVASION of France, the collapse of French military power, and the acceptance by France of an armistice with Germany and Italy indicated a great shift in the geopolitics of the Second World War in Europe. Hitherto an ally of Britain, the government of Bordeaux and then Vichy surrendered all autonomous action, and in so doing abandoned all formal allied connections with Britain. Although promise of a united government had been offered by the United Kingdom, this was set aside by the rapid turn of events.

On 4 July 1940 Winston Churchill, the Prime Minister, announced to the House of Commons measures taken to prevent the French Fleet from falling into German hands. The Bordeaux government had been given a chance to save the Fleet, and to allow it to sail unhindered to various British ports. Naval emissaries had with painful necessity appealed to French admirals to allow the ships to pass to the Royal Navy – and had failed in their task. London decided to destroy French naval units. At the time, and later in hindsight, British admirals – Cunningham, Somerville and North – thought that London's forceful policy of bringing the matter to a crisis by attacking French warships at the naval port of Oran, Mers-el-Kébir, was wrong. Churchill disagreed with the admirals: the capital ships of the French navy would have been placed within the power of Nazi Germany under the Armistice terms signed in the railway coach at Compiegne. 'The transference of these ships to Hitler would have endangered the security of Great Britain and the United States. We therefore had no choice but to act as we did, and to act forthwith. Our painful task is now complete.' And so the deadly stroke was executed, and Churchill never shied away from his responsibility in this. As General Wolfe remarked, 'war is an option of difficulties'.

On 20 August 1940 Churchill outlined in review the situation presented as to the disposition of the French Fleet. 'Shielded by overwhelming sea power, possessed of invaluable strategic bases and adequate funds, France might have remained one of the great combatants in the struggle.' Now all was changed.

That France alone should lie prostrate at this moment is the crime, not of a great and noble nation, but of what are called 'the men of

Vichy'. We have profound sympathy with the French people. Our old comradeship with France is not dead. In General de Gaulle and his gallant band, that comradeship takes an effective form. These free Frenchmen have been condemned to death by Vichy, but the day will come, as surely as the sun will rise tomorrow, when their names will be held in honour, and their names will be graven in stone in the streets and villages of a France restored in a liberated Europe to its full freedom and its ancient fame.

French defeat formed another chapter of sorrow to the British cause, for already the Norwegian campaign had ended in British withdrawal, the British army had been evacuated from Dunkirk, and Italian forces were powerful in the eastern Mediterranean, threatening the British base at Alexandria. With the fall of France all efforts of the French in the Mediterranean and in eastern Africa disappeared. Diplomats of the United States showed little faith that Britain could stand alone, inviolate, and suggested that the Royal Navy be based in Canadian and American east coast ports. These then were the desperate circumstances that Churchill's government faced when it acted to seize the French port of Dakar in Senegal in order to keep it out of German naval hands as a U-boat base (it would be a threat to convoys round the Cape to the Middle East) and gain a critically important toehold of empire for General de Gaulle and those who called themselves Free Frenchmen. Admiral Raeder had stressed to Hitler the advantages Dakar would give Germany and the critical role it could play in upsetting British maritime supremacy. There was much at stake. But the whole went horribly wrong.

The generalities of the history of this campaign were known when the American historian Arthur Jacob Marder (1910–1980) came to examine it. Marder was then a high ranking historian of the Royal Navy, author of the magisterial five-part *From the Dreadnought to Scapa Flow: The Royal Navy in the Fisher Era, 1904–1919* (1961–1970; reprinted by Seaforth Publishing and Naval Institute Press, 2013–2014). After that work's completion he turned to various high-intensity subjects in British naval history that were to take him through the inter-war years and right into the naval war against Imperial Japan. The volume here reprinted is one of these subjects (or rather two, for they are a pairing), large enough in complexity and documentation for significant historical analysis. They address subjects of perennial fascination.

It bears noting that Marder was barred from writing a general history of the Royal Navy in the inter-war period because his great rival, Captain Stephen Roskill, the official naval historian who had authored *The War at Sea* (three volumes of four, 1954–1962), had gone on to produce the two volumes entitled *Naval Policy between the Wars* (1968–1976; reprinted by Seaforth Publishing and Naval Instute Press 2016). As Marder put it, Roskill 'had preempted the period'. Marder thus determined to work away at case studies. One such, 'The Royal Navy and the Ethiopian Crisis of 1935-1936', appeared in the *American Historical Review*. Another, '"Winston is Back": Churchill at the Admiralty, 1939-1940' – all about Churchill's return to the Admiralty, where he had been from 1911 until May 1915 – was a case study showing that, contrary to widely-held views, Churchill did not dominate Admiral Sir Dudley Pound, the First Sea Lord. A third, 'Oran, 3 July 1940: Mistaken Judgement, Tragic Misunderstanding, or Cruel Necessity?' brought Marder into the core of Anglo-French naval relations, and revealed his many contacts with retired British naval officers (or keepers of their papers).

Each of these case studies constitutes a commentary on the Royal Navy in those very circumstances that tested its mettle during war or in phases of peace in the run-up to the Second World War, more specifically during the years 1939 to 1941. Marder provides insights into the relationships between statesmen and admirals, the complexities of naval administration, and the higher management of war policy. Marder remained fascinated by 'the war behind the war'. As Stephen Roskill commented in *Churchill and the Admirals*:

> The Admiralty, unlike the War Office and Air Ministry, was an operational centre as well as an administrative department, and the Board of Admiralty was invested with wide powers of instruction to and direction of naval forces. The extent to which those powers were used depended chiefly on the personalities, preferences and outlook of the First Lord and the First Sea Lord.

And at, or near, the centre was that remarkable agent for directing the war, Churchill, whether First Lord or Prime Minister (or Minister of Defence). Roskill's undisclosed premise was that in naval matters the Navy must be presumed right. Churchill, since his days with Admiral Lord Fisher at the Admiralty, assumed he knew the business of the Admiralty better than the admirals. Therein lay the difficulties, 'the war behind the war'.

For years Marder compiled notes on Churchill and naval affairs and these grew into his 'Winston Churchill' project. He had opened correspondence with retired naval officers and civil servants, notably Admiralty secretaries knowledgeable about those years. As Marder's fame spread, the number of correspondents increased. An initial exchange of letters could lead to several revelations, with Marder pressing on his opposite for answers to this issue or that question.

As an example, Sir Eric Seal, who had served at the Admiralty before the war and became Churchill's private secretary at the outbreak of hostilities, held that interference from Whitehall was not Churchill's work but the spontaneous action of the Naval Staff and in particular Admiral Sir Dudley Pound and Vice Admiral Sir Tom Phillips (Vice Chief of Naval Staff). To Marder Seal put it this way:

> The plain fact of the matter was that Dudley Pound, who had recently been C-in-C Med, found it very difficult to keep his hands off the control of the fleet, and he certainly had more and better information. But much suspicion attached to Winston, partly as an echo of the Dardanelles, and partly because it was generally known that he was always in the War Room, to which he was irresistibly attracted. Being aware of the Dardanelles legend, I was very alert to the problem. I am quite satisfied that Winston took scrupulous care not to transgress the proper limits of Naval and Political responsibility, and not to force his view on any professional decision.

Seal continued in defence of Churchill, his chief: 'May I say that I think that I am almost the sole survivor of those who were close to Winston as First Lord, senior enough to know what it was all about, and I feel a corresponding responsibility.' Seal recounted how Churchill, when reading the draft text, had become disturbed by Roskill's official *The War at Sea*, 'which enlarged upon the undoubted fact that the Admiralty had intervened seriously in Naval operations in the early years and suggested, quite falsely, that the prime factor in this was Churchill's influence as First Lord'. When the text of the first volume of Roskill's *The War at Sea* came to the Cabinet Committee for approval in advance of publication, Churchill, then Prime Minister, grew alarmed by Roskill's inference that the First Lord had meddled in naval operations in Norway. Churchill then sent Seal to examine the Norway campaign records; he had found that there was no undue interference on the part of the First Lord. In the end, the irritated and emotionally exhausted Roskill was obliged to make some changes and then the work was released for printing and binding. This was 1954 and Seal had not forgotten.

In contrast to Roskill, Marder saw naval relations from a different perspective. Widespread opinion existed within the Navy that politicians usually misunderstood or bungled the affairs of state in regards to defence matters. Marder took a contrary view. Two themes stand out. First, he argued, the Navy was not an expensive toy placed at the disposal of admirals in wartime: it was an instrument of national policy. Churchill had a clear idea of what the Navy could do, and Pound was in accord with this view. Secondly, he contended, because Churchill was an historian of considerable merit, 'it could not have escaped him that throughout English naval history, when the admirals had been left to their own devices, they had made a mess of things, and that it was only when there had been strong political direction at the top, as in the Seven Years War and the Napoleonic War, that the Navy had really achieved the full measure of its capability'. Marder tipped the scale in favour of the professionals yet at the same time concluded that Churchill did not dominate his professional advisors. Did, therefore, Churchill infuse a new climate of morale into the administration of the Navy? Was this his greatest gift? And was Pound immune to Churchill's independent judgments and schemes that others classified as ill thought out? Reading Marder's account '"Winston is Back": Churchill at the Admiralty, 1939–1940' we can see Seal's influence on every page. 'Read this account and shudder', commented the *Navy News*, July 1972. 'The factual account of Churchill's forays into professional realms, and the general muddle of the early war months, require the reader to remind himself constantly of Winston's morale-building influence, lest the conclusions become distorted.'

Marder's next subject offered the first fully documented account of the British attack on French warships at Oran. If in Churchill's mind the end result was never in doubt, to almost everyone else the whole was problematic, fraught with difficulty, and even regarded as morally reprehensible. The whole constitutes an extraordinary episode in modern annals. No dramatist could ever have conceived of it. The human dimensions run deep, charged as they are with pathos and sympathy. There is the sense of the inevitable, too, though Marder had always wondered if a more skilful handling of negotiations might have avoided all the bloodshed and the bitterness. 'It was an absolutely bloody business to shoot up those Frenchmen who showed the greatest gallantry,' commented Admiral Sir James Somerville of Force H that steamed from Gibraltar to execute orders from London (if a final attempt at naval diplomatic relations with the French admiral failed, which they did).

Did Churchill really have realistic fears about Germany using the French warships? Marder makes a convincing case that the respective governments and their respective naval negotiators could not avoid the calamity. Churchill was ruthless. Perhaps he exaggerated the danger of the French fleet falling into enemy hands. On the other hand, as Peter Kemp put it in his *Victory at Sea*, 'the whole balance of sea power, now the only hope left to Britain of winning the war hung poised precariously on the integrity of the German assurances to France. And there was no lack of evidence as to the value of a German assurance'. Churchill acted under the pressure of circumstances and at a time of great British weakness. Britain's fortunes and prestige were then at their lowest ebb. The attack was 'a cruel necessity'. Churchill, in his own history of the event, described the arc of the story as a Greek tragedy, and in his analysis Marder follows equally strongly. Here is an example of Marder at his best – a master of his sources, specific in his definition of the historian's tasks, organised in his narrative, and capable of telling a story with conviction and appeal. (These studies, with others, were published in updated and expanded form in *From the Dardanelles to Oran: Studies of the Royal Navy in War and Peace 1915–1940* (1974; reprinted by Seaforth Publishing and Naval Institute Press, 2015).

From his study of the Oran operation of 3 July 1940 Marder turned his attention to the expedition of September 1940. Marder's agenda was the Dakar adventure. This became *Operation Menace: The Dakar Expedition and the Dudley North Affair* (1976). While the operation was being planned, the Battle of Britain was being waged; invasion was expected daily; and a crisis in the Middle East appeared imminent.

In theory the Dakar expedition of 3 July 1940 seemed sound enough. General Charles de Gaulle, newly arrived in London to raise the standard of Free France, would be landed at the Senegal port with a small force. The transporting and covering of the force would be, in the main, a British commitment. Once placed ashore the force would raise the flag. The locals would rally round the new but relatively unknown leader. A new anchor of a non-Vichy France could be established. Any move by Hitler or Pétain in West Africa would be forestalled.

So far so good. The unravelling tragedy had comic beginnings. De Gaulle, never one to shy away from the press, arrived at Simpson's Piccadilly to be kitted out in tropical dress, explaining in booming voice that his destination was West Africa. Nearby, in Jermyn Street, Free French officers filled the restaurant Ecu de France with stirring toasts of 'à Dakar!' At Euston Station (en route to the embarkation port, Liverpool) a case of leaflets addressed 'Aux habitants de Dakar' broke open and were scattered in the breeze. Incredibly, neither Vichy nor the enemy got wind of the operation.

Independent of these comic turns in Piccadilly and Euston, the Vichy government had decided to send three cruisers and three destroyers from Toulon to Dakar. The British consul in Tangier and the British naval attaché in Madrid learned of this Vichy squadron, and independently passed secret messages to London that the French warships would pass through Gibraltar Straits on 11 September. But the messages sat in an in-tray, and by the time the Admiralty was alert to proceedings the French ships had passed through in broad daylight and clear, unobstructed waters lay ahead. They reached Dakar. When the Anglo-Free French force, with de Gaulle, his officers and men aboard, arrived off Dakar, heavy fog lay off the coast. In an ill-judged contest with guns ashore the Royal Navy suffered damage, and after two days, now in brilliant sunshine, the force made its humiliating withdrawal. Churchill ordered the termination of the mission.

An integral aspect of this sorry saga was the highly controversial story of Admiral Sir Dudley North, then Flag Officer commanding at Gibraltar. He had injudiciously told the Board of Admiralty that he disagreed with the previous Mers el-Kébir (Oran) operation, when the Royal Navy had bombarded the French fleet at anchor. By taking no action against the French warships passing through the Strait of Gibraltar he invoked Admiral Sir Dudley Pound's ire. Churchill had wanted North removed after the Oran signal. North now had to go. He was superseded in his command for negligently allowing a French naval squadron to pass out of the Mediterranean, thus jeopardising the Dakar operation. We will return to this presently.

Marder revealed that as a military operation Menace was undertaken at the insistence of Churchill, its enthusiastic chief sponsor, against all professional advice. 'Churchill was eager during July for a military adventure somewhere that might divert the Germans from the British Isles, enhance British prestige and raise morale at home.' It proved a tragic farce. In Marder's words: '"Menace" exemplifies ... all that can go wrong in warfare: an operation fouled up by unforeseen contingencies, the accidents of war, and human error, and against a background of undue political interference, inadequate planning, and half-baked co-operation between Allies.' Marder saw in this a tale of classic, tragic-comic proportions specifically illustrative of the fog of war. In reviewing Marder's book, in *The English Historical Review*,

Professor Brian Bond was so struck by the many similarities between Dakar and the Dardanelles that it was tempting to blame Service advisors of 1940 for neglecting the 'lessons of history'; Churchill had been the prime mover on both occasions, when political considerations overrode professional advice. In fact, the Joint Planning Staff had told Churchill directly that an operation that relied on the co-operation of the enemy (Vichy France) did not provide a sound basis for planning. In the end there were few if any Germans in Dakar and it was the soldiers of Vichy France who put up stout resistance. The Germans were so impressed by this show that they saw no need to occupy Morocco or French West Africa.

Seldom do books of historical scholarship, written by academics, receive exalted acclaim. Yet such was the case with *Operation 'Menace'*. Reviewers John Litchfield, A B Sainsbury, A J P Taylor and Ronald Lewin gave it their highest praise. They (and others) spoke of the book as being the last word on the subject, the definitive treatment. They were equally excited about the example it offered of war being the extension of politics by other means, as Clausewitz said. Litchfield wrote that, 'Marder, as ever, writes with real understanding of the Royal Navy, of whose ways and leading characters he has, in some miraculous way as an American acquired an extraordinarily accurate perception.' Sainsbury, with a keen eye on the Marder-Roskill dispute (as told in detail in my *Historical Dreadnoughts*) took pains to set Marder's new appraisal against Roskill's 'official history'. Time and new evidence had deepened the story.

> Its construction is a microcosm of Marder's methodology. The diligent use of published sources, the hunting down and use of private papers and of individual recollections; the distillation of all this energetically accumulated evidence into a readable text, spiced with a mixture of some occasionally questionable and other more magisterial *obiter*.

Marder had not told much more than his confrere Stephen Roskill had done in *The War at Sea*, but that had been published in 1954. However, the scope allowed Marder more promise: 'Hence, we are grateful for his expanded and racier account, with more detail than was available to or could be used by the official historian.' Sainsbury had brought the Marder-Roskill dispute into the review pages. Taylor, with a wider view, comparing Marder's book to *The Guns of Dakar*, written by criminologist and historian John Williams and published concurrently, thought the latter slighter and less austere: 'It also fills Marder's one deficiency: a reluctance to look over "the other side of the hill" to discover what the enemy (in this case the Vichy French) were doing.' Lewin, comparing the same two books, set the tone of his review at the outset:

> Come home, Evelyn Waugh: all is forgiven. How often has it seemed that your brilliantly sardonic and deflationary novels merely present a minor truth about the British at war, whilst ignoring the main point. Your soldiers, hilarious boobies, rarely look like matching up to Alamein or Normandy. But now, on the unimpeachable evidence of these two books, we discover that your picture in *Men at Arms* of Operation Menace (where you were among those present) is not just one of your idiosyncratic caricatures. As you sit with Voltaire, please accept this signal admitting that you told the truth, nothing but the truth, and a great deal less than the grotesque pathetic reality. After the fiasco, one of *Ark Royal's* pilots, who had had a rough time, explained: 'Operation Menace' – I call it Operation Muddle!

It is said that at White's, Waugh's London club, the story of the fiasco was regular repertoire, and true it is that a scriptwriter had no need to embellish the details. They stood on their own. The particulars and anecdotes were not lost on Marder who gave them extended life in brilliant description. He had no shortage of eyewitnesses. Though Waugh's *Men at Arms* had enshrined the story, Marder had written the true history.

Marder's book offered a cautionary tale for those tempted to believe that 'war is too serious a business to be left to the generals'. At the same time the Dakar fiasco showed that war is too professional a business to be left to political strategists. But to this discussion was added a second part: Marder's treatment of the controversial Dudley North affair, which was indirectly connected with the events at Dakar. Marder's book thus offered two tickets of admission for the price of one, as John Terraine noted. Few incidents in the Second World War led to such accusations of injustice, which involved, besides North, Pound and, by implication, Churchill, then Prime Minister. After five years in command of the Royal Yacht Squadron, North was appointed to Gibraltar as Flag Officer North Atlantic. Pound had chosen him for the job, a safe hole and essentially an administrative position. With the fall of France the appointment assumed greater importance. North imprudently expressed strong feelings about the Navy's recent attack on the French fleet at Oran. Twelve days before Operation 'Menace' was put in motion three Vichy French cruisers and three destroyers were allowed to pass through the Strait of Gibraltar; North took no steps to intercept them, shadow them, or ascertain their destination.

On Pound's advice, their Lordships, having lost confidence in North who failed 'in an emergency to take all prudent precautions without waiting for Admiralty instructions,' relieved him of command. But the Board went beyond that: they spelled out their reasons in terms that amounted to a charge of negligence. North demanded a court martial to clear his name. Their Lordships declined. North remained alive and would prove litigious. Marder followed the saga through its seventeen years (eight successive First Sea Lords were burdened by it) until in 1957 the Prime Minister, Harold Macmillan, cleared North's honour without endorsing his actions. Four years later, North died.

Marder's revisiting of Roskill's treatment of the Dudley North affair enhanced an already public conflict between the two historians. Marder's interpretation – that Pound played the key role in North's downfall – is more convincing, for it rests upon North's limitations as an officer of flag rank and on Pound's own personality traits when confronted by what he viewed as incompetence. Both Marder and Roskill remained conscious that North received punishment far harsher than the rather foggy evidence of his supposed negligence could ever justify. Indeed, all parties involved – North, Admiral Sir James Somerville (C-in-C Mediterranean), the Admiralty, Churchill, Pound and even the Foreign Office (for neglecting to decode promptly the original Tangier message) can all bear some measure of blame in this unfortunate but all too common wartime occurrence when the chains of command and responsibility are not clearly articulated.

It is worth noting that Roskill's correspondence shows that Churchill ordered North's dismissal. When Roskill's first volume of *The War at Sea*, then in draft form, came to the Admiralty for discussion it faced difficulties. From a safe in his office, Sir John Lang, the Secretary of the Admiralty, produced a letter written by Churchill ordering that North be dismissed.

Marder died in 1980 in his seventieth year. His friend Peter Kemp, naval officer and historian of note, paid him the great compliment of calling Marder the supreme historian. What Kemp identified in Marder, many others had witnessed first hand: Marder's great courage in redoing that segment of *From the Dreadnought to Scapa Flow* lost to the incinerator in consequence of janitorial error, and Marder's great happiness in his work. Kemp stated that Marder demonstrated a marked modesty, and he was right, for modesty was the handmaiden of Marder's simplicity of approach and his insistence on forming no preconceived notions, let alone conclusions. He had opposed military historians 'of the drum and bugle type' and had sought something much more comprehensive, something more substantial. He liked to cite Homer's 'After the event any fool can be wise'. Right to the end Marder defended his historical method of using details and particulars to sustain a powerful narrative. In his journal articles and book chapters he was necessarily more constrained, owing to circumstances. Resisting any desire to tilt at historical windmills or take on the theories of other historians, Marder stuck to the historical records. Of course, he was not faultless in the selection of materials, and on occasion he failed to weigh correctly the testimony of various informants; in certain cases or episodes, he may be said to have gone overboard by the needless recounting of supporting evidence. In disputatious matters he liked to have the last word. But these, his critics noted, did not appreciably weaken his great work. It is a fascinating fact that those who endeavour to rework his historical corpus deal almost exclusively with only the first three volumes of *From the Dreadnought to Scapa Flow* and then only on specific aspects. The feud between Marder and Roskill may provide titillations for naval historians who know those times or have followed these 'historical dreadnoughts' by reputation. But it is not the essential factor in how we judge historians of Marder's elevated class, or of Roskill's either. Roskill had put it best, in 1966, when he wrote graciously about Marder: fortune had smiled on the Royal Navy when a scholar of Marder's distinctions and abilities had come along to write its history. That is why Marder still commands our attention.

As to Churchill's responsibilities and abiding influences in the Dakar episode and the North affair, his influence is clear. He dominated wherever and whenever he could – and he was often wrong. 'Menace' cost the Navy a battleship out of action for a year and a cruiser for six months, plus nineteen aircraft destroyed. There was an additional cost in terms of Britain's prestige, as Correlli Barnett explains. The American military attaché in London regarded 'Menace' as 'probably another of Churchill's military inspirations, like Antwerp,' writing that it 'appears to have been as great a mistake as the attempt upon Norway'. Barnett makes clear that 'Menace,' coming on top of Norway, taught Churchill nothing: 'his enthusiasm for quickly cobbled up combined operations still remained quenchless.'

Sources

Churchill speeches quoted or cited are in Winston S Churchill, *Blood, Sweat, and Tears* (1941). A survey of Churchill and Dakar is in Martin Gilbert, *Finest Hour: Winston S. Churchill, 1939-1941* (1983) based on Churchill papers (now in Churchill Archives Centre, Cambridge) and Premier files (The National Archives, Kew). See also, Martin Gilbert (ed) *The Churchill War Papers: Never Surrender, Volume 2, May 1940 – December 1940* (1995). On Churchill: David Jablonsky, *Churchill, the Great Game and Total War* (1991). For a concise account of Dakar revelatory of Churchill's penchant for combined operations: Correlli Barnett, *Engage the Enemy More Closely: the Royal Navy in the Second World War* (1991). Peter K Kemp, *Victory at Sea 1939-1945* (1957). Differences between Marder and Roskill (also Roskill's difficulties with Churchill re: Norway campaign and other naval operations, including Dakar) may be followed in Barry Gough, *Historical Dreadnoughts: Arthur Marder, Stephen Roskill and Battles for Naval History* (2010). This last contains a bibliography of Marder's works and, necessarily, one of his sparring partner Roskill. Roskill's rejoinder to Marder's '"Winston is Back"' (as it first appeared in *The English Historical Review*, Supplement 5, 1972) is published as 'Marder, Churchill, and the Admiralty' *RUSI Journal*, December 1972. For Roskill's commentary on Marder and a general appreciation of Churchill's direction of the war in regards to Dakar, see his *Churchill and the Admirals* (1977), reviewed analytically by Ronald Lewin, in *International Affairs*, July 1978. On Pound, Robin Brodhurst, *Churchill's Anchor* (2000).

Among reviews of Marder's *Operation 'Menace'* are: John Litchfield, *Naval Review*, April 1976; A B Sainsbury, *The Mariner's Mirror*, 62, 1, 1976; A J P Taylor, *The Observer*, 8 February 1976; Ronald Lewin, *The Listener*, 18 March 1976. Also, David Stafford, *American Historical Review*, 82, February 1977; E J Grove, *History*, October 1977; Bryan Ranft, *War and Society*, 1976; John Terraine, *Daily Telegraph*, [?] February 1976; Brian Schofield, *RUSI Journal*, June 1976; *Navy News*, February 1977; *Globe & Laurel* (Royal Marines), May–June 1976; *Economist*, 7 February 1976; Michael Wolff, *The Times*, 5 February 1976; Correlli Barnett, *Eastern Daily Press*, 27 February 1976; C V Collinet, *Revue d'hist 2e Guerre*, 111 (1978); J-M d'Hoop, *Revue historique*, 257 (1977).

BARRY GOUGH
Victoria, BC, Canada

Preface

I was attracted to the subject of this volume by various considerations. The Dakar expedition was in some respects a sequel to the Oran (Mers-el-Kébir) operation of 3 July 1940, which had constituted the last chapter of my last book.* Dakar continued the sad story of the confrontation of two Fleets, allied but a short time before, and it highlighted, as had Oran, the controversial role of Churchill as Prime Minister in the making of strategy. Was Dakar but another example of Churchill as an amateur and meddlesome strategist, as his critics would have it? There was also the attraction of becoming acquainted with that most fascinating of Frenchmen, de Gaulle, and of studying the subsequent fortunes of two of the main characters in the Oran affair, Admirals Sir Dudley North and Sir James Somerville, to whom I had become attached. There were yet other considerations. 'Menace' exemplifies, in its genesis, planning, and execution, all that can go wrong in warfare: an operation fouled up by unforeseen contingencies, the accidents of war, and human error, and against a background of undue political interference, inadequate planning, and half-baked co-operation between Allies. I thought it would prove an interesting, and perhaps even a useful, exercise if I treated 'Menace' as a sort of case history in how an operational plan comes into being and all that can go wrong with it. Marshal of the Royal Air Force Sir John Slessor had piqued my interest in 'Menace' with the assertion in a letter that it was 'a fantastic affair if ever there was one', and Admiral of the Fleet Earl Mountbatten of Burma had done the same for the North facet of 'Menace' by declaring that 'he was sacked under the most disgraceful conditions—*absolutely* inexcusable'.† Was that an accurate description? Could there be more to the story? Finally, the paucity of detailed published accounts of Dakar or the North Affair was an invitation to proceed.‡

* *From the Dardanelles to Oran: Studies of the Royal Navy in War and Peace, 1915-1940* (London, 1974), pp. 179-288.

† Lord Mountbatten in a taped interview with Mr. Richard Hough, 28 June 1973, for the latter's book *Louis and Victoria* (1974).

‡ As I write, there have been only two full-length studies of 'Menace': Jacques Mordal's *La Bataille de Dakar* (1956) and an 'intimate personal account' from the angle of the Spears Mission to de Gaulle, by Colonel John A. Watson: *Échec à Dakar* (1968). There is one detailed, though journalistic and hastily compiled, treatment of the North

I owe a special debt of gratitude to Lord Mountbatten and Sir John Slessor for encouraging me to undertake this study, and to the former for answering many questions, via correspondence, on the North Affair (he was the First Sea Lord in 1955-7, when the Affair was coming to a boil) and to the latter for putting his papers on the case at my disposal and reading the manuscript with care. Slessor, who was Director of Plans at the Air Ministry at the time of 'Menace', had planned a study of the North aspect. To this special company I must add Captain J. S. S. Litchfield (Joint Planning Staff in 1940), who also provided me with relevant contemporary diary extracts, Lieutenant-Commander P. K. Kemp (the onetime Head of the Naval Historical Branch and Naval Librarian, Ministry of Defence), and Mr. Richard Hough, all of whom read the manuscript to its great profit. My warm thanks also go out to Colonel John A. Watson (Personal Assistant to General Spears during 'Menace'), Captain P. N. Walter (CSO to Admiral Sir John Cunningham), Commander T. C. Crease (Cunningham's Staff Officer (Operations)), and Colonel C. Hettier de Boislambert (a close associate of de Gaulle's in 1940), for a constructive reading of Part I, and to Colonel Pierre Gotscho-Granville (with the Free French Forces) and Lieutenant-Colonel Pierre Julitte (Signals Officer of the Free French Forces), who read selected portions of Part I and made a number of valuable suggestions. All the above-mentioned gentlemen patiently answered a great many queries. The usual assurance is in order: I, and I alone, am responsible for any errors, whether of fact or interpretation, that remain.

I am thankful to the following, who generously shared their recollections: Admiral of the Fleet Sir Algernon Willis, Admirals Sir William Davis (VCNS, 1954-7) and Sir Richard Onslow (Inter-Services Planning Staff, 1940, Naval Secretary to the First Lord, 1952-4) (the latter also read the first three chapters); Vice-Admiral Sir Peter Gretton (Naval Assistant to the First Sea Lord, 1950-2); Rear-Admiral T. L. Eddison (Gunnery Officer of the battleship *Resolution*); Captains G. R. G. Allen (Churchill's naval expert when he was writing his *History of the Second World War*), L. H. Bell (Naval Assistant to VCNS, 1939-41), who also furnished me with pertinent excerpts from his diary, Geoffrey Bennett (on the staff of the C-in-C, South Atlantic), R. P. S. Grant (a junior officer in the

Affair: Noel Monks, *That Day at Gibraltar* (1957). For good local colour and perceptive observations on 'Menace' there is Major-General Sir Edward Spears's splendid *Two Men Who Saved France* (1966).

cruiser *Devonshire*), Ford Hammill (commanded the cruiser *Cornwall* in the preliminaries to Dakar), A. H. Hillgarth (Naval Attaché, Madrid), H. F. Layman (commanded the destroyer *Hotspur*), who also sent me various papers of interest, and R. R. Stewart (commanded the cruiser *Australia*); Commanders A. J. Cobham (a lieutenant in the battleship *Barham*), N. R. Corbet-Milward (a Swordfish pilot in the aircraft carrier *Ark Royal*), and J. R. Lang (a lieutenant in the *Ark Royal*); General Lord Bourne (ISPS, 1940), General Sir Ian Riches (Brigade Major to Brigadier St. Clair-Morford, commanding the Royal Marine Brigade), the late Major-General Sir Edward Spears, Bt. (Head of the British Mission to de Gaulle), who also loaned me his invaluable Dakar diary, and Major-General A. N. Williams (who as a lieutenant-colonel commanded the 2nd Battalion, Royal Marines); Majors A. S. Irwin (a 2nd lieutenant on the Command Staff in the operation), who provided important source materials, and R. P. Owen, RM (*Devonshire*); the Rt. Hon. James Callaghan, H.M. Secretary of State for Foreign Affairs (he played a role in the North Affair, post-war), Messrs. John Biggs-Davison and G. C. B. Dodds (both 2nd lieutenants, RM—and the latter was a Principal in the Military Branch, Admiralty, 1945–50); Sir Jock Colville (Assistant Private Secretary to Winston Churchill, 1940–1, and his Joint Principal Secretary, 1951–5), Sir John Lang (Permanent Secretary of the Admiralty, 1947–61), and the tenth Earl of Selkirk (First Lord of the Admiralty, 1957–9).

Most kind also were Admiral of the Fleet Sir Caspar John and Admiral Sir Guy Grantham, for sharing their knowledge of the Navy and its personalities of the period under study; Vice-Admiral Sir Ronald Brockman, Secretary to the First Sea Lord, 1940–3, for putting his expertise at my disposal; Rear-Admiral P. N. Buckley, until recently Head of the Naval Historical Branch and Navy Librarian, Ministry of Defence, for making available certain invaluable records, and, with his undermanned but valiant staff, especially Mr. J. D. Lawson, answering a never-ending stream of queries with dispatch and good humour; Dr. M. A. Hoskin, Keeper of the Archives, Mr. A. D. Childs, onetime Deputy Librarian, Miss Angela Raspin, onetime Archivist, Churchill College, Cambridge, for answering queries and facilitating my use of the Edwards diary and the A. V. Alexander (Lord Alexander of Hillsborough) and Somerville Papers; Professors Kendall E. Bailes, of the University of California, Irvine, for his translation of certain Russian material,

Alvin D. Coox, of the California State University, San Diego, for encouragement when it was most needed, and Henri Diament, now of the University of Haifa, and Patricia O'Brien, of the University of California, Irvine, for elucidating the mysteries of French 'navalese'; Lady Edwards, for permission to quote from the diaries of Admiral Sir Ralph Edwards; Lady Beatrix Evison, for permission to cite material from the A. V. Alexander Papers; Rear-Admiral Fliche and his staff at the Service Historique de la Marine, for answering a number of challenging queries with promptness and efficiency; Major-General G. C. A. Gilbert, Commandant of the Joint Warfare Establishment, for extracts from 'History of the Combined Operations Organization, 1940–1945', which was prepared in 1956 by Amphibious Warfare Headquarters, London; Mrs. J. H. Godfrey, for the privilege of examining the papers of Admiral J. H. Godfrey, the wartime DNI; Professor Paul G. Halpern, of the Florida State University, for material from the Keyes Papers; Major-General J. L. Moulton, RM, for valuable leads to Marine officers who had participated in 'Menace'; Lady North and Mr. Roger North, with the co-operation of Mr. Ralph Barker, for permitting me to make copies of selected documents in the North Papers before they were deposited in the Churchill College Library; Mrs. Mary Z. Pain, for allowing me to examine the late Commander M. G. Saunders's notes (now at Churchill College) for a book on the French Navy in 1940–2; Brigadier C. M. Paton, for personal observations on General Irwin; Mr. A. W. H. Pearsall, Custodian of Manuscripts, National Maritime Museum, Greenwich, for being helpful in various ways; Miss Cathy Smith, for once more producing a model typescript from unpromising raw materials; Lieutenant-Commander J. A. F. Somerville, for permission to use his father's papers and for deciphering diary extracts and letters from the Admiral to his wife; Mr. Roderick Suddaby, Keeper of the Department of Documents, Imperial War Museum, for assistance with the Irwin Papers; Dr. E. K. Timings and Mr. N. E. Evans, of the Public Record Office, for innumerable courtesies and extraordinary patience; and the University of California, Irvine, for continued support.

I am grateful to Mr. Noel Atherton, the onetime Chief Civil Hydrographic Officer in the Admiralty, for preparing the charts with his usual skill.

An overdue tribute is due to my very dear friend and incomparable editor, the late Geoffrey Hunt. It is impossible to set down on paper all that his patience, understanding, breadth of learning, and superb editorial skills have meant to me, not only for this volume, in whose initial preparation he was involved, but for the half-dozen OUP volumes that have preceded it.

Grateful acknowledgement is made for permission to quote from the copyright material indicated: Weidenfeld & Nicolson (Publishers) Limited, and Simon and Schuster, Inc., from Charles de Gaulle, *War Memoirs*, i. *The Call to Honour, 1940–1942*, and Eyre & Spottiswoode (Publishers) Ltd., and Stein and Day/ Publishers, from Major-General Sir Edward Spears, *Two Men Who Saved France: Pétain and de Gaulle*. Transcripts of Crown-copyright records in the Public Record Office appear by permission of the Controller of H.M. Stationery Office.

ARTHUR MARDER

Irvine, California
8 March 1975

A Note on Sources

This volume is based on these unpublished primary source materials in the Public Record Office: Prime Minister's Office: operational papers (PREM 3/276); War Cabinet papers: WP series (CAB 66/10, 12) and minutes (Conclusions: Confidential Annexes): WM series (CAB 65/9, 14–15); Chiefs of Staff Committee minutes and papers: COS series (respectively, CAB 79/5–7, 55, CAB 80/14–21, 56); Joint Planning Committee minutes and papers: JP series (respectively, CAB 84/2, CAB 84/17–19, 21); various Admiralty files, especially ADM 1/19177–19190 (genesis and early development of the Dudley North Affair), ADM 199/817 ('Menace' signals), ADM 199/906 (Admiral Cunningham's voluminous report), 907, 1931, ADM 202/413 ('War Diary'), ADM 205/6; the FO/371 files of the Foreign Office, especially records indexed under the 'Dakar' subject heading; and a War Office file: WO 106/2858 (General Irwin's report). I have also profited greatly from the Irwin Papers in the Imperial War Museum (IRW 1/1–4); the Richmond Papers (North correspondence of 1941–6) at the National Maritime Museum, Greenwich (RIC 7/4); the North and Somerville Papers in the Churchill College Library (respectively, NRTH 1/1–10 and SMVL 1/31, 3/22, 7/4, 26); materials in the Naval Historical Branch, Ministry of Defence; General Sir Edward Spears's 'Dakar Diary' of 30 August–28 October, which includes a daily log prepared during and after the operation ('War Diary, Spears Mission').

I must single out for special mention three important unpublished official studies of 'Menace': 'The Dakar Operation' (PREM 3/276, also ADM 205/6), a history prepared by the Naval Staff in the week after the operation; Hist. (A) 1 (Final), 'The Dakar Operation', 5 Feb. 1941 (PREM 3/276, also ADM 199/207), which was 'prepared by Colonel Yule from the papers available in the War Cabinet Offices in October, 1940, and represents the story as seen in London. It gives clearly the information on which the decisions of the War Cabinet were taken. It was written before the Commanders' reports were available in London'; and, above all, Hist. (A) 2, 'The Dakar Operation, August and September 1940', May 1942 (ADM 199/907), which includes in a set of annexes the principal documents—directives, signals, etc. It was 'written by Brigadier R. Chenevix-Trench from the first narrative compiled by Colonel Hyslop from the Commanders' reports and from an unofficial document "Devant Dakar".' The last-named, by Lieutenant-Colonel P. R. Smith-Hill, RM, who was General Irwin's GSO 1 during the operation, is an unofficial 'light account' (ADM 199/907). ADM 199/907 also contains an important lecture on Dakar given by General Irwin at the Staff College, Camberley, on 23 September 1941.

Abbreviations used in the text

(whether official or in common Service usage)

AA	anti-aircraft
ACNA	Admiral Commanding North Atlantic Station
ALC	assault landing craft
A/S	anti-submarine
CAS	Chief of Air Staff, Air Ministry
C-in-C	Commander-in-Chief
CIGS	Chief of Imperial General Staff, War Office
COS	Chiefs of Staff Committee
CSO	Chief Staff Officer to an Admiral Commanding
DDOD(H)	Deputy Director, Operations Division (Home), Naval Staff
DMI	Director of Military Intelligence, General Staff
DNI	Director of Naval Intelligence, Naval Staff
DOD(F)	Director, Operations Division (Foreign), Naval Staff
D of P	Director of Plans Division, Naval Staff, etc.
EPS	Executive Planning Section of the Joint Planning Staff
FOCNA	Flag Officer Commanding North Atlantic Station
GOC	General Officer Commanding
GSO	General Staff Officer (Grade 1, etc.)
ISPS	Inter-Service Planning Staff
JPS	Joint Planning Sub-Committee (JPC) of the COS: Joint Planning Staff (JPS) from 6 September 1940
MT ships	ships carrying mechanical transport
NA	Naval Attaché
NCO	non-commissioned officer
NID	Naval Intelligence Division, Admiralty
RM	Royal Marines
RNVR	Royal Naval Volunteer Reserve
R/T	radio telephony
SNO	Senior Naval Officer
TSR	'torpedo, spotting, and reconnaissance' aircraft (Swordfish)
VCIGS	Vice-Chief of Imperial General Staff, War Office
VCNS	Vice-Chief of Naval Staff, Admiralty
V/S	visual signalling
W/T	wireless telegraphy

Contents

PART TWO

The Story of Dudley North: WAS JUSTICE DONE?

List of Illustrations

(The ultimate rank and title are the ones given)

List of Charts

Calendar of Events

'Menace'
1940

Last days of July   De Gaulle-Spears-Morton Dakar plan worked out

August

4   Churchill approves operation
6   Churchill evolves a new plan with de Gaulle
8   Churchill directs the COS to prepare a plan forthwith
12   Appointment of Cunningham and Irwin as Force Commanders
13   War Cabinet approval of the plan
19   The Vice Chiefs of Staff point out surprise descent is no longer possible
20   Reversion to the plan of 6 August
26   Convoy 'M.S.' sails
26–29   Equatorial Africa rallies to de Gaulle
27   The War Cabinet give their final approval to the operation
28   *Barham* sails for Gibraltar
29   The examination of Commander Rushbrooke and Captain Poulter
31   The remainder of the armada sails

September

9   (4 p.m.) Force Y sails from Toulon
9   (6:24 p.m.) Dispatch of signal from Consul-General, Tangier
10   (6:09 p.m.) Dispatch of signal from Naval Attaché, Madrid
11   (4:45 a.m.) *Hotspur*'s sighting report
11   (5:45 a.m.) Somerville orders *Renown* to one hour's notice for steam
11   (8:45 a.m.) Force Y passes through the Straits of Gibraltar
11   (12:39 p.m.) The Admiralty order *Renown* to raise steam for full speed
11   (1:47 p.m., 2:29 p.m.) The Admiralty signal instructions to Somerville
11   (4 p.m.) *Renown* sails
12   (3 a.m.) Somerville institutes a patrol off Casablanca
12   (4 a.m.) Force Y leaves Casablanca and heads for Dakar
14   (12:16 a.m.) Admiralty message to Cunningham that Force Y has left Casablanca

14   (1 a.m.) Conference of Cunningham, Irwin, and de Gaulle in *Westerland*

14   (noon) Arrival of the French cruisers at Dakar

14   (6 p.m.) Patrol line to intercept Force Y established—too late

15   (5.15 p.m.) Churchill directs the COS to cancel 'Menace'

16   (2 p.m.) The Admiralty direct de Gaulle to land at Duala

16   (4:42 p.m.) The Force Commanders protest cancellation of 'Menace'

16   (11:52 p.m.) Admiralty telegram to the Force Commanders giving them liberty to examine the whole situation and advise the War Cabinet

17   (a.m.) The Force Commanders and de Gaulle confer in Freetown; de Gaulle and Spears appeal to London not to abandon 'Menace'

18   (12:46 a.m.) The Force Commanders reply to the message of 11:52 p.m./16th

18   (1:20 p.m.) The War Cabinet inform the Force Commanders that the operation is to go forward

19–20   Chase of the French cruisers

21   The Allied expedition sails from Freetown

23   (5 a.m.) The expedition arrives off Dakar. First day of Operation 'Menace': 'Plan Charles'

24   Second day of 'Menace': the two bombardments

25   Third day of 'Menace': torpedoing of *Resolution*. Abandonment of the operation

27   The expedition, less *Barham* and *Resolution*, arrives at Freetown, the two battleships on the 29th

October

3   De Gaulle's forces leave Freetown for Duala

8   They arrive at Duala. Churchill's statement on Dakar in the Commons

24   Churchill asks the COS to prepare a plan for the British capture of Dakar

29   At a meeting with the Joint Planning Staff Churchill concedes it is not practicable

Part One

The Story of 'Menace'

A STUDY IN
THE FOG OF WAR

The story of the Dakar episode deserves close study, because it illustrates in a high degree not only the unforeseeable accidents of war, but the interplay of military and political forces, and the difficulties of combined operations, especially where allies are involved. To the world at large it seemed a glaring example of miscalculation, confusion, timidity, and muddle.

Churchill, *Their Finest Hour*

Chapter One

'Menace' is Born

I thus undertook in an exceptional degree the initiation and
advocacy of the Dakar expedition.

Churchill, *Their Finest Hour*

(Charts 1, 5)

(1) The Situation in July 1940

THE vigorous British action in the first week of July to prevent
the major French naval units from falling into enemy hands
had met with only partial success but had (especially Oran,
3 July) precipitated a grave crisis in Anglo-Vichy French relations.
Marshal Pétain, 'Chief of the French State', made official the rupture
of diplomatic relations with Great Britain that had existed since the
departure of the British Ambassador and his entire staff from
France on 22 June. Although war had been averted, sources of
friction remained. Anglophobia in Vichy was fed by the stepped-up
British propaganda against the new régime, including the dropping
of leaflets in Morocco; by the development of the Free French
organization in London, with official British approval and support
(Vichy considered de Gaulle a British puppet); by the efforts,
through British agents, to provoke the French colonies, particularly
in North and West Africa, to declare their independence of Vichy;
and by the announcement in the House of Commons on 30 July of
a War Cabinet decision of 13 July, that the blockade of Germany
would be extended to French North Africa. (A decision of 25 June,
made known in the Commons on 2 July, had already extended the
blockade of Germany to the whole of metropolitan France, occupied
and unoccupied.) The blockade could easily lead to open hostilities
between Britain and Vichy France, if it proved effective and thereby
provoked the French to try to force it. In practice, the extension of
contraband control to North Africa was nominal, since there were
not enough ships to enforce it. To sum up, tensions had increased
dangerously in the weeks following Oran. One serious incident

might bring on outright war. On the other hand, the French Admiralty and Foreign Office, as will be brought out in due course, were giving signs of a more friendly disposition.

The absence of direct official relations was a severe handicap in ironing out differences and misunderstandings. The exchange of diplomatic correspondence through the British and French ambassadors in Madrid, and the retention in London by Vichy of the French Consul-General as Acting French Agent to liquidate French economic interests, were *pis-allers*, no more. The Foreign Secretary, Lord Halifax, was 'doubtful whether even unofficial relations with France will stand the strain of the action we are taking in the matter of French ships, in the French colonies, in encouraging the resistance of free Frenchmen, in conducting propaganda, in blockading and bombarding France.[1] Two months later the British precipitated a crisis that put the tenuous British-Vichy relationship under an almost unendurable strain.

The catalytic agent was that remarkable personality, General Charles de Gaulle, whom the British Government had recognized on 28 June as the 'leader of all free Frenchmen wherever they might be, who will rally to him in support of the Allied cause'. The catalytic event stemmed from de Gaulle's African schemes.

A pen portrait of de Gaulle at this time reads:

A strange-looking man, enormously tall; sitting at the table he dominated everyone else by his height, as he had done when walking into the room. No chin, a long, drooping elephantine nose over a closely-cut moustache, a shadow over a small mouth whose thick lips tended to protrude as if in a pout before speaking, a high, receding forehead and pointed head surmounted by sparse black hair lying flat and neatly parted. His heavily-hooded eyes were very shrewd. When about to speak he oscillated his head slightly, like a pendulum, while searching for words.[2]

De Gaulle's weaknesses are well known. He was an exceptionally difficult man to deal with—proud to the point of arrogance, aloof, direct, autocratic, austere, irascible, stubborn, self-righteous, vain, hyper-sensitive in some ways, thick-skinned in others, and trusting no one completely. Though of a retiring disposition, he was, in a social situation, neither dour nor lacking a sense of humour. He was

[1] WP (40) 288, 'Relations with France. Memorandum by the Secretary of State for Foreign Affairs', 27 July, CAB 66/10. Part I dates, in text and reference footnotes, are to 1940, unless otherwise stated.

[2] Major-General Sir Edward Spears, *Assignment to Catastrophe* (2 vols., London, 1954), ii. 139.

a man of vast culture, with a powerful brain, and an enormous capacity for work and to lead men. 'Certain men,' he once wrote, 'have, one might almost say from birth, the quality of exuding authority.' In military matters his decisions were quick and generally sound. He passionately hated the Germans, but at the same time had a fundamental distrust of Britain and her rulers. Major-General Spears, who as Churchill's personal representative with de Gaulle ('Head of the British Mission' to him) came to know the General well, writes: 'He could neither understand nor accept that when we said we had no territorial ambitions at France's expense, we meant it, nor believe that we would not somehow, sometime, succumb to the temptation to help ourselves to a tempting morsel of the French empire'.[3] Never in dispute were de Gaulle's fervid nationalism—his belief in and love of France—and his absolute faith in the eventual restoration of her independence and her greatness. 'His one ambition was to serve the goddess he revered more than all the saints in heaven—France' (Spears). In spite of the difficulties and differences between de Gaulle and the British Commanders in the Dakar operation, the latter could not but admire his utter dedication, dignity, and belief in himself.

In July 1940 no part of France, metropolitan or colonial, had rallied to de Gaulle. His supporters were few and he had himself been sentenced to death *in absentia* by a court martial in Toulon late in June. Where to begin to build the Free French movement into a national endeavour? 'It all really began in Africa', a Gaullist remarked after the war. Why Africa? De Gaulle gives us the *raison d'etre*, of which this is the most cogent part:

To take part in the Battle of Africa with French forces and territories was to bring back, as it were, a fragment of France into the war. It was to defend her possessions directly against the enemy. It was, as far as possible, to deflect England—and perhaps one day America—from the temptation to make sure of them on their own account, for their fighting needs and for their advantage. It was, lastly, to wrench Free France free from exile and install her in full sovereignty on national territory.

[3] Spears, *Two Men Who Saved France: Pétain and de Gaulle* (London, 1966), p. 144. Spears, who, incidentally, had brought de Gaulle to London in June, thereby initiating the Free French movement, maintains that the General's foibles, specifically, his 'harshness and irascibility', were intensified by the treatment he received at British hands in his early days in London, for example, the obstacles to his recruiting drive. '... it was the intolerable strain of constantly recurring rebuffs and disappointments that were, in part at least, responsible for his unfair and unjust suspicions, his vindictiveness and outbursts of ugly temper.' Ibid., p. 212.

But where should we start upon Africa?[4]

Prospects were poor in French North Africa, where a 'wait and see' attitude, together with much hostility to de Gaulle, prevailed. Even a very large force would be received with hostility, he believed, and especially since Oran. But 'the fire was smouldering' in the French Cameroons and the Equatorial African territories, which had close economic ties with the British colonies in West Africa.[5] On 13 August three Gaullist 'missionaries' (Major Claude Hettier de Boislambert, General Philippe Leclere, and René Pleven) arrived in Lagos (British Nigeria) with the object of rallying these French territories. Meanwhile, de Gaulle was preparing to carry out the other part of his African plan, the rallying of French West Africa and its principal city and capital, Dakar, in the Vichy-controlled colony of Senegal.[6] The General had a special motive here. Establishing a seat for his government in such a large and strategically important centre as Dakar would enhance the prestige of the Free French movement and its leader, while at the same time checking any British designs on that great naval base and its prize, the uncompleted 35,000-ton battleship *Richelieu*, damaged but repairable. De Gaulle was confident that Dakar, itching to be free, would rally to the Cross of Lorraine. There were other players and other stakes.

The British interest in Dakar was primarily strategic. Located on the westernmost point of Africa, it had all the requisites of a good port. The approach was easily fortified, there was no bar such as existed in most West African coastal ports, and the reasonably deep-water harbour was well sheltered. The large artificial harbour protected by breakwaters was perfectly sheltered and free from swell. Intelligence reports suggested that the Germans were planning to make use of the port. In German hands Dakar would provide a very effective base for operations by U-boats, surface raiders, and aircraft against British sea communications in the North and South Atlantic, and particularly against the shipping and troop convoys

[4] De Gaulle, *War Memoirs*, Vol. i (2 parts), *The Call to Honour, 1940–1942* (London, 1955), Pt. I, p. 111. All citations hereafter from the *War Memoirs* are to Pt. I, with one exception to be noted.

[5] The Cameroons were 161,000 square miles in area, with a population of 2,400,000. Equatorial Africa had 867,000 square miles and a 3,500,000 population, and consisted of four colonies: Gabon, the Middle Congo, Ubangi-Shari, and the Chad.

[6] French West Africa (1,807,000 square miles, 14,800,000 population) was composed of the colonies of Senegal, Mauritania, French Guinea, the Ivory Coast, Dahomey, the French Sudan, and the Niger. The capital of Senegal was St. Louis, farther up the coast, not Dakar.

around the Cape of Good Hope. These routes were vital, since communications with the Middle East, India, and Australia via the Mediterranean and Suez Canal were hazardous after Italy entered the war in June 1940. Also, the Germans, if they acquired Dakar, would pose a threat to British communications with their West African colonies, the enclaves of Gambia, Sierra Leone, the Gold Coast, and Nigeria, on the southern coast of French West Africa. The Germans, moreover, would have a base for offensive action against these colonies and for depriving the British of the use of Freetown, thereby complicating their task of convoying ships by the Cape route. There were, then, weighty reasons for keeping the Germans out of Dakar. But there were equally important advantages to Britain in seizing Dakar for her own use. If available to British convoys and escorts, it would be a useful addition to the limited resources of Freetown in Sierra Leone, the only British naval base in West Africa, as a base for anti-submarine operations. Other rich prizes at Dakar were the *Richelieu*, and the vast quantity of Belgian and Polish gold, amounting to 65 billion francs, which the Banque de France had transferred to Dakar in June. Finally, there was a political prize to be won. The whole of French West Africa under Free French control would serve as a buffer against German penetration from Dakar, about which the British administration in Nigeria, above all, had nightmares. On instructions from the Chiefs of Staff, the Joint Intelligence Sub-Committee examined the question of a German or Italian offensive against Dakar and concluded: 'If the British Navy were no longer able to use Gibraltar as a base and had therefore no base between Plymouth and Freetown, we think that an enemy expedition against Dakar would have a very fair chance of evading interception.'[7]

The British concern over Dakar was paralleled and reinforced by the attitude of the United States. Though still neutral, the Americans had a powerful stake in the future of Dakar. U-boats operating from that base would threaten American as well as Allied shipping, and the proximity of Dakar to the bulge of Brazil (1,700 miles) posed another potential danger to American interests. To keep an eye on the developing situation in Dakar, in August 1940 the Americans decided to reopen their consulate. (It had been closed in 1931 for economy reasons.) The Consul, Thomas C. Wasson,

[7] COS (40) 637 (JIC), 'Possibility of a German or Italian Occupation of Dakar', 17 Aug., CAB 80/16.

arrived in Dakar on 15 September, a week before the sudden appearance of an Allied armada off the port.

We must bear in mind the persistent reports in London and Washington that the Germans were infiltrating into Dakar as emissaries of one kind or another, or under the guise of 'tourists'. In the words of a British official announcement issued after the abortive expedition (25 September), 'H.M. Government were all the more ready to afford General de Gaulle this support as information had reached them that German influence was spreading to Dakar'. The Diplomatic Correspondent of *The Times* (26 September) wrote of the 'clear signs' being received at de Gaulle's London headquarters for some weeks before the Dakar operation that 'the Germans and Italians were gently laying their hands on the port: their officers were arriving by air on various excuses'.

We know that Grand Admiral Raeder, C-in-C of the German Navy, would have liked the use of Dakar as a U-boat base for attacks on important convoy routes in the Atlantic.[8] He first stressed its extreme value to Hitler at a conference on 20 June, in the course of discussions on the terms of an armistice with France, and again on 11 July. But Hitler then appeared to be more interested in one of the Canary Islands, which he thought he might get free from Spain in exchange for French Morocco. On 6 September, when unbeknown to German intelligence the Anglo-Free French expedition was on its way to Dakar, Raeder once more stressed the value of Dakar for Germany. He pointed out that now that French Equatorial Africa had (as we shall see) sided with de Gaulle, the unrest and uprisings might spread to the colonies in West Africa. 'An agreement between the colonies and Britain, and revolt against France would jeopardize our own chances of controlling the African area; the danger exists that strategically important West African ports might be used for British convoy activities and that we might lose a most valuable source of supplies for Europe. The danger of an attack on the part of the U.S.A. is not entirely out of the question . . .' Nothing happened. The German Naval War Staff

[8] For what follows I have relied on *Fuehrer Conferences on Naval Affairs, 1940* (7 vols., Admiralty, 1947), ii. 58, 65, 95 (*Fuehrer Conferences on Matters Dealing with the German Navy, 1940*, U.S. Navy Department, Washington, 1947, has a different pagination), and Admiral Kurt Assmann's draft official work on the German Naval Staff and Franco-German collaboration, 1940–2, *Die Bemühungen der Seekriegsleitung um ein deutsche-französisches Zusammengehen gegen England und um die Behauptung des französischen Kolonialreichs in Africa.* I have used the microfilm copy in the Naval Historical Branch, Ministry of Defence. Assmann's main sources were the *Kriegstagebücher* (War Diaries) of the German Naval War Staff (*Seekriegsleitung*).

continued to stress Dakar's great value for a successful prosecution of the war in the Atlantic, but this, too, was of no avail. The Naval War Staff realized that the OKW (Supreme Command of the Armed Forces) were too exclusively absorbed in purely Continental questions to appreciate the urgency and importance of the problem of North and West Africa, and that in consequence Hitler was inadequately briefed by the OKW on these problems. From the remarks in the 'SKL' (*Seekriegsleitung*) diary it is obvious that the Naval War Staff were too weakly represented in the OKW and could not get their views across.

The point I would establish here is that the British and American fears of a German presence in Dakar were grossly exaggerated. At the time of the British-Free French attack in September there were perhaps two or three Germans in all of French West Africa.[9]

Vichy had no desire to see the Germans entrenched in North or West Africa, which, with the Fleet, constituted one of their few trump cards. Accordingly, when on 15 July Hitler asked for authorization to use eight air bases in Morocco and the Mediterranean ports of metropolitan France (Unoccupied France), as well as those of French North Africa, the Vichy Government bluntly refused (18 July). It was no better disposed to the rallying of French Equatorial and West Africa to de Gaulle. Apart from the natural desire to retain these important bargaining assets, there was the fear that the Germans would react strongly to transgressions of the

---

[9] According to the American Consul, there was none. 'Except for four or five Jewish refugees, there were no Germans in Dakar while I was there [15 September 1940–10 February 1942]. And apart from certain specific German officials who passed in transit through French West Africa . . . there were no Germans in all of French West Africa.' Thomas C. Wasson, 'The Mystery of Dakar: an Enigma Resolved', *American Foreign Service Journal*, xx (Apr. 1943), 214–17. In sworn testimony (October 1944) Wasson declared 'without hesitation that there were no Germans in Dakar, nor German activities in French West Africa, during my time as Consul.' Daniel Chenet, *Qui a sauvé l'Afrique?* (Paris, 1949), p. 202. There is also contemporary evidence by Wasson. On 28 September 1940 he had telegraphed the Secretary of State: 'The Governor General assured me on September 26 that there was not one German in this city or in Senegal. All of my other sources of information confirmed this.' He added that there were a few Italians in Dakar, mostly building contractors, all of whom had resided there for many years. 740.0011 European War 1939/5798, National Archives, Washington. But a number of Germans had arrived some weeks earlier. Between 27 July and 10 August two German transport planes had made seven trips to Dakar for the purpose of repatriating 165 interned Germans. Wasson to Secretary of State, 20 Sept. 1940, 740.00115 European War 1939/567. And I have it on the authority of Colonel Hettier de Boislambert that these planes had brought an armistice commission, of which several members remained in Dakar, and that during his time as a prisoner at Dakar at the end of September he was interrogated by a German officer of this commission. De Boislambert's letter to the author, 24 Jan. 1975.

armistice. The French Government had agreed in the very first article to cease hostilities against Germany 'in France, in French possessions, colonies, protectorates, and mandated territories, and at sea'. Their worried Foreign Minister, who described himself as 'not an unbending anglophil', confided to his diary (2 September): 'Very bad news is reaching me from Wiesbaden [site of the Franco-German Armistice Commission] concerning the intentions of the Germans in respect of French Africa. They seem determined to establish themselves there in order to stop the spread of disaffection in the colonies of Chad and West Africa . . . What new folly on the part of England will provide them with an excuse?'[10] To the Vichy Ambassador in Madrid he sent this telegram for the British Ambassador, Sir Samuel Hoare:

> The British Government has of late greatly intensified its support of M. de Gaulle's movement, and it has strongly seconded the spread of this movement to the French African possessions. Its attention should be drawn to the consequences of its action, for this may lead to results diametrically opposed to its interests. The truth is that there is every reason to fear that if the attempt to detach from the French Government the territories of our African Empire continues, not only will the French reaction cause serious incidents between England and France, but, given our weakness, Germany and Italy will secure the defence of our colonial Empire with their own forces. If they are successful in this the consequences would be extremely detrimental to British interests. Thus there is a danger to which the British Government should be alive.[11]

This summarizes the French position. It was, therefore, as Vichy viewed the matter, essential to maintain its authority in French West and Equatorial Africa. The vigorous Gaullist propaganda against the 'so-called Government of Vichy' and the 'traitors' who headed it only hardened Vichy's resolve.

(2) Genesis

Churchill was eager during July for a military adventure somewhere that might divert the Germans from the British Isles, enhance British prestige, and raise morale at home. For a while he thought of Casablanca, the French naval base on Morocco's Atlantic coast, which sheltered the powerful unfinished battleship *Jean Bart*. Then

---

[10] *The Private Diaries of Paul Baudouin (March 1940 to January 1941)* (London, 1948), p. 227.
[11] Ibid., p. 228.

his thoughts turned towards Dakar, where the situation looked promising. On 4 July the Colonial Office transmitted to the Chiefs of Staff a telegram of 2 July from the Governor of the Gold Coast based on reports from British liaison officers in French West Africa. The message reported the existence of a 'strong feeling' among the French military and civil authorities in the French Ivory Coast in favour of continuing the war in association with Great Britain, and of the immediate British occupation of Dakar. 'But it is evident that, unless a decisive lead is given very soon, the local French authorities in West Africa will succumb to defeatism and acquiesce in any measures which the French Government, under enemy inspiration, may impose on them. It will be appreciated that this would result in a serious strategical threat to our position in West Africa.'[12]

The British Consul-General in Dakar had reported on 4 July (nine days before he and his staff were forced to leave) that the Mayor considered that

a show of force should be made by British fleet if possible by July 10th. Later on the situation may be more difficult without considerable loss of life, whereas arrival in force in the near future might have the desired effect without much bloodshed. . . .

I know that semi-official groups of French European patriots are planning a coup d'état in various centres and would be ready to seize vital positions. Chief Mohammedan religious heads of Senegal have been in conference and are determined to join us. Two have visited me to convey this information. Black population would back action, but lack own leaders.[13]

Churchill immediately picked this up. Off went a minute on 5 July to the Deputy Secretary (Military) of the War Cabinet, Major-General Sir Hastings Ismay: 'This appears to be of the utmost importance and it should be possible for the Fleet to make contact almost by the date mentioned.' He suggested sending de Gaulle out to Gibraltar by air that day, so as to embark with a small staff in a British ship. 'There is no time to organize the movement of French troops from here.' He asked that his plan be considered by the Chiefs of Staff forthwith. His expectation apparently was that a naval demonstration by 'Force H', the Gibraltar-based squadron in

---

[12] FO 371/24384. A telegram of 3 July from the Governor of Nigeria strongly recommended the immediate occupation of Dakar 'in friendly form', that is, through support to the French civil, military, and naval authorities who were prepared to rise—provided that it was considered that such action had a reasonable chance of success. Ibid.

[13] This and the following documents are in PREM 3/276.

the Western Mediterranean, would bring Dakar over to the British cause.

Ismay's appreciation (5 July) made these principal points. Dakar was defended by eight 9·4-inch guns, submarine patrols, and the *Richelieu*. 'Consequently a naval operation is impracticable, unless we can be *positive* that the coast defence guns will not fire on us, either when we are approaching the harbour, or subsequently. Unless, therefore, these batteries are definitely in the hands of friends the risk of entering the harbour would be unjustifiable.' The political objection was as weighty. 'Hitherto we have confined ourselves to ensuring that the French Fleet does not fall into German hands. To seize French territory ourselves would be a new departure. If this is to be done, it should be done by French forces hostile to the Bordeaux [Vichy] Government, i.e. de Gaulle.' On Ismay's instructions Spears approached de Gaulle for his reactions (5 July). The latter endorsed action at Dakar, 'but considers that to go himself with a few men would be courting defeat and would be entirely lacking in panache. He did not say so but French people always have in mind the ridiculous figure cut by Napoleon III at Boulogne.'[14] De Gaulle's idea was that Admiral Muselier, the C-in-C of the Free French Naval Forces, should sail for Dakar with as many French ships as he could—a couple of submarines and a destroyer probably could be manned—under the French flag, in company with British units, sail in, communicate with the Governor-General, take over the coastal batteries, and negotiate with the *Richelieu*. On news of Muselier's success, de Gaulle would at once sail from England with a battalion of French legionaires and whatever other forces could be collected and transported in time. The plan foundered on French pride. 'It cannot be emphasized sufficiently', Spears reported, 'that neither de Gaulle nor Muselier will march unless they have some French ships flying the French flag . . .' De Gaulle would be unable to man more than 'a very limited number of French ships', which was not enough.

By the last week of July telegrams from the Governors of Nigeria and the Gold Coast on the latest developments in French West and Central Africa revealed that there had been a general deterioration in the situation. Various indications, such as the dissemination of anti-British propaganda from Dakar and Abidjan (Ivory Coast) and the rumoured arrival of German and Italian officers at Dakar,

---

[14] The fiasco of Prince Louis Napoleon, as he then was, in 1840. With a few followers he landed at Boulogne and tried to rally the garrison. He was rebuffed and arrested.

pointed to an attempt by Vichy to assume active control of the French colonies in Africa. The Vansittart Committee on French Resistance recommended on 22 July that the Chiefs of Staff consider the possibility of seeking to improve the situation in the French West African colonies through a show of force.[15]

The Service Chiefs understood that 'the object of a show of force would be to rally the doubtful and wavering elements in the Dakar area'. It could be effective only '(a) If the French elements whom it is desired to rally were sufficiently strong and well organized to take advantage of it in order to seize control, or (b) If we were prepared to follow it up by Military action.' Latest reports showed that there was little justification for assuming that the conditions in (a), above, existed. They would therefore have to back up a show of force with military action. There were three possibilities here: a naval bombardment, but this was not consonant with the Government's policy of not exacerbating relations with Vichy; an air bombardment with aircraft from a carrier, but this was open to the same political objection, and a mere demonstration over Dakar would have little effect; a military occupation in face of French opposition, but this 'would be an operation of some magnitude for which we have not at present the forces available. We therefore conclude that the proposals to make a show of force in the Dakar area are not practicable from the Military point of view.'[16]

Prospects of a Dakar operation were, then, not bright at the end of July. Yet Churchill was still restless for action somewhere. On 25 July he asked the newly installed Director of Combined Operations, Admiral of the Fleet Sir Roger Keyes, for 'three or four proposals for medium-sized action, i.e. between five and ten thousand men', to take place in September and October.[17] It was at

---

[15] FO 371/24384.

[16] COS (40) 585, 'French Colonial Possessions in Africa', 29 July, CAB 80/15. In an appreciation of 16 July the Chiefs of Staff, after warning against the possibility that Vichy might permit the Germans the use of Dakar, had confessed that, given the strength of the garrison there, they could not hope to seize it in the face of opposition. The destruction of the port facilities by naval bombardment or by air attack from carriers was all they could contemplate. COS (40) 543, 'Implications of French Hostility', CAB 80/14. The Service Chiefs were Admiral of the Fleet Sir Dudley Pound (First Sea Lord and Chief of Naval Staff), Air Chief Marshal Sir Cyril Newall (Chief of Air Staff), and General Sir John Dill (Chief of the Imperial General Staff).

[17] Brigadier Sir Bernard Fergusson, *The Watery Maze: the Story of Combined Operations* (London, 1961), p. 55. Churchill's direct request to submit proposals for action without reference to the Chiefs of Staff was surely rather unconstitutional and can be explained only by his close personal relations with Keyes and his inexperienced impatience with the COS system.

this juncture, apparently before Keyes was able to respond, that a fresh Dakar proposal was presented to Churchill.

An equally restive de Gaulle was already planning his next move in anticipation of the successful rallying of Equatorial Africa, which had been put in hand. He admits this 'new phase bid fair to be much more arduous'. The military strength of his movement was negligible: a few planes, a few warships and merchantmen, and some 7,000 men, mainly volunteers, lacking tanks and heavy guns, but spoiling for a fight. Obviously, de Gaulle's forces would stand no chance in a direct attack from the sea on a strongly defended naval base. 'Besides, I considered it essential to avoid a large-scale collision. Not that—alas!—I indulged in illusions about the possibility of achieving the liberation of the country without blood ever being shed between Frenchmen. But at such a moment and on that particular ground, for us to engage in a big battle would, whatever its outcome, have gravely diminished our chances. The course of the Dakar affair cannot be understood if it is not realised that that was the conviction which dominated my mind.'[18]

In the last days of July de Gaulle worked out with two of Churchill's collaborators, Spears and Morton, a plan in outline for an indirect attack on Dakar. Spears was a man of dominating personality—he was tough and tenacious and held definite ideas—coupled with an exceptional brain, great moral courage, and imagination. He had considerable administrative talents and a mastery of spoken French and the art of conversation. His Assistant during the time of 'Menace' contributes this pen portrait of an extraordinary person:

He was of medium height, somewhat sturdily built and with a very strong character, which rather explained the reputation he had of being 'difficult'. He did not put up with any nonsense, did not allow anyone to impinge upon his prerogatives and knew exactly what he wanted. He was remarkably intelligent, he had an astonishing memory and spoke and wrote French like a Frenchman. Furthermore, he was quite fearless . . . He was an indefatigable worker, even in the tropics. He detested sloppiness and insisted upon sound and regular administration, with no frills. Finally, he wanted to know about, and control, everything that was within his province.[19]

---

[18] De Gaulle, *War Memoirs*, i. 119–20. My study casts new light on de Gaulle's mentality, for we shall see from repeated instances how very cautious he was in operations. There was none of the absurd *'tout le monde à la bataille'* about him.

[19] Colonel John A. Watson, *Échec à Dakar* (Paris, 1968), pp. 45–6.

Major Desmond Morton, Personal Assistant to the Prime Minister, was a man with a good mind, who, unfortunately, was a self-important amateur. In the opinion of Spears, who worked with him closely at this time, he 'will exasperate people in the end, giving the impression of being too pleased with himself, making too much of his power to obtain the PM's backing'.[20] Although in his *War Memoirs* de Gaulle writes of 'my initial plan', all three men were in fact responsible for it. Inebriated by his patriotic ardour, de Gaulle may have been the first to suggest the central idea—that a few Free French troops, with the assistance of the Royal Navy, would suffice to rally West Africa.[21]

The essentials of the outline plan may be stated briefly: (1) de Gaulle and his Free French Forces in Britain (two battalions, one company of tanks, one section of artillery, a fighter squadron, a bomber squadron, and support units) would be ready to sail for West Africa on 15 August, with the object of 'hoisting the Free French Flag in French territory in West Africa, the occupation of Dakar and the consolidation under the Free French Flag of the Free French Colonies in West and Equatorial Africa'. (2) The British were to provide the necessary arms and equipment, shipping —with the ships to be manned as far as possible by French crews— and naval escort, with some of the naval units, if possible, to be commanded and manned by Free French officers and men. (3) If successful, the operation would be followed by the rallying of French North Africa through the intervention of Gaullist elements in those colonies. General Catroux, the recently deposed Governor-General of French Indo-China, would be in command in North Africa. 'The exact port of arrival to be decided in the light of

[20] Spears, 'Dakar Diary,' 30 Aug. 1940, Spears MSS. As collaborators without responsibility who had the ear of the Prime Minister, Spears and Morton were, as the Chiefs of Staff and the Joint Planning Sub-Committee viewed them, mischievous influences at the centre and a pain in the neck for them, as perhaps all unofficial advisers are bound to be when they indulge in special pleading without full knowledge of or responsibility for the conduct of the war as a whole. I might add that there was no love lost between the two men.

[21] The DMI, Brigadier F. G. Beaumont-Nesbitt, believed that Spears was 'the chief instigator of the scheme', as well as being 'mainly instrumental in obtaining Churchill's approval . . .' Journal entry, 2 Oct., James Leutze (ed.), *The London Observer: the Journal of General Raymond E. Lee, 1940–1941* (London, 1972), p. 76. Lee was the American Military Attaché in London. But General Spears's version is probably closer to the truth: 'As regards the germ of *Menace* I cannot remember exactly who originated the idea. I think it emerged in general discussion between myself, members of my Mission and de Gaulle's staff, as we all wanted to take some military action in the summer of 1940.' Letter to the author, 7 Nov. 1973.

future events.'[22] De Gaule had Konakry, in French Guinea, Duala in the French Cameroons, or Freetown in mind. He favoured Konakry, far to the south of Dakar, which was linked with Dakar by road and rail. From the port 'a resolute column would proceed towards the objective rallying as it went the territories through which it passed and the elements which it encountered. One might hope that in this way the forces of Free France, growing by contagion, would reach Dakar by land.'[23]

Churchill was powerfully attracted to the plan, as he grasped the immense political and strategical importance of a successful assault. Although not committing himself immediately to de Gaulle, he lost little time in setting the operation in motion. The normal and indeed the correct way to set about the planning of this (or any other) operation was through a minute from the Prime Minister to the Chiefs of Staff explaining his ideas and requesting their views. The Chiefs would first have investigated whether the plan was practicable and desirable from the military point of view. If their conclusions were unfavourable, they would have reported to the Prime Minister to that effect. They might then have had to withstand heavy pressure, perhaps from Churchill; but if they had stuck to their guns, there would have been no expedition. If, on the other hand, the Chiefs had agreed that the project was practicable and the resources available, they would have instructed the Joint Planning Sub-Committee to prepare an outline plan of the form the expedition should take, the resources required, and the date on which it could be launched.

But on this occasion Churchill very much kept things in his own hands, not using the planning machinery in the normal way. What happened when the Prime Minister rang through early on 4 August is told by Rear-Admiral A. D. Nicholl, then Naval Assistant Secretary to the War Cabinet.

I happened to be holding the fort in the War Cabinet office when the P.M. rang through [from Chequers] on the scrambler phone. He asked for Ismay and then told me that he wanted the Chiefs of Staff to make a plan for the capture of Dakar on the basis of an outline plan which had been prepared by de Gaulle, General Spears, and Major Morton, and to make the necessary forces available. And he added (though I do not remember the exact words) that it was entirely a political decision and that he didn't want a lot of military objections put up by the Chiefs of

[22] WP (40) 301, ' "Operation Scipio",' 4 Aug., CAB 66/10.
[23] De Gaulle, *War Memoirs*, i. 120.

Staff. I rang round to Ismay and the Chiefs and they met later in the day. They were extremely disgruntled about the whole thing, and especially over the fact that they were faced with the decision to implement a plan which their Planners had not previously examined. There was a very grumpy discussion and clearly the Chiefs felt that there was far too much optimism about the reception de Gaulle would get at Dakar. I think I summed up the general feeling when I passed a chit to Ismay at one point, 'Why not let the first flight be our Marines—dressed as Frenchmen if necessary but ready to fight like Royal Marines?' Ismay grimaced his agreement but of course said nothing.[24]

Churchill sent Operation 'Scipio' (WP 301, above) to the War Cabinet on the 4th with a covering minute that he approved the operation, 'subject to anything that the Foreign Office may have to say in general', or the Admiralty about the naval escort. The plan would be brought before the War Cabinet the next day, and 'meanwhile all preparations should go forward'.

The Chiefs of Staff called the Joint Planning Sub-Committee into an emergency meeting in the morning of 4 August to consider 'Scipio'. The Joint Planners directed the Inter-Service Planning Staff to examine 'the administrative problems involved in organising and despatching the proposed expedition'. When the JP met again in the afternoon to consider the operation, the Foreign Office representative present reported that Lord Halifax was disposed to agree to the operation, if the Service Chiefs had no objections to it. But the Colonial Office spokesman declared that the Colonial Secretary, Lord Lloyd, 'was apprehensive of the possible implications of the failure of the proposed operation'.[25] The report of the ISPS was introduced and the bulk of it incorporated in a

[24] Admiral Nicholl's letter to the author, 31 May 1967. Incidentally, Ismay makes no mention of the Dakar operation in his memoirs, perhaps because, as Nicholl suggests, he 'deliberately left out Dakar and the inevitable need to criticise his great leader, well knowing that if he put it in, the episode would be seized on and high-lighted when his memoirs were published'. Ismay, Nicholl adds, was wrathful over criticism of Churchill by lesser men.

[25] JP (40) 79th, 80th Meetings, CAB 84/2, JP (40) 376, 'Operation Scipio,' 4 Aug., CAB 84/17. The Chiefs of Staff Committee were served by the Joint Planning Sub-Committee, which was headed by the Joint Planners—the three Service Directors of Plans (the JP, as they were colloquially called): Captain C. S. Daniel, Air Commodore J. C. Slessor, and Brigadier I. S. O. Playfair. They were quite often in disagreement with the COS. Though having as a subordinate sub-committee to accept the decisions of the COS, the Joint Planners never failed to express their own views or to argue the point in discussion when there was disagreement. Men like Charles Daniel and Jack Slessor were forceful characters and very able debaters. For the details of the planning organization, see below, pp. 30–1.

JP draft report on 'Scipio'. It was distinctly cool to the whole idea. It called attention to the conflict between the Government's policy of working to improve relations with Vichy and the policy of encouraging dissident elements in the French colonies to continue the fight against Germany (which policy was it in their military interest to pursue?), that there was little hope of French colonial administrators in French West and Equatorial Africa rallying to de Gaulle and the British, although important elements would rally to their side, given a strong lead. The conclusion was: 'Unless there is substantial evidence that such a revolt could be launched with good prospects of success and without having undesirable repercussions elsewhere . . . it would be to our advantage from the military point of view to seek a *modus vivendi* with the local French administration in each Colony and to avoid an open breach with the Vichy Government on the Colonial issue.'[26]

The Chiefs of Staff accepted the substance of the JP report when they met that evening. Their support of 'Scipio' was reluctant. They approved it only on the three important assumptions that (1) the force would be equipped and loaded so that it could land in any French West African port; (2) the expedition was to consist entirely of Free French troops (2,260): the only British element was to be the naval escort and part of the shipping; (3) the expedition would land without opposition in French territory. That is, the matter must be settled as between Frenchmen in advance of the landing. The only French West African ports with the necessary facilities for disembarking mechanical transport were Dakar, Konakry, and Duala. If War Cabinet approval were immediately forthcoming, the transports and storeships would sail from Liverpool on 13 August, and, to synchronise with their arrival at the port of debarkation, the troopships would sail between the 19th and 23rd, depending on the debarkation point chosen. The expedition would reach Dakar on 28 August, or Konakry on the 30th, or Duala on 5 September, depending on the port chosen. These views were set

[26] JP (40) 369, 'Policy in Respect of French Colonial Possessions in West Africa', 4 Aug., CAB 84/17. Though it is not reflected in their report or minutes of their meetings, the JP were also concerned about Dakar's defences. As Marshal of the Royal Air Force Sir John Slessor has written to me: 'The JP and COS meetings leading up to Menace were very rushed affairs, and it does not surprise me that not all the arguments deployed against it were recorded in minutes. But my memory is quite clear that we did take into account the defences of Dakar—we should have been very wrong not to do so, and I remember particularly being nervous about the presence of *Richelieu* with her 15-inch guns.' Letter of 19 Nov. 1964. And see further, below, p. 25n.

forth in a paper of 5 August that was available for the War Cabinet meeting of 11.30 a.m. the same day.[27] Among the points made in the discussion was that the operation would be 'a French responsibility and it was for General de Gaulle to take the operational decisions'. A premise of the plan was that the landing would be unopposed, 'but there could be no certainty that this would be possible'. The First Lord of the Admiralty, A. V. Alexander, was not happy that the naval escort might find itself committed to action against French warships, should Vichy attempt to stop the expedition. The War Cabinet approved the operation in principle.[28]

As a result of the War Cabinet decision, the First Sea Lord held a conference on the same afternoon (5 August) with de Gaulle, Spears, Morton, and the VCNS, Acting Vice-Admiral Sir Tom Phillips. It was quickly apparent that de Gaulle's conception of the operation differed from that of the Chiefs of Staff. There might, he maintained, be opposition at sea from French warships. This would make it necessary for the British escort to accompany the Free French ships to the anchorage, and possibly to sink the Vichy ships. He agreed that such a situation should not be allowed to develop. If air reconnaissance revealed the presence of French warships in the harbour selected for landing, he would proceed to the nearest British colony and use it as a base of operations for the land invasion of French territory. He stipulated that the expedition should be guaranteed against the arrival of Vichy reinforcements in the French colony at which he had landed or which he was invading from a neighbouring British colony. This would involve greater and more lasting commitments than the British had foreseen, and it appeared that the expedition was beginning to lose its Free French character. As a COS minute for the Prime Minister summed up the matter: they had 'visualised that the operation would be essentially of a "free French" character, British assistance being strictly limited and as unostentatious as possible. Nor had we visualised commitments anything like so great or so enduring as those which General de Gaulle's suggestion involves.'[29]

As a result of this development, Churchill evolved a new plan with de Gaulle at No. 10 on 6 August that emphasized a psycho-

---

[27] COS (40) 246th Meeting, CAB 79/5, COS (40) 603, 'Operations in West Africa', 5 Aug., CAB 80/16.

[28] WM (40) 219, CAB 65/14.

[29] 'Note of a Conversation between the First Sea Lord and General de Gaulle', PREM 3/276, COS (40) 249th Meeting, 5 Aug., CAB 79/5.

logical approach and a peaceful takeover of Dakar.[30] The Prime Minister was at his eloquent and imaginative best as he strode up and down the Cabinet Room, all the while talking with animation. 'We must,' he told the General, 'together gain control of Dakar. For you it is capital. For if the business goes well, it means that large French forces are brought back into the war. It is very important for us. For to be able to use Dakar as a base would make a great many things easier in the hard Battle of the Atlantic.' He stressed the importance of a swift operation, since the naval force was needed back home and in the Mediterranean as quickly as possible. This ruled out a slow land advance from Konakry, which would necessitate keeping the warships in West African waters for months. Churchill proceeded to paint an alternative proposal in 'the most picturesque tints' and with tremendous conviction:

Dakar wakes up one morning, sad and uncertain. But behold, by the light of the rising sun, its inhabitants perceive the sea, to a great distance, covered with ships. An immense fleet! A hundred war or transport vessels! These approach slowly, addressing by radio messages of friendship to the town, to the Navy, to the Garrison. Some of them are flying the tricolour. The others are sailing under the British, Dutch, Polish or Belgian colours. From this Allied force there breaks away an inoffensive small ship bearing the white flag of parley. It enters the port and disembarks the envoys of General de Gaulle. These are brought to the Governor. Their job is to convince him that, if he lets you land, the Allied fleet retires, and that nothing remains but to settle, between him and you, the terms of his co-operation. On the contrary, if he wants a fight, he has every chance of being crushed.

During this conversation between the Governor and your representatives, Free French and British aircraft are flying peacefully over the town, dropping friendly leaflets. The military and the civilians, among whom your agents are at work, are discussing passionately among themselves the advantages offered by an arrangement with you and the drawbacks presented, on the contrary, by a large-scale battle fought against those who, after all, are the Allies of France. The Governor feels that, if he resists, the ground will give way under his feet. You will see that he will go on with the talks till they reach a satisfactory conclusion. Perhaps meanwhile he will wish, 'for honour's sake', to fire a few shots. But he will not go farther. And that evening he will dine with you and drink to the final victory.

De Gaulle allowed himself to be seduced by Churchill's eloquence

---

[30] The account that follows is based on de Gaulle's version in his *War Memoirs*, i. 120–2. The VCNS may have been present.

and arguments, though, like Churchill, he did not envisage a frontal attack on Dakar. He had made it clear to Churchill that he would have no part in a fight between Frenchmen. A *coup de main* through a 'mixture of persuasion and intimidation' would do the job. He realized, anyway, that if he did not consent, the British would probably go ahead, sooner or later, on their own, and this would not serve Free French interests. The next day, the 7th, as if to seal the bargain, Churchill signed an agreement with de Gaulle spelling out British obligations to the Free French movement, including the promise of 'the integral restoration of the independence and grandeur of France' when victory had been won.

The Chiefs of Staff accepted the essential point in the Churchill-de Gaulle plan when they met in the evening of 7 August, with the Prime Minister, who, remember, was also the Minister of Defence, in the chair. Agreement was reached that the only really effective place to land de Gaulle's force was at Dakar—that is, a direct attack—*and that British troops would accompany the expedition* in order to ensure its success. What troubled the Chiefs most was that the overland expedition would require too much time. They would not risk tying up a sizeable naval force and other resources for an indefinite period. And as on 29 July, they expressed uneasiness over the conflict between the policy of improving relations with Vichy and the policy of rallying the French colonies against Vichy, which could lead to war with Vichy France and the colonies under its control. In the end the Chiefs gave a cautious approval to the new plan: they would recommend that the expedition go forward if reports from British and Free French agents in West Africa indicated that its prospects of success were good.[31]

In the early morning hours of 8 August, after the meeting had adjourned, Churchill prepared an 'ACTION THIS DAY' minute for the Chiefs of Staff which showed his impatience with them and his desire to have the expedition proceed regardless of the reports from West Africa. He cited a telegram from the Governor of Nigeria showing the danger of the spread of German influence in French West Africa.

Unless we act with celerity and vigour, we may find effective U-boat bases, supported by German aviation, all down this coast, and it will become barred to us but available for the Germans in the same way as the western coast of Europe. . . .

It would seem extremely important to British interests that General de

[31] COS (40) 253rd Meeting, CAB 79/5.

Gaulle should take Dakar at the earliest moment. If his emissaries report that it can be taken peaceably, so much the better. If their report is adverse, an adequate Polish and British force should be provided and full naval protection given. The operation, once begun, must be carried through. De Gaulle should *be used to* impart a French character to it, and of course, once successful, his administration will rule. But we must *drive him on and* provide the needful balance of force.

The Chiefs of Staff should make a plan for achieving the capture of Dakar. For this purpose, they should consider available: (a) De Gaulle's force and any French warships which can be collected. (b) Ample British naval force, both to dominate French warships in the neighbourhood and to cover the landing. (c) A Brigade of Poles properly equipped. (d) The Royal Marine Brigade which was being held available for the Atlantic Islands, but might well help to put de Gaulle ashore first; or alternatively commandoes from Sir R. Keyes' force. (e) Proper air support, either by carrier or by machines working from a British W.[est] A.[frican] Colony.

Let a plan be prepared forthwith . . .

It is not intended, after Dakar is taken, that we shall hold it with British forces. General de Gaulle's administration would be set up, and would have to maintain itself, British assistance being limited to supplies on a moderate scale, and of course preventing any seaborne expedition from Germanized France. Should de Gaulle be unable to maintain himself permanently against air attack or airborne troops, we will take him off again after destroying all harbour facilities. We should, of course, in any case take over, under the French flag, *Richelieu*, and have her repaired. The Poles and the Belgians would also have their gold recovered for them.

In working out the above plan, time is vital. We have lost too much already. . . .

The risk of a French declaration of war and whether it should be courted is reserved for the Cabinet.[32]

This directive, in the use which it contemplated of British forces, naval, military, and air, was a marked advance in the commitments which had so far been accepted. On receipt of this directive, the Chiefs of Staff instructed the Joint Planning Sub-Committee to draw up a plan based on it. One was hurriedly prepared by the Inter-Service Planning Staff. The object was stated to be the installation of de Gaulle in Dakar, where he would hoist the Free French flag and rally the French West African colonies to his standard. As for the two methods of achieving this object, an

[32] ADM 199/207. Churchill, *The Second World War* (6 vols., London, 1948–54), Vol. ii, *Their Finest Hour*, pp. 421–2, reproduces the document with minor changes, mostly in punctuation, but it diplomatically omits the words I have italicized. Note that the pagination of the American edition of the volume is entirely different.

unopposed entry into the port of Dakar 'cannot be contemplated as a serious proposition unless the port and fortress are known to be under the control of friends of General de Gaulle, and the absence of suitable beaches precludes an unopposed landing elsewhere in the vicinity'. The rest of the paper—nine closely typed sheets—was concerned with a combined operation to capture Dakar against opposition. The plan called for a dawn attack on the widest possible front: a combination of simultaneous landings at six beaches on the north, west, and south shores of the Cape Verde Peninsula (Yof, N'Gor, Cape Verde—a small beach just south— Atlantic Coast immediately west of Dakar, Cape Manuel, Hann Bay), with a seventh landing on Gorée Island. The plan depended for its success on the use of highly trained British forces (five battalions of Royal Marines, two independent companies, and one field company), tactical surprise, dispersing the effort of the defences, and on the supposedly low morale of the French. French troops would not be used in the main attack. They were 'not suitable in any way for inclusion in the assault owing to need for careful preparation and high standard of training'. De Gaulle's force, proceeding in separate convoy some hours astern of the British assault, would disembark in the port immediately local resistance had been overpowered, or his landing could be ensured in safety. This would not happen until the British troops had secured military control of the city. It was not recommended that Polish troops take part in the operation: there were none which could be trained in time. An approximate timetable was given which set the date for departure from the United Kingdom at 23 August (de Gaulle's force) and 30 August (British force), and for the operation at 8 September.[33]

The Chiefs of Staff approved the plan on the afternoon of 9 August and sent it to the Prime Minister the next day with a commentary which stressed, among other things, that the operation must be carried out by highly trained British forces, with the Free French Forces kept below the horizon until the British had taken over the town and de Gaulle could enter the harbour unopposed. The Chiefs supported the recommendation against the inclusion of a Polish force in the expedition: they could not be trained in time, it was undesirable, politically, to mix the French and Poles, and, besides, de Gaulle did not want their participation.[34]

[33] ISPS 77th Meeting, 9 Aug., ADM 199/207.
[34] COS (40) 257th Meeting, CAB 79/6.

Churchill discussed the plan with de Gaulle, who expressed himself as in general agreement. The General, however, failed to win acceptance of two of his pet ideas. He was anxious that, to give the expedition an inter-allied flavour, Polish and Belgian contingents should be included. (This was contrary to the impression of the Chiefs of Staff that he wanted no Poles.) And he emphasized the importance of giving the impression that his forces were making the landings, to which end he suggested that the British troops be dressed in a uniform resembling the French and that British aircraft carry French markings. The Service Chiefs had no sympathy for this proposal, feeling that 'it would be a mistake for the British Forces to attempt to sail in under "false colours", and little would be gained by this ruse as the vital phase of the Operation would probably take place in half-light'. De Gaulle continued to hope that the operation would not meet with resistance, especially if elements of the Foreign Legion accompanied the first landing parties. In the event of opposition, however, he would issue instructions that the French elements with British troops would fight, if necessary.[35]

On the same day (13 August) Churchill explained the 'drastic change of plan' to the War Cabinet—that instead of landing de Gaulle at Konakry or Freetown and going overland, there would be a *coup de main* on Dakar by a joint British and Free French military and naval operation under British command. It was, he said, based on the fact that Dakar was defended by only 2,500 Senegalese troops and about 200 French officers. He promised that 'every endeavour would be made to secure the place without bloodshed, on the plea that an Allied force had come to prevent the Germans seizing Dakar, and to bring succour and help to the Colony'. He admitted that Vichy might declare war. This was unlikely (in *Their Finest Hour* he says that 'I felt in my finger-tips that Vichy France would not declare war'), but 'it would not perhaps matter very much if they did'. The War Cabinet approved the new plan, subject to hearing further from the Foreign Secretary, who wished to have 24 hours in which to consider Vichy's possible reaction.[36]

[35] COS (40) 262nd Meeting, 13 Aug., CAB 79/6.
[36] WM (40) 225, CAB 65/14. Halifax raised no objections after consulting the pre-Vichy British Ambassador to France, Sir Ronald Campbell, on the 13th. The latter summarized his views the next day. The operation would 'of course infuriate' the Vichy Government, which would use the incident 'to create as much bad blood as possible between the French people and this country. It is very doubtful however whether it would provoke them to declare war.' An important factor in favour of the operation was the probable German design on Dakar as a U-boat base. FO 371/24338.

And so 'Menace', the new code name for the operation, was given life.[37] One fails to detect very much enthusiasm on the part of the Chiefs of Staff. Churchill spotted the principal reason:

The most serious danger was prolonged fighting. But these were days in which far more serious risks were the commonplaces of our daily life. I conceived that our resources, albeit strained to the last inch and ounce, could just manage it. With invasion looming up ever nearer and more imminent, we had not shrunk from lending half our tanks to Wavell for the defence of Egypt. Compared to that, this was a pup. Our national War Cabinet, Tory, Labour, and Liberal, were hard, resolute men, imbued with an increasing sense of playing a winning hand. So all the orders were given, and everything went forward under unchallengeable authority.[38]

If Churchill had forced 'Menace' through with the lukewarm support of the Chiefs of Staff, he did so in opposition to the Joint Planners. As the then Director of Plans, Air Ministry, states:

The JP were very opposed to 'Menace' from the beginning, but W.S.C. [Churchill] put very severe (and I think improper) pressure on us—even to the extent of coming in to us in Committee and bullying us. Actually, tempers got rather frayed—we made him angry by saying we thought it was an operation which could only succeed with the hearty co-operation of the enemy, which we did not think was a sound basis for planning! However, one concession W.S.C. did make was that the exercise should be called off if the French heavy ships left the Mediterranean for the Atlantic.[39]

[37] The mention of 'Menace' as a code name for an operation, however abortive, brings to mind the extraordinary use of girls' names in the United States for hurricanes. How can anyone name a killer 'Fifi' or 'Gladys'! Churchill hit it on the head when he insisted that no mother would like to hear that her son had been killed during 'Operation Wendylove'.

[38] *Their Finest Hour*, p. 423.

[39] Marshal of the Royal Air Force Sir John Slessor's letter to the author, 7 Aug. 1972. Elsewhere Slessor writes: 'I used to be under the impression that the condition was if the French warships moved out into the Atlantic. Having since studied the actual facts and dates, I think now it must have been if the French warships reinforced *Richelieu* in Dakar before the arrival of *Menace*.' Slessor's memorandum, 'Operation Menace: the Attack on Dakar. Personal Recollections and Reflections', 22 Oct. 1972; copy in the author's possession. Slessor has told the author that the Joint Planners were 'quite sufficiently sceptical about the success of *Menace* against the then existing defences of Dakar to be certain in our minds that the addition of a formidable squadron like Force Y [see below] would be decisive against us.' Memorandum for the author, 30 Oct. 1974. The JP minutes in CAB 84/2 show no such meeting in August as described by Slessor, when the Prime Minister descended in person upon the Committee. But he is positive on the point, and it is probable that the meeting took place on 6 Aug. (JP 82, 10.30 a.m.), though possibly between 9 Aug. (JP 85) and 24 Aug. (JP 87). No minutes were issued for either JP 82 or JP 86; the latter meeting does not even have a date.

Note that the events described above were all crammed into about a week. It had been a case of hurry, hurry, hurry from the start, with the Prime Minister pushing hard for the launching of an immensely tricky and hazardous combined operation thousands of miles from home. He had his way by issuing what was virtually a ukase for the operation on 8 August. This seems to me to be a copy-book model of how to court disaster in the circumstances of 1940. Indeed, we shall see as our story proceeds that 'Menace' is an object lesson on how a combined operation should *not* be conducted by politicians and High Command in Whitehall.

*   *   *

There was at that time a controversy between the Prime Minister and the Service Chiefs over the status and role of the Joint Planning Sub-Committee after Churchill had issued an extraordinary directive on 24 August.[40] It made the JPC part of the Minister of Defence's office directly responsible to the Minister, Churchill, for working out 'the details of such plans as are communicated to them' by him. In effect, the JPC were to operate as Churchill's own staff. This was contrary to the established constitution of the COS organization and channel of responsibility, under which the JPC took instructions from the COS and reported to them. Indeed, the JPC were the most important part of their staff. (Slessor is 'amused to remember that Newall's (C.A.S.) pragmatic and objective re-action to the ukase . . . included the guess that, if we resisted the P.M.'s desire, he would soon be setting up a Joint Planning Staff of his own—which, Newall suggested, would probably include Desmond Morton and Tommy Thompson, W.S.C.'s Naval A.D.C.!'[41]) After a great deal of argument and rowing, a compromise was reached under which the Prime Minister reserved the right to issue 'prayers' to the JPC direct, while the COS maintained their right to have the JPC reports submitted through themselves. The incident was, in the judgement of a member of the JPC, 'a reflection of the PM's sense of frustration at that time; and in practice very little change resulted, except that the JP's work was increased by constant demands direct from the PM to report on so-and-so by such-and-such a time.[42]

[40] Annex to JP (40) 421, CAB 84/18.
[41] Slessor's memorandum, 'Operation Menace: the Attack on Dakar'.
[42] Captain J. S. S. Litchfield's letter to the author, 24 Sept. 1973. See Slessor, *The Central Blue* (London, 1956), pp. 299–302, for more on this curious episode.

Chapter Two

Commanders, Planners, and Planning

The word 'Dardanelles' was in the minds if not on the lips of the planning Staff.

> Commander T. C. Crease, in a letter to the author,
> 22 November 1973

The Planners made three points: (a) An all-British Force. (b) Absolute secrecy. (c) No ultimatum to Dakar. In the event: (a) Free French joined in. (b) Secrecy was absolutely broken. (c) An ultimatum *was* given. Result: complete failure.

> Admiral Sir Charles Daniel, in a letter to the author,
> 29 July 1973

. . . the plan as so far declared to me won't work. The comment of one Marine field officer was 'Caesar couldn't have got away with this against the ancient Britons' arrows.'

> Lieutenant (RNVR) R. T. Paget to A. V. Alexander,
> 29 August 1940

(Charts 1, 5)

(1) Commanders and Planners

WITH the direct British military involvement in 'Menace', Churchill insisted on British commanders, brushing aside de Gaulle's objections. Appointed as Force (Joint) Commanders on 12 August were Vice-Admiral J. H. D. Cunningham, to command the naval forces, and Major-General N. M. S. Irwin, to command the military forces. The Joint Commanders were brought together early the next day—and lived together happily ever after. They found themselves 'in complete agreement and accord' (as Irwin said afterwards) when they were called on to make combined decisions.

The two choices were solid officers. Cunningham had been

commanding the 1st Cruiser Squadron, which had been on Northern Patrol duty in the North Atlantic. Overshadowed by his more glorious namesake, Andrew B. Cunningham (no relation), John Cunningham was seldom in the public eye until after the war. He was a stocky man of middle height who usually held himself with his neck a little bent forward. Like Dudley Pound, he was dour and not easy to know. He was ready to stand up to anybody and had a reputation for not suffering fools gladly. Commander T. C. Crease, who had served under Cunningham's command in a battleship and was his Staff Officer (Operations) during 'Menace', says: 'He had a wickedly sarcastic tongue with fools, who to him were some 95 per cent of his fellow human-beings.' His sharp wit, 'earthy' tongue, and lightning repartee were famous in the Service, as were a sense of humour that belied his somewhat funereal expression, and a temper which when aroused made it desirable to say, 'Yes, Sir', and to leave his presence quickly. He was not an easy man to serve, being a strict disciplinarian and insisting on 100 per cent efficiency. He kept everyone on their toes and tolerated no slackness or sloppiness. (Though no sadist, he had the unpleasant habit of sticking the points of his dividers into the backsides of midshipmen on the bridge when he thought they were not keeping a sharp enough look-out!) To those who served him well he was very considerate and understanding; but you had to put the Service first and be up to and on top of the job. Throughout the years that Commander Crease served under him, he never remembers him bestowing praise either verbally or by signal. On the other hand, he remembers going to him and confessing to having made a mistake. 'Instead of the telling off I expected, he could not have been nicer. It would, I think, have been different had the mistake occurred through slackness or had I attempted to make excuses.' He was, in the Commander's estimation, 'a Great Man who with the addition of some more humanity might have been like his namesake a Very Great Man.'

But if few people really liked him, everyone respected him and, in difficult situations, trusted him completely, because he was an eminently sound, practical, and level-headed officer of the highest professional competence and endowed with a splendid brain. Captain P. N. Walter, his CSO in 'Menace', considers that 'he and Philip Vian had the quickest brains of any officers with whom I served in action'. Admiral Sir William Davis, who knew Cunningham well over many years, rates his 'one of the quickest and best ordered brains I know'. Admiral of the Fleet Lord Mountbatten claims that 'Andrew Cunningham did not have John Cunningham's intellectual attainments but had ten times the fire in his belly and the leadership'. Admiral of the Fleet Sir Caspar John is of the same opinion: 'Whereas A.B.C. was a leader of men, John was a thinker, with a considerably superior brain.' But if we accept Field-Marshal Lord Montgomery of Alamein's definition of leadership as 'the capacity and the will to rally men and women to a common purpose, and the character which will inspire confidence', John Cunningham was a leader, even if he lacked A.B.C.'s panache. Both were great men who exercised leadership in entirely different ways, but both effectively.

Altogether, John Cunningham was an impressive man of forceful character—one who was obviously a commander of men and ships, and clearly a man of authority. Surprisingly perhaps, during 'Menace' he remained on friendly and understanding terms with that not easiest of Frenchmen, de Gaulle. The latter found the Admiral 'sometimes troublesome to work with, but an excellent sailor and a man of feeling'. Out of deference to de Gaulle's pride and sensitivity, Cunningham was to issue orders to the French naval units only with the General's concurrence.

General Irwin had taken the 6th Infantry Brigade to France and led it with great distinction. After Dunkirk he was commanding the 2nd Division (and 'very ably', said Churchill'), re-forming in the United Kingdom, when appointed Joint Commander of the Dakar expedition. He was of athletic build, just under six feet in height, always well turned out—a typical British officer of that period, fit, not overweight, confident, nice-looking, a gentleman. But he was more than that—a forceful character, with an immense reserve of energy, and one of those fortunate people who are not in the least discommoded by either personal danger or hardship. His record in the First War was truly remarkable. He ended the war aged 26, with the Military Cross, DSO and three bars, the French Croix de Guerre, and five mentions in dispatches. Major-General A. N. Williams, who as a lieutenant-colonel commanded the 2nd Marine Battalion in 'Menace' and who knew Irwin in 1938–9, when both were serving in Hong Kong, had the strong impression that war was a horror to him. It was, he says, not any question of losing his nerve—he was exceptionally brave—but rather a realization of the misery, the horror, the loss of life that resulted. 'I always remember him saying that he would hate to have to do the things again which he did in the First World War.'

The Admiral brought three of his staff of six officers (the six included Commander Rushbrooke, on whom see below), who did not include his CSO for 'Menace', Captain P. N. Walter. (Indeed, the two had never so much as met before, but they got on very well.) Irwin was not so fortunate. A GSO 1 detached from a marine brigade was the first of his staff of eight officers (including Captain Poulter—see below) to show up. He was Lieutenant-Colonel P. R. Smith-Hill. The General was invited to select the rest of his staff; but he found that impossible, as he had much else to do. In the end the War Office hustled together his staff. 'They did their best,' Irwin remarked later, 'but it was not a staff who had worked together before but were just individuals thrown at me from here, there and everywhere.' Smith-Hill and Walter were able staff officers who worked together well. De Gaulle was not so fortunate in his Chief of Staff, Commandant (Major) Tissier. He 'appeared to be ill-served by his Chief of Staff', Cunningham noted in his Report, and General Spears referred in his diary to 'that perfectly useless fellow Tissier'.

The Commanders met the Chiefs of Staff on the morning of 13 August. The Chiefs agreed that, after the British Commanders had discussed the plan with de Gaulle and his Staff Officer the following morning, the Commanders would work out detailed plans with technical advice from the Staff of the Directorate of Combined Operations. Arrangements for embarkation and loading, shipping, and escorts would be made through the ISPS. A few details on the planning organization are in order.

Most of the work was done in the Cabinet War Room (CWR). This comprised an underground labyrinth of rooms beneath the Government offices at Storey's Gate (at the south-east corner of St. James's Park, where Great George Street enters the Park and becomes Birdcage Walk). It has been described as 'a rather spartan version of Hitler's bunker'. It was in one of these rooms, the 'JP Room', that the Directors of Plans, who normally worked in their own ministries, met collectively as the Joint Planning Sub-Committee to consider the larger picture—broad strategy and policy—clear of detail.[1] The Joint Planners were served by a tiny central

---

[1] The Joint Planners and Chiefs of Staff also met occasionally in a conference room in Richmond Terrace, a fine Georgian terrace lying off Whitehall, near the present Ministry of Defence, between Whitehall and the river. The Chiefs of Staff met in the Cabinet Room in the CWR, as did the War Cabinet when things were rough outside. Churchill had rooms in the CWR for working and sleeping. (He also used No. 10 Downing Street when things were quiet. No. 10 was not bomb-proof.) We have a

staff of nine officers from the three Services, the 'Staff of the Joint Planning Sub-Committee', which used the JP Room in the CWR. It kept the general strategical situation under constant review. Also working under the Joint Planners was the Inter-Service Planning Staff (ISPS), which was accommodated in an offshoot of the CWR. It dealt with the logistics of specific operations like 'Menace' in the stage following strategical appreciation.[2]

The final plan was the product of many cooks: the ideas of Churchill, the Chiefs of Staff (assisted by the Vice Chiefs of Staff), the Joint Planners and their staff and the ISPS, the Force Commanders and their staffs, and, so far as the plan affected the Free French Forces, de Gaulle and his staff. And so was the biblical injunction (Proverbs xxiv:6) fulfilled: 'For by wise counsel shalt thou make thy war; and in multitude of counsellors *there is* safety.' The Force Commanders and their hard-worked staffs had three rooms in the Admiralty: 97, 98, 99, with the Commanders in 99, where they 'worked in comparative calm and dignity'. The naval and military staffs got on well: everyone was cheerful and there was

---

picture of him in action there which I particularly like. 'Mr Churchill—the "Old Boss," as we called him—would trundle in wearing his siren suit, with dragon-decorated slippers and a cigar. At once each Minister would passionately press his claim to priority. The "Old Boss" would pass by, unruffled, to take his seat, and then ask Ismay what was on the agenda. As Ismay replied, Churchill would toss the butt of his cigar in the fire bucket behind him. He never took aim, but rarely missed.' James Leasor, *War at the Top* (London, 1959), p. 10. The volume is 'based on the experiences of General Sir Leslie Hollis', who had been an Assistant Secretary in the office of the War Cabinet during the war.

[2] The staff of the Joint Planning Sub-Committee expanded and reorganized on 6 Sept., when it was divided into a Strategic Planning (or S) Section, which carried on the work already performed by the Joint Planners, and an Executive (or E) Section, which took over the functions of the ad hoc ISPS. The S Section continued to work in the subterranean rooms of the Cabinet War Room. The E Section (EPS, or 'Eeps' as they were verbally referred to) were not always in session, but met as necessary in one of the Service ministries unless a meeting with the S Section or the Ds of P was convened in the JP Room in the Cabinet War Room. For the sake of completeness I should mention that a third section, the Future Operational Planning Section (or FOPS), was also constituted on 6 Sept., consisting of nine officers who were accommodated in Richmond Terrace and dealt with long-term contingency planning. The three sections, (S), (E), and (O), worked under and reported to the three Ds of P. The whole caboodle constituted the Joint Planning Sub-Committee or JPC, renamed on 6 Sept. the Joint Planning Staff, or JPS. JP, JPC/JPS, and 'Joint Planners' were interchangeable (the first and last were the more colloquial), though only the Ds of P were officially *the* JP, etc. The members of the JPC/JPS were all appointed to the Plans Divisions of their own Service ministries, with which they maintained close contact; and thus the official views and policy of the Naval, General, and Air Staffs were brought together and co-ordinated in the Joint Planning Staff. The details of the 6 Sept. reorganization are in JP (40) 421, 'Joint Planning Arrangements', 6 Sept., CAB 84/18.

no quarrelling. De Gaulle, accompanied by Spears, who acted as interpreter, often came to the Admiralty for conferences with Cunningham and Irwin in room 99. He was, as one would have expected, generally difficult and touchy.[3]

(2) Evolution of the Plan

Since the full details would make for tedious reading, besides which only a part of the plan was carried out, it may be sufficient to indicate the major problems and twists and turns, and the thrust of the final plan.

At a meeting in the evening of 15 August the Chiefs of Staff made clear to the Force Commanders that they were not to be in any way bound by the outline plans prepared by the ISPS for the Joint Planners. They instructed the Commanders, however, to prepare and submit for their approval a plan based on the following considerations: (1) The object of the operation was to establish de Gaulle in Dakar, without force if possible, but if necessary with all the force at their command. (2) The British Force would withdraw after installing de Gaulle. (3) Free French troops would be used to impart the essentially French character to the operation.[4] The Commanders continued to plan on the basis of 'Surprise rather than Force'. On the 16th they met with de Gaulle and Spears and proposed these alternative plans: (a) All-French operation, relying on a peaceful entry in broad daylight with flags flying, etc. The British Force would lie off, preferably out of sight unless required.

---

[3] Admiral Sir Richard Onslow, then a commander in the ISPS, worked with de Gaulle, almost exclusively on cleaning up logistical problems concerned with shipping and its loading. Onslow *'couldn't stand the man!'* 'Terrible aloofness; almost undisguised contempt of junior officers working with him; even at that date you could almost hear him thinking, "Moi, de Gaulle". He never smiled and never as far as I could make out showed any sign of gratitude for all we as a nation did for him.' Admiral Onslow's letters to the author, 6, 11 Dec. 1973. It is only fair to point out that Frenchmen see nothing unusual about the aloofness of their senior Army officers in their relations with subordinates. See Colonel Watson's interesting commentary on this point in his *Échec à Dakar*, pp. 89–90. General Lord Bourne, then a major in the ISPS, remembers how 'very haughty, unco-operative, and uninterested in the details' de Gaulle was in the one or two meetings he came to at the War Office. Letter to the author, 20 Jan. 1974. General Spears performed yeoman service as a buffer between de Gaulle and the British authorities. 'Day in and day out,' he noted in his diary late in August, 'I have fought thro' the trammels of Departs. & fiercely torn down the network of prejudice, hesitation & procrastination'—and making '60 enemies a day', in the opinion of his secretary. As Head of the British Mission, Spears had an extremely difficult task demanding of him exceptional understanding, skill, and patience.

[4] COS (40) 266nd Meeting, CAB 79/6.

(b) The British Force would go in as originally planned, i.e. a surprise landing, with a French element in the van to give the leading flights a French character. (c) All-British operation: air and sea bombardment would reduce the forts before a landing was attempted. De Gaulle rejected (a) on the grounds that his force would be unable to overcome the degree of resistance which might be encountered, and (c) because this would inevitably produce what he most wished to avoid, a definite war incident. He considered (b) the best plan, but accepted (c) if further study proved (a) and (b) to be impracticable. It was accordingly agreed that the Force Commanders would proceed to draw up a definite plan for (b) as soon as possible.[5]

The situation changed dramatically by 18 August. It was realized that all chances for surprise had vanished, and that it was 'a senseless proceeding [in the words of the Vice Chief of the Air Staff] "to bang at a girl's door at 3 a.m. when it is pitch dark and ask to rape her in the friendliest manner" and yet expect to be well received without one word of prior warning or any attempt to secure consent.'[6]

It all began on 18 August when the Commanders, having made a detailed examination of the ISPS plan in the light of their directives, asked to see the Chiefs of Staff at once. They represented that careful analysis of the operation had revealed two points which rendered the chances of a surprise descent on Dakar, which was an essential factor in the ISPS plan, remote. They were emphatic that if surprise failed, it would be impossible at the last moment to transform the operation from a peaceful takeover into a violent assault. The Vice Chiefs of Staff Committee (in the absence of the Chiefs of Staff) summed up the new situation on the 19th:

> The original conception of Operation 'Menace' was that we should do everything possible to install General de Gaulle at Dakar without bloodshed. This was not because we wished specifically to avoid a fight, but because it was clear that the best chance General de Gaulle would have of successfully raising his standard in West Africa was to get the Dakar garrison and people to rally to him by their own choice, and not as a result of force. With this view General de Gaulle was in full agreement.

[5] Cunningham's Report on 'Menace', 24 Oct., Pt. I, p. 4, ADM 199/906, Irwin's Report on 'Menace', 7 Oct., Ch. I, p. 3, WO 106/2858 (hereafter 'Cunningham's Report' and 'Irwin's Report'), 'War Diary', 16 Aug., ADM 202/413. These sources vary somewhat in their description of the alternatives and de Gaulle's reaction.

[6] Entry of 21 Aug. 1940, diary of Acting Captain L. H. Bell. He was Naval Assistant to the VCNS.

The corollary of this was that the initial landing should achieve tactical surprise.

New intelligence, they went on, had led to a material alteration in the plan. First and most important was the confirmation that swell and surf conditions made the projected landings on the north and west coasts of the Cape Verde Peninsula (to use the words in Cunningham's Report) 'quite impracticable' (N'Gor and Yof) or 'probably impracticable' (Cape Verde and 'Atlantic Coast', apparently meaning Fann Point). This reduced the possible landing beaches in the peninsula as proposed by the ISPS to the two on the south coast of the peninsula, Cape Manuel and Hann Bay, immediately north and south of the harbour, both sheltered within the Gulf of Gorée and both covered by heavy gun defences and lights. The second point was the existence of a line of hydrophones well to the seaward (3 miles) of the A/S net boom covering Dakar harbour. (We shall see that there were no hydrophones: below, p. 146n.) To avoid detection as long as possible, it was originally considered necessary to transfer the landing parties from troopships to landing craft about 8 miles from the landing beach, a distance much in excess of that normally considered desirable. It would now be necessary to extend this distance to 11 miles in order to avoid hydrophone detection. The conclusions of the Vice Chiefs were:

(i) The chance of the landing parties escaping detection until they are on the beach is remote.

(ii) If they are detected, they will be unable, in the dark, to establish their peaceful intentions.

(iii) If, as seems most likely in these circumstances, they were fired upon by patrols or coast defences, they would be out of reach of any supporting fire from our own ships, which might be anything up to eleven miles away.

We would then have fallen between two stools. All hope of a successful bloodless operation would have vanished; and at the same time the dispositions which had been adopted with this end in view would preclude any hope of a successful *coup de main*.

In these circumstances the Commanders have reluctantly come to the conclusion and, on the information available, we agree that we must abandon all idea of a bloodless landing on the lines originally conceived.

The Vice Chiefs put forward (on behalf of the Chiefs of Staff) as a promising alternative to a surprise descent on Dakar the delivery of an ultimatum, followed, if this were rejected, by the use of force and an opposed landing. The difficulty was, they stated, that de

Gaulle would not associate himself with this plan. 'He is prepared to risk incidents but not to take part in a deliberate assault on his countrymen.' The Committee went on to discuss a de Gaulle memorandum of that day proposing that if the operation as planned turned out to be impossible, or resulted in failure, they should fall back on an 'emergency' operation. This was the seizure of St. Louis, 100 miles north of Dakar, at the mouth of the Senegal River, through a landing there of the whole expeditionary force. It would then advance on Dakar by road and rail, while at the same time negotiating with the authorities and appealing to the population. The Vice Chiefs saw no merit in the scheme: only very shallow draught vessels could negotiate the bar at the entrance to the river, 'and from the navigation point of view the landing of an expedition of the size contemplated is considered impracticable'. The best they could suggest, however, was to fall back on the original Konakry project, which had been ruled out on account of its great distance from Dakar. If 'Menace' were regarded as no longer feasible, the installation of de Gaulle at Konakry as a first step in rallying West Africa might well be the best course. 'This would be a relatively simple operation which could be carried out without delay.'[7]

It was already 19 August and they were back in square one! On the evening of 20 August what turned out to be a decisive meeting took place, of the Vice Chiefs at No. 10 with Churchill presiding and de Gaulle and Spears present. The Prime Minister pointed out that in view of the new information about the defences of Dakar, a night landing would be difficult and surprise would be lost. He outlined a new plan, which was actually a reversion to his original plan of 6 August, whereby the Free French Forces, both naval and military, would lead the advance on Dakar in daytime, the British force remaining on the horizon in order to take part if this should subsequently prove necessary. The Anglo-French armada would arrive off Dakar at dawn; aircraft would drop leaflets over the town appealing to the soldiers, sailors, and townspeople (two million were prepared); the British squadron would remain on the horizon while the Free French ships advanced towards the port; about an hour and a quarter after dawn, a picket boat flying a white flag and

---

[7] COS (40) 643, 'Operation "Menace",' 19 Aug., CAB 80/16, COS (40) 646, 'Operation "Menace"' (de Gaulle's memorandum), 19 Aug., CAB 80/16. The Vice Chiefs were Acting Vice-Admiral T. S. V. Phillips, Air Marshal Sir R. E. C. Peirse, and Lieutenant-General Sir R. H. Haining.

a tricolour would enter the harbour bearing a letter from de Gaulle to the Governor announcing the arrival of de Gaulle and his Free French troops. The letter would stress that de Gaulle had come to deliver Dakar from the danger of imminent German aggression, that they were bringing food and succour to the garrison and the people. It would emphasize that this was a French enterprise but that a British squadron had accompanied it. If the Governor welcomed de Gaulle and his Free Frenchmen, the British squadron would not advance on the port. All would be well if the Governor were prepared to welcome de Gaulle's entry. He might, however, refuse to receive de Gaulle's emissary and follow it up by a show of resistance. If the resistance were serious, de Gaulle would ask the British squadron to close in. 'If the firing continued the British warships would open fire on the French gun positions but would use the utmost restraint in the initial stages. If it was clear that the coast batteries and possibly the battleship *Richelieu* were determined to make a fight, the British force would use all the force within their power to break down their resistance. It seemed unlikely however that French opposition would be severe in the face of the overwhelming force which would confront them. The action outlined above would be carried out deliberately and without undue hurry so as to give the Frenchmen ashore time to realize the uselessness of resistance.' When de Gaulle had established himself on shore, parleys would follow, and he would, it was hoped, take control of Dakar peaceably. The British squadron would withdraw once de Gaulle was master of Dakar. One or two British battalions might have to be landed to support de Gaulle in the initial stages. It was, in any case, essential that he be in control of Dakar by nightfall. De Gaulle expressed his agreement with the plan as outlined by the Prime Minister, as did the Vice Chiefs.[8]

The plan was explained to the Commanders the next morning (21 August) by the Vice Chiefs. It was agreed that, if practicable, French aircraft would be flown off a carrier to land at Dakar (the Cape Verde Peninsula airfield of Ouakam) as early as possible and persuade the Vichy French pilots not to leave the ground. The Committee instructed the Commanders to consult with de Gaulle and submit their outline plan and programme that evening. A combined plan on the lines of the new programme was submitted to the Prime Minister in the evening and accepted. It included details of the naval and military forces necessary.

[8] COS (40) 275th Meeting, CAB 79/6.

De Gaulle, who was present at the meeting on the 21st, thought it was quite likely that the Governor would not receive his emissary. He 'stressed the necessity for carrying out the Operation deliberately and without undue hurry in order to allow French action at Dakar to become subject to decision and argument.'[9] In deference to his wishes, the final plan placed no restrictions on the length of time to be devoted to the operation.

It was hoped, the Force Commanders stated in a Combined Naval and Military Instruction,

that a firm yet conciliatory approach by the Free French Forces, preceded by a parley and leaflet dropping, and supported at a distance by powerful British forces manœuvring in the offing, will lead to the peaceful establishment ashore of General de Gaulle and his force.

Should only formal or sporadic resistance occur it may be neutralised by resolute handling of the Free French units, assisted if necessary by a limited employment of British force.

While it is desired to use as little force as possible and to stress always the French nature of the expedition, yet, if serious resistance is offered the British Forces will be employed to overcome it and will use all the force necessary to obtain possession of the Port.

The intention is to capture Dakar and install General de Gaulle with as little bloodshed as possible.[10]

This meant that, if it came to it, British troops, the Royal Marine striking force, would land with the Free French troops, though not before naval gunfire had silenced the main shore batteries, and take Dakar. Originally, de Gaulle had insisted that force must not be used under any circumstances—that the operation must be no more than a demonstration ('*comme une fête*'). He would not accept Irwin's argument that, persuasion failing, they should use limited force, so that the Dakar authorities could satisfy their honour by fighting, then claiming that they had been overcome. 'We argued,' Smith-Hall, Irwin's GSO 1, relates, 'but finally de Gaulle stood up, shook hands with each of us in silence, and went off to his hotel. However, the next day Spears said: "The General says Joan of Arc spilled French blood, and he is prepared to do the same".'[11] It was,

[9] COS (40) 276th Meeting, CAB 79/6.
[10] 'Naval and Military Instruction No. 1' (short title, M.N.G. 1), Admiralty, 27 Aug., ADM 199/906. The Instruction 'gives a general idea of the projected operation and forms the basis upon which operation orders will subsequently be issued'.
[11] Anthony Heckstall-Smith, *The Fleet that Faced Both Ways* (London, 1963), p. 127. He had apparently interviewed Smith-Hall after the war.

nevertheless, at least de Gaulle's expectation that the show of force would mean no more than a few rounds of fire by Cunningham's ships, since the forts would offer only a token resistance.

The Combined Instruction included a schedule with approximate timings and plans for three alternative 'situations'. These were given the code names of 'Happy', 'Sticky', and 'Nasty'. 'Happy' would be applicable if the defenders welcomed de Gaulle's emissaries, and de Gaulle and his troops were securely established in control of Dakar. Irwin would land to confirm whether this was so. No operations would be necessary, though they might have to land some British troops to support de Gaulle temporarily. 'Sticky' described this situation: 'Formal or sporadic resistance leading to a position of uncertainty regarding the issue, followed by a request from General de Gaulle for assistance if his own ships cannot deal with it.' In that case, the British squadron would close 'and may subsequently bombard specific targets, using every endeavour to restrict damage'. 'Nasty' would indicate 'organized resistance'. A sea and air bombardment would reduce the fortifications, and then British troops would be landed to destroy enemy resistance ashore and occupy Dakar. It might be necessary to land at any or all of these beaches: Hann Bay (possible objectives, Bel-Air battery, Ouakam airfield, and the harbour and town of Dakar); Bernard Bay, north of the harbour (batteries at Cape Manuel and Madeleine); Gorée Island (batteries on the Island); and Rufisque (the road and rail communications).[12]

The War Cabinet gave 'a general approval' to the plans for the operation on 27 August. They considered that, 'having regard to the value of its objects, the Operation was one which we should be justified in undertaking. The danger of the Vichy Government declaring war as a result was not rated very highly.'[13] The target date was then 18 September. The planning stage was completed so far as the authorities in London were concerned, but neither information, staff, nor time were available to prepare before sailing the operation orders, bombardment plans, and other details for an opposed landing.

---

[12] See further on the landing plans, below, pp. 65-6.
[13] WM (40) 235, CAB 65/14.

Chapter Three

Problems: Intelligence, Security, Delays, and Doubts

The business asketh silent secrecy.

Shakespeare, II *King Henry IV*

Three factors will appear which fought against success. These were the miscalculation of the resistance which would be encountered, the urgent need for haste, and, lastly, the persistent ill-luck which dogged the operation from beginning to end.

'The Dakar Operation' (official account of May 1942)

(Charts 1, 5)

(1) Intelligence Failures

CHURCHILL later wrote that they 'certainly had bad luck'. It was all of that, and much of it predated the operation itself. 'Menace' was, let us face it, a muddle from the start. Almost everything went wrong, beginning with the intelligence situation. The success of the operation depended, in the first instance, on a correct appreciation of the state of feeling in Senegal and in particular at Dakar, since the plan was predicated on the peaceful establishment of de Gaulle and his force. The political objective of the operation and indeed the success of the operation if it came to serious shooting were to a considerable degree founded on the hope and expectation of little, if any, bloodshed.

But de Gaulle grossly overestimated the extent of his backing. He was influenced by the receipt at his London headquarters of messages of sympathy and support from many Frenchmen in Dakar and other towns in Senegal. His agents in West Africa assured him that 70 per cent of the Dakar garrison supported his cause, that 20 per cent were neutral, and that a mere 10 per cent favoured Vichy. He was, moreover, encouraged by intelligence that the crews of four

French armed merchant cruisers at Dakar had refused to fight the British at the time of their attack on the *Richelieu* (8 July), that the crews had been imprisoned, and that there had been strong resistance in Dakar to orders from Vichy to attack the British colony of Gambia. These acts may have been due to nothing more than war weariness. It was Irwin's expectation that, generally speaking, 'The Senior Officers and the Navy (particularly *Richelieu*) are likely to be unfriendly, while the majority of Junior Officers, garrison troops, and population are expected to be in sympathy with General de Gaulle'. Much closer to the true position was the estimate of an officer of the French submarine *Ajax* at Dakar, who classified the French population there on the eve of the Allied attack as: 20 per cent favourable to de Gaulle, comprising mainly those with a vested interest—merchants or producers of peanuts, who wanted at any cost to sell their produce; 50 per cent indifferent, desiring above all to be left at peace; 30 per cent, mostly the naval and military elements, who wanted to resist *à outrance*.[1] The most rabidly Anglophobe elements in Dakar were the naval officers, who were still bitterly resentful over the Mers-el-Kébir humiliation. Nor had the subsequent attack on the *Richelieu* won any friends for the British in the French Navy. (A torpedo-bomber attack from the aircraft carrier *Hermes* on 8 July had resulted in damage to the *Richelieu*'s hull.)

It was easy afterwards to pin the responsibility for the miscalculation of the strength of the Free French sympathizers on de Gaulle. But Churchill, the War Cabinet, and the Services were not blameless. De Gaulle's information on the state of opinion in Dakar and Senegal—reports from emissaries and local informants—were *never shown to Spears or the higher-ups*: he merely reported the happy tidings. There was, then, no opportunity for the evaluation of the reports. Apparently, nobody pressed the point.[2] 'We had,' said Halifax later, 'perhaps accepted too readily the rosy estimate of the operation which had been given by General de Gaulle's supporters, and we had been misled by people on the spot as to the feeling of the French forces at Dakar.'[3] They accepted de Gaulle's assurances and those of their own agents in West Africa, in spite of uncertain reports from West Africa. Thus, on 4 July, the C-in-C, South Atlantic, Vice-Admiral Lyon, had described the situation in

---

[1] Vice-Admiral E. M. Muselier, *De Gaulle contre le gaullism* (Paris, 1946), p. 84.
[2] Author's interview with General Sir Edward Spears, 17 Dec. 1973.
[3] WM (40) 258, 25 Sept., CAB 65/15.

Dakar as he had observed it during a visit on 25–26 June. General Barrau, commanding the Army in French West Africa, told him that there were three classes of people in Dakar: the Service element, who would obey their senior officers; the commercial element, who were concerned with protecting their own interests and were awaiting some statement of French policy; and the remainder of the white population, chiefly 'the unintelligent and "scallywags" who were obviously ready to join up with whichever party, Britain or France, gave the best promise of advantage to them'. This estimate was, unhappily, somewhat undercut by Captain J. G. L. Poulter, the British Military Liaison Officer, who told the Admiral that Barrau and the Army were pro-British.[4] On 4 August the Colonial Office had reported that the dissident elements in the French colonies were hardly in control, nor were they likely to be:

Our first aim on the collapse of France was to induce the French colonies to fight on as our allies. We established close contact with the local French administrations and offered substantial financial inducements. The reaction leaves no doubt that there are French elements ready to rally to our side. But the Vichy government is in a position to exercise strong pressure on the local officials who have been in a defeatist and wavering frame of mind; and there is no doubt that the official policy of the local administrators is now one of obedience to Vichy and refusal to co-operate with us.[5]

Certainly there was no reason to believe that the High Commissioner for French West and Equatorial Africa would be disloyal to Vichy. Pierre Boisson was a veteran of the First War (he had lost a leg in it) who had been Governor of the French Congo until ousted by the Free French. This brilliant, energetic, and determined colonial official—a leading Gaullist called him 'a very prickly customer'—was of extreme Rightist sympathies and therefore found

[4] Vice-Admiral G. H. D'O. Lyon to Admiralty, FO 371/24321. Poulter was a bit wobbly. Cf. his later opinion, below, pp. 44–5. On 31 July the C-in-C, South Atlantic, reported, on the authority of the Captain of a Polish merchant ship which had escaped from Dakar, that 80% of the population at Dakar were against the Vichy Government, that there was much unrest in the Services, and that the food situation was bad apart from meat and bread, of which there was sufficient for three months. On 13 August Admiral Muselier, Commander of the Free French Navy, told Spears that the *Richelieu* was the only French naval unit at Dakar that was strongly anti-British. These two reports are in 'Dakar: Morale, Various Reports', part of an NID file of August. Major A. S. Irwin kindly furnished this document to me.

[5] J. R. M. Butler, *The History of the Second World War. Grand Strategy*, ii (London, 1957), 312.

the Vichy régime to his taste. Of greater importance, he was as anti-German as de Gaulle himself; but he was convinced that the surest way to attract the Germans to French Africa was by joining the Free French and the British, which would give the hated enemy a pretext. French Africa was for him, as for Vichy, France's one remaining trump, apart from the Fleet, and should not be thrown away by a premature move. Boisson would not have tolerated more than a token German presence in Dakar.

We can only conclude with General Spears: 'A further mistake was to base a serious military operation on unverified and unverifiable political assumptions,' that is, to believe the over-optimistic information which was fed to them by the Free French and their own sources that Dakar was essentially pro-de Gaulle and would welcome the General if he arrived there.

Strategic intelligence was as faulty as political intelligence, and here the Services were directly to blame. Section 6 of NID played an interesting role in the planning. This was the Topographical Section ('topography' included information on hygiene, suitable clothing, and flora). On 19 August they were urgently asked to collect all information on Dakar. They performed a small miracle in a week's time, preparing a detailed report, with photographs, maps, and plans of Dakar—all the intelligence that Cunningham's staff seemed to require. For example, the London School of Hygiene and Tropical Medicine contributed an estimate of probable casualty rates from malaria among troops moving across marshy ground in tropical areas like the Dakar hinterland.[6] Neither NID nor the Military Intelligence Directorate of the War Office were very helpful as to the defences of Dakar.

The combined staff for the operation suffered from a lack of information about Dakar's defences.

---

[6] This paragraph is based on *The Naval Memoirs of Admiral J. H. Godfrey* (8 vols. in 11, privately printed, 1964–6), v, Pt. 2, pp. 358–9. He was DNI, 1939–42. But Commander Crease, who was on Admiral Cunningham's staff, remembers being sent by the Admiral to NID to collect all available material on Dakar. 'I returned with a thin file containing nothing of any value. The Admiral was *not* pleased. He remarked that, as he had feared, between the wars the department had made no efforts to collect information but had lapsed into a filing office. If my memory is correct, we obtained our most valuable information from the Admiralty Sailing Directions.' Crease's letter to the author, 22 Nov. 1973. How does one reconcile the major discrepancy in these two sources? It could be that Crease's visit coincided with the request to NID to prepare a report. On the other hand, we do have evidence to indicate that NID was indeed wanting. See the 'typical' photograph (Major A. S. Irwin) from NID opposite p. 71, on which General Irwin and his staff were expected to plan their beach assault!

The military plan was dependent on the over-riding consideration that no landings were to be attempted until the main shore batteries had been silenced by naval gun fire. It was recognised that naval guns are usually unable to silence shore batteries but reliance was placed on the assurance (received from several quarters) that the crews of the batteries were not whole-heartedly in favour of Vichy and would take the first opportunity of supporting the Free French movement under General de Gaulle. In any case General de Gaulle was confident that the defenders would not open fire on Free French Ships.[7]

It was, nevertheless, important to have reliable information about the gun defences: how many batteries, of what calibre, and their positions.

Although the Navy had been using Dakar for nearly a year, for both aircraft and warships, and the British had had two liaison officers stationed at Dakar before the fall of France—Commander Jermyn Rushbrooke and Captain Poulter, whom the French authorities had forced to leave at the end of June—the overstrained Intelligence departments seemed to find it difficult to produce an accurate picture of the shore batteries and other defences, as well as the true situation as regards the landing beaches. At a meeting of the Chiefs of Staff and the ISPS on 10 August the need for the most up-to-date local knowledge was emphasized and the decision was taken to have Poulter flown home from Freetown in a flying boat. Rushbrooke, who was also at Freetown, was soon added. The flying boat detailed for their transport was undergoing repairs in Lagos that were not completed until 19 August. Then the commander in Freetown, General Giffard, who was not informed that the officers were wanted post-haste, used the flying boat on other business for several days before he made it available to transport the two officers. They did not arrive in London until nearly midnight on 28 August, which was some 24 hours before the Commanders were due to catch the night train to the Clyde, from where they were to sail on the 31st. They were cross-examined in rather hurried fashion by Cunningham and Irwin at the Admiralty early the next morning (29 August), and, 'as so often happens with even

---

[7] Smith-Hill, 'Devant Dakar 1940', p. 4. The advantages of shore batteries in a duel with naval guns were practically axiomatic in the Navy. The fixed gun platform, unlimited width of rangefinder angle, offshore hydrophones, and plotted shot sections gave shore batteries an excellent chance to defeat ships, which in 1940 still relied on a physically limited rangefinder and an unsteady gun platform. It would require over-whelming naval strength, good visibility, and aircraft spotting to overcome the batteries.

the most promising "contacts" neither officer could elucidate the points that were in doubt!'[8]

The Atlantic swell might render a landing impracticable, since it broke on the West African coast so many days in the year that a single calm day could never be relied upon. The only possible landing places on the Cape Verde Peninsula, upon which Dakar is situated, were several small beaches on the coast west and north of the town, at Yof, N'Gor, Cape Verde, and Fann Point. Three of these (all but N'Gor) were commanded by shore batteries and all could be easily defended by infantry posts and by wire. Beaches above Dakar, on the north side of Gorée Bay between Bel-Air Point and Rufisque, were more sheltered, although modern batteries at Bel-Air Point, Gorée Island, and Cape Manuel commanded them. Still, one of the points that particularly required elucidation was the precise surf conditions at all the possible landing beaches. But the guidance of the informants 'was in the nature of "It may be rough and it may not".'[9]

The intelligence on the landing conditions on the beaches remained lamentable. They had originally intended to land on the Atlantic beaches to the westward of Dakar. But when they could not find out from any source what sort of conditions of surf to expect on these exposed beaches, they had to rule these out completely as potential landing places, although they were by far the best, if conditions were right, for the object. In the end they decided on the sheltered beaches inside the bay. (See above, pp. 23, 34, 38.)

The two officers from Freetown were, however, firm on two crucial points, one of which was that *Dakar would not rally to de Gaulle.* The Governor-General and the Dakar garrison were loyal to Vichy and would put up a determined and effective resistance to any attempted landings. De Gaulle would not be welcomed by any important section of the community. Poulter, in particular, felt that Dakar would resolutely oppose any attempt by de Gaulle. The responsible authorities would not accept this assessment. There was, for one thing, little time (the Force Commanders and their staffs were due to leave London on the 30th to embark in the *Devonshire* in the Clyde), and there was little inclination to examine in detail an opinion which if taken seriously could result in a last-

[8] Godfrey, *Naval Memoirs*, v, Pt. 2, pp. 359–60.
[9] Rear-Admiral L. E. H. Maund, *Assault from the Sea* (London, 1949), p. 72. Maund was then in the Directorate of Combined Operations.

minute cancellation of the operation. It was too late for that. 'The lists were set and the adventure had gathered a momentum which was not to be deflected.'[10]

The other important point on which Poulter and Rushbrooke were firm was that the defences were much stronger than the planners had believed. (The approximate date of the information about Dakar handed to the Commanders before sailing may be judged from the statement in it that the construction of certain buildings was projected for *1919*!) On the basis of Poulter's information, Admiralty draughtsmen worked through the night, correcting the charts of the defences. They were rushed to the *Devonshire* for distribution to the Force on arrival at Freetown, whither, we shall see, the expedition was to go prior to Dakar. There not being time to get all the information out of Poulter and Rushbrooke, it was decided to take them along in the flagship.

The more up-to-date information revealed by Poulter was an eye-opener. The naval and military forces allotted to the operation were based on information ('gross misinformation', in Cunningham's words) that Poulter proved to be inaccurate. Whereas the Commanders had been told by the Chiefs of Staff on 15 August that the coast defences included five 9·4-inch guns, eight 5-inch, and four 4·8-inch, they now learned that the coast artillery was about twice as strong. It included eight 9·4-inch guns, which was nearly accurate, twenty-five 5·4-inch, and eighteen 3-inch or 4-inch H.A./ L.A. (high angle, low angle) guns. And the operation itself revealed the existence of batteries whose location and calibre had been unsuspected. That was not all. When they were at sea, Poulter surprised the Commanders by producing a copy of the French West African Defence Scheme, which he had sent to the War Office in June and about which they knew nothing. This document showed that the field troops in Dakar were considerably stronger than the figures given to Cunningham and Irwin on 15 August.

---

[10] 'There is a conflict of evidence as to the emphasis which Captain Poulter laid on the loyalty of the garrison to Vichy. He maintains that his words, in his interview with the joint commanders, were "Not one man, woman or child is pro-de Gaulle." The joint commanders do not admit that he was so emphatic.' Hist. (A) 2, 'The Dakar Operation, August and September 1940', p. 9n. And see 'Notes by Major-General N. M. S. Irwin, C.B., D.S.O., M.C., on the "Dakar Operation",' n.d. (late 1940), Irwin MSS., IRW 1/2. These were notes on a 20 Nov. 1940 draft of what became Hist. (A) 1 (Final), 'The Dakar Operation', 5 Feb., 1941. See above, p. xii. Poulter came out with the expedition in the *Devonshire* as a member of Irwin's staff. (Rushbrooke joined the Admiral's staff.) Captain Walter remembers how 'he consistently maintained that Dakar would never accept de Gaulle, but we all regarded him as a Jeremiah. Alas, he was perfectly right.'

Instead of only seven garrison companies of Senegalese infantry, that is, approximately 1,400 men, there was, in addition, it was now revealed, a regiment (three battalions) of Senegalese infantry, for a total of some 7,000 (including French officers).[11]

(2) Security Leaks

The two dangers, once the decision to go forward was reached on 5 August, were, in Churchill's words, 'delay and leakage, and the first aggravated the second'. The Chiefs of Staff and the War Cabinet, in their meetings on 5 August, had recognized the great importance and the extreme difficulty of keeping the preparations top secret. 'The troops,' declared the Service Chiefs, 'have to be concentrated and equipped for service under tropical conditions and it is inevitable that this will give rise to speculation as to their destination. It will be essential that both officers and men should be provided with some pretext for the preparations which will not divulge the real intention.'[12] Yet the gaff was soon blown, for there were, as Marshal of the Royal Air Force Slessor puts it, 'completely Gilbertian breaches of security in London'. If intelligence was lamentable, security was nil. In his report on the operation, Irwin declared that he 'was most disagreeably impressed with the number of officers I met in the War Office who seemed to know all about the operations. I daresay this is inevitable . . .'

Security was breached by what Donald McLachlan has called 'the careless competition of the Three Service Ministries in the collection of information'. The situation resulted in a needless overlapping and duplication of effort which multiplied the possibilities of leaks. One hears of a young officer who appeared at a City firm and openly and directly asked for a plan of Dakar. The Poles, who were originally intended to form part of the expedition, were responsible for further leakage.

[11] Hist. (A) 2, 'The Dakar Operation, August and September 1940', pp. 4, 5n., 11n., Irwin's Camberley lecture, Cunningham's Report, Pt. 1, p. 8, App. 1, p. 1. The Admiral added: 'Actually Captain Poulter's estimate of the probable defences, received verbally only, on the eve of sailing, proved in the end fairly accurate, but in the complete absence of confirmation, if not of actual contradiction from other sources well qualified to judge, his estimate was only partially accepted by the Force Commanders.' The information on French air strength given to the Commanders on 15 August was incorrect, or at least it was so by the time of the operation: 34 Glenn-Martin bombers at Dakar, etc. For the complete picture of the garrison and defences of Dakar, see below, pp. 107-8, which is derived from official French sources.

[12] COS (40) 603, 'Operations in West Africa', 5 Aug., CAB 80/16.

The principal transgressors were the Frenchmen in England. A JP report of 19 September on the leakage of information asserted:

> It is alleged that the destination of the force was widely known. This was in fact the case and we attribute it principally to the total indifference to security measures, and the lack of discipline of the French officers and other ranks. Our opinion is based upon the following reports:
>
> (a) That General de Gaulle, when purchasing a considerable quantity of tropical equipment at 'Simpson's' in Piccadilly, remarked in public that his destination was West Africa.
>
> (b) That at a dinner in a restaurant in Liverpool [Adelphi Hotel] the French officers toasted 'Dakar'.
>
> (c) That, according to a special intelligence report received by the Inter Service Security Board, 'Dakar' was common talk amongst the French troops.[13]

This was all very true, but was scarcely half the story.

Rumour, well-founded as it happens, had it that at a great 'hurrah' party in a London restaurant (the Écu de France in Jermyn Street) on the eve of departure patriotic young Free French officers, carried away by enthusiasm and wine, made stirring toasts '*à Dakar*' and '*à de Gaulle*'.

Then there was the famous incident at Euston. The Spears Mission and de Gaulle and his staff left Euston (the station for Liverpool) at 10 a.m. on 30 August in 'a blaze of glory, or, should I say publicity? I have never seen so many people from V.I.P.s, civil and military, to wives and girl-friends gathered together to see off the heads of an ultra-secret expedition.'[14] Security went out with the wind, literally, when the train was about to move out of the station. A porter came running up, trundling a large case on a barrow. There was a collision, the case fell off the barrow and burst open, revealing blue, white, and red leaflets headed '*AUX HABITANTS DE DAKAR*'. They danced about in the wind until hurriedly gathered together and put back into the case.[15]

A similar misfortune occurred at the Clyde about a week before the sailing. A lighter came alongside the *Devonshire* with a con-

---

[13] JP (40) 465 (E), 'Operation "Menace"—Security Arrangements', a joint report by EPS and the Inter-Service Security Board, CAB 84/19. In Liverpool bars and restaurants prior to the sailing Free French soldiers in tropical uniforms raised their glasses in toasts '*à Dakar*'.

[14] Watson, *Échec à Dakar*, p. 51.

[15] Ibid., p. 52. Other witnesses have testified to this incident as well as to the fanfare that marked the entire episode of the departure. See especially Sir Ronald Wingate, *Not in the Limelight* (London, 1959), p. 159. He was with the Spears Mission.

signment of large paper packages. During embarkation of these by a working party of the ship's company, one or more of these packages accidentally broke open, revealing leaflets in blue, white, and red, inscribed in French: '*FRANÇAIS DE DAKAR! Joignez-vous à nous pour délivrer la France!* Géneral de Gaulle.' A quantity of these leaflets was circulated among the ship's company, and it is generally accepted that a number of these found their way ashore and circulated in the pubs of Glasgow and Greenock, where there was a fair sprinkling of French at the time.[16]

Then there was the shipment of landing craft from Portsmouth to Liverpool, 'loaded onto trollies without any covering and paraded across England like the Durham Ox "to the wonder and consternation of the countryside".' And the troops who guarded them wore tropical kit. On arrival the landing craft were open to the 'unobstructed inspection' of Swedish and other neutral ships. These charges were made by a Lieutenant, RNVR, R. T. Paget, who commanded a section of assault landing craft in the expedition, in a letter to A. V. Alexander, the First Lord, on 29 August. (Halifax and the Force Commanders had some days earlier expressed dismay over the leakage of information.) 'The Germans must know by now of the existence and composition of the expedition and they must further know that its destination is in the tropics and an assault landing is contemplated somewhere. They may or may not know of our precise destination. I do; not because I have been let into the secret but because I have picked up sufficient clues to enable me to identify the place. Before I knew this I was told of our destination by a man on the Liverpool docks. . . . I have since been told by a Marine Officer that he was not only told of our destination by a docker hand but was also told of the precise composition of our escort.'[17] The officer who brought the back pay to the French-

---

[16] Among those who refer to the incident is Evelyn Waugh, in his hilarious novel *Men at Arms* (1952) about the 'Royal Halberdiers'. Though fictional, the story is founded on Waugh's service in the 1st RM battalion. The latter part is concerned with the Dakar expedition.

[17] After some unflattering remarks about the loading of the ships at Liverpool and other inanities, and the weaknesses of the operational plan, Paget concluded that he was 'fully aware that I am committing a court martial offence in writing you this letter. I am doing it entirely on my own responsibility because I consider it my duty to place the facts before you and I leave myself entirely in your hands.' ADM 199/1931. Churchill minuted this extraordinary document (4 Sept.): 'No action is possible except to make sure that the faults alleged by the writer do not recur next time. The writer is granted [protection?] by me, & must not be proceeded against in any way.' EPS and the Inter-Service Security Board examined the letter (JP (40) 465 (E), above), as did the Chiefs of Staff after the operation, on 4 October, the latter making these observations: '(a) The

manned merchantmen at Liverpool (see below) informed Commander Onslow, on returning to London the next day, that the destination of the convoy was common knowledge around the docks. General Irwin commented in his Report on how 'the destination of Dakar was being openly discussed' at Liverpool. Elsewhere he stated: 'That people knew that the entire force was being inoculated for yellow fever there is no doubt.'

Although the indiscretions and leakages resulted in the Pétain Government being aware that an expedition was leaving for Freetown, they did not, *mirabile dictu*, suspect that its ultimate destination was Dakar. It was, we shall see, not until almost the eve of the attack that the authorities at Dakar had some inkling what was up.[18] They were apparently misled by knowledge that all convoys for the Mediterranean round the Cape called at Freetown. More important, perhaps, was point (a) in the Service Chiefs' appreciation (below, n. 17). Major Morton's Committee on Allied Resistance, when they became aware early in August of leaks of information, collaborated with the Chiefs of Staff in taking action calculated to confuse the enemy. In particular, they used the Security Service to spread abroad false rumours of the nature and destination of the expedition. As soon as the operation was set on foot, the Inter-Service Security Board had it put about that the British were sending a Free French expedition to Egypt. The local security people in the Middle East assisted the deception by marking out camp sites

---

"cover" plan was discreetly spread and subsequent information showed that the hoped for leakage of the "cover" had in fact taken place. (b) The passage of the landing craft across England and their presence in Liverpool could not be hidden but, in any case, their movements could be accounted for under the "cover" plan. (c) With the exception of the garrisons in Iceland and the Faroes all soldiers going abroad are issued with tropical clothing. This, in itself, was therefore no indication of any particular destination. (d) Shore leave would not have been granted after arrival at the port of embarkation if the ships had been sailing immediately, which they were not. (e) It appears that there was a general leakage of information through French sources. Even General de Gaulle himself had remarked in public that his destination was West Africa. It is very unlikely that anyone, other than the immediate staffs of the two Commanders, had any knowledge of the actual plan of the Operation before the expedition sailed. . . . The Chiefs of Staff consider that it is virtually impossible to *prepare* a large expedition in complete secrecy, but the use of suitable "Cover" should prevent knowledge of its *destination* leaking out.' ADM 199/1931 (also PREM 3/276). The First Lord found the reply 'not wholly convincing'.

[18] The French Government knew as early as 8 September, through a telegram of 6 September from the Spanish Ambassador in London whose content was passed on by the Spanish Ambassador in Vichy, that de Gaulle had left England for Africa and would attempt a landing in Africa with British ships. But here again they were not aware that the objective of the expedition was Dakar. See Yves Bouthillier, *Le Drame de Vichy* (2 vols., Paris, 1950), i. 162, and below, pp. 96–7.

in the Canal zone for a supposed contingent of Frenchmen arriving from England. Egypt remained the 'cover' for 'Menace', although Churchill suggested, unsuccessfully (24 August), that Martinique be used as 'cover', whether as additional or alternative to Egypt he did not make clear. 'We may believe,' asserted Morton, 'that this action [Egypt as "cover"] has had some success since two well-known agents of the Vichy Government are now under the impression that General de Gaulle is about to sail round the Cape to Egypt.'[19]

EPS and the Inter-Service Security Board were confident that the French did not know the real destination of the expedition, and Churchill to a degree shared that feeling. Irwin refused to get ruffled. As he explained in his Camberley lecture, 'That everybody knew that we were all going somewhere there is no doubt. . . . Yet so many rumours and counter-rumours were going about that I don't believe serious harm was done.' Yet there was a widespread apprehension in the upper echelons of the expedition that Vichy was indeed aware of 'Menace'. This is brought out in Cunningham's Report: 'The lack of secrecy by Free French Forces which characterised the final preparations for the sailing of the expedition from England was deplorable and there can be little doubt that Vichy was fully aware of the project and only in doubt as to the exact date.' This attitude dampened confidence in the success of the operation. Of equal importance is that both the 'Menace' Force and Whitehall blamed the subsequent sailing of the French cruisers from Toulon (see below) on the total lack of security among the Free French. This feeling gave de Gaulle and the Free French a poor reputation and led to suspicion between the two sides.

(3) Delays

Churchill was more worried by the mounting delays than by the leakage, as this not only increased the chances of the Germans and French getting wind of the operation, but it tied up desperately needed men and *matériel*. The original time-table for the plan prepared by the ISPS fixed the operation for 8 September. The date was based on the movements of the slowest unit, that is, the

[19] Minute of 29 Aug. to the Prime Minister, PREM 3/276. The Joint Report by EPS and the Inter-Service Security Board (JP (40) 465 (E), above) was able later to add other bits of evidence that indicated that 'the destination of this force was not as widely known as has been supposed', for example, an intercept which stated that six divisions were sailing from Scapa to the Middle East.

French MT convoy (the ships carrying the mechanical transport). French ships were chosen because, as originally conceived, the operation was to have been of an entirely French character. This convoy was assumed, on the available information, to have a speed of 12 knots, and that it would be able to sail from Liverpool on 23 August and make Dakar in sixteen days. But as the planning proceeded, actual examination of the MT ships disclosed that their speed was unlikely to exceed 8 to 9 knots. This fact did not become clear until a stage of preparation had been reached—the ships were already partly loaded—when to substitute faster British ships could only have led to further delay. The discovery added about five days to the time of passage and brought the date of the operation to 13 September. This was regarded as the latest date on which a landing should be attempted, from the point of view of moon and tide conditions.

On 17 August the Force Commanders proposed a postponement to 10/11 October, which was the next date when the moon and tide would be suitable for execution of the plan. The main consideration was that they badly needed intelligence on French defences and the state of the beaches from Poulter and Rushbrooke, who were not expected before 25 August.[20] This was too much for Churchill:

Is it true that Admiral Cunningham says that the only suitable day for 'Menace' is September 12, and that if this day is missed owing to storm, no other days will be open till 27 or 28, when tide and moon will again be satisfactory? All this raises most grave questions. The Admiral cannot take up a position that only in ideal conditions of tide and moon can the operation be begun. It has got to be begun as soon as possible, as long as

[20] COS (40) 642, Cunningham's untitled paper, CAB 80/16. The VCIGS (Haining) submitted a memorandum the same day which added several military arguments for postponement—they emanated from the Commanders—of which the most cogent pertained to the marine brigades detailed for the operation. Somebody had discovered that they had not been trained for their special role. Most were wartime recruits, and only a few NCOs had had boat training. The Commanders had arranged with Keyes (16 August) to send the marines to Scapa Flow for a crash training programme in boat work. They were due to arrive in four troop transports about 22 August (bad weather delayed their arrival until the 26th), which would give them only three or four days for disembarkation practice. More thorough training for this 'particularly complicated form of attack' was desirable. Also, weather conditions in the Dakar area would greatly improve with postponement (it was doubtful, Cunningham realized, whether landings in September were feasible on the north or west shores of the peninsula on account of the Atlantic swell), and several more landing craft, which were very important for the operation, would be available at the end of August. The VCIGS noted that the Commanders would consider a fortnight's delay acceptable, if a four-week postponement were not possible, though the state of the moon would exclude a landing in total darkness, which was desirable. COS (40) 641, 'Operation "Menace",' CAB 80/16.

conditions are practicable, even though they be not the best. People have to fight in war on all sorts of days, and under all sorts of conditions. It will be a great misfortune if there is any delay beyond the 8th. Pray report to me on this to-day.[21]

This left the date at 13 September.

When preparing their final plan, the Force Commanders realized that it was essential for the main force to go first to Freetown, which lies 550 miles *beyond* Dakar, before carrying out the operation. If they went directly to Dakar, the destroyers, and even the battleships, would be short of fuel within 24 hours. There were other reasons for the Freetown detour: the need for obtaining the latest intelligence, making the final adjustments of troops between transports, conferences, and the issue of orders. This further two days' delay moved the operation to 15 September. (Another reason for the decision to put into Freetown developed after the departure of the expedition, when water began to run short.)

Further delays occurred at Liverpool in loading the stores and vehicles of the troop convoy—*Ettrick*, *Kenya*, *Karanja*, and *Sobieski*. They had been stowed without much reference to the operational plan, and consequently the weapons and other *matériel* needed for a landing were scattered among the various ships, 'and so stowed that there were neither the facilities nor the time to remedy the mistakes' before the convoy sailed.[22] 'In fact,' says Irwin, 'no one had the least idea of what actually was down below decks.' It was the Dardanelles (1915) and Norway (1940) all over again. In the end an officer from the Directorate of Combined Operations (established at the Admiralty in June 1940 under Keyes) hustled up to Liverpool and spent three days (18–20 August) in restowing the ships tactically to the best of his ability. There was time only to repair the worst of the mistakes.

There were difficulties with the French crews of the MT ships, which owing to their slower speed were to sail a few days before the rest of the convoy. On the eve of their departure from Liverpool, the Staff Officer there telephoned the ISPS to say that one of the ships had not been paid for three months and would not sail until the crew got their money, and that de Gaulle was on his high horse

[21] Minute of 19 Aug. to Ismay, PREM 3/276.
[22] Spears, *Two Men Who Saved France*, p. 191. The difficulty stemmed from the fact that the marines and the ships had been standing by for two other overseas operations (independent operations to capture bases in the Portuguese Atlantic Islands of the Azores and Cape Verdes), which had been displaced by 'Menace'. These operations were expected to be unopposed, which is why the ships had not been tactically loaded.

because he had not been provided with a suitable motor-boat for use at Dakar. This last-minute requirement was to carry the General's emissaries ashore to the Governor-General in Dakar under a flag of truce—something faster than was available onboard any ship present flying the French ensign. The ISPS had omitted such a boat in the logistic planning, although the sending of an emissary ashore formed part of the plan. 'There was a very real fuss about it,' Admiral Onslow remembers, 'and a last minute fuss at that with talk about delay to the sailing of the convoy until it could be provided.' Onslow spent the whole night on the telephone and managed to get de Gaulle a suitable boat, which had to travel from Plymouth to Liverpool by road. 'The money was easier, but the formalities required to prise out of the Treasury several tens of thousand pounds of banknotes in the middle of the night were beyond belief. Eventually, I succeeded, but only after obtaining the First Sea Lord's signature; and the RNVR Sub. Lt. who was our office "dogs-body" caught the first train to Liverpool, and the French sailors were paid.'[23]

The crews then refused to sail unless champagne and pâté de foie gras were included in their rations. The rations were adjusted, but still the ships refused to sail. It seems that the captain of one of the ships had lost his mistress, without whom he would not sail. This matter was settled by Cunningham's staff. Finally, the convoy sailed, but before they had left the Mersey two ships collided and had to return to Liverpool for repairs. At last the MT convoy did sail, on 26 August.[24]

In all, there was a ten-day delay: five due to the miscalculation of speed of the French ships, two due to the decision to go to Freetown, and three due to the loading troubles at Liverpool and the 'misbehaviour' by some of the French crews. 8 September had become 18 September by 22 August, and the convoy's departure

[23] Admiral Sir Richard Onslow's letters to the author, 6, 11 Dec. 1973, 8 Jan. 1974. It developed that the boat was of somewhat ancient vintage, and this led to an argument with the *Devonshire* later, during the voyage to Freetown, as the Free French endeavoured to winkle a more suitable craft from the British. In this they were eventually successful at Freetown. In naval parlance a 'dogs-body' is a young officer, especially a midshipman.

[24] This paragraph is derived from Smith-Hill, 'Devant Dakar 1940', p. 4. No Frenchman will believe for one moment that French merchant seamen, at that time, could possibly have insisted on having foie gras and champagne in their rations. Yet Smith-Hill is positive on the point. The official version, probably derived from this source, speaks of 'misbehaviour by some of the French crews': 'The crews would not sail without arrears of pay and improvement in messing, nor the captain of one ship without his mistress; these matters were adjusted.' Hist. (A) 2, 'The Dakar Operation', p. 8.

from Liverpool, scheduled for 23 August, was moved to the 26th because of the loading troubles. On 2 September, after the main force had sailed, Cunningham signalled that they could not arrive at Freetown until 36 hours late. He gave no reasons, but it was assumed at the Admiralty that they were navigational. What had happened was that it had been discovered that the speed of the convoy, particularly the foodship *Belgravian* and the British transport *Ettrick*, was less than expected. This meant putting off the operation for one more day, to 19 September. Finally, the diversion of the expedition in manoeuvres designed to intercept the French cruisers which had sailed through the Straits of Gibraltar *en route* to Dakar (see below) led to a further three-day postponement, to 22 September. On 20 September there was a final postponement to the 23rd, in order to give de Boislambert enough time to arrive at Dakar and to effect the destruction that he was planning. (See below, pp. 108–9.) This proved to be the actual date.

A month after the operation Churchill excoriated the Naval Staff for the delays in an unfair and intemperate criticism:

It does not seem to be appreciated by the Naval Staff that time is the essence of success in war. Delays are accepted tamely and readily, instead of violent efforts being made to overcome the difficulties and to keep the timetable. . . .

I have been looking at the records of what happened in the Dakar expedition. I see in my first directive, that I prescribed extreme urgency, and that the date September 8 should be kept. The actual reference was as follows:

'In working out the above plan, time is vital. We have lost too much already. British ships are to be used as transports whenever convenient, and merely hoist French colours. No question of Orders in Council or legislation to transfer British transports to the French flag need be considered. August 8, 1940.'

Yet five or six days later I am told that the French ships are found only to go 8 knots instead of 12; that it is now too late to take up British transports and fit them; and that five days retardation must be accepted. Anyone can see what a part this delay played in our discomfiture.

There seems to be an air of negativism, and of undue yielding to difficulties, and a woeful lack of appreciation of the time factor in some of the naval proceedings, which is not in accordance with the best traditions of the Admiralty.[25]

[25] Churchill's minute to the First Lord, 22 Oct., ADM 205/6.

(4) Doubts

On 24 August Irwin submitted a memorandum to the War Office emphasizing the principal military weaknesses of the plan after his further examination. The principal point was that success depended 'almost entirely' on conditions in Dakar being favourable to de Gaulle. 'A miscalculation in this appreciation will have serious results.' He was apprehensive of the effect on the population of any heavy British attack, fearing that de Gaulle would not receive a welcome behind British guns and bayonets. If full-scale opposition developed, the reduction of the three main forts and the airfield by ships' fire would be no easy task without air support, yet the air forces placed at their disposal appeared inadequate (approximately 45 aircraft). The landing-craft production programme having only just got under way, there was a shortage of assault landing craft: a mere 15 (and primitive in the extreme, let me add), and a want of training by the troops in their use.[26] This was the gravamen of his memorandum, which the VCIGS circulated to the Chiefs of Staff on the 27th.[27] The Chiefs agreed that it called for no specific reply (30 August).

[26] A battalion required 15 ALC for an opposed landing, or 60 if all four battalions were to land simultaneously in one flight, without allowing for Force Headquarters or attached troops. 'It would be unusual for all battalions to land simultaneously in addition to all battalions landing in one flight, but in average circumstances about 50 ALC would be desirable. The only craft in fact available were 15 ALC, 1 SLC [support landing craft, which carried a mortar as well as automatic weapons] and 2 MLC [motor landing craft, capable of carrying one Bren carrier each]. It was thus apparent that some flights would be required to land in ships lifeboats towed by motor boats [with inadequate engines].' Smith-Hill, 'Devant Dakar 1940', p. 5. Hardly anyone realized that this was not a good way to carry out such operations. The small number of landing craft available was largely responsible for Irwin's decision to employ no more than four battalions under one brigade headquarters. On 18 August he ordered one brigade headquarters (102nd Royal Marine) and one battalion (the 8th Argyll and Sutherland Highlanders) to disembark from their ships at Liverpool. The four transports left Liverpool for Scapa on 24 August. One, the *Karanja*, had to return when she sustained damage to a propeller on departure, thus depriving the battalion she was transporting of any training. The other three transports arrived at Scapa on the 26th, which gave the troops four days for training in boat work before their sailing on the 31st. Irwin saw the troops under his command and the commanding officers for the first time on 27 August, when he flew to Scapa. 'The Battalions of the Royal Marines impressed me most favourably and their officers and N.C.O.'s seemed excellent.' Irwin's Report, Ch. I, p. 9. I must insert this sidelight on the disembarkation practice at Scapa. The last two days there featured a full-dress rehearsal for the landings at Dakar. The equipment of the men had been 'scientifically scaled down so that we could carry the maximum amount of ammunition—though I learned that Evelyn [Waugh]'s batman struggled ashore with a knapsack containing two excellent bottles of Châteauneuf du Pape!' John St. John, *To the War with Waugh* (London, 1974), p. 41.

[27] COS (40) 672, 'Operation "Menace",' CAB 80/17. Commander Crease remembers

Another fleet commander was a doubter—Vice-Admiral Sir James Somerville, Commanding Force H in the western Mediterranean. During a visit to the Admiralty on 10–11 August, asked for his opinion of an expedition against Dakar, he replied emphatically that the project ought to be dropped unless it was likely that the expedition would be received peaceably. His reasoning was that it was exceedingly rash to further antagonize Vichy when invasion threatened at home and the Fleet was stretched to the limit in the Mediterranean.

The pessimism of the Force Commanders was shared in the highest quarters. 'The whole Board was against it but they didn't resign,' claimed the Deputy Director of Operations (Home).[28] The Naval Staff were, from the Chief of Naval Staff (Pound) down, against 'Menace', regarding it as an unacceptable and relatively unimportant diversion of their meagre resources. One should also remember the conditions prevailing in London at the time. They were facing a precarious military situation in the Middle East, where the Italians were poised to attempt an invasion of Egypt from

---

that on this occasion (25 August), as well as on an earlier one (14 August), when Cunningham had expressed doubts, the Force Commanders were invited to dine at Chequers with the Prime Minister, 'and returned the following morning with renewed enthusiasm!' Letter to the author, 22 Nov. 1973. Irwin in his Report admits that 'the operation and its weaknesses were discussed [25 August], but general optimism prevailed as to its outcome'. But he goes on to say: 'I must record the fact that in the face of such determination and optimism it was difficult to underline the dangers and risks so strongly as to cause one to withdraw in face of them,—a decision which would presumably result only in a change of commander at the last and most difficult moment and not in the abandonment of the expedition.' The War Diary entry for 29 August reveals the continued scepticism of the Commanders and suggests the real reason for their unwillingness to draw back: their awareness of the strategic and political gains to be won. 'Force Commanders lunch with Prime Minister at No. 10 Downing Street, and on this, as on previous occasions, emphasize the military weaknesses of the operations. Prime Minister assures Commanders that the risks were known and accepted in view of the great results which [would] accrue from a successful operation. For this reason the operation must be pressed home and that the Government would accept responsibility for any result.' That afternoon, however, Irwin 'saw C.I.G.S. and again emphasized that considerable military risks were being run for a political end'. ADM 202/413. In his covering letter to his Report on the operation, Irwin was more specific: '. . . although the Military plan was full of weaknesses which were well-known to the Commanders, represented by them at appropriate times and places, they were accepted by them because of the great political and strategical gains which would result from a successful operation carried out on the lines laid down by the Prime Minister in consultation with General de Gaulle.'

[28] Diary of Captain Ralph Edwards 25 Sept., REDW, 1/2 (Churchill College). The reference must be to the attitude of individual members of the Board of Admiralty, since there were no Board meetings during the gestation period of 'Menace' (after 2 July until 5 September), and there is no mention of the operation at the 5 September meeting.

Libya. (They did on 13–15 September.) At home the threat of invasion seemed very real, and remained so through September. This, naturally, engaged much of the attention of the Staff, with 'Menace' regarded, in the words of the Naval Assistant to the VCNS, 'as an irritating and irrelevant side show'.[29] When the operation started, this officer wrote: 'An ill-omened operation, sponsored on us by the P.M. in spite of bitter opposition from the Service Chiefs. It is part of the price we pay for having Winston as P.M. . . . I hate this operation. We don't want to dissipate our strength fighting the French, when every blow we can strike should be delivered against the Germans or Italians.'[30]

When the Force Commanders and their staffs left London, 'the unanimous opinion of the naval and military staffs was that unless received with open arms we were in for a defeat, ships' guns being no match for shore guns'.[31] In other words, they banked on Situation 'Happy'. Although Cunningham, Irwin, and their staffs were not sanguine about their prospects, they drew what comfort they could from de Gaulle, who constantly informed them that his name and presence would carry the day.[32]

A morale problem of another sort prevailed among the officers and men. The officer who commanded the 2nd Royal Marine Battalion says: 'Inevitably, there was a feeling of regret that if there was to be an "enemy", it would be the French—and not the known and established enemy, the Germans.'[33]

There was one encouraging development. The Gaullist 'missionaries' (see above, p. 6) had done their work very well indeed. On 26 August, at Fort Lamy, the capital, the Chad Colony proclaimed its adherence to Free France. In the next days a *coup de main* by a mere 25 or so Free French troops in the port of Duala brought the French Cameroons into the Gaullist camp. Brazzaville, in the Middle Congo, the capital of Equatorial Africa, joyously

<hr>

[29] Captain L. H. Bell's letter to the author, 25 Nov. 1973.

[30] Bell diary, 23 Sept. He did not like the operation for another reason (20 Aug.): 'It ought to be solely a French (de Gaulle) undertaking; if our hand appears in it it is likely to fail in its real object.'

[31] Commander T. C. Crease's letter to the author, 22 Nov. 1973. When J. M. ('Jack') Mansfield, in command of the *Devonshire* as Cunningham's Flag-Captain, saw the operation orders the day before sailing, he told the Admiral that there was an obvious misprint in the passage, 'If situation "Nasty" . . . the Fleet will proceed systematically to reduce the Forts.' For 'Forts', read 'itself', he said. Captain J. S. S. Litchfield's diary, 23 Apr. 1941. Litchfield had discussed Dakar with Mansfield that day.

[32] Admiral Sir Richard Onslow's letter to the author, 6 Dec. 1973.

[33] Major-General A. N. Williams's memorandum for the author, 5 Dec. 1973.

followed suit, as did Ubangi-Shari. By the end of August, and with no blood having been spilt, only Gabon, in the south of Equatorial Africa, remained loyal to Vichy, and that largely because of the appearance of a small naval squadron loyal to Vichy and a detachment of loyal Senegalese infantry at Libreville, the capital of Gabon.

The news as the expedition prepared to sail of the Free French successes in Equatorial Africa (announced by the BBC) cheered de Gaulle and the Force Commanders but did little to cut through the pervading pessimism and gloom.

Chapter Four

The Odyssey of Force M: I

This chapter of accidents sealed the fate of the Franco-British expedition to Dakar.

Churchill, *Their Finest Hour*

In war we must always leave room for strokes of fortune, and accidents that cannot be foreseen.

Polybius, *Histories* (*c.* 125 B.C.)

Events, especially in war, do for the most part depend upon fortune, who will not be governed by, nor submit unto, human reason or prudences.

Michel de Montaigne: *Essays* (1580)

(Charts 2, 5)

(1) The Expedition Sails

ON 28 August the Admiralty issued the final orders for the operation to Cunningham. The naval covering and escorting forces allocated to the expedition, known collectively as 'Force M' ('M' for 'Menace', naturally), were drawn from the Home Fleet: the 31,000-ton battleship *Barham*,[1] the 8-inch cruiser *Devonshire* (the flagship, in which were embarked the Force Commanders and their staffs) and the 6-inch cruiser *Fiji*, and 4 destroyers (*Escapade, Echo, Eclipse, Inglefield*); from Force H at Gibraltar: the 29,150-ton battleship *Resolution*, the 22,000-ton aircraft carrier *Ark Royal* (25 Swordfish torpedo bombers and 21 Skua fighters were 'serviceable', and there were two small 'Lucioles', French tourist planes, originally on board the *Fiji*, which were embarked at Freetown), and 6 destroyers (*Faulknor, Fortune, Fury, Foresight, Forester, Greyhound*); and from the South Atlantic command, to come under Cunningham's orders on arrival of

---

[1] One of the squadron's bombardment units, the *Barham* had only recently been recommissioned following the completion of a major refit after torpedo damage to her bows. The Dakar operation was in lieu of the usual shake-down cruise.

Force M at Freetown: the 8-inch cruiser *Cumberland*, 2 sloops (*Bridgewater*, *Milford*), and a boom defence vessel (*Quannet*). Only one aircraft carrier was included instead of the two proposed by the Commanders, and no submarines, although two had been asked for. The absence of submarines was to have an effect on the operations. The embryo Free French Navy provided 3 sloops (the *Commandant Dominé* and *Commandant Duboc*, small minesweeping sloops of 630 tons (two 3·9-inch guns) which tossed around like corks, and the considerably larger *Savorgnan de Brazza*: 1,969 tons and a primary armament of three 5·5-inch guns) and a patrol vessel (the armed trawler *Président Houduce*).

Twelve merchant ships had been assembled at Liverpool to carry the expedition and its equipment. Four of these were troop transports (the British *Ettrick*, *Karanja*, and *Kenya*, and the Polish luxury liner *Sobieski*) for the British military force ('Force A'). This consisted of the Headquarters Staff, four battalions of Royal Marines (101st Marine Brigade, 2,560 men, commanded by Brigadier St. Clair-Morford), an independent company (270), ancillary troops (1,410), and French liaison troops (30), for a total of 4,270 men. The transports also carried the landing craft. The marines, as indicated, were not fully trained. Apart from perhaps half a dozen senior officers, no one had any experience of warfare. The regular officers had grown up in peace-time, and the temporary officers (the large majority) were of very good quality and reasonable training, but they were quite ignorant of what might lie ahead. This went for the men, too.[2] No artillery was included, and but a handful

---

[2] On 22 August, after a conference the night before with Keyes, the War Secretary (Eden), and the VCNS, the Prime Minister decided that the Royal Marine Brigade detailed for the operation be replaced by a smaller number of more highly mobile trained troops, independent companies and commandos (1,500 men), offered by Keyes. One Regular Army battalion and one Marine battalion would go out as a reserve. But, as the Vice Chiefs of Staff patiently explained to Churchill, the substitution was not advisable for various practical reasons. It would, for instance, be necessary to alter the loading of the ships, which would entail a delay of four to five days in the operation. COS (40) 277th Meeting, 22 Aug., CAB 79/6. Churchill pulled back gracefully. This led to a typical letter of reproach fron Keyes to Churchill (24 August): 'Are you going to risk failure at Dakar? Do you think for one moment that if you had sent me to Oran, I would not have:—(1) gone in myself and used all my personal influence and prestige with the French Navy to persuade the Admiral to accept the honourable terms offered. (2) If unsuccessful, that I would not have insured the destruction of all the French vessels of military value before nightfall. I could not have laid off like Parker at Copenhagen. However I have faith in Almighty God—and you—and Orion is blazing in the southern sky. . . . [I am] confident that I will, before long be given the opportunity of proving that the youth of the Navy and Army will act as offensively overseas and face death as contemptuously as the young Knights of the Air do every day.' PREM 3/276.

of tanks (Free French), nor was the expedition organized for a protracted operation or for an occupation of long duration. Additionally, there were the British oil tanker *Ocean Coast* and the food-ship *Belgravian*, which carried 3,000 tons of food supplies for the inhabitants of Dakar and was intended as a propaganda tactic.

The Free French troops, numbering 2,400, were mostly tough and disciplined troops: a battalion (three companies) of the Foreign Legion, which had fought in Norway, and a battalion of mixed infantry (one company each of French Marines, mixed troops, and a machine-gun company). It was unfortunate that there had been no time to train the French troops in boat work, though they needed it as badly as the Royal Marines. The French troops were embarked in the 16,000-ton Dutch liners *Pennland* and *Westernland*, which were largely manned by Dutch seamen. De Gaulle and his staff and the Spears Mission were also in the *Westernland*: this 'poor foreign ship, with no guns [actually, she had a 4-inch], with all lights extinguished, was carrying the fortunes of France' (de Gaulle). Her Dutch Captain, Piet Lageay, deserves a mention. He was dedicated, efficient, and, in Spears's words, 'a remarkable person as a man and as a sailor. He was made of steel.'

There were also four Free French MT and storeships among the twelve merchantmen (*Nevada, Fort Lamy, Casanance, Anadyr*), loaded with guns, tanks (9), vehicles, aircraft, and supplies. But the aircraft (4 bombers, cased, and 2 in reserve, and 6 fighters, cased, and 2 in reserve) were not available until after the operation. These four ships and the British oil tanker, being slower than the troop-ships, were formed into a separate convoy ('M.S.'). It was the first to sail, departing Liverpool on 26 August, attached to a British outbound convoy and escorted by the *Savorgnan de Brazza* and the *Président Houduce*. On the 30th the five ships left the convoy when it dispersed at the Western Approaches and, with its escort, made for Freetown, arriving on 15 September.

The remainder of the armada left the United Kingdom on 31

Keyes never got over the fact that the Directorate of Combined Operations had scarcely been involved in the planning of 'Menace', beyond the contribution made to straightening out the 'shipping miscarriage' (above, p. 52). He told the Chiefs of Staff on 9 December 1940 that the plan for capturing Dakar was 'fantastically foolish. . . . The Naval and Military Commanders had the civility to call on me but my offer to help in any way was simply ignored. . . . The Admiral's only response to my suggestion that I might help was: "Oh, you had 6 months to prepare for Zeebrugge—we have to be ready to sail within a very few weeks." ' Keyes MSS., KEY 13/5 (Churchill College). Keyes's remarks were not recorded in the minutes of this COS meeting.

August in three groups. One section of Convoy 'M.P.' (*Westernland, Pennland, Belgravian, Karanja*), escorted by three destroyers, sailed from Liverpool, and the other section (*Ettrick, Kenya, Sobieski*), escorted by the *Fiji* and four destroyers, from Scapa Flow. From the Clyde (Greenock) the *Devonshire, Commandant Duboc*, and *Commandant Dominé* sailed to rendezvous with the Liverpool section of Convoy M.P. north of Ireland, which they did at 6 a.m. on 1 September, and with the Scapa section off the Western Approaches, at 9 a.m. on 2 September. The destroyer escort parted company that afternoon. The *Fiji* was torpedoed by the *U-32* at 5.20 p.m. on the 1st and had to return to the Clyde. She was replaced by the 8-inch cruiser *Australia* from the Home Fleet. (She sailed from the Clyde on the 14th and joined Force M early on the 16th). This inauspicious beginning was only the first of the many frustrations that dogged the enterprise from beginning to end. It was, indeed, an Odyssey, but with the Iliad a disaster and at the wrong end.

The *Barham* and four destroyers had sailed on 28 August for Gibraltar, arriving on 2 September and proceeding into the Atlantic four days later in company with the greater part of Force H. This force joined Convoy M.P. in the afternoon of 13 September.

As the armada got under way, Churchill was already looking beyond 'Menace' and the expected happy denouement at Dakar. As soon as the place had been occupied and de Gaulle had established himself there, they should deploy the ships and troops and try to repeat 'the process of Menace' in Morocco, this operation to be called 'Threat'.[3]

---

[3] Churchill's minute of 1 Sept. to Ismay for consideration by the Chiefs of Staff, COS (40) 696, CAB 80/17. The Joint Planners, at the request of the Service Chiefs, examined this question and concluded that the success of 'Threat' would depend 'on a sufficiently favourable political atmosphere in Morocco as is likely to result in a virtually unopposed landing. If General de Gaulle is established ashore at Dakar without any serious opposition, there should be little difficulty in re-embarking the bulk of the forces in Operation "Menace" with a view to repeating, without much delay, a similar operation in French Morocco. If Operation "Menace" meets with serious opposition, however, it is most unlikely that the necessary favourable political conditions will be created in Morocco. Moreover, in these circumstances, the bulk of General de Gaulle's Free French force will be required to stabilise the situation at Dakar and will not be available for operations elsewhere. The British forces engaged may have suffered considerable casualties and will be in no position to undertake an operation of a similar nature elsewhere. In any event, a purely British force could not achieve the object of rallying Frenchmen to General de Gaulle's flag. We therefore consider that it would be impracticable to undertake Operation "Threat" except in the conditions envisaged in the Prime Minister's minute viz: If "Menace" succeeds "with little or no bloodshed".' JP (40) 430, 'Operation "Threat",' 10 Sept., CAB 84/18. The Chiefs of Staff approved

Having the Force Commanders and de Gaulle in separate ships, and largely out of touch with each other during the operation, was not a bright idea. It complicated communications unnecessarily. On 10 September the *Devonshire* had signalled the *Westernland* suggesting that better control of operations, particularly in Situation 'Nasty', might result from de Gaulle being in the Combined Headquarters ship. De Gaulle would not play, giving these reasons:

(i) Chances of French success would be greatly diminished if directed from a British Ship.

(ii) He would not wish to direct a purely French Operation from a British Ship.

(iii) A successful French Operation directed from a British Ship would have unfavourable later repercussions.

(iv) De Gaulle does not wish to be on a British Ship in case of NASTY. To have been on a British Ship during shelling of French Forces would not only be very distasteful, but would have impossible repercussions on the eventual operation.[4]

Then there was the difficulty that Irwin, in the flagship, was practically cut off from his troops, because of the complete wireless silence imposed while at sea. Only visual signals (by lamp) were permitted between ships during the voyage to Freetown and subsequently from Freetown to Dakar. This was a great handicap to Irwin, since discussion with heads of Administrative Services, who were in the transports, was only possible at Freetown. We shall see how grave were the consequences during the course of the action of this separation between the Commander of the British troops and the Commander of the Free French Forces—consequences all the more serious because of the imprecise command relationships, on which more below.

It was a long, slow passage to Freetown, 3,000 miles away, partly because the transports were slow and partly because of evasive routing to avoid U-boats. The *Sobieski* sighted a submarine periscope on 7 September, and the next day the *Commandant Dominé* reported a torpedo had passed astern. This report was considered very doubtful in the flagship.

---

the recommendation, but, subsequently, on 20 September the Joint Planners definitely recommended against 'Threat' even if 'Menace' were an unqualified success. The evidence now was that the establishment of Free French Forces in Morocco, especially if with direct British support, would lead to an open clash with Spain in Morocco, or to a German move into Spain, either of which would probably lose the British the use of Gibraltar. JP (40) 463, 'Operations "Threat", "Alloy" and "Shrapnel",' CAB 84/19.

[4] Cunningham's Report, Pt. III, p. 4.

Intelligence reports continued to reflect optimism. One from Gambia contained intelligence received from a demobilized French airman who had been in Dakar for a month until 5 September, actively engaged in pro-British propaganda. 'He had interviewed at least 100 leading people of all sections in Dakar and found them pro-British. Estimated each would have a following of at least 10 persons. Some people not yet made up their minds but only small proportion actively pro-Vichy, commercial people 100 per cent pro-British. People were very anti-German and all Germans have left Dakar. . . . Africans in favour of British for economic if not other reasons. . . . Considered Free French forces should take Dakar. Could be easily accomplished . . . should be French and not British as if the French came there would be no firing.'[5]

In the *Devonshire* work never stopped. Due to the lack of staff and time, and especially the absence of information about Dakar's defences, it had not been possible to prepare detailed plans before sailing.

After sailing, no conferences with subordinate commanders and heads of services, and no issue of orders, would be possible until arrival at Freetown. Major-General Irwin realised that the two days in that port would not suffice for the brigade commander to assimilate the orders from Force Headquarters: hold his conferences, make his plans and get out his own orders: for battalion commanders to follow in their turn and for detailed orders to reach companies and platoons. Vice-Admiral Cunningham was faced with a similar difficulty. In consequence, the most detailed orders were written during the voyage, at Force Headquarters, for the action of units and sub-units in the event of an opposed landing being necessary; that is, if the successive stages of peaceful emissary, ultimatum, display of British naval power, restricted bombardment and full bombardment should fail, in turn, to secure a welcome for General de Gaulle. . . .

The plans had to be completed in detail and with no possibility of discussion with the brigade commander who was to carry them out, with the heads of services or with General de Gaulle, who were all in other ships. The brigadier and General de Gaulle were, however, kept informed by signal of the broad outline of the plans as they developed.[6]

The Force Commanders continued to change the operation orders as more information came in ('maddening amendments', Captain Walter calls them) and to heap detail upon detail, 'inundating us,'

---

[5] To the Colonial Office, 7 Sept., transmitted to the 'Menace' force *c.* 9 Sept., PREM 3/276.

[6] Hist. (A) 2, 'The Dakar Operation, August and September 1940', p. 11.

writes Spears, 'with the result of their labours. Their industry was in fact amazing . . . at the time I hardly knew them and wondered at the amount of paper they jointly produced, which reached us every few days in disconcertingly large bundles, plans to meet every emergency, excepting, as it turned out, the one with which we were presently faced.'[7]

No operations would be necessary if de Gaulle were welcomed and Situation 'Happy' were in effect. 'Sticky', as pointed out, involved a limited naval bombardment of the defences. The military plans covered three main operations in the event of 'Nasty' prevailing. The one selected would depend on the course of events, and this hinged on the attitude of the defenders, particularly of the Senegalese battalions and the coast defence companies. 'Rufus' called for a landing at Rufisque, 15 miles east of Dakar, and an overland advance on Dakar; 'William', for a landing at Hann Bay in the centre of the defences; and 'Conqueror', a combination of 'Rufus' and 'William', the Rufisque landing preceding the Hann Bay landing by some hours. In addition to the main landings, two subsidiary ones might be ordered: 'George', a small landing at Gorée or Bernard Bay, and 'Alfred', a direct assault by a naval landing party from destroyers or sloops into the centre of the inner harbour, i.e. on the quays in Dakar harbour.[8]

Irwin regarded 'William' as 'the most unlikely although it offered the quickest road to success, because it assumed the ability to move the transports well into Dakar Roads in the face of or after the neutralization of the forts and batteries defending the harbour.' 'Rufus' was 'the least favourable against opposition, because this overland advance would meet two important defiles, both of which

[7] Spears, *Two Men Who Saved France*, p. 190. The orders were transferred from the cruiser to a destroyer by line, and then by the same method to the *Westernland* and the other transports. Operation orders (excluding naval orders) ran to something approaching 200 pages, and 205 copies had to be run off and distributed.

[8] The details are in M.N.G.2, 12 Sept., ADM 199/206. But see also Smith-Hill, 'Devant Dakar 1940', pp. 8-9. Captain Walter, CSO to the Admiral, had the fun of inventing the names of the three 'situations' and, afterwards, when the expedition was at sea, the names of the landing plans in case of 'Nasty': 'Plan Rufus', which was obvious for a landing at Rufisque (also because Rufus was a 'bad king!'), and from which Walter derived 'Plan William' and 'Plan Conqueror' (William the, of course). 'Plan George' and 'Plan Alfred' were both named after kings, since Walter had started with kings. Over the French landing at Rufisque which was planned in Freetown Walter's 'tired imagination failed and I called it "Charles" [he now wishes it had been 'Henry' or 'Richard'], which was also the name used for de Gaulle, and I remember we got a signal during the battle from Spears, "Charles keen on Charles", which sounded rather bizarre!' Walter's letter to the author, 21 Mar. 1974.

would presumably be well defended, and it would have to rely on Naval gun support, which is seldom satisfactory for an infantry advance, even if it could have been given in face of the forts and batteries'. The General hoped he would be able to order 'Conqueror', for it had 'the advantage of pinching out a great part of the mobile (as opposed to the fixed) defences, before proceeding to the occupation of Dakar with Free French Troops in closest co-operation'. There was for the Force Commanders a *sine qua non* to making any of the plans practicable: the shore batteries and the *Richelieu* would have to be reduced or sufficiently neutralized by naval gunfire to permit the transports to close the shore with reasonable prospects of doing so without being destroyed.[9]

Neutralization could be achieved with the demoralization of the opposition. We must remember that there was no artillery and only 18 landing craft (the remnants from Norway). But, writes Captain Walter, 'we felt that our four battalions of Marines could cope with an indefinite number of sulky Frenchmen provided they *were* just sulky'. This was a crucial point. 'All these plans,' Irwin declared in his 1941 Staff College lecture, 'depended on prior reduction, or at least neutralization, of the forts by fire from H.M. Ships—a feat ships have not yet succeeded in accomplishing and were only expected to do so on this occasion because it was believed that the defence would not in fact put up, at worst, more than spasmodic and undetermined resistance.'

Another consideration of extreme importance was the time factor. Cunningham and Irwin believed that French reinforcements (up to nine battalions of Senegalese troops from French West Africa) would take between three and seven days to arrive, by road and rail. There was also the possibility of air reinforcements after the third day. 'Altogether it was obvious that if we wanted to succeed with the least damage we must do so within three days from our first appearance.'[10]

The Combined Staffs worked against time (there was a haunting fear that the operation orders would not be ready for distribution on arrival at Freetown) and under the most trying conditions. There was considerable overcrowding in the *Devonshire*, which was not designed to accommodate a military as well as a naval staff. Thus, Walter's 'desk' in the Admiral's after cabin was a large

[9] Irwin's Report, Ch. 11, pp. 1-2.
[10] Irwin's Camberley lecture. Smith-Hill stresses the same point in 'Devant Dakar 1940', p. 8, which also mentions the expectation of submarine reinforcements.

board fitted against the ship's sternpost, the position of maximum vibration in a ship under way. Because of the very limited accommodation on the flagship, Irwin's staff was small—eight officers, a small signal detachment, and three inexperienced clerks. Only one of the latter was able to type accurately and at a fair speed. Working conditions for the military staff left something to be desired. The cabin used as an office was about seven feet square and permanently closed down; only one of the three typewriters worked regularly, and the duplicator often broke down; they ran out of duplicating paper; paper clips, file covers, ink pots, and other necessities had not been supplied by the War Office. 'All the members of the Military Staff will probably look back on their time in the *Devonshire* as a nightmare. As it was forbidden to open the scuttle in the improvised office, and as work continued to all hours, day and night merged into an infernal, sweating, twilight.'[11] The temperature was about 90 degrees F.

The troopships had a much better time of it. There were no pressures and there was comfortable living on board. The British ships (the *Ettrick* was a P & O boat, the *Karanja* and *Kenya*, BI, British Indian Steam Navigation Co.) were still largely on a peacetime trooping basis, which meant early morning tea in cabins, long menus, five-course meals, gin at a penny a tot, white-coated stewards, and a general air of semi-luxury compared with, later, the *Queen Mary* crossing the Atlantic with each berth occupied by three persons for eight hours each day. This, of course, referred to the officers; for the men even peace-time trooping was hard, but on this trip it certainly got no harder. The troopship *Sobieski* was a Polish luxury liner, on her maiden voyage when war broke. She came under British control soon after, but the interior of the ship remained as for a prewar luxury cruise for some time. Thus, the band was there during the expedition! This was due to nobody having got round to putting the ship on a war footing by that time. The good living and other conditions on board the troopships may have produced an uncalled-for euphoria, but did not necessarily make any worse fighting men. They carried out intensive physical jerks and other training on board.

The pace in the *Westernland* was more leisurely still, though conferences took place to discuss problems that might arise in the action. The atmosphere was almost picnic-like. Spirits were high. The rallying of most of French Equatorial Africa to the Cross of

[11] Ibid., p. 7.

Lorraine at the end of August buoyed up the Free French. British and French raconteurs spun their stories (Spears saw the usually undemonstrative de Gaulle 'laugh then as I never did again'),[12] and there were a boxing exhibition, sing-songs, concerts, and a parade of their troops by the Free French officers. The dozen or so English and French girls, who had been taken on as nurses, some of them very pretty indeed, helped to enliven matters. Contrary to gossip among the British in the expedition, there was no question of setting up what in the French Army was called a B.M.C. (*Bordel Militaire de Compagne*). Although the girls were definitely not '*filles à soldats*', there were, as was to be expected in the circumstances, some romantic interludes: '*idylles*' is the term used by an officer on de Gaulle's staff. (Three of these ended in marriage.)[13]

'All on board gay and light hearted,' Spears recorded in his diary (4 September). Some of this disappeared when the expedition neared tropical waters on the 6th and the terrific and often clammy heat became a problem. 'We slowly melt,' Watson (with the Spears Mission) entered in his diary on the 6th. The temperature in his cabin was by the 13th 'somewhat akin to that of the inside of an oven in full blast'. On that day startling news reached the *Westernland*. An extraordinary event had occurred at Gibraltar.

(2) The Saga of the French Cruisers

When Vichy received news on 27 August that the Chad Colony

---

[12] 'When told a good story he lifts his head, turns it aside, laughs and invariably lifts one hand and clasps it on the other.' Spears, 'Dakar Diary', 10 Sept.

[13] The girls were volunteers, regularly enrolled members of the Free French Forces in uniform, commanded by a lieutenant, Miss Ford. There were qualified nurses among them and probably some assistant nurses and ambulance drivers. They seem to have done well (at least two later covered themselves with glory), but Colonel Watson does not think that de Gaulle and his staff were pleased at having them onboard. Nor were Cunningham and Irwin when they learned of the situation in Freetown. They could not accept having women onboard ships which were to spearhead an 'invasion' against a possibly hostile port. They may have also thought that nursing and/or ambulance driving could be only one reason for their presence. The Force Commanders intended to order them to be landed at Freetown and asked Admiral Raikes, C-in-C, South Atlantic, to arrange for their accommodation, etc., at least until Dakar had been effectively seized. He readily agreed to do so. Upon getting wind of what was up, Spears radioed a strong personal protest to Churchill, who promptly told Raikes, Cunningham, and Irwin, in effect, 'hands off de Gaulle's nurses'. This left the Force Commanders with no option but to rescind the order. On this contretemps I have relied on Captain Geoffrey Bennett (memorandum of 11 Jan. 1975), who was on Admiral Raikes's staff. There is some foundation for the gossip in the British ships about the mistresses of the French officers in the small Free French ships being taken to the scene of action. See above, p. 53.

had declared allegiance to de Gaulle, fear that the risings might spread to neighbouring colonies convinced the Government that they must send out a strong naval force to re-establish order in French Equatorial Africa and prevent the spread of the Free French movement. Vichy knew that Germany would judge the will and the capability of France to defend her empire by her success against the dissident movement in Equatorial Africa.[14] On 27 August Rear-Admiral Jean Bourragué, commanding the 4th Cruiser Squadron, received orders to constitute a special force from his three ships and the three super-destroyers of the 10th Flotilla. On the 30th the squadron officially became 'Force Y'. Its true destination was soon known by everybody. They were openly talking about it on the quay of Toulon harbour. (It is unfortunate for the Allies that this common knowledge never extended to any of their agents.) But under the terms of the armistices, the French Government were compelled to seek German and Italian permission to move their warships from one port to another. Vichy duly applied to the German Armistice Commission (30 August) for permission to send Bourragué's squadron from Toulon to French West Africa to help restore the status quo. On the recommendation of the Naval War Staff, which feared that the unrest and revolt would spread to French West Africa and open strategically important ports there for British convoys, Hitler consented, subject to Italian agreement. This was given only after some hesitation (1 September), and with the stipulation that the ships would resist any attacks that might be made and would be scuttled if captured by British forces.

The sailing of Force Y was set for 4 p.m. on 9 September, and the speed was calculated so that the ships would be at the entrance to Gibraltar right after daybreak on the 11th. The idea was to avoid error by having the vessels pass through the Straits in daylight. At the appointed time the squadron left Toulon: the cruisers *Georges Leygues*, *Montcalm*, and *Gloire*, accompanied by the super-

[14] On 6 September Raeder drew Hitler's attention to the serious military and economic consequences of French West Africa following French Equatorial Africa in declaring for de Gaulle. On the 11th General von Stülpnagel, the Chairman of the German Armistice Commission, warned the French delegation of German intervention if the dissidents in Equatorial Africa were not brought into line immediately. *Documents on German Foreign Policy, 1918–1945*, Ser. D (1937–45) (13 vols., London, Washington, 1949–64), ix. 61. The same document emphasized that 'irrespective of the release, effected or still to follow, of certain units for Equatorial Africa, the basic requirement of disarmament of the French Navy and Air Force (also in metropolitan France) will be maintained'. Ibid., p. 72.

destroyers *Le Fantasque*, *L'Audacieux*, and *Le Malin*.[15] Their Commander, Bourragué, was an officer with a profound knowledge of men and the sea. His orders were to go to Dakar, after a short stop at Casablanca, and put himself at the disposal of the Governor-General of French West Africa for all police actions or liaison missions that would appear necessary to him.

There now began a chain of mistakes and misfortunes which contributed to the eventual failure of Operation 'Menace'. At 8.45 on the evening of the 9th, Admiral Sir Dudley North, Flag Officer Commanding North Atlantic Station (FOCNA), at Gibraltar (based ashore, and also in charge of Gibraltar Dockyard), received a signal from A. D. F. Gascoigne, the British Consul-General at Tangier (dispatched at 6.24 p.m.). It reported information obtained from a highly reliable source (graded 'A'), Captain Luizet, a French intelligence officer who had secretly joined Free France, that a French squadron might try to pass through the Straits of Gibraltar within the next 72 hours, destination unknown. (All Tangier intelligence reports were sent to the nearest British naval command.) North took no action beyond ascertaining whether the message had been repeated to London. He was told that it had been. He had no reason to suppose that the Admiralty would fail to receive this message. What happened was that the signal had been repeated to the Foreign Office at 6.50 p.m. (this was natural, being from the Consul-General), to be passed to the Admiralty. It was not received at the Foreign Office until 7.50 a.m. on 10 September. It was popped into a basket among the huge file of messages received from ambassadors, etc. from all over the world and had to take its turn for decoding. 'It was not marked important, and, owing to arrears and to stopping of work in air raids, it did not reach the Admiralty till the [forenoon of the] 14th.'[16]

Churchill was probably only repeating what he was told at the time when he wrote in *Their Finest Hour* (p. 292) that the delay was due to the accumulation of work in the cipher department of the Foreign Office. 'At this time we were under almost continuous bombardment in London. Owing to the recurrent stoppages of work through the air raids, arrears had accumulated in the cipher branch. The message was not marked "Important" and was

---

[15] *'Contre-torpilleurs'*, often translated as 'light cruisers', and so officially designated by the French Admiralty in October 1943. There was no similar class in the Royal Navy. They were of 2,569 tons, carried a main armament of five 5·5-inch guns, and were capable of better than 40 knots. All times in the text are Greenwich Mean Time.

[16] Hist. (A) 2, 'The Dakar Operation, August and September 1940', p. 12.

General Spears and General de Gaulle confer off Dakar

Governor-General Boisson, Governor of French West Africa, with members of the Dakar Municipal Council

Admiral Sir James Somerville

Admiral Sir John Cunningham;
a photograph taken in 1948

Les basaltes de la presqu'île du Cap-Vert (Dakar).

Intelligence briefing on landing beaches at Dakar; the comments were
added by Major A. S. Irwin, A.D.C. to his father during the operation

deciphered only in its turn.' Is this explanation to be passed off as transparent rubbish? The difficulty with Churchill's explanation is that he admits that the night air raids on London for the ten days following 7 September 'struck at the London docks and railway centres, and killed and wounded many other civilians, but they were in effect for us a breathing space . . .' (By 'breathing space' Churchill is referring to the attacks on the RAF airfields, which had been so savagely damaged.) And there were only insignificant day raids on the 9th, 10th, and 11th. On the 10th, the day the Tangier message arrived, there were only four daylight air-raid warnings, all in the afternoon, totalling an hour and 29 minutes. The simpler and probably more accurate explanation of what had gone wrong was that a message which bore no special priority mark and was repeated for information to the Admiralty stood little chance among the IMMEDIATES, especially since the Foreign Office Communications Department was in a bad state at this time.

Gibraltar and London received a second intimation, this time with specifics on the composition of the French squadron. The British Naval Attaché in Madrid, Captain Alan Hillgarth, was described by the Ambassador, Sir Samuel Hoare, as 'the embodiment of drive'.[17] Hillgarth had been friendly before the collapse of France with their Naval Attaché in Madrid, Captain Delaye, a 'decent fellow', and had welcomed his suggestion that in spite of the armistice, they should keep in touch, because who knew when it might not be useful. Accordingly, they met occasionally, and now and then the Frenchman told Hillgarth things that he was obviously meant to pass on. Hillgarth was, therefore, not surprised when the French Attaché came to his flat in the late afternoon of 10 September to tell him that a French squadron of three cruisers and three destroyers had left Toulon.[18] He did not say that he was speaking

[17] This paragraph owes much to Captain Hillgarth's letters to the author, 28 Oct. 1973, 12 Feb., 3 Apr. 1974.

[18] The information to Hillgarth was in line with the French policy of avoiding any error. But we know that Vichy waited until almost the last moment to inform the British, so that the latter would not have time to make 'malevolent [*malveillantes*] dispositions'. French Admiralty to Naval Attaché, Madrid, 6 Sept., Naval Historical Branch (Ministry of Defence) records. When, on 18 September, the French deputation to the German Armistice Commission reported that the squadron had passed through the Straits in broad daylight, they tactfully stated that the British had not been given prior warning. This explained to German satisfaction why the British had been so surprised that it was not until later that they had sent out a naval force. German Naval War Staff, BA-MA Marinearchiv, Case 571, I 14 D-2, p. 130, Naval Historical Branch (Ministry of Defence) records.

4

officially, though it was quite clear to Hillgarth that he was acting under orders, and he did not tell him the destination of the ships. Immediately his visitor had gone, Hillgarth went to the embassy and sent an 'Immediate' priority signal to the Staff Officer (Intelligence), Gibraltar (6.09 p.m.), repeated, for information, to the DNI, Admiralty: 'French Admiralty to me begins: "Please advise naval authorities Gibraltar departure from Toulon September 9th three cruisers type *Georges Leygues* and three French cruisers *Le Fantasque* class which will pass Straits a.m. September 11th." Ends. Destination not known.' 'I did not know the forces' destination,' writes Captain Hillgarth (there was a tacit agreement between the two Naval Attachés that Hillgarth did not ask questions), '*and had no knowledge of Operation Menace*, but I did appreciate that the movement was significant. Hence my sending the signal "Immediate", which should have been enough, but I realize now that I ought to have made doubly sure by marking it "Most Immediate", a label normally only employed when the enemy is in sight.' However, that aside, the 'immediate' prefix should have ensured that the message would be taken at once to higher authority. Captain Hillgarth sees that the real error was that they in Madrid were not warned of what was afoot. 'Personally, I feel very strongly that in circumstances like those ruling at that juncture and with such a vital project in contemplation it was foolish not to warn me to watch for some French naval movement of the kind and to tell me about operation Menace. Had I known of it, I would have marked my signal "Most Immediate" and "Personal for First Sea Lord".' He concludes from this incident that, in the words of Donald McLachlan, 'too much security about operations can be stultifying, and even dangerous.'[19]

What happened was that the message reached the Admiralty at 11.50 p.m. on the 10th, and as soon as deciphered was sent to the

[19] McLachlan, *Room 39: Naval Intelligence in Action, 1939–1945* (London, 1968), p. 199. In passing, let me note that at about the time the French Attaché was talking to Hillgarth, the Spanish Foreign Minister, Colonel Beigbeder, had summoned Hoare to give him the same piece of information, which had been sent to the Spanish Navy. In his book *Ambassador on Special Mission* (London, 1946, p. 85) Hoare says: 'As there was not a moment to be lost, I thanked him for the news and at once went to the Embassy where I telegraphed it to Gibraltar.' In an article in the *Sunday Dispatch* on 30 May 1954 ('The Case of Admiral North') his imagination was even livelier: 'I stayed with the Minister for only two or three minutes and hurried off to my naval attaché's flat, where, together, we drafted two most urgent telegrams to the Admiralty and the admiral at Gibraltar.' There is no record of any such telegrams emanating from Hoare, nor did he ever come round to Hillgarth's flat that day, or have anything to do with the drafting of Hillgarth's signal. Captain Hillgarth's letters to the author, 11, 28 Sept. 1974.

Duty Captain. He, in turn, showed it to the Director of Operations (Foreign), Captain R. H. Bevan (about 12.30 a.m., 11 September). Despite its 'Immediate' priority and the fact that this officer knew about 'Menace', he, unfortunately, chose not to disturb the First Sea Lord's sleep (Pound often slept in the Admiralty) and merely added the telegram to the pile awaiting distribution at 8 a.m. The probability is that the DOD(F) had utterly failed to appreciate the significance of the Naval Attaché's message.[20] It was not brought to Pound's attention until the forenoon of the 11th, some nine hours after its arrival at the Admiralty. For this egregious error in judgement, the offending officer was relieved on 20 September and received an expression of 'their Lordships' displeasure'.

Hillgarth's signal reached Gibraltar just after midnight on the 11th (12.08), eighteen minutes after it had reached the Admiralty. It was decoded by about 12.30 and was shown to North's Chief of Staff, Captain Gordon Duke, who telephoned it direct to the Admiral. Again North took no action beyond asking Duke whether the message had been repeated to the Admiralty (he was assured that it had been directed to them, and they should have got it just as soon as they at Gibraltar, or possibly sooner) and informing his destroyers (2.15 a.m.), three of which were on patrol about 120 miles to the eastward of Gibraltar, hunting a suspected submarine, that French ships might be expected, and ordering them to report immediately if they sighted the squadron. (Whether it was North who was responsible for this signal is a moot point, on which see below, p. 213n.) The matter was none of his business, the Admiral thought, since he knew from the prefixed addresses that the Admiralty were the principal addressee. He assumed that the Admiralty would inform him and Admiral Somerville of any action to be taken. 'The fact that no instructions of any sort with regard to the interception of these ships had been received by me from the Admiralty after the Consul General's Tangier message, confirmed this conclusion, and I decided that no action should be taken to interfere with their passage through the Straits unless of course the Admiralty ordered

---

[20] Captain Bevan 'was in bed when the signal was brought to him and failed to take immediate action which he acknowledged he should have done by reporting the signal at once to his Senior Officers.' Pound, 'Points which Admiral North Has Made', minute of 23 Jan. 1941, ADM 1/19187. To be fair to Bevan (I can find no record of any case he may have made for himself), he may not have regarded the message as especially significant when read in the light of current Admiralty policy. This could be interpreted to mean, as it was by Admiral North and Somerville, that the avoidance of incidents was the governing factor. See below, pp. 215–16. One who knew 'Bob' Bevan describes him as 'a very nice chap but unlikely to set any river on fire'. And see addendum, p. 225.

me to intercept them.'[21] What did he make of these French ships?
'In view of what had so recently transpired it appeared clear to me
that this force was taking advantage of an opportunity to leave
Toulon for Casablanca in order to escape from the German and
Italian control liable to occur at the former port.'[22] I must emphasize that neither North nor Somerville had been informed of
'Menace'. But they were aware of the operation, certainly since the
arrival of the Home Fleet ships on 2 September. When they left on
the 6th with ships from Force H, the two Gibraltar Admirals knew
their destination and objective, even if they did not have the actual
operation orders.[23]

The destroyer *Hotspur* was the pawn which made the opening
move a few hours later. Commander H. F. H. Layman, commanding
the destroyer division on patrol east of Gibraltar, had received the
messages from Tangier and Madrid. He had decided to shadow the
French squadron, if indeed it did appear, although he had no orders
to do so. 'Coming from Toulon, in Metropolitan France, it seemed
to me to be most improbable that a Vichy French Squadron could
be in any way helping the British cause. I had, of course, copies of
the policy signals about French warships [see below, pp. 214–15],
but thought these would be overridden by the sudden appearance of
such a large Vichy force, whose destination was unknown. In any
case, it is a cardinal principle that it is essential to keep in touch
with any "enemy" ship sighted, so long as this is feasible or unless
orders to the contrary are received.'[24] At 4.45 a.m. on 11 September
the *Hotspur* reported the sighting of six ships, burning navigation
lights, 50 miles east of Gibraltar steaming west at high speed and
that she was shadowing them. The *Hotspur* had to light up extra
boilers to keep up. North received the message at 5.12 a.m. At
5.55 a.m. he ordered the *Hotspur* to cease shadowing and to take no
action, since the French had officially notified the British of the
passage of the squadron (Hillgarth's message).[25] North informed
the Admiralty of the contact at 6.17 a.m. (received at 7.40 a.m.):
'HMS *Hotspur* sighted lights of six ships probably warships steering

[21] 'Extracts from a letter from Admiral Dudley North', n.d. (probably 1945),
Richmond MSS., RIC 7/4.
[22] Ibid.
[23] The North and Somerville aspects of the incident are treated in more detail below,
in Part II.
[24] Captain Layman's memorandum for the author, 11 Jan. 1974.
[25] Layman was astonished to be ordered to cease shadowing and resume his patrol.
Thinking he must have made a bad blunder, he made another signal to North, saying
that he had disengaged from the shadowing without being sighted by the French. Ibid.

west at high speed 36° 03′N., 004° 14′W. I have directed *Hotspur* to take no action.' An hour later (7.11 a.m.) he reported that he was using air reconnaissance and would report the probable destination of the French ships. Both signals were marked 'Immediate'.

North had, as he says, 'every reason to believe that the Admiralty must have received the message from the Naval Attaché Madrid some two hours before it was received by me, and that they had therefore known since about 10 p.m. that the ships were approaching Gibraltar. I had naturally thought therefore, that the movement was taking place with the full knowledge and approval of the Admiralty.'[26] Upon receiving *Hotspur*'s sighting report, North had consulted with Somerville, who agreed that the Admiralty evidently wished no action to be taken. But in case of a change in policy, at 5.45 Somerville ordered the battle-cruiser *Renown* to one hour's notice for steam, also the only destroyer immediately available, the *Vidette*. The significance of this was that, if ordered out, he could have been ready to go to sea at 7 a.m. (or 7.15—both times are mentioned in the records), which allowed ample time to intercept the French ships. Somerville did not think of doing more, as he was certain the Admiralty were 'fully in the picture'. Having received no instructions from Whitehall, with North's approval (10.20) he decided to revert to the normal two hours' notice for steam (executed at noon). By this time the French ships were in the Atlantic.

At 8.30 that morning of the 11th the Port War Signal Station at Gibraltar had sighted Bourragué's squadron. At about 8.45 it passed through the Straits (Europa Point, at the southern tip of the Rock) at high speed (25 knots) and, to the great amazement of all, without hindrance. The leading ship, the *Georges Leygues*, in reply to a request signalled their names in international call letters, receiving a 'thank you' from the station. North recognized the ships: some of them had served at Gibraltar under his command. 'As it seemed so obvious that they were friendly' (he later wrote), he had the Port War Signal Station make a friendly gesture: a 'Bon Voyage' signal was flashed. There was still no suspicion that anything was wrong. 'The continued silence from the Admiralty confirmed us in our opinion that we were acting in accordance with Admiralty wishes. I had kept the Governor of Gibraltar [General Sir Clive

---

[26] North's memorandum for the Admiralty, 'Passage of Three French Cruisers and Three French Destroyers from Toulon through the Straits of Gibraltar on 11th September 1940', 8 Dec. 1940, ADM 1/19187.

Liddell] informed by telephone as to what was happening and he agreed with me that everything pointed to it being a pleasant sign that the French Navy was now coming to its senses.'[27]

Although North's signals of 6.17 a.m. and 7.11 a.m. (above) were received at the Admiralty at 7.40 a.m. and 7.42 a.m., respectively, and the information of the passage of the French ships through the Straits, at 10.43 a.m. (via a 9.17 a.m. signal from North), *the first that Pound knew about the French ships was when North's signal of 6.17 a.m. passing the Hotspur's sighting report was brought to him by an alert officer during a Chiefs of Staff meeting in the late morning of the 11th.* At once grasping the significance of the report, Pound telephoned the Admiralty to order the *Renown* and all available destroyers to raise steam for full speed. This signal of 12.39 was received by Somerville just after 1 p.m. Pound would do no more without War Cabinet approval. After getting off the signal, he attended the War Cabinet meeting that had begun at 12.30 p.m.

The War Cabinet discussed the instructions to be sent to North. Once in the Atlantic, it was brought out, the French force might (1) turn north to a port in occupied France; or (2) turn south for Casablanca, if they had left Toulon in expectation of a German occupation of southern France; or (3) proceed to Dakar, 'with a view to putting a stop to Operation "Menace".' Speaking of the first possibility, Pound said that they had all along made it clear to Vichy that they reserved the right of action if French warships attempted to reach German-occupied ports. As between (2) and (3), the former was preferable in the War Cabinet's view.

The question arose, however, whether, if we said that we would let them go to Casablanca but not to Dakar, this would show that we had some interest in Dakar. But this would not be material if the object of the French in sending the ships to Dakar was to forestall an operation of which they had obtained knowledge.

It was agreed that it would be most undesirable to allow these French ships to go to Dakar, where their arrival might make all the difference between a favourable and an unfavourable attitude when the 'Menace' Expedition arrived. Further, we could argue that we had information that Dakar was German-controlled, but that Casablanca was not.

On Churchill's initiative, and with War Cabinet concurrence, the Admiralty were instructed to inform North that the French

[27] Ibid.

ships would not be permitted to reach Biscay ports or Dakar.[28]

In pursuance of the War Cabinet directive, an Admiralty telegram of 1.47 p.m. to Somerville (received at Gibraltar at 2.06 p.m.) instructed him to 'proceed to sea and endeavour to obtain contact with French force. Further instructions follow.' These were dispatched at 2.29 p.m. (received at 3.46 p.m.) and read:

A. If French Force is proceeding Southward inform them there is no objection to their going to Casablanca but that they cannot be permitted to go to Dakar which is under German influence.

B. If Force appears to be proceeding to Bay Ports inform them this cannot be permitted as these ports are in German hands.

C. In A and B minimum force is to be used to enforce compliance.

The Admiralty's signal of 1.47 p.m. irritated Somerville, who knew that the French ships were over five hours ahead of him. The signal of 2.29 p.m. evoked a still stronger response. 'They must be mad!' he told his Flag-Lieutenant—'mad' because it was too late for him to be able to carry out this last order, the French having got such a start. Besides, Force H, reduced by Force M on 6 September to the *Renown* and six destroyers (under North's command, but allocated to him), was no match for the Vichy squadron. ('How the hell I was expected to stop all six I don't quite know,' he wrote his wife the next day.) Unable to get an adequate destroyer escort for the *Renown* for several hours, it was not until 4 p.m. that the battle cruiser and three destroyers sailed (joined early the following afternoon by the other three, who had been hunting the Italian submarine). Minutes later, aircraft from Gibraltar which had been shadowing the French ships reported that they had entered Casablanca (150 miles south of Gibraltar) and the protection of its powerful batteries at 4.10 p.m.

In accordance with fresh Admiralty instructions (8.06 p.m., 11 September), Somerville instituted a patrol to the southward of Casablanca (3 a.m. on the 12th) to intercept the French ships if they sailed south—this with his old battle cruiser and a few old destroyers. He patrolled between Cape Blanco (N)[29] and Agadir. Somerville was handicapped by his inability to spread his small force—he would not chance leaving the *Renown* unprotected against submarine attack—and by the haze which blanketed the harbour. It

---

[28] WM (40) 247, CAB 65/15.

[29] So referred to in order to distinguish it from a promontory of the same name much farther south, in Rio de Oro.

was not until late afternoon of the 13th that aircraft were able to search the harbour conclusively. They spotted no French cruisers: the birds had flown. Bourragué had planned to refuel and take on stores before proceeding southward in the afternoon of the 12th. When the French Admiral at Casablanca learned (at 5.30 p.m. and at 7.45 p.m. on the 11th) through a lookout at Cape Spartel (a headland on the African side of the Straits of Gibraltar) of the presence of a British squadron, he instructed Bourragué to speed up the refuelling and provisioning and get under way rather than risk being bottled up or suffering the fate of the French fleet at Mers-el-Kébir. The squadron slipped out unseen at about 4 a.m. on the 12th and turned south towards Dakar, 1,300 miles distant. Somerville returned to Gibraltar on the 14th to refuel his destroyers.

Pound asserted after the event that in order for the *Renown* to have been in a position to intercept the French ships as they passed through the Straits, it would have been necessary to take action previous to the *Hotspur*'s sighting report, but that 'even if everything had gone right there could have been no certainty whatever that these French ships would not have been able to evade the patrol which *Renown* and other ships were maintaining south of Casablanca. The interception of ships of the high speed of the French ships is a very difficult thing unless a very large number of ships are available to do this.'[30]

It had been an extraordinary series of mistakes and errors of judgement. Churchill has summed up the 'ifs':

But through the coincidence of this failure of two separate communications—one from the Consul-General in Tangier and the other from the Naval Attaché in Madrid—and through lack of appreciation in various quarters all was too late. If the Consul-General had marked the first message 'Important', or if either of the admirals at Gibraltar, even though not in the secret, had so considered it themselves, or if the Foreign Office had been working normally, or if the Director of Operations had given the second message the priority which would have ensured the First Sea Lord's being woken up to read it immediately, the *Renown* could have stopped and parleyed with the French squadron pending decisive orders, which would certainly have been given by the War Cabinet, or, till they could be summoned, by me.[31]

Precautions were taken against the possibility of active French

[30] Pound's minute to the First Lord for the Prime Minister's information, 4 Oct., ADM 1/19180. The rationale for the first statement is not clear. See below, pp. 212–13.
[31] *Their Finest Hour*, p. 426.

hostility resulting from Operation 'Menace'. On 12 September the Chiefs of Staff approved recommendations from the Joint Planning Staff. The JPS deemed the most probable forms of French hostility to be air attacks on Gibraltar and Malta, submarine attacks on British Atlantic trade, active operations by the French fleet in Mediterranean ports, and, if 'Menace' failed, air attack and a 'light scale of land attack' on British West African colonies, particularly Freetown. A variety of measures to meet the threat were recommended before the commencement of 'Menace' (the alerting of all Cs-in-C to the operation, the preparation of plans to re-route their Atlantic trade farther to the westward, the drawing up of plans for an air attack on the French fleet in Toulon, etc.) and in the event of French hostility (air attack on the naval units in Toulon, an attack on Casablanca by Force H, the occupation of the Azores and the Cape Verde Islands, if Gibraltar became unusable and they failed to secure Dakar or Casablanca, etc.).[32] On the 14th all Naval and Military Cs-in-C in the Atlantic, Mediterranean, and Middle East were warned that 'certain operations which are contemplated in immediate future in the West African theatre may conceivably result in the Vichy Government either declaring war or ordering reprisals by air against Malta and Gibraltar and against any of H.M. Ships met at sea. You will take all preparatory measures to meet situations as affecting your command.'[33]

In mid-afternoon of 11 September, when he was about 300 miles north-west of Dakar, Cunningham received news from Admiral North of the passage of the French force westward through the Straits. The *Westernland* did not get the news until 5 p.m. on the 13th, when they heard the BBC's Empire broadcast. The news, which was confirmed by the *Devonshire*, caused 'immense concern' in the ship. Spears believed the destination of the French squadron was Dakar or other French ports on the west coast. 'If they arrive Dakar before we do fatal.'[34] He immediately conferred with de Gaulle. The two Generals considered that the implication of the

---

[32] JP (40) 431, 'Implications of French Hostility Arising from Operation "Menace",' 10 Sept., CAB 84/18.

[33] COS (40) 3rd Meeting (O), CAB 79/55. The 'O' minutes of the Chiefs of Staff (like the 'O' memoranda) dealt with matters of particular secrecy.

[34] 'Dakar Diary', 13 Sept. 'Had the Vichy government heard of our plans, we asked ourselves, as they well might have done, and was this an attempt, with German connivance, or perhaps on German orders, to thwart them? . . . The most likely explanation that occurred to us was that Marshal Pétain had wished to make sure that no more French colonies rallied to de Gaulle and if possible to try to induce those who had done so to return to the fold.' Spears, *Two Men Who Saved France*, p. 188.

news was so grave as to justify a conference with the Admiral (signal of 7.05 p.m.). Cunningham agreed (7.21 p.m.) to see them 'immediately on arrival' at Freetown. This was not good enough, and at 8.15 p.m. de Gaulle sent the Admiral a message suggesting that everything possible must be done to intercept the French ships. 'If they reach Dakar it is most unlikely the place will surrender to him [de Gaulle].' He proposed that his sloop the *Savorgnan de Brazza* should accompany the fleet on this mission, carrying a letter from him ordering the French ships to place themselves under his orders and withdraw to Casablanca or take the consequences.

Cunningham's hands were to some extent tied by his observance of wireless silence, and therefore he could not obtain Admiralty instructions before they themselves initiated them. On the evening of that day (13 September) Churchill had presided over a Chiefs of Staff meeting which decided to use every available ship of Force M to prevent the French ships from reaching Dakar, even if it meant another postponement of 'Menace'. Shortly after midnight, Cunningham received an Admiralty message of 12.16 a.m. (14 September) that the French cruisers had left Casablanca, and ordering him immediately to do what in fact de Gaulle and Spears had proposed. He was to use every available ship, including the *Ark Royal* (if unavoidable, without her destroyer screen), to prevent the French ships reaching Dakar. The signal reached Cunningham when Force M was some 350 miles south of Dakar and approaching Freetown. He promptly signalled the *Westernland* (12.39) that he was coming over. The *Devonshire* and *Westernland* were stopped, and at 1 a.m., in brilliant moonlight—it was a fine sight—the Admiral's barge came alongside the *Westernland*.

The conference of Cunningham, Irwin, and de Gaulle took place in the captain's cabin and lasted but twenty minutes in view of the importance of speed. 'It was,' Spears narrates, 'a strange council of war, held in that dark and hideously hot and airless cabin, where the participants with shining, streaky, yellow faces clutched long glasses containing warm whiskey, as they discussed the situation, the Englishmen at great pains to ensure that de Gaulle understood all that was said. A queer night, certainly a very queer night.'[35]

It was agreed that, since there would be little chance of taking Dakar without a fight if the French ships were making for, and reached, Dakar, Cunningham would try to intercept them north of Dakar and force them to return to Casablanca. But he could only

[35] Ibid., p. 189.

collect the *Ark Royal* and three cruisers for the job (*Devonshire*, *Australia*, and the *Cumberland* from the South Atlantic Station, which had just been put under his orders). The capital ships had to go on to Freetown to get water. All idea of an overwhelming show of force was therefore gone. Another obstacle was that Cunningham judged the only good French ship available to carry de Gaulle's message, the *Savorgnan de Brazza*, was too slow to accompany the British ships, and they could not imagine the Vichy ships taking orders from the British Admiral. Spears had a 'brain wave': let them send d'Argenlieu in the *Devonshire* with de Gaulle's letter, should contact be made with the French ships. 'It was just possible he might get a word in—a French voice better than nothing.'[36]

Commander Thierry d'Argenlieu ('this dapper little monk,' Spears calls him) was a professional naval officer who had retired before the war and joined the Carmelites. He returned to active service on the outbreak of war and was among de Gaulle's first adherents. Spears's suggestion that he 'should embark in a destroyer and personally order the Vichy ships to turn about was accepted. I thought they might find it easier to obey so humiliating an order if it was conveyed by a Frenchman, whilst not missing the point that it must be obeyed since it was given from the deck of a British warship. On this occasion the fact that d'Argenlieu was a monk proved very useful, for a man of God has few possessions. His preparations were the fastest I have ever seen. He was ready in well under ten minutes.'[37] But this was too long for an impatient Cunningham, who said every moment counted. D'Argenlieu returned with Cunningham and Irwin to the *Devonshire* about 2 a.m. De Gaulle's letter was an invitation to the French Admiral 'either to rally immediately to the Free French Forces under my orders and in consequence to carry out my instructions, or to return without delay to Casablanca'. He would not be permitted to go to a port in French Equatorial or West Africa.

Ten precious hours had been lost. 'Had he conferred with us when we suggested 6 hours ago, what time w^d have been gained— 6 hours one way, not 6 hours back because of increased speed, but anyway 10 hours lost.'[38] As de Gaulle summed up the situation: '*Un vendredi treize est toujours un jour à redouter.*' ('Friday the thirteenth is always a day to beware of.')

---

[36] 'Dakar Diary', 14 Sept.
[37] Spears, *Two Men Who Saved France*, p. 190.
[38] 'Dakar Diary', 14 Sept.

The convoy of transports went on their southward way with a destroyer escort,[39] while the *Ark Royal* and *Devonshire*, soon joined by the *Australia* and later by the *Cumberland*, turned at 2.30 a.m. on the 14th and made for Dakar, about 350 miles distant (*Devonshire* and *Ark Royal* had not moved much after about 12.30 a.m.), at maximum speed. The *Ark Royal* raced on ahead. Note that the Military Commander by his presence in the flagship was removing himself from his command at about 27 knots. The *Barham* and *Resolution* (the Admiral had a second thought about their use), with the remainder of the destroyers, co-operated by moving to a position a little west of north from Dakar, distance 75 nautical miles. The patrol line to intercept the French ships was established by 6 p.m. on the 14th. But again the Navy was too late by a few hours, Bourragué and his three cruisers having reached Dakar at noon. (He had sent the three escorting super-destroyers back to Casablanca on the 13th during the dash south: their lack of range would be a handicap in the event of complications while *en route*. But they subsequently sailed, on the 16th, and were at Dakar by the 20th.) Air photographs taken by two Skuas from the *Ark Royal* confirmed the presence of the cruisers. The aircraft also reported there was no evidence that the French authorities were aware of the impending operation: the *Richelieu* and the three cruisers had their awnings spread, preventing rapid use of the guns, and were moored in positions that would partially mask their gunfire to seaward.

Given the fuel situation, there was nothing for it but to proceed to Freetown to refuel and to get on with the operation as planned. Leaving only the *Cumberland* to keep watch south of Dakar, Cunningham turned his ships back towards Freetown in the afternoon of the 15th. He did so with a feeling of relief. He had no stomach for intercepting and perhaps having to turn his guns on the cruiser *Montcalm*, in particular. She had sailed with him at the end of April 1940, when he commanded the 1st Cruiser Squadron, which force had evacuated the troops at Namsos in the Norwegian campaign.

In the afternoon of 16 September a bombshell burst as the force was once more nearing Freetown.

[39] When the troopships arrived at Freetown in the afternoon of the 14th, the Africans who came out in canoes to do business or dive for coins greeted the men with the chorus, 'Massa, you going Dakar?' So much for secrets in wartime!

Chapter Five

Odyssey: II

Our advice to continue the operation in face of this access of strength to the defences of Dakar was based too much on the information that the people were ripe for General de Gaulle, and not enough on the obvious military reinforcement to the defence, and it was, in consequence, and in my opinion, not sound.

General N. M. S. Irwin, in his Report of 7 October 1940

(Charts 2, 3)

(1) Crisis in London

ON Saturday, 14 September, fairly late in the evening, the Duty Officer from the Cabinet War Room came up to show Air Commodore Slessor, the D of P, Air Staff, a signal reporting the arrival of the French cruisers at Dakar. It was probably one from the Admiralty reporting a Vichy broadcast that evening which had announced that three French cruisers and three destroyers—the latter was incorrect—had reached Dakar. (Why Slessor? He was the only senior officer of the Air Staff remaining in the office. But why did the signal not go to his opposite number in the Admiralty?) He got straight on to the scrambler telephone to the Chief of the Air Staff, Newall, at Chequers, where the Chiefs of Staff were weekending, told him the news, and asked for instructions. Ten minutes later Newall rang back, said that the Prime Minister agreed that 'Menace' should be called off, and that Slessor was to assemble the Joint Planners, who should be prepared to advise the Service Chiefs when they returned to London the next morning as to what should be done with the 'Menace' Force. 'I said,' writes Slessor, 'that was an easy one—that we had always thought that if Free French influence was to be boosted anywhere in West Africa, it should be through the Cameroons, which would be easy.'[1] The Joint Planners met the next day (15th) and so

[1] Slessor, 'Operation Menace: the Attack on Dakar'. Significantly, it took Newall

advised the Service Chiefs when they gathered in the early evening. The latter also had before them a directive from the Prime Minister.

Churchill, for whom the arrival of the cruisers had 'revolutionised' the situation at Dakar—'New life would have been put into the defence of Dakar', he had told the Chiefs of Staff on the 14th—directed them to cancel 'Menace' and replace it with the original operation, 'Scipio'—actually, a variant. The 'Menace' force, or part of it (not all Free French), would land at Konakry in French Guinea and move up the railway so as to cut Dakar's communications on the landward side. At the same time a naval force would blockade Dakar. The 'utmost dispatch' was called for: if they did not get there first, the Vichy forces at Dakar might proceed up the railway towards the frontier of French Equatorial Africa, 'which might produce a situation of great gravity'.[2]

The Chiefs of Staff declared such an operation to be impracticable —on the land side, the difficulty of communications to Bamako after a landing at Konakry, and on the naval side, the impossibility of a close blockade of Dakar with the naval forces available. They added their old bugaboo: 'Until the threat of invasion has either been dealt with or has receded, and until our reinforcements have reached the Middle East, we are definitely of the opinion that we must do nothing which might result in active hostilities with the Vichy Government.' Their recommendation was that de Gaulle use his forces to consolidate the Free French position in French Equatorial Africa, using Duala as his base.[3] Churchill was won over. As he wrote in his war memoirs:

I had no doubt whatever that the enterprise should be abandoned. The whole scheme of a bloodless landing and occupation by General de Gaulle seemed to me ruined by the arrival of the French squadron, probably carrying reinforcements, good gunners [for the Dakar shore batteries], and bitter-minded Vichy officers, to decide the Governor, to pervert the garrison, and man the batteries. It was possible however to cancel the plan without any loss of prestige, so important to us at this time, and indeed without anyone knowing about it. The expedition could be diverted to Duala and cover General de Gaulle's operations against the

---

but 10 minutes or so to get Churchill's authority to cancel the operation. It was presumably done on the basis of the concession to the Joint Planners referred to above, p. 25.

[2] Desmond Morton's notes on a telephone message from Churchill, at Chequers, to him at No. 10 Downing Street (5.15 p.m., 15 Sept.), PREM 3/276.

[3] COS (40) 4 (O), 'Operation "Menace". Report', 15 Sept., CAB 80/56.

French Cameroons, and thereafter the ships and transports could be dispersed or return home.[4]

And this is how the crisis was resolved initially.

The War Cabinet that met at noon on the 16th to discuss the new situation had the Chiefs of Staff report before them. The Prime Minister explained that the arrival of the French cruisers at Dakar 'had altered the whole situation'. They might carry troops, and an attempt on the place, under the new circumstances, was likely to lead to bloodshed, with all its repercussions on their relations with Vichy. He considered that 'Menace' should be cancelled. '. . . a fiasco had undoubtedly occurred, and it was to be hoped that it would not too much engage public attention.' The War Cabinet accepted the recommendation of the Service Chiefs that de Gaulle should land his force at Duala and use it to consolidate his position in the Cameroons, Equatorial Africa, and the Chad Colony, and extend his influence to Libreville, while the British force remained for the present in Freetown. The plan was to be carried out forth-with, an Admiralty telegram of 2 p.m. to the Joint Commanders declared, 'unless General de Gaulle has any strong objections'.[5]

The Government's decision reached Cunningham and Irwin when they were approaching Freetown that afternoon. They had it retransmitted to de Gaulle, with a message that they would discuss it with him on reaching Freetown the next day. At 4.42 p.m. the Commanders fired off a strong protest to the Admiralty. The presence of the cruisers 'does not materially alter the previous naval situation except that both HMS *Cornwall* and HMS *Cumberland* can be included in Force M (? to provide) adequate force to deal with cruisers if they put to sea. At present cruisers have awnings spread and 2 are so berthed as to be virtually impotent and present excellent bombing targets.' The military situation was not altered by the arrival of the cruisers, the only point in doubt being whether

---

[4] *Their Finest Hour*, p. 427. It was also the fear of the Force Commanders that 'the Vichy ships must have brought a considerable number of Vichy militia, indoctrinated Fascist troops, to Dakar. These, we thought, might have succeeded in cowing the town, for we had been led to believe by Gaullist elements that, left to themselves, the population and the garrison would take the first opportunity to rally to de Gaulle.' Spears, *Two Men Who Saved France*, p. 196. In fact, there were no 'bitter-minded Vichy officers'—only 120 gunners of the coastal defence, whose arrival at Dakar enabled the authorities to send back to the *Richelieu* the sailors who had been transferred to man the guns of Cape Manuel in July, as well as the battery at Bel-Air. Jacques Mordal, *La Bataille de Dakar* (Paris, 1956), p. 163.

[5] WM (40) 250, CAB 65/15.

this had raised the morale at Dakar.[6] The message was received at 8.28 p.m. On reading it, Churchill authorized a telegram from the Admiralty to the Joint Commanders at 11.52 p.m. on the same day, giving them full liberty to examine the whole situation themselves and to consult with de Gaulle, and promising that the War Cabinet would give careful consideration to their advice. 'The whole question is largely affected by reference in your Part 3 as to whether arrival of cruisers has raised morale, and if this can be ascertained and how soon. Have you considered the possibility of French cruisers having taken reinforcements to Dakar.' The Prime Minister's own view, as expressed to the War Cabinet that met at noon the next day (17 September), was that, 'if there was any danger of having to use considerable force, it was better not to proceed with the Operation. But there could be no harm in hearing what the Officers in charge of the Operation had to say in regard to the situation.'[7]

At 6.30 a.m., 17 September, the fleet anchored in Freetown, where de Gaulle and the convoy awaited the Commanders. The latter found de Gaulle and Spears much upset by the talk of cancelling the operation. For Spears it was 'frightful & worst ex[ample] of pusillanimity encountered yet. Terrible blow to de G., who went [? clammy] & right into his shell.'[8] So strong were their feelings that each had fired off a protest to Churchill that morning. De Gaulle appealed to Churchill not to abandon the plans for the consolidation of the Free French position in French Africa through Dakar. The great majority of the African population, who were presently friendly, would hear of his arrival and of that of the British forces at Freetown, and it was therefore essential to act before Vichy could succeed in undermining this favourable attitude. He emphasized the strategic importance of Allied control of bases in French Africa. If the British Government gave up the Dakar operation, he requested British naval and air support for an alternative operation that he would personally lead overland with his

[6] Cunningham and Irwin felt that the information they had been getting pointed to improved prospects of a friendly reception at Dakar. This as well as the evidence that the French ships were in no mood for fighting (from their being anchored with awnings spread) explained their signal to London. Irwin's Report, Ch. II, p. 3.

[7] WM (40) 251, CAB 65/15. In *Their Finest Hour* Churchill does not mention the 4.42 p.m./16th message from the Force Commanders and he makes it appear (pp. 428–9) that his own 11.52 p.m./16th resulted from the vehement reactions of 'all the leaders' on the 17th. Logically, this is an absurdity, the result of careless writing. Moreover, the 11.52 p.m. message begins: 'Your 1642/16.'

[8] 'Dakar Diary', 16 Sept.

own troops against Dakar, proceeding from Kaolack (100 miles south-east of Dakar on the Saloum River) via Thiès.

Spears was even more outspoken in his telegram.

If changes in policy are often puzzling in London they are heart-breaking here.

It is impossible to understand why naval action under most unfavourable circumstances, British alone against French, was boldly faced on Friday [13 September] whereas on Monday [16 September] the prospect of tackling these same ships now lying helpless in harbour under awnings is considered impracticable.

De Gaulle's presence here must inevitably be known, and it is quite clear that if he fails to seize the opportunity so obviously within his grasp, of rallying West Africa, and agrees to vegetate at Duala, his power to rally any other part French Empire is gone for ever.

If fleet departs leaving De Gaulle here, the accusation of having abandoned him to his fate will swing French opinion totally against us in France as well as in Africa. . . .[9]

The rallying of the Cameroons and Equatorial Africa and the convictions of de Gaulle and his emissaries that the people and the soldiers of Dakar (though not the sailors) would welcome him played an important role in the determination of the Joint Commanders to go on with the operation. The arrival of the Vichy cruisers at Dakar had, in their view, not appreciably increased the risks.

The War Cabinet discussed the de Gaulle and Spears telegrams in the evening of 17 September. The First Sea Lord, looking at the matter from the naval point of view, said that the preoccupation of the Naval Staff was twofold: they should not get embroiled in a war with the Vichy Government, and it was not possible to provide adequate force for the blockade of Dakar involved in de Gaulle's alternative operation. Otherwise, he saw no reason why 'Menace' should not go forward, as he did not consider that the morale of the Vichy forces would be greatly affected by the presence of the French cruisers. Their fighting strength was not great. Churchill agreed that the arrival of six medium-sized warships did not add greatly to Dakar's strength, although they might strengthen the determination of the pro-Vichy forces in Dakar. That was the vital consideration. In particular, the coastal batteries might now be resolutely manned. The new factor in the situation, he said, was the

---

[9] The de Gaulle and Spears telegrams are annexes to WM (40) 252, 17 Sept., CAB 65/15. I have made a few minor alterations in the two telegrams on the basis of the copies in 'Dakar Diary'.

eagerness for action of the Commanders on the spot. 'Were the War Cabinet prepared to say to them "If you, the Commanders on the spot, are anxious, after due consideration, to proceed with the original plan, we will back you"?'

'It was clear,' the Prime Minister went on to say, opening a discussion of the political aspects of the problem, 'that the War Cabinet did not rate highly the dangers of any hostile reactions from Vichy', since they had been prepared to take strong action against Vichy warships, as on 3 July ('They had lived to bless the day on which they had decided upon the "Oran" Operation') and only a few days earlier in the case of the six warships from Toulon. Also, they had been prepared to force their way into Dakar, if peaceful persuasion failed. The Prime Minister thought that not enough attention had been paid to the moral effects of a failure of 'Menace'. 'If our expedition came back with its tails between its legs we could hardly hope that the fact would escape notice.' To Sir Alexander Cadogan, the Permanent Under-Secretary of State of the Foreign Office, it was conceivable that Vichy would react strongly to the destruction of their warships in Dakar harbour. But Lord Lloyd, the Colonial Secretary, and Alexander, the First Lord, were more sanguine about the prospect of French hostility.

On balance, Eden, the War Secretary, Sinclair, the Air Secretary, Greenwood, Minister without Portfolio, Chamberlain, Lord President of the Council, and Attlee, Lord Privy Seal, favoured proceeding with the operation. The argument that weighed heavily with them was the thought that de Gaulle would have no political future and the Free French Forces in West Africa would disintegrate, if 'Menace' were cancelled. Although the general opinion was definitely for going on, the First Lord wanted a direct opinion from Cunningham on the crucial point of the morale of the Dakar garrison. 'Was it likely to have been improved by the arrival of the French cruisers? Would the fire of the coastal batteries be more effective as a result?' The War Cabinet took this line, deferring a final decision until the next day.[10] On that day, 18 September, the desired opinion arrived in a signal from the Admiral in reply to Churchill's 11.52 p.m. of the 16th. But we must go back.

On 17 September, in Freetown, Cunningham, Irwin and their staffs had conferred at length with de Gaulle and his staff on board the *Westernland*. They were somewhat shaken in their resolve by the fact that on the preceding day the French cargo ship *Poitiers*

[10] WM (40) 252, CAB 65/15.

had set herself on fire rather than surrender to the *Cumberland*.[11] Also, de Boislambert, who had rejoined de Gaulle at Freetown, had immediately informed him of all the risks of a frontal attack on Dakar and imparted his anxieties, as well as those of General Leclerc. It was under these influences that agreement was reached on a new plan of operations that was dreamed up rather hurriedly: 'Plan Charles', a modification of 'Rufus', under which the Free French forces would land at Rufisque, should the unopposed entry into Dakar fail and Situation 'Sticky' develop. It was intended that 'Charles' should be as Free French in character as possible, but full British naval and air support would be provided, if necessary. The Plan would be a final attempt to effect a peaceful Free French landing. Should it fail, the operation would be continued as already arranged for Situation 'Nasty', with British landings under Plans 'Conqueror', 'William', or 'Rufus'. There was a discussion of how morale at Dakar would be affected by the arrival of the cruisers. This was seen to be an important point, since the Admiralty had made this question the touchstone of whether the operation could go on or not. De Gaulle and Colonel de Boislambert (he was to head de Gaulle's agents in Dakar) said frankly this would take some time to ascertain, and even then they could not be certain.

There was a further conference on the captain's bridge in the evening. De Gaulle declared that, if necessary, he would use his entire force in full co-operation with the British forces. He would, he realized, be held personally responsible for the resulting bloodshed and damage to Dakar. This might lead to his eclipse as the leader of the Free French, and it would be extremely harmful to the cause of Free France. But he had to accept these risks, for 'he considered himself and his Forces to be allied to the British, and that it was obligatory for allies to use all their forces, if the need arose, without any reservations'. His officers and men, he added, subscribed to his views.[12] The Force Commanders were, naturally,

---

[11] The *Poitiers* had sailed from Dakar on 15 September for Equatorial Africa. Libreville, her ultimate destination, was 2,500 miles from Dakar. She had on board 2,300 tons of sand, eleven railway passenger cars, and other non-military cargo. A day and some 100 miles out of Dakar, the *Poitiers* was stopped by the *Cumberland*, which prepared to board her. Realizing that he could not save his ship from capture, the Captain scuttled her, according to his orders, and made for land in life-boats. The *Cumberland* forced them to stop and took the crew prisoner. The *Poitiers*, which was slowly sinking, was finished off by gunfire from the cruiser. See further on the incident, Watson, *Échec à Dakar*, p. 125n.

[12] 'Notes on Conference held on board S.S. *Westernland* at 2130 hours, 17 Sept. 1940', ADM 202/413.

very favourably impressed with the General on this occasion. De Gaulle, on his part, was greatly relieved to know that the Joint Commanders were confident of success and anxious to go ahead with 'Menace'.

Following this conference, the Force Commanders sent a full report to the War Cabinet (12.46 a.m., 18 September). It was a response to the message of 11.52 p.m. on 16 September (above, p. 86) and made these principal points. De Gaulle was pressing for early action at Dakar. He considered the arrival of the cruisers was unlikely to have an important effect on morale, though it would be impossible to verify this within a reasonable time; and he was advised that substantial support for him in Dakar was likely to be found, if his agents, who were ready at Bathurst, were sent to foster this feeling and if a too British complexion of the operation were avoided. He wished to go ahead with the original plan, under which the Free French would try to enter the harbour unopposed. If this failed, his new proposal was that his troops should attempt a landing at Rufisque, supported by British naval and air action, if necessary, and then advance on Dakar. British troops were to be put ashore only if called upon after a bridgehead had been established. The message went on to state the view of the three Commanders that the scuttling of the *Poitiers* might show a stiffening of anti-British feeling, but that French seamen were notoriously anti-British and French troops and civilians were not necessarily affected. A favourable factor was the discovery that the coastal batteries were manned by native troops and not by naval ratings.

The recommendation was: 'After careful consideration of all factors we are of the opinion that the presence of these three cruisers has not sufficiently increased the risks, which were already accepted, to justify the abandonment of the enterprise. We accordingly recommend acceptance of De Gaulle's new proposal and that, should he fail, landing of British troops should be undertaken to install him as previously undertaken. Increased strength in naval forces is however considered essential. The operation could be carried out four days after decision of H.M. Government is received.' Irwin felt so strongly about the recommendation that he telegraphed independently to the CIGS (4.48 a.m.): 'As you know I have already accepted risks in this operation not fully justified on purely military grounds. New information possibly increases these risks but I consider them worth accepting in view of obvious results of success. De Gaulle has also committed himself to complete co-operation with British troops in case of need and has not shirked responsibility of fighting between Frenchmen.' The CIGS replied: 'I will support the attitude you have taken up. May good fortune attend you.'

The War Cabinet that met at noon on the 18th had the message from the Joint Commanders before them. The Prime Minister found the changed attitude of the Commanders (he especially had Irwin on his mind) a refreshing 'twist in the situation. It was very rare at this stage in the war for commanders on the spot to press for audacious courses. Usually the pressure to run risks came from home. . . . I was therefore agreeably surprised at the evident zeal to put this complicated and semi-political operation to the test. If the men on the spot thought it was a time to do and dare, we should certainly give them a free hand.'[13] When he met de Gaulle later in the year, Churchill told him that (in the General's words) he had been 'surprised and enchanted by this insistence' that they be allowed to attempt the operation.

The War Cabinet confirmed the provisional decision of the previous evening that the operation should go forward and authorized the Admiralty to send this telegram to the Admiral: 'We cannot judge relative advantages of alternative schemes from here. We give you full authority to go ahead and do what you think is best in order to give effect to the original purpose of the expedition. Keep us informed.'[14] There could be no turning back now. 'Menace' was definitely on, with the Force Commanders having, as an official British account puts it, 'a free hand such as is seldom enjoyed by the leaders of an overseas expedition in unbroken touch with their government'. The operation was now scheduled for 22 September, but was postponed 24 hours on the 20th, after de Gaulle had urgently requested this in order to give his agent, de Boislambert, more time to get into Dakar, where he was to attempt to influence opinion in advance of the operation.

Three reports reaching Freetown that day (18 September) on the situation in Dakar raised hopes. The British Consul in St. Vincent stated: 'Feeling for De Gaulle now strong and would fight for him if strong lead shown.' The Governor of Gambia learned 'from fairly reliable source that most French Europeans in Dakar are now anxious for Dakar to join with Free French movement'. And it

[13] *Their Finest Hour*, pp. 428–9.
[14] WM (40) 253, CAB 65/15. The telegram, which was sent at 1.20 p.m. on the 18th, was drafted by Churchill at the request of the War Cabinet.

transpired from an interrogation of the personnel of the *Poitiers* by d'Argenlieu that, although they were decidedly pro-Vichy, their morale was low, as was that at Dakar.[15]

(2) The Chase

A new factor was added to the already complex tale of moves and counter-moves. The three French cruisers, each with a detachment of 80 Senegalese infantry, slipped out of Dakar unobserved at 5 p.m. on 18 September. They headed at full speed for Libreville, still under Vichy control, and, as originally planned, would try to force the dissident colonies back into Vichy control. There was special concern over Gabon, since the strong Gaullist sentiments in neighbouring Pointe Noire in the Middle Congo, and the presence of the British cruiser *Delhi* at Pointe Noire since 6 September, threatened to bring Gabon over to the Free French standard. Admiral Bourragué had no suspicion that a strong British naval force was ahead of him. There being no fuel stocks at Libreville, the tanker *Tarn*, escorted by the cruiser *Primauguet* (Captain Goybet), had been sent ahead to Libreville on the evening of the 14th. She was expected to arrive there on the 22nd to refuel the cruisers, which were due four days later. The idea was that Bourragué's ships could, if desired, operate from Libreville or Pointe Noire.

On the morning of the 19th the *Australia* (Captain R. R. Stewart), on her way to relieve the *Cumberland* (Captain W. H. G. Fallowfield), on patrol south of Dakar, sighted three French cruisers 150 miles north-west of Freetown, steering south-east at 15½ knots. At noon the *Cumberland* joined her in shadowing the cruisers, while Cunningham in the *Devonshire*, with three destroyers, left Freetown at high speed (2 p.m.) in the hope of intercepting before dark. The *Barham*, escorted by two destroyers, followed to back up these measures. Cunningham appreciated the importance of dealing with the French ships. If they escaped, and were bound for Equatorial Africa, as seemed likely, they would be able to recapture Pointe Noire and Duala. This would alter the whole situation in the Cameroons and the Congo, since the cruisers could cover landings of troops from Dakar, Konakry, or Abidjan. Note that when Cunningham sailed off again, the entire military staff were transferred at shortest notice to a troopship. This turned out to be fortunate, as it gave Irwin additional time to discuss the whole plan in Freetown with his force.

On instructions from the Chiefs of Staff (at a meeting chaired by the Prime Minister), the Admiralty dispatched a 'most immediate' signal to Cunningham and Admiral Raikes (C-in-C, South Atlantic) in the late afternoon of the 19th: 'Do not allow French cruisers to return to Dakar. Tell them that we consider it under German influence and after parley make them either surrender and enter Freetown or proceed under escort and proper safeguards to Casablanca.'

Meanwhile, towards noon on the 19th, the *Primauguet* and *Tarn* were intercepted by the cruisers *Cornwall* (Captain Ford Hammill, whose ship had been placed under Cunningham's command by Raikes) and *Delhi* when in the Gulf of Guinea, between Freetown and Duala, about 1,000 miles ahead of the French cruisers and 640 miles from Libreville.[16] The *Cornwall* pulled across the *Primauguet*'s bows. Hammill had received a signal from his C-in-C at Freetown, instructing him to intercept the French ships and insist on their going to Casablanca, using force if necessary. He was to give the Captain of the *Primauguet* a message from de Gaulle—the one originally intended for Bourragué (see above, p. 80)—urging him to join the Free French. Hammill signalled the *Primauguet* to stop, which she did. The *Delhi* went ahead and closed her, while the *Cornwall* patrolled about 10,000 yards ahead across the course of the French ships, ready for anything, with guns trained fore and aft. The *Delhi* delivered de Gaulle's letter to Captain Goybet and an official one from Hammill telling him what he must do. There was also a personal letter from Hammill which stressed his friendly feelings towards France and the French. They were, he reminded Goybet, a product of his three years as Naval Attaché in Paris before the war, when he 'had got into the habit of considering myself as a brother of the French Navy'. He implored Goybet to turn round with the *Tarn* and sail to Casablanca, 'without forcing me to do what I would deplore all my life'. His hatred of the thought of having to sink a French ship was fortified by pleasant memories of the summer of 1939, when the *Cornwall* and *Primauguet* were at Shanghai together and entertained each other, and by his fear that sinking another French ship after Mers-el-Kébir could well detonate something much bigger. A more persuasive argument

[16] My account of the *Primauguet* incident owes much to a memorandum of 25 Nov. 1973 from Captain Hammill.

than the letters was the eight 8-inch guns of the *Cornwall* and the six 6-inch of the *Delhi*, to which Goybet could only oppose eight 6·1-inch. Goybet was unable to shake Hammill's resolve with such arguments as that 'We are not at war. It is not admissible that you should prevent us from doing for the loyalists what you yourselves are doing for the dissidents.' He asked Hammill for time to receive instructions. Hammill was agreeable, but he set a 5 p.m. deadline. Goybet appealed by radio to the naval command in Dakar (3.45 p.m.), saying that he was faced with a decision to fight the two British cruisers or to comply with their ultimatum by 5 p.m. to make for Casablanca. At 4.45 nothing had happened. It was an 'uneasy time' for Hammill. At 4.53, the *Primauguet*, having received the order—it came from Bourragué at 4.25—to accept the British demand, got under way, followed by the *Tarn*, and turned west at 12 knots. Captain Hammill was immensely relieved. 'My feelings were, I expect, the same as those of a naughty girl who has discovered that she is not going to have a baby—this time.'

From then on the French behaved admirably, showing stern lights at night, which made Hammill's task of shadowing easy and unobtrusive. (The *Delhi* was detached for refuelling on the 22nd when near Freetown.) On the 26th, the *Cornwall* signalled that she was authorized to discontinue the escort, if Goybet promised to go direct to Casablanca with the *Tarn*. His reply was: 'I gave this promise implicitly when I turned back. I now give it explicitly.' The episode closed, to everyone's relief, with an exchange of friendly messages as the ships parted company. The French ships reached Casablanca on 1 October. (Sent to engage the American fleet approaching for Operation 'Torch' in November 1942—the Allied North African landings—the *Primauguet* was sunk in her hopeless task.)

The diversion of the *Primauguet* and *Tarn* meant that Bourragué must abandon his mission, for there was no point in reaching Libreville only to be paralysed by a lack of fuel. Moreover, his path was blocked by superior force. Resolved not to risk a pitched battle, Bourragué decided to give up the operation. At 6.30 p.m. on the 19th, a little before nightfall, he suddenly turned round, increased speed to 29 knots, and made a dash for Dakar. The *Australia* and *Cumberland* hotly pursued at their best speed, but were unable to close. At 12.54 a.m. on the 20th the *Cumberland* signalled the French ships: 'My Government instructs me to inform you that it cannot allow you to go back to Dakar, because it considers it to be under German domination. You are either to go back with me to Freetown to discuss this or to go to Casablanca under escort.' A few minutes later the *Cumberland* added: 'Surely we can find a better way than that of fighting one another.' Bourragué contented himself with assuring the *Cumberland* that in no case would he allow his ships to pass under German control.

The *Cumberland* continued to shadow the cruisers, but owing to torrential rain she lost touch with them. The heavy rain persisted until about 3 a.m., reducing visibility at times to a few yards and never exceeding two miles. Touch was regained at 5.30 a.m., distance 10 miles and when the Frenchmen were only 30 miles from Dakar. The attempts at parley having failed, and there being no possibility of intercepting the cruisers, the *Cumberland* abandoned the chase at 6.55 a.m. It was just as well, since she was alone by now. Bourragué brought his flagship, the *Georges Leygues*, and the *Montcalm* into Dakar at 7.50 a.m. (20 September). What had happened to the third cruiser, the *Gloire*? And to the *Australia*?

Towards 9 p.m. on the 19th the *Gloire* had developed engine trouble which reduced her speed to 23, and eventually to 4, knots. She headed for Konakry, but was overtaken at 11.45 p.m. by the *Australia* and two destroyers, which had dropped out of the chase to handle her. The *Devonshire* and the destroyer *Inglefield* joined later, and after Cunningham had parleyed with the *Gloire*, she agreed early on the 20th to proceed to Casablanca under escort of the *Australia*. The British accepted her Captain's word, when the *Gloire* was about 190 miles south-west of Dakar (morning of the 21st), that he would proceed to Casablanca without escort. The *Australia* now parted company with her and rejoined Force M, which had just sailed for Dakar. The *Gloire* anchored in Casablanca on 24 September. But for the *Australia*, Cunningham's ships were back in Freetown on the morning of the 20th.

These various contacts on the high seas between British and French warships were characterized by a running exchange, not of shells, but of polite messages that reflected the mutual anxiety to avoid the use of force. Considering the linguistic difficulty and the delicacy of the situation, it is not surprising that the wording of these messages ranged from the pathetic to the farcical. But let us return to Bourragué.

Bourragué had shown wisdom and skill in getting out of a delicate situation. This was recognized by the Governor-General, Boisson, who congratulated him on the 20th for managing to avoid an action which could have had serious consequences for French West Africa and the mother country. But the Admiral's conduct—he was held responsible for the failure of the operation—incurred the displeasure of Darlan, Minister of Marine and C-in-C of the French Navy. Vichy had placed great hopes in Force Y's mission. Had it succeeded, it would have placed France in a much stronger position to resist the Germans and the Italians. Darlan was furious over the interception of his cruisers. As soon as he was informed of the incidents of the night of 19–20 September, he renewed the order to fire on all British ships encountered within 20 nautical miles of French shores, an order of 8 July that had been cancelled a few days before, and without even waiting for Bourragué's report sent him a telegram relieving him of his command (20 September). His replacement, Vice-Admiral Émile Lacroix, Commander of the 3rd Squadron at Toulon, was immediately thrust into a plane and sent to Dakar, arriving in the evening of the 21st. The kindly and courteous Bourragué left Dakar with the unanimous regrets of the officers and men of Force Y, who saw him off in a rather funereal atmosphere. Darlan eventually got over his pique and, six months later, promoted Bourragué to vice-admiral and appointed him to the Naval Staff.

It was only now that Vichy, drawing the logical conclusion from the recent contacts and exchanges of messages, realized that the objective of the Allied expedition was Dakar. Boisson altered the defences to be prepared for anything. The Dakar naval authorities were, however, more fearful of a British naval blockade than of a direct attack on the town, which was not envisaged at that time. Less than twelve hours before the arrival of Force M, Lacroix signalled the French Admiralty: 'Latest events show that the English are definitely determined to use force in order to prevent the reduction of the dissident movement in French Equatorial Africa. . . . The impression gathered from the British ultimatum [to Force Y] is that any force gathered at Dakar represents an obstacle to the British. Logically, this must induce them to attack Dakar. For the moment this attack would appear to be risky. However, a blockade is possible, and this would lead to the complete strangling of West Africa. . .'[17] The arrival of the expedition in sight

[17] Telegram of 6.40 p.m., 22 Sept., Daniel Chenet, *Qui a sauvé l'Afrique?*, p. 189. On 21 September General Doyen, the head of the French armistice delegation at Wiesbaden, discussed the incidents of 19–20 September in the Gulf of Guinea with General Stülpnagel and presented a request for rearming naval reinforcements to be sent to West Africa, including the battle cruiser *Strasbourg*, two 10,000-ton cruisers

of Dakar apparently provoked complete surprise. This is confirmed by de Boislambert, who was in Dakar at the moment of the attack, and later by the Historical Section of the French Navy.[18] Admiral Cunningham's measures had succeeded in barring Libreville to four Vichy cruisers and had diverted two of them to Casablanca. And the fact that the cruisers had turned tail when ordered north had encouraged the idea that they would not fight. The Allied Commanders, however, had second thoughts about these events. De Gaulle summed them up: 'But after congratulating ourselves on having made our adversaries' plan come to nothing, we had to admit that our own was gravely compromised. In fact, the Dakar authorities were henceforward on their guard and had received a most valuable reinforcement of ships. We learned almost at once, through our intelligence agents, that to serve the shore batteries naval gunners had been substituted for the men of the colonial artillery, who were considered less reliable. In short, our chances of occupying Dakar appeared, from now on, very small.'[19]

The episode was viewed optimistically at the Admiralty. Pound 'thought that the return to Dakar of the two Cruisers, after being chased in, but without having been fired on, would not have a very inspiring effect on the morale of the other French ships. Indeed, he thought the effect on stiffening the morale of the pro-Vichy forces would have been greater if the two ships had limped into harbour after having been fired on and with a number of wounded on board.' Churchill considered that 'the result was by no means unsatisfactory. It was true that two of the three French Cruisers had got back to Dakar, but the *Primauguet* was no longer there. The French Naval forces were therefore only one ship up on balance.'[20] It is ironic that the two Vichy cruisers had been chased back to the place where they could do the most damage to the operation that was about to commence. Heckstall-Smith acutely observes: 'How much wiser it would have been had we left them to

---

a 7,500-ton cruiser, and super-destroyers. He made a similar request for the air force. The German Naval Staff was convinced of the French Admiralty's determination to offer resistance if the situation demanded it, but still required further clarification of the action taken by the French cruisers. Accordingly, the French request was refused.

[18] Colonel Hettier de Boislambert's letter to the author, 24 Jan. 1975, Watson, *Échec à Dakar*, p. 51.

[19] De Gaulle, *War Memoirs*, i. 127. In his Report (App. I, p. 1), however, Cunningham said that it appeared to the Force Commanders that the 'tame submission' of the *Primauguet* and *Gloire* 'betokened a considerable lowering of their former morale and so more than discounted the accession of strength to the garrison . . .'

[20] WM (40) 255, CAB 65/15.

sail on their lawful occasions. In Libreville, where they were bound, there were no oil tanks, and it would not have been long before the supply of fuel carried there in the *Tarn* was exhausted. Then, these ships really would have been immobilized thousands of miles beyond the enemy's reach.'[21]

(3) On the Eve

Freetown has a magnificent anchorage, and the approach from the estuary is beautiful—reminiscent of Dublin Bay, thought Spears. The town itself has a lovely setting, nestled in a hollow at the foot of fairly high dark green hills. The troops had a chance to stretch their legs after being cooped up in transports since 31 August. There was no relaxation for the Allied Commanders. Two contretemps marred the days before the departure of the expedition, the first straining the harmony between the British Commanders, particularly Irwin, and de Gaulle.

The question of command which arose on 18 September saw de Gaulle at his intransigent best. Who was to exercise command in the event of a landing? The Chiefs of Staff had explained to the Joint Commanders on 13 August that they were in sole charge of the operation, and that 'General de Gaulle's responsibility for the conduct of operations would only begin when the British Military Commander had secured control of the objective and had issued an invitation to General de Gaulle to enter'. (The directive to Irwin, of 28 August, stated: 'Command of the expedition, until the British military forces are established ashore, will be exercised by you jointly with the Naval Commander . . .') De Gaulle protested that he had not been consulted about these orders, knew nothing about them, and would not accept them. He insisted on being on the same level as Cunningham and Irwin, whereas the latter was determined to retain control of land operations in his own hands so long as British troops were engaged on land. This was in accordance with Churchill's uncompromising attitude on the question. The discussion was resumed when de Gaulle and Spears dined with the Force Commanders in the *Devonshire* that evening. Spears tells the rest of the story in his diary (18 September):

Quite pleasant evening, then bomb dropped. Irwin asked de G to sign copy of instructions. All the amendments had been inserted save one, the most important . . . De G has a keen eye & spotted it at once: they had

<hr>

[21] *The Fleet that Faced Both Ways*, p. 144.

left in the words 'Command of this expedition is exercised jointly by Vice Adm^l. C. & Maj^r. G^l. Irwin.' No mention of de G. He flatly refused to sign. I backed him. There was considerable asperity. De G's point was that it was inadmissible that it s^d be said he had no say in the command of an expedition in which he played so prominent a part—that in fact in every hypothesis envisaged he, de G, played a most prominent part with his troops, & to deny this was to deny a plain fact. There was a further point which I made: these Instructions will become a historical document. From these it w^d appear for ever that this was purely a Brit expedition in which de G was a mere puppet.

I[rwin] pressed me & so did C[unningham] but neither de G nor I w^d budge. When C said to me meaningly, not to say threateningly, 'We sail the day after tomorrow—are you coming?' I said we had better put off the discussion till tomorrow.

There had been some talk previously of the Brit carrying on alone.

So we left, de G naturally deeply resentful—&, this is [the] fate [of a] Liaison Officer always—not too keen on me tho' I had fought his case harder than he had.

The denouement is contained in Spears's diary of the following day. 'An extraordinarily nice letter from Cunningham arrived which more than made amends for what occurred last night. Presently he announced he was coming. . . . C before he left [*Westernland*] said some v. nice things. Before going he wanted to make certain there was not the shadow or the substance of a misunderstanding. I told him his letter had made best pos[sible] impression. Irwin who does not shine in all this made no sign all day tho' there are many things to deal with.' Cunningham had given up the British claims gracefully: the paragraph in the instructions to which de Gaulle had objected to so strenuously had been omitted. De Gaulle's position was accepted, in return for which he agreed to commit himself to 'complete co-operation with the British Commanders in case of need'.

The other contretemps also involved de Gaulle, this time in a less favourable light. He telegraphed 'MOST IMMEDIATE PERSONAL' to the Prime Minister in the small hours of 21 September, protesting against the British Government's invitation to General Catroux, who had rallied to de Gaulle, to go to Syria. It had been done without de Gaulle's consent. Spears got him to tone down his answer. Even then it was sharp. 'I consider this procedure not in conformity with engagements concluded between that Government and myself. . . . General Catroux can only act on territories of Levant under French Mandate in capacity of representative of free Frenchmen of which I am recognized leader. He can consequently only act on a mandate delivered by myself. Were it otherwise I would be compelled to disown any action which he undertakes. I am most anxious to be informed with least possible delay of steps British Government intend taking on observations I am now submitting.' Churchill's reply in the afternoon of the 22nd is a masterpiece of tact, so important when combined operations, especially those involving Allies, are concerned.

From every quarter presence of General Catroux was demanded in Syria. I therefore took the responsibility in your name of inviting the General to go there. It is, of course, perfectly understood that he holds his position only from you, and I shall make this clear to him again. Sometimes one has to take decisions on the spot because of their urgency and difficulty of explaining to others at a distance. There is time to stop him still if you desire it, but I should consider this was a very unreasonable act.

All good fortune in your enterprise tomorrow morning.

That was that. There was no response from the General!

The expedition was already well on its way. The Free French storeships and the British tanker had sailed on the 18th, the troopships and Force M on the morning of the 21st. Cunningham had on the 20th transferred his flag to the *Barham*, and Irwin moved his headquarters to her for the operation. The choice had been between the *Resolution*, fully efficient but much as she had been in 1916, and the *Barham*, partially modernized, faster, and with more accommodation. The latter, however, had only recently recommissioned with a new crew, and her gunnery left much to be desired, though this could not have made much difference to the outcome. Conditions in the *Barham* were even worse than in the *Devonshire*. In Smith-Hill's vivid account:

The heat and lack of office accommodation had been remarkable in the *Devonshire*. The heat was more intense and the officer accommodation more restricted in the *Barham*. . . . At night it was almost impossible to sleep in the cabins. Some slept on the quarter deck if they had mattresses; some slept in chairs in the wardroom. The water served in the wardroom with lime juice or whisky was not just warm, but hot—about the temperature of a hot cup of tea. It seemed that the hot water system went wrong and that the water invaded the cold water circuits. There appeared to be no arrangement for the supply of cool or iced drinks. The troops were no worse off than the officers. It seemed that their only meals during the three days of the battle of Dakar consisted of a sandwich made of bully beef which was so hot that it melted and, on the last day, so old that it stank.[22]

During the passage from Freetown, the ship's officers in the *Devonshire* (as in the *Westernland* and presumably the other ships) were briefed—in the case of *Devonshire*, by the Gunnery Officer, Lieutenant-Commander Becher, Royal Australian Navy, and were told that they were to expect one of three situations to materialize: (1) The Vichy French forces and people of Dakar would respond to the appeal to capitulate, and there would be no fighting. (2) They would capitulate after token resistance. (3) There would be total resistance. Those responsible for the operation considered that situation (3) was unlikely to rise. The whole tone of the operation was set during the briefing by the declared intention that in the event of situation (3) arising, naval gunfire would be directed at vast stacks of groundnuts piled on the harbour wall at Dakar, which would be set on fire, and thus persuade the defending forces to capitulate! Recalls a lieutenant in the *Devonshire*: 'The assembled officers found it difficult to believe that this was intended to be taken seriously, but apparently it was.'[23]

There apparently was good reason to expect that either of the first two situations would prevail. As Force M steamed towards Dakar, the latest intelligence reports pointed to a happy ending. 'It has been reported to Governor of Gambia by a fairly reliable source that most Frenchmen in Dakar are now anxious for Dakar to join Free French movement. Provisions scarce. Opposition reported from troops and mercantile marine against anti-British elements of Navy. . . . The unwillingness of the French cruisers to face an engagement indicates that the morale of the Naval forces (which are the most anti-British) is not high. Airmen at Thies are said to be pro-British. The business community is pro-British in the belief that this attitude will assist towards the resumption of more normal trading.' Another report, on the 'Present Situation as known or believed in Dakar' on 20 September, introduced a note of caution: 'Morale of population said to be apathetic. Estimates of public

[22] 'Devant Dakar 1940', p. 10.
[23] Major R. P. Owen's memorandum for the author, 9 Jan. 1974. Commander A. J. Cobham, then a lieutenant in the *Devonshire*, says that during the operation the Fleet Air Arm tried to set fire to a large mound of groundnuts in the hope of producing smoke interference. This was not successful. Memorandum for the author, 8 Jan. 1974. But there is nothing about groundnuts in the operation orders as possible targets of ships or aircraft.

feeling vary from 60 per cent pro-British to 90 per cent, but these reports may be wishful thinking.'[24]

Morale was only fair. French reconnaissance planes had been over Freetown, and ships' companies were beginning to get an inkling of what lay ahead. The officers in the *Ark Royal* were pretty hopeful that, with the considerable Allied force, de Gaulle would be well received. There was considerable over-confidence among the Free French officers and men in the *Ark Royal* about the nature of their reception. An officer in the *Resolution* does not think that 'anybody at my level expected anything but a painless operation with a rallying to the cause of General de Gaulle. It was difficult not to be optimistic.'[25] On the other hand, many officers were not exactly bursting with optimism. Certainly the general morale on board the *Devonshire* was not high. One of the junior officers writes of the mood as the fleet prepared to leave Freetown: 'We had recently taken part in the Norwegian campaign, which had ended with the evacuation of King Haakon, his family and the Cabinet from Tromsö, and we, or certainly I, regarded this Dakar operation as another ill-conceived venture. I doubt whether anybody on board *Devonshire* expected the operation to succeed as it was launched.'[26]

Churchill was on the side of the optimists when he wrote to Field-Marshal Smuts (22 September), Prime Minister of the Union of South Africa:

Naturally the risk of a bloody collision with the French sailors and part of the garrison is not a light one. On the whole I think the odds are heavily against any serious resistance, having regard to the low morale and unhappy plight of this French colony, and the ruin and starvation which faces them through our sea control. Still, no one can be sure till we try. The argument that such a risk ought not to be run at a time when French opinion, encouraged by British resistance, is veering towards us even at Vichy, and that anything like a second Oran would be a great set-back, has weighed heavily with us. Nevertheless we came to the united conclusion that this objection might not turn out to be valid, and must in any case be surpassed by the dangers of doing nothing and of allowing Vichy to prevail against de Gaulle. If Vichy did not declare war after Oran, or

[24] Both reports represented summaries of 21 Sept. from the Intelligence Officer of the military staff of 'Force A'. ADM 202/413.

[25] Rear-Admiral T. L. Eddison's letter to the author, 10 Jan. 1974. He was a lieutenant-commander at that time.

[26] Captain R. P. S. Grant's letter to the author, 26 Nov. 1973.

Band of the Foreign Legion practising on board S.S. *Pennland* during the voyage to Dakar

Washing day on board the French sloop *Commandant Duboc* during operations

Aerial view of Dakar taken by an R.A.F. observer during operations

under the pressure of our blockade, there is no reason why they should do so if there is a fight at Dakar. . . . Anyhow, the die is cast.[27]

In the evening of the 22nd de Gaulle gave a dinner party in the *Westernland*. An iced cake symbolized the hopes of the expedition: inscribed with white sugar on pink were the words: '*À la Victoire*'.

[27] *Their Finest Hour*, p. 431.

Chapter Six

The First Day of the Operation: Situation 'Sticky'

No plan survives contact with the enemy.

Attributed to Field-Marshal Helmuth von Moltke
('The Elder')

The attitude of the defence as a whole was of course the problematical factor and the one on which we finally crashed.

Major-General N. M. S. Irwin, in a lecture at the
Staff College, Camberley, 1941

Having begun we must go on to the end. Stop at nothing.

Churchill to the Force Commanders,
evening of 23 September 1940

(Charts 3, 4, 5)

(1) Prologue

CHURCHILL refers to the operation as 'a further good example of bad luck'. How much was the result of bad luck, and how much of faulty planning or execution, or of the unexpectedly stout French defence (which itself may have stemmed from faulty planning), is a moot point. But there can be no doubt that the operation was initially plagued by bad luck.

The expedition arrived off Dakar in the dark at about 5 a.m. on 23 September. (Dawn was about 5.30, sunrise about 6.) The *Westernland*, *Pennland*, and the Free French sloops were 16 miles S.W. by W. off Cape de Nazé; the British troopships, *Devonshire*, and three destroyers were five miles farther south; the French storeships were still farther south; and the battle fleet (the 2 battleships, 3 cruisers, *Ark Royal*, and 6 destroyers), 11 miles west of the French transports and sloops, steering east at 15 knots, the battleships and cruisers in single line ahead. The battle fleet closed the shore before dawn (5.15), to about 30,000 yards from the coast and remained under way. This was well beyond the range of the shore batteries, though not of the *Richelieu*, yet within what was normally the visual distance of the people and defenders of Dakar.

The Chiefs of Staff had emphasized on 9 August that the success of the project depended upon the weather. 'With North-East trade wind conditions, it seems probable that the weather will be suitable.'[1] Further meteorological information confirmed this favourable prognosis. July to October was the rainy season, with a September norm of 5·2 inches. Tornadoes, which were likely to reach gale force, were a feature of the Dakar weather, but they were said to be less frequent and less severe in the rainy season. The rain, high temperature (77° to 90°), and high relative humidity made for an unpleasant climate in September, but this need not affect the operation. The important thing was that visibility was rated as 'good, as there are no Harmattan dust storms in September or October. May be ½ mile *when* there is Harmattan or Dry Tornado.' Dry tornadoes occurred in October and November. *There was no mention of the likelihood of fog or mist at this time of the year, and there were no plans to meet conditions of low visibility.*[2] Spears maintains that they were 'shocked to learn later that fog was a common phenomenon on the coast at this time of year. It seems incredible that the naval authorities were not aware of this, for had they been they would surely have taken care to ensure that the operation was not started while there was any likelihood of fog.'[3] This must be viewed as a criticism of the meteorological experts, not of the Joint Commanders, Chiefs of Staff, or other high authorities.

When the armada arrived off Dakar, a fog shrouded the coast—'the dark, dripping, warm wetness of the tropical fog', which was not dispelled by the sun as it rose. It has also been described as a thick mist or thick haze, all of which come to pretty much the same thing. Visibility, only three to five miles on arrival, worsened throughout the day, closing to between two and three miles. It did not, however, extend to any height. The sky and sea were blue, but the horizon was blurred. Unseasonable or not, the fog spoiled the

---

[1] COS (40) 257th Meeting, CAB 79/6.

[2] Part V, 'Meteorology', of the 'Intelligence Summary' appended to M.N.G.I.1. See above, p. 37n. The Summary was got up by NID. Part IV, on the beaches, stated: 'The most favourable period for the landing of a large combined expedition would be during the season which begins between October and December and ends in June.' The planners had been forced to ignore this, given the strategic necessity for launching the operation as soon as possible.

[3] *Two Men Who Saved France*, p. 195.

Allied stage management of the approach upon which they had greatly relied. It ruled out the moral, or psychological, effect on the population of Dakar, of seeing a great armada majestically steaming towards them, as Churchill had imagined the scene when first discussing the project with de Gaulle. The fog, moreover, would hamper the *Ark Royal*'s reconnaissance and spotting planes if it were decided to bombard the port; and Cunningham's battleships and cruisers would have to open fire at short range against the 9·4-inch guns of the batteries and the 15-inch guns of the *Richelieu*. The Admiral did not for a moment consider postponing the operation in the hope that the fog would clear. It was impossible to forecast how long this would take, and it was imperative that he get on with the job, given the urgent need for his ships in waters nearer home and the expected heavy French reinforcements in a few days. Thought Major Watson, Spears's Assistant, as his eyes tried to pierce the 'clammy curtain': 'First, the Vichy cruisers, now, the fog. Our luck is out! Our best chances of success are gone.' This opinion must have been widespread. The weather, we shall see, continued to be a major factor through the second day, affecting decisions and inhibiting actions. Each morning the shore was shrouded in fog which was slow to clear.[4]

At the risk of some repetition, it may be worth comparing the opposing forces. The major units of Force M consisted of a heterogeneous collection of archaic vessels of First War vintage and modern ships: the battleships *Barham* and *Resolution*; Britain's one modern aircraft carrier, the *Ark Royal*, which had survived several near misses and acquired a certain personality (21 Skuas and 30 Swordfish, several of which were not serviceable);[5] the 8-inch cruisers

---

[4] Major R. P. Owen well remembers 'the harassed naval meteorological officer in *Devonshire* being ceaselessly badgered by agitated senior officers for forecasts on local weather conditions. It was abundantly clear that he had no more idea than anybody else.' Many of the officers were convinced that, had 'the most wonderful opportunity' for combined operations been taken advantage of, 'we should have had the port by breakfast or soon after. The Almighty produced the most perfect conditions for a surprise landing, but de Gaulle had to throw this away, in his fervent desire not to hurt a Frenchman.' Commander A. J. Cobham's memorandum for the author, 8 Jan. 1974. See further, below, p. 165.

[5] The Blackburn Skuas were erratic fighter-dive bomber monoplanes, the Swordfish, vulnerable but versatile and manoeuvrable biplanes which gave a splendid account of themselves in the war. They were known as TSRs, standing for torpedo, spotting, and reconnaissance. The Captain of the *Ark Royal* was our old friend of Mers-el-Kébir days, who had conducted the negotiations with Admiral Gensoul—'Hooky' Holland, so named after his powerful nose and the Hook of Holland. He was a sympathetic and emotional character. See *From the Dardanelles to Oran*, pp. 239–52.

Devonshire, Australia, and *Cumberland* (the *Cornwall* and *Delhi,* which had been escorting the *Primauguet* towards Casablanca, were not available for the operation), and the 6-inch cruiser *Dragon* (allocated from the South Atlantic Squadron to replace the destroyer *Eclipse,* which had developed engine trouble); and 9 destroyers. There were 4,270 British troops and 2,400 Free French. But any landings made and bridgeheads established would be in danger because of the absence of artillery and armoured support and the chaotic nature of the signals arrangements.

The major units of the French fleet at Dakar comprised the immobile new battleship *Richelieu* (eight 15-inch guns, fifteen 6-inch), lying protected by the breakwater; the Force Y cruisers *Georges Leygues* and *Montcalm,* and super-destroyers *L'Audacieux, Fantasque,* and *Le Malin*; the destroyer *Hardi*; and the submarines *Ajax, Bévéziers,* and *Perseus.* The *Hardi* and *Fantasque* were not available until the 24th. The *Richelieu* had left Brest on 18 June, before the completion of the mounting of her guns. On 23 September they had just been mounted but had not had any practice firings. Only the No. 2 turret of the main armament and one of the five 6-inch turrets were serviceable, owing to the detachment of gunners to man the Cape Manuel batteries. The presence of 54 merchant ships in the harbour robbed the warships of their manoeuvrability. The defences included searchlights and anti-submarine and anti-torpedo booms. There was a naval reconnaissance squadron of seven seaplanes at Bel-Air, a fighter group, two squadrons of 19 Curtiss, at Ouakam, and a bomber group of 22 Glen-Martins 40 miles away at Thiès. As for land forces, there were five regiments of troops in and near Dakar.

Geographically, the situation at Dakar was not unlike that of Gibraltar. It is a small peninsula jutting out from the African mainland and joined to the latter by a low, narrow isthmus about 20 miles wide, which rendered defence against a landward attack a simple problem. Again like Gibraltar, the naval base lay facing a bay which could be fully covered by coast-defence guns, and the approach to the entrance had to be made round the strongly defended point at Cape Manuel.

The fixed coast defence batteries of Dakar consisted of four 6-inch at Yof, three 9·4-inch and one 3-inch at Mamelles (Cape Vert), two 9·4-inch and one 3-inch at Cape Manuel, four 5·4-inch at La Madeleine, two 9·4-inch, four 5·4-inch and two 3·5-inch at Gorée, two 9·4-inch at Bel-Air Point, and two 3·7-inch at Rufisque.

The Allies learnt afterwards that shortly before their arrival 'all the possibly friendly colonial gunners in charge of the coastal batteries had been replaced by naval gunners who were certainly hostile'.[6] Actually, these batteries were manned by native gunners, except for Bel-Air and Cape Manuel. (See above, p. 85n.) Only the Gorée and Cape Manuel batteries, however, were involved in the operation.

The French high command was headed by the Governor-General, Boisson. Under him were General Barrau, the C-in-C, Army, French West and Equatorial Africa, Rear-Admiral Landriau, the C-in-C, Navy, French West and Equatorial Africa, Vice-Admiral Lacroix, Commander of Force Y, and General Gama, the Commander of the West African Air Force. Boisson was described in a British intelligence report of this time as 'deafened and lost a leg in the last war. Is very pro-Vichy and was specially promoted to his present position. Good character—anti-British.' Barrau was rated as a 'very honourable and delightful man. Fine military record. Will certainly obey orders from Vichy.'[7] A French source describes Lacroix as a foul-mouthed 'hairy old sea-wolf, who looked as though he were hewn with an axe. He had the reputation of being a "war lover".'

Dakar at this time had 112,000 inhabitants, of whom about 12,000 were Frenchmen (4,000 in the Navy, 2,000 in the Army, 300 in government service, and the rest were civilians). Sheltered inside the hook of Cape Verde, the town was, for the American Consul-General, one of 'slumbering streets and still courtyards, filled with antique charms'.

Nothing went according to plan from the beginning. A 'fifth column' of three French officers under a dashing and highly intelligent leader, the short, blond, robust-looking Commandant (Major) Hettier de Boislambert, was to infiltrate Dakar before the expedition arrived. It was to sabotage communications, try to win over as many officers as possible, then welcome de Gaulle's emissaries when their boats arrived at No. 2 Mole. They had left Bathurst in a rowboat and disembarked on the 22nd at Foun-Diougne, on the Senegal-Gambian border, obtained a car, and driven to Dakar. They arrived, wearing civilian clothing, of course, in Dakar in the evening of the 22nd. De Boislambert was unable to contact the Colonel commanding one of the Senegalese regiments in order to persuade him to join the Gaullist troops when they landed.

---

[6] Spears, *Two Men Who Saved France*, p. 197.
[7] 'Personalities' (mainly Frenchmen in Dakar), n.d., ADM 202/413.

He then tried to win over the Colonel commanding the coastal artillery, but received a cold welcome at his lodgings. This officer had, moreover, been relieved recently and was no longer in command of the coastal artillery. Slowly it dawned upon de Boislambert that the information on which de Gaulle had conceived the whole operation was not accurate—that the co-operation of the Army was simply not going to be forthcoming, and that the population was far from favourably disposed to the Free French. Unfortunately, he had no way of getting this vital intelligence to de Gaulle. 'If I had been able to communicate with General de Gaulle,' de Boislambert said later, 'I would have tried to dissuade him from pursuing the operation.' Instead of welcoming d'Argenlieu on the quayside on the morning of the 23rd, he had to go into hiding. He had been able to achieve this much: the cutting of all the telephone lines between Staff Headquarters in Dakar and the Cape Manuel and Gorée batteries, as well as the telephonic and telegraphic communications between Dakar and Thiès and the Dakar-Thiès railway. All this led to what Colonel de Boislambert describes as 'absolutely incredible confusion' in Dakar, and which, he maintains, would have been of great assistance to the operation based on Rufisque. De Boislambert was captured a few days later, after the failure of the operation, at the Gambian border. He was imprisoned and in June 1941 condemned to death by court martial. This was commuted to hard labour for life, but he escaped to England after 31 months of prison in conditions that were often 'atrocious'. Ironically, he was later French Ambassador to the Republic of Senegal (1960–2).

The other preliminaries went no better. At 5.35 a.m. two unarmed French Luciole planes, small passenger craft with French insignia (they rather resembled the De Havilland Tiger Moth), were flown off the *Ark Royal*. They made a surprise landing at 5.54 on Ouakam airfield, a fighter base on Cape Verde Peninsula, a few miles from the town, and put down four Free French airmen. Their mission was to persuade the Vichy pilots to throw their lot in with de Gaulle, so that the Allied armada need not fear air attack. This was extremely important to the attackers, since they had only about 50 Fleet Air Arm machines, and these were slower than the French. The extreme vulnerability of the transports to air attack was a further cause of anxiety. The Commander of the airfield, de la Horie, advanced in all innocence to greet the Free Frenchmen, but when he showed no interest in rallying to de Gaulle, they promptly tied him up and laid out the pre-arranged 'success' signs by means of ground strips. This signified that the airfield was now able to receive aircraft from the *Ark Royal*. As a result, a Swordfish which had accompanied the Lucioles disembarked three more French airmen (6.08) and took off with no opposition. Minutes later, while keeping the airfield under observation, the Swordfish was attacked by a Curtiss fighter.

For the 'success' signal had been premature. Some of de la Horie's men, quickly grasping the situation, had rushed up, freed him, and made the intruders prisoner. They found on the person of one of them a list of Gaullist supporters in the town. Again, fiasco. Like the de Boislambert failure, it was not immediately known to the Allied Commanders.

At about the same time, six Swordfish left the *Ark Royal* and flew over the harbour and the town in the fog, scattering tricoloured leaflets and carrying out reconnaissance and photography. All the leaflets were signed by de Gaulle. Some contained a special appeal to the French sailors and were supposed to be dropped on the ships in harbour: 'French Sailors! Rally to the French Fleet which fights for our Country!' Others, to the soldiers, were meant to be dropped on the barracks: 'French Soldiers! Your duty is to fight alongside us for France!' Another proclaimed: 'We are here to defend Dakar alongside you. We are here to bring food to Dakar!' One read simply: 'Frenchmen of Dakar! Join us to set France Free!' The longest leaflet read:

Dakar is threatened by the enemy and by famine!
We must save Dakar for France!
We must resupply Dakar. [The food supply was adequate: there was no rationing.]
This is why French forces under my orders have arrived at Dakar.
Powerful Allied forces are ready to support them.
I urge the civil and military authorities to co-operate with me.
I ask that all elements of the land, sea, and air forces remain at their posts and contact the French troops which are coming to reinforce them.
I invite the population to demonstrate their patriotism by remaining calm and welcoming my troops.
Long live French Dakar!
Long live French Africa!
Long live France!

Still another leaflet, 'to the population of Dakar,' declared that very important announcements would be broadcast on 45 metres, and urged the people to listen on this wave length. The evidence is that most of the leaflets remained untouched and unread. At Boisson's orders, at 6.10 AA fire from the *Richelieu* welcomed the unexpected visitors. It damaged one of the planes. Curtiss fighters also challenged the Swordfish. The hostile French reaction was regarded in Force M as a bad sign—'quite upsetting', as Spears noted in his diary.

In the next phase Gaullist emissaries were supposed to land at Dakar and present important messages to Boisson and the military commanders. A favourable reply within two hours would be expected, failing which de Gaulle would call on British support to force the surrender of Dakar.

At 5.25 a.m., when Force M was about ten miles to the south of Cape Manuel, de Gaulle ordered the Free French sloop *Savorgnan de Brazza* to proceed alone towards the harbour. (A sloop was chosen because it was thought she would not appear menacing.) With the benefit of resemblance to Vichy ships of the same class, she proceeded unmolested. At 5.55, when three miles south of the boom entrance, she stopped and lowered two unarmed motor-boats flying a large tricolour with the Cross of Lorraine and white flags of truce, and carrying de Gaulle's emissaries. In the first boat was Commander d'Argenlieu, the head of the delegation, and thirteen officers and ratings, including Captain Henri Bécourt-Foch, grandson of Marshal Foch. All were in French uniform. The second boat carried an armed 'security detachment' of a dozen men. Its role, presumably, was to reinforce the first party, if necessary.

The boat carrying the emissaries came alongside Mole No. 2 and tied up at 6.55, while the other remained a short distance away. Both boats kept their engines idling. The hope was that the second party would soon be able to land. The Free French airmen, after landing at Ouakam, were supposed to arrange for motor cars to meet the landing parties at the quay. The parties would then proceed to the Governor-General's residence, accompanied, it was hoped, by enthusiastic crowds. Rockets would announce the success of the mission. It did not quite work out that way.

On landing, the emissaries were threatened by a naval lieutenant with a revolver. Minutes later they were met by the Chief of the Navigation Police, Lieutenant-Commander Lorfèvre, who had been alerted to their arrival by the Navigation Police Station at the entrance to the harbour. (British sources identified him as the 'Harbour Master and a Key Man', who was written off as anti-British.) Asked about the purpose of his mission, d'Argenlieu replied that his instructions were to hand important letters to the three supreme authorities in Dakar—the Governor-General and the Army and Navy Cs-in-C.[8] When d'Argenlieu refused a request to hand over his letters, Lorfèvre dispatched his Second-in-Command, Lieutenant Geoffrois, by car to report to the Admiral at his home, 500 yards away, and to receive his orders. There was a somewhat heavy silence. D'Argenlieu inspected his surroundings, then suddenly remarked to Lorfèvre:

You have a nice little fleet here.

Lorfèvre: Yes, and it is ready to defend itself.

D'Argenlieu, after a painful silence: We, too, are a group with a lot of esprit de corps.

Lorfèvre: You belong to a religious order and I am myself a believer. We know how to examine our conscience. I have examined mine and I am absolutely convinced that I have done my duty.

D'Argenlieu: Our duty was first of all to fulfil our obligations to England.

Lorfèvre: I obey my legitimate orders.

D'Argenlieu: Our superiors have betrayed us.

Lorfèvre: What about Mers-el-Kébir?[9]

At this point in the spirited exchange Geoffrois returned with the Admiral's instructions. Let us turn back.

Landriau had just had one of the leaflets which had fallen on the town brought to him. He knew of the landing at Ouakam and that British ships were off the town. A large-scale operation was evidently about to commence, and he had already alerted his naval forces. Without consulting Boisson, the Admiral first ordered that the emissaries should leave the port immediately. This was the message that Geoffrois brought to d'Argenlieu. The latter argued heatedly with the Lieutenant. Then he saw armed men running towards him. What had happened was that Landriau had had a second thought. He now feared that the arrival of the delegation might well coincide

---

[8] The letters were identical. They were dated 18 September and signed by de Gaulle. They asked the French authorities to join him 'and carry on the war for the liberation of our country'; mentioned the presence near by of 'important' forces, which had come to reinforce the garrison, protect the place from any surprise attack by the enemy, and furnish supplies to the colony; and declared de Gaulle's intention to disembark his Force and the supplies. 'I cannot imagine that any opposition will be met with.' If, contrary to expectation, there was resistance, this 'would involve intervention by the Allied Forces which accompany me, whose mission is to prevent, by all means at their disposal, any risk of the Dakar base falling into the hands of the enemy'.

[9] Maurice Martin du Gard, *La Carte impériale: histoire de la France outre-mer, 1940–1945* (Paris, 1949), pp. 112–13, Chenet, *Qui a sauvé l'Afrique?*, pp. 55–6.

with an attempt at a *putsch* within Dakar. He telephoned Lorfèvre and ordered the arrest of d'Argenlieu and his companions. D'Argenlieu reacted swiftly. He incapacitated the sergeant of the guard with a kick in the crotch, made a dash for his motor-boat, shouting, 'Into the boats. Let's go!', and was followed by his companions. They leapt into the boat and made off. It was 7.15 a.m.

Both boats, their white flags still flying, made for the open sea at high speed, chased by an old tug which quickly fell behind. There were a few bursts of harmless machine-gun fire in the direction of the motor-boats from the tug and from the AA post at the extreme end of the southern jetty, at the entrance to the harbour. A burst of machine-gun fire, apparently from Gorée, severely wounded d'Argenlieu and another officer in his boat when it was passing the northern end of the island. Boisson was afterwards accused of a violation of the well-known laws of war, *The Times* Diplomatic Correspondent, for example, charging (26 September) that the Governor-General had 'fired without warning on the flag of truce— a gross breach of international law, which indicates that he himself feared the effect of parleys'. This was as far from the truth as one could get. Boisson was completely unaware of the action of the gunners, not learning of it until the boats were far away.

The motor-boats reached the waiting sloop at the harbour entrance, to the south-east of Gorée, at 7.55 a.m., and it withdrew into the fog under fire from the *Richelieu*'s secondary armament and the Gorée batteries. At 9.45 the *Savorgnan de Brazza* joined the *Westernland* and transferred the two wounded officers, who came on board 'full of pep'. D'Argenlieu was hospitalized for six weeks in Duala.

The repulse of the mission threw the *Westernland* into gloom. 'It was', in Spears's view, 'a dastardly action.' Cunningham, in his Report, was critical of de Gaulle's timing: 'The entry of the Emissary in the harbour and the arrival of Free French Sloops at the Boom also [as with de Gaulle's first broadcast, below] took place before the pre-arranged time and far too early for any appreciable effect to have been made by the leaflets.'

In the meantime, just after 8 a.m., at de Gaulle's order, the sloops *Commandant Duboc* and *Commandant Dominé* had reached the boom (one hour ahead of the time-table) and tried to penetrate the harbour and land special detachments that had been put on board the ships. They were to incite the crew of the *Richelieu* to join the Free French. Suddenly revealed by the shifting fog, the sloops were quickly forced to retire by machine-gun fire from the southern jetty, which just missed the bridge of the *Commandant Dominé*, and by a few rounds from the *Richelieu*'s secondary armament, which fell just ahead of the *Commandant Duboc*. The sloops were surprised and shaken by the reception from their compatriots.

The *Commandant Dominé* had escaped almost certain disaster through a ruse employed by her Commander, Jacquelin de la Porte des Vaux, who was noted for his originality and sense of humour. In order to leave the harbour he would have had to sail alongside the *Richelieu*. Realizing, as he approached the battleship, that her big guns were being lowered and would blow him out of the water when he passed in front of them, he ordered his bugler, who was beside him on the tiny bridge, to 'sound attention' (*garde-à-vous*). That is, he was to play the tune which ordered the sailors to come to attention. The bugler obliged and, deeply moved, he held the sound so long as the *Commandant Dominé*, bolting at top speed, was under the mouth of the big guns. No shot was fired from the *Richelieu*, whose sailors believed (or seemed to believe), so close was the sloop, that it was in their own ship that the *garde-à-vous* had been sounded! They were, consequently, immobilized. By the time they discovered their mistake, the fog had shrouded the *Commandant Dominé*.

Afterwards, when Jacquelin de la Porte des Vaux was back in Freetown, he telegraphed his annoyance at his little ship being fired on in a telegram to the Captain of the *Richelieu*, Paul Marzin. After chastising Marzin in mocking fashion for rendering proper honours to his ship with a gun salute, he remarked with feeling that 'after all, it is for the liberation of our families that we, each of us believing he is doing his duty, are fighting, for the liberation of our sons, who are sitting on the same bench in the same school in Brest. I do not want to believe that reconciliation has become impossible. . . .'

By this time the Allied Commanders were under no illusions as to the attitude of the authorities in Dakar. At 9.05 Cunningham warned Force M that the situation was developing towards 'Sticky'. Nor were the Dakar authorities under any illusions about the attackers. At 8.15 a state of siege was declared, followed by the arrest of fourteen suspected Gaullist sympathizers, including the Mayor and the President of the Chamber of Commerce. A mere fourteen out of a population of over 100,000. Let it be said here that no Gaullist demonstrations occurred in Dakar during the operation to hinder the defenders. This is not to say that the population was hostile to the Free French. An apparently reliable informant, a European businessman from Gambia who had been in Dakar during the battle, reported some days later: 'The [European] civil population was almost entirely in favour of de Gaulle, but the Governor and the military obeyed Vichy orders. . . . The native element at Dakar remained perfectly calm and was for the most part interested in the evolutions of the planes and the fighting of the ships.'[10]

After seeing d'Argenlieu and the Captain of the *Savorgnan de Brazza*, de Gaulle signalled the Admiral (10.30) that Situation 'Happy' would have to be considered as having come to an end, and suggesting that 'Sticky' should be put into operation. As a first step, he proposed that his sloops should try again to enter the harbour under cover of naval fire directed at the *Richelieu* and Gorée, and that, if they were repulsed, they should attempt Plan Charles that afternoon.

And so concluded the prologue to Act I. De Boislambert's mission had been an abject failure; the attempt at Ouakam had failed; the emissaries had been forced to flee; the sloops had been compelled to retire. No attempt had been made to take advantage of the fog by a swift combined operation. Now it was too late. Two courses remained: to retire or to fight. Allied plans called for the latter.[11]

* * *

[10] As reported by Colonel Ellis, Press Attaché, Tangier, 4 Oct., FO 371/24333. There was at least one exception to the apparent lack of concern of the natives. At the request of de Boislambert, the Grand Marabout of Tidjanes, El Hadj Seydou Nourou Tall, a Gaullist sympathizer and one of the highest Moslem religious authorities in Africa, led a crowd of about 20,000 natives towards the palace of the Governor-General. It was an attempt to persuade Boisson to yield to the entreaties of de Gaulle and his Allies and give up a useless fight. (As I write, the Grand Marabout is alive at 106!) Boisson dispersed the crowd roughly. Watson, *Échec à Dakar*, pp. 171–2, Colonel Heittier de Boislambert's letter to the author, 24 Jan. 1975. Mordal, who reflects the Vichy point of view, makes light of this incident. 'The influx of the native population towards the Governor's palace at the moment of the first bombardments has been presented as a pro-Gaullist demonstration. In fact, these were people who were crazed with fear and who were seeking shelter.' *La Bataille de Dakar*, p. 205. De Gaulle learnt after the operation that a French precaution taken immediately before the operation was to draft 'a kind of semi-military Fascist body of young toughs'. War Diary of the Spears Mission, 28 Sept. Spears heard at this time from men who had been in Dakar during the Allied bombardment that 'groups of police & sailors at every cross roads overawed population, and mgs [machine guns] manned by sailors were trained on the civil part of the town'. 'Dakar Diary', 30 Sept. I can find no confirmation of this in French sources, beyond a mention in Mordal that the town was carefully patrolled against any actions by a fifth column; but if true, these reports would help to explain the quiescence of the civilian population, European and native.

[11] When it was obvious that the Anglo-Free French Forces would not receive an official welcome, and a landing or landings would have to be made, writes a then

At a conference in Freetown before the expedition left, Spears had suggested that he could personally make a contribution in one of two ways. Should the French authorities not take d'Argenlieu at his word that the British had no intention of landing, unless forced to, and did not dream of annexing Dakar, he could send for Spears, who would support him. If the emissaries were not allowed to land, Spears would go into the harbour in a British motor-boat, under a white flag, and try by persuasion to avoid an engagement.

It was my intention to explain the last thing we wanted was to bombard Dakar, our only care being to ensure that the Germans did not gain possession of the place and that some understanding with General de Gaulle was therefore necessary. I had meant to suggest that the Governor or the Admiral should come out in one of their own boats and have a conversation with General de Gaulle and, if need be, with our own Commanders. The latter would however not hear of the idea and considered that from the time the French emissaries had been rejected, the situation was in their hands and must be dealt with by them. I was told that if I wished to carry out this idea I must obtain authority from London. This I declined to do as it was impossible to explain, by signals, so complicated a story and it would, I felt, have given the impression of a squabble and lack of unity of views, so I dropped the idea. Looking back on events as they actually occurred I am far from believing that such a step would have been successful. Nevertheless Capt. d'Argenlieu . . . believes it would have had a very fair chance. He puts the odds as high as 70%. If only contact could have been established the whole thing might have been avoided or the position at least clarified.[12]

If Mers-el-Kébir offers any guidance, I would say that Spears's hunch was right, that probably nothing useful would have come of either of his proposals. On the other hand, I subscribe to Desmond Morton's dictum, in a marginal note on the letter: 'A gamble. Much of war is a gamble'.

(2) The First Bombardment

De Gaulle's hourly broadcasts from the *Westernland* on the wave length announced in many of the leaflets reflected his growing pessimism over the likelihood of a peaceful solution, and with it a more threatening tone. The speeches were 'admirable in themselves',

---

2nd Lieutenant of Marines, 'the suicidal nature of the plan was borne in upon us. We young officers thereupon ran up huge Mess bills which we thought we would never have to pay.' John Biggs-Davison's letter to the author, 11 Apr. 1974.
[12] Spears to Ismay, 30 Sept., PREM 3/276.

but General Spears 'wondered whether the sailors, enclosed and isolated in their ships, or the officials at their desks, even heard them, or if they did whether, under the eye and supervision of their chiefs, they could have responded to his call had they wanted to. Did any of the native population hear him and would they have realized what it was all about if they had?'[13]

The first broadcast, a few minutes after 6 a.m., which was delivered three-quarters of an hour before the agreed time, was afterwards criticized by Cunningham as a premature move. It gave no time for the leaflets to be picked up and to have their effect, and for de Gaulle's emissaries to reach the harbour. Moreover, the Admiral thought that the broadcast may have alerted the defences. The first broadcast announced de Gaulle's arrival with troops to strengthen the defences of Dakar and to resupply the town, and that he had sent officers to request of the authorities the unopposed landing of the Free French troops and the supplies. The 'powerful British fleet and numerous British troops' which accompanied him would not intervene 'if all goes well'. De Gaulle's third broadcast (the second was at 7), at 8.07, was threatening: 'I am awaiting a reply to my questions, before disembarking. . . . But you have just fired on the *Savorgnan de Brazza*. If such opposition continues, the powerful Allied Forces which are supporting me will come into action and the consequences will be very serious. . . .' At 9 a.m. a new message threatened that 'if my ships and my French troops cannot fulfil their mission, the enormous Allied forces which follow me would step in and take charge of the entire business. Come, good Frenchmen of Dakar, there is still time. Impose your will on the guilty ones who are firing on Frenchmen.' At 10.20 de Gaulle broadcast what was practically an ultimatum: 'The Authorities of Dakar have refused to negotiate with the officers I have sent to them. The *Richelieu* and the battery at Gorée have fired on the *Savorgnan de Brazza*, the *Commandant Duboc*, and the *Commandant Dominé*. The French ships and troops which are accompanying me must enter Dakar and, if they meet with resistance, the large Allied Forces which are following me will take the matter in hand.'

After de Gaulle's last broadcast, the Dakar authorities speeded up defensive preparations. Fearing that mines might have been laid in the entrance to the harbour, Landriau ordered two sweepers to clear the channel. An additional gate was made in the net barrage to facilitate ship movements to the sandy beaches east of the town,

[13] *Two Men Who Saved France*, p. 197.

where landings might be attempted. A reconnaissance aircraft was sent up. It reported a large fleet, including troop transports, south and south-west of Cape Manuel. The authorities were now certain that a landing was imminent.

Towards 9, to demonstrate that they meant business, Cunningham had begun to close. The 9·4-inch guns of Cape Manuel opened sporadic long-range fire on the British ships at 10.05, causing the Admiral immediately to warn the French authorities by wireless in plain language (10.07): 'If fire is continued on my ships, I shall regretfully be compelled to return it.' The reply, from Barrau, was prompt and sharp: 'If you do not wish me to fire remove yourself more than twenty miles from Dakar.' Cunningham continued to approach until he was 4,000 yards from the forts, which brought the fleet close under their guns. His instructions were to fire only in self-defence or against warships leaving the harbour. But at 11.04 the British ships finally replied, engaging the *Richelieu* and the forts. It was a weird sort of duel in the fog that still prevailed. The Admiral soon ordered a cease-fire, and at 11.35 the fleet altered 40° to the southward and withdrew out of range. Cunningham had ordered the cease-fire 'partly because a peaceful solution was still hoped for and partly because it had been agreed that no more force than was necessary to overcome sporadic resistance should be used'. Another consideration may have been the unsuitability of visibility conditions for this kind of action, in which in any case the advantage lay with the forts.

Whereas the *Barham* and *Resolution* had fired over a hundred rounds of 15-inch shells without effect, the 9·4-inch guns on Cape Manuel and Gorée, as well as the big guns of the *Richelieu* (two-gun 15-inch salvoes), had been surprisingly accurate.[14] The destroyers *Foresight* and *Inglefield* were hit by the shore batteries, suffering minor damage, when pursuing the submarines *Ajax* and *Persée*. A 9·4-inch shell from the Cape Manuel batteries hit the cruiser *Cumberland* amidships (11.29), piercing the port side just above the armour belt and bursting above the lower deck. The hit wrecked

---

[14] Each of the French shore batteries as well as the *Richelieu* had its own colour scheme to distinguish its own salvoes for fire-control purposes: black for the big guns of the *Richelieu*, yellow for Cape Manuel, white, red, blue, green, and purple for others. This is the first recorded use of coloured shell bursts to simplify spotting. 'These coloured, feathery water spouts had the prettiness of a wedding cake.' They also worked to the British advantage, being a 'tremendous help in manoeuvring the *Australia* [and presumably the other British ships] to dodge being hit'. Captain R. R. Stewart's letter to the author, 3 Dec. 1974.

the main switchboard and did serious damage in the engine-room. Her best speed reduced to 10 knots, the *Cumberland* turned and steamed out of range, later withdrawing to Bathurst (Gambia) for repairs.

There was some offset. The *Persée*, ignoring Cunningham's warnings that French ships would be forced to return if they left harbour (10.30, 10.50), was sunk while proceeding on the surface south of Cape Manuel to her patrol position in the Bay of Yof. The *Barham* nearly sank the *Persée* with 6-inch shell; depth charges finished her off, and she sank at 11.37 about a mile and a half E.N.E. of Cape Manuel Lighthouse. French craft rescued most of her crew.

The French cargo vessel *Porthos* was hit by a 15-inch shell. Some damage was done to the dockyard and to houses in the town, including a native hospital. There were no public shelters against bombardment in Dakar. On the 23rd the European residents hastily dug trenches in their gardens, shallow affairs which managed to give the illusion of security. The natives took no precautions, and when a few British 'overs' fell in the native quarter, it provoked a general panic, the inhabitants fleeing in every direction. Panic gradually yielded to an orderly evacuation to the interior.

The first bombardment had succeeded only in bolstering the morale of the defenders and their determination to resist. At 11.44 Cunningham received a message from the Governor-General, who was replying to de Gaulle's broadcast of 11.20, urging the Vichy authorities to signal that they would 'no longer oppose the entry into the port of French ships and the landing of troops under my orders'. Boisson confirmed that all landings would be opposed. 'You have taken the initiative in causing French blood to flow. Keep this responsibility, for blood is already flowing.'

The situation, when the fleet withdrew, appeared to be as follows: 'Opposition to General de Gaulle a hundred per cent from the Authorities, substantial from the French Navy and partial from some of the batteries. Civilian population incapable of or unwilling to support. Opposition to British Forces whole hearted from Authorities, Forts and probably French Navy. French Air adopting a passive attitude toward both Free French and British. Attitude of French Troops unknown, but possibly General de Gaulle's Agents in Dakar might have had some success with Army as they appear to have had with the Air Force.'[15] On the whole, a perceptive assessment. At 12.20 p.m. the Joint Commanders informed the Force that the

[15] Cunningham's Report, Pt. V, p. 3.

situation was 'Sticky', i.e. that de Gaulle had met with partial opposition and needed some help from British guns and aircraft.

(3) Plan Charles

By midday, writes Spears, 'it was becoming difficult to suppress the feeling that impetus was being lost, that the fog, like a slimy jelly-fish, was gradually enfolding us, depriving us of movement'. To the Force Commanders the state of opinion in Dakar and the vigour of the defenders boded ill for a landing attempt at Dakar. They therefore 'considered it inadvisable further to inflame feelings on shore by engaging with the British Forces until General de Gaulle had been given an opportunity of attempting an unopposed landing at Rufisque'. This was Plan Charles, a final attempt at a peaceful landing by Free French troops at Rufisque, from where they could proceed by rail or road to Dakar. The Commanders thought that the fog might help them in carrying out the plan. According to intelligence reports, the anchorage of Rufisque in depths of $3\frac{1}{4}$ to 7 fathoms was dangerous at that time of year owing to heavy swell. There were several jetties with depths of about 9 feet at their head facing the town. Landing on beaches west and east of Rufisque was considered possible, but dependent on surf conditions, which were frequently difficult. The great advantage of 'Charles' was that Rufisque was beyond effective gun range from Dakar.

The fog was thicker than ever, obscuring everything beyond about 3,000 yards. De Gaulle's ships literally disappeared, we shall see. The *Westernland* was hardly able to see the other transport, the *Pennland*, a couple of cable lengths away. Occasionally, they got a glimpse of the destroyers and once of the battleships. The wretched visibility made visual signalling possible only spasmodically, and this completely congested the wireless transmission sets. R/T and W/T communication between the flagship and the *Westernland*, satisfactory at first, deteriorated progressively during the afternoon. Cunningham attributed this to 'the jambing of R/T by *Westernland*'s own transmissions, which included heavy traffic on French Army lines, between *Westernland* and the Free French sloops. *Westernland* was always clearly readable in *Barham*. As far as W/T was concerned there was slight delay due to congestion, but the serious lag appears to have resulted from the time taken in *Westernland* to code and decode and distribute messages.'[16] Whatever the precise causes

[16] Ibid., Pt. V, p. 1.

of the poor communications, and we shall have to return to this, there was a great delay in getting out and receiving messages. There were two-hour delays on important messages as the available lines became more and more congested. What follows is a somewhat simplified account of the 'strange and baffling phase of confusion and uncertainty', as Irwin referred to it. Signals were arriving in the wrong sequence, there were long delays, and in some cases the British and Free French forestalled one another in the questions and answers. It was a period of 'cross questions and crooked answers', as the official account puts it.

At 11.58 Cunningham signalled de Gaulle: 'What about Charles now? He ought to do well.' This was followed by one at 12.15 asking for immediate information on de Gaulle's intentions. The War Diary of the Spears Mission reflects the confusion that reigned during the afternoon. Thus: '1215. We received a message requesting immediate information as to our intention. We on the other hand were waiting to be told whether the situation was ripe for "Charles".' At 12.25 de Gaulle's reply to the 11.58 signal was received in the *Barham*: 'Charles is all for Charles but would like to know situation.' At 12.34 a message was received from de Gaulle asking whether opposition, especially from the shore batteries, was believed to be wholehearted. At 1.25 the Force Commanders signalled that bad visibility prevented effective engagement of the batteries, but would help to hide 'Charles'. At 1.39 de Gaulle's reply was received to the message of 12.15: he pointed out that he had already said in a message of 12.50 that apparently was not received or understood in the *Barham* that he was in favour of the immediate application of 'Charles'. This last message from de Gaulle crossed one to him of 1.40 giving zero hour for Charles as 3.30 p.m., if his ships could be in position by then. This was sent in desperation (under the plan, de Gaulle was to fix zero hour), since the Commanders had received no further reply as to de Gaulle's intention. At 2.45 a message, timed 2.20, was received from de Gaulle that he was still awaiting instructions to execute 'Charles'. This increased the confusion, as the Joint Commanders had by that time assumed that the Free French ships were already in position to commence the landing. The answer went out promptly, arriving in the *Westernland* at 3.06: 'Carry out "Charles". Report zero hour.'

'Charles' was on, but de Gaulle first made a last attempt to reason with the Dakar authorities. He 'most earnestly' requested them to signal that they would not oppose the entry of his ships into the harbour and the disembarkation of his troops. At 3.42 a signal was made to the *Westernland* proposing to issue a one-hour ultimatum to the Governor-General, the landings to continue meanwhile. Did de Gaulle agree? The signal was received at about 4.15. De Gaulle's reply of 4.20 was, however, not received in the flagship until 6.05, after 'Charles' had been cancelled (see below). It announced that, in view of the ultimatum, he was suspending landings from the troopships till the situation changed, but that he proposed meanwhile to land troops from the sloops. This was the first information that the Joint Commanders had that the landing was about to take place. The next thing de Gaulle knew was that 'Charles' had been cancelled. Again we must go back.

Two British destroyers were to have co-operated in the 'Charles' operation by following the Free French ships to Rufisque to provide covering fire on the flanks of the landing parties, if needed. It was, therefore, necessary to get in touch with the Free French ships. But nobody knew where they were. At 1.35 Cunningham had altered course to the eastward to get in touch with the *Westernland*, and he shaped courses until 4.31 in an endeavour to locate her, or even some unit that had recently seen her. Despite requests for position, course, and speed, at 2.15 and 3.02, no information on the whereabouts of the French transports was received until 4 o'clock. The *Barham* then received the *Westernland*'s signal of 2.45 giving her position, course, and speed, leading away from Rufisque. Since these referred to the position of an hour and a quarter earlier, it was not sufficiently accurate to warrant Cunningham sending the supporting destroyers to her. It was not until 4.15 that the *Westernland* was seen and reported by the *Devonshire* (received in the *Barham* at 4.43), steering for Rufisque, though still 20 miles from it.

The late hour at which the *Westernland* had been sighted 20 miles from Rufisque made it clear to the British Commanders that it was too late to complete the landing before dark. At the same time, aircraft reported the movement of two French cruisers towards Rufisque and the presence in that neighbourhood of one and possibly two submarines. Cunningham's job was to protect the Free French Forces against warships issuing from Dakar. It had not been intended to take the heavy ships into the shoal waters to the southward of Rufisque Bay to give close support to the landings. In any case, the fog and gathering darkness ruled this out. The Commanders accordingly decided to call off the operation. A signal of 4.42 conveyed this decision to de Gaulle, asked for acknowledgement, and ordered the whole of Force M to withdraw south from 5 p.m. At 5.20 a signal, timed 4.35, was received from de Gaulle saying: 'Expect to arrive 16.50 [4.50 p.m.] which will be zero hour.' The signal was timed seven minutes before the message of cancellation was sent. It was received in the *Westernland* at 4.39. What happened then? All we know for certain is that it was over an hour before de Gaulle's cancellation signal was received in the *Savorgnan de Brazza* (see below), by which time 'Charles' had failed.

At 2.40 p.m. the Free French sloops, joined by the *Président Houduce*, had headed for Rufisque at 14 knots, with the transports making their way somewhat more to the south. De Gaulle had decided that the first wave of the landing forces would comprise only the marines who had been embarked in the sloops. The men of the Magrin-Vernerey Brigade (the Foreign Legion) would remain in the *Westernland* and *Pennland*, to be stopped about four miles south-east of Rufisque, in order to constitute a second wave.[17]

At first de Gaulle had proceeded with doubts about the wisdom of his decision. General Spears explains:

> There was a v. curious little interlude when, his soul sorely puzzled, de G consulted me. He felt Charles was pretty desperate & wanted to get out of it, but he had just told C he w^d do so (he often changes his mind like that). The only excuse was that C had signalled the batteries as well as the ships were in whole hearted opposition [1.01 p.m.]. I made a suggestion which he adopted, but later came to me as I was working on his text & tore it up saying he w^d do Charles. I am glad he did. It was rather a Gethsemane for him.
>
> We proceeded towards Ruffisque [*sic*], not really knowing where we were in the mist. We saw the M.T. Transports, & the Brit destroyer which was to cover us, but presently it disappeared in the mist. Soon we saw land, & advanced along the coast. It had been settled we w^d stay further away from Rufisque than had been intended, but in fact we proceeded really not knowing at what point we were. The French sloops disappeared ahead in the mist.[18]

At 4.48 the *Westernland* stopped near Cape Rouge, 7½ miles from Rufisque.

[17] Colonel Raoul Charles Magrin-Vernerey, alias Monclar (to hide his identity from the Germans and the Vichy authorities), commanded the 13th Half-Brigade of the Foreign Legion, one of the most famous units in the French Army. He was the finest type of French soldier, with about sixteen medals already in 1940. Colonel Watson describes him as 'a legendary figure, a born leader, a magnificent fighter and one of the most courteous and entertaining personalities that I have ever met'. He never stopped fighting and was still at it (in Korea) after the war.

[18] 'Dakar Diary', 23 Sept.

The sea was calm and the chances for landing were, in Spears's judgement, 'unique'. On the other hand, de Gaulle's transports were being shadowed by a French aircraft at 2,000 feet. (The fog had lifted at that height). Presently Major Watson came running up with a signal from the Admiral (*Ark Royal* aircraft had sighted the cruisers and were reporting their movements) that two cruisers had broken out of Dakar and were but two miles off, and that the British ships were unable to afford any protection. 'De Gaulle knew as well as I did,' writes Spears, 'that if the cruisers opened fire on us, defenceless and undefended as we were, it would mean a holocaust. Our ship, packed with troops, would burn like a torch until it sank into that shark-infested sea.'[19] At Spears's suggestion, towards 4 de Gaulle turned away to sea. What were the two cruisers doing in the area?

At 4.20 p.m., in response to a report from a patrolling aircraft (3.35) which had sighted the transports, accompanied by light vessels, some 12 miles to the south-west of Rufisque, heading east, the super-destroyer *L'Audacieux* had sailed out to investigate. She was followed by the cruisers *Georges Leygues* (Lacroix) and *Montcalm* and the super-destroyer *Le Malin*, which force threatened the approach of de Gaulle's sloops to Rufisque. As the *Audacieux* passed out through the gate in the boom between Gorée and the shore (i.e. east of Gorée) that had been created that morning, she was sighted by the *Australia* and the destroyers *Greyhound* and *Fury* at 4.24 and engaged minutes later at point-blank range (about 4,000 yards). She was then smothered by British fire. An 8-inch shell blew away her bridge and instantly converted her into a blazing wreck. The Second-in-Command had two torpedoes launched, fearing that they might explode. He was merely getting rid of them. They were not aimed at any particular ship and hit nothing.

The sloop *Surprise*, though under British fire, succeeded in rescuing 186 men of the *Audacieux*, among them about 100 wounded; 81 men had been killed. The ship burned for more than 36 hours. The flaming wreck drifted slowly to the shore, where it ran aground the next day between Rufisque and Popenguine. (Refloated in March 1941, the *Audacieux* managed to reach Bizerte, where she was finished off by American planes in 1943.)

The French cruisers and the super-destroyer, which had sailed at 4.40 to reconnoitre the Bay of Rufisque, had heard the firing, but did not realize what was taking place less than 3,000 yards away.

[19] *Two Men Who Saved France*, p. 201.

They arrived in Rufisque Bay after the British scouting forces had left and a few minutes before the Free French ships appeared. They passed to the north of Résolue Bank and, at 5.20, when one mile from Rufisque Lighthouse, turned around without discovering anything, and at 5.50 were back in Dakar harbour. The exceptionally poor visibility near the coast had prevented the French ships from seeing the sloops, which precisely at the moment the French ships were off the lighthouse were off Rufisque and about to attempt a landing. The French cruisers had thrown a scare into de Gaulle, who, as noted, had received news of their presence and of their course, which might lead them to the *Westernland* and *Pennland*. De Gaulle's transports were at one point less than 15,000 yards south of the cruisers, and his sloops were even closer. The thick mist had saved them. 'De Gaulle really v. upset at this. The thought crossed my mind he feared they might demand his surrender on pain of sinking us. We w^d not have done so & they w^d have sunk us anyway. We turned about & made off slowly inshore.'[20]

It was subsequently learned what had happened at Rufisque. At about 5.15 the three sloops, each carrying 60 *fusiliers marins*, boldly entered Rufisque Bay. The *Savorgnan de Brazza* stopped three-quarters of a mile from the beach and lowered her landing craft into the water to disembark her marines on the beach. The two smaller sloops proceeded inshore and got their bows close to the eastern jetty (5.20). Before they could land any marines, however, accurate point-blank fire was opened on the sloops from the 3·7-inch guns at the foot of the lighthouse, and soon after by machine guns. The order to fire was given by a very junior French army officer (*aspirant*) named Coustenoble, who was decorated by Boisson some days later and who, as he later declared, had no intention of continuing the action once it became dangerous to do so. What happened was that, upon the *Commandant Duboc* suffering a direct hit from a 3·7-inch shell (three men were killed), both vessels retired under cover of smoke screens. The *Savorgnan de Brazza* destroyed the lighthouse and apparently silenced the battery with her 5·5-inch guns. (In fact, the guns had not been hit.) There followed an attempt to land upon the beach farther south, with the marines being towed in by the *Savorgnan de Brazza*'s motor-boats, and the other two sloops covering the operation as close inshore as possible. When within about 300 yards from the beach, isolated rifle shots (not a hail of bullets, as is sometimes said) from the regiment of Senegalese

[20] 'Dakar Diary', 23 Sept.

infantry stopped the boats before they reached the shore. At 5.58 a signal was received from the *Westernland* that 'Charles' was abandoned, whereupon the *Savorgnan de Brazza* recalled her boats and re-embarked the landing parties. By 6.38 the three sloops were withdrawing to a position south-west of Cape de Nazé.[21]

All this time the *Westernland* and *Pennland* were 7½ miles away. It would have taken at least 40 minutes to reinforce the marines.[22] There was much criticism afterwards, from Spears among others, of the performance of the marines. '. . . the opposition from a company of native troops had been of the lightest, apparently half-hearted and supported by most ineffective rifle fire. A few hits had been scored on the Free French sloops by a field battery but not enough to have stopped troops with a minimum of training. But the Free French *fusiliers marins* had neither leadership nor training, nor even the minimum required for brave men to dash for an objective. . . . It was pathetic.'[23] This is true enough. The Rufisque operation was feebly conducted by men who lacked the training and felt that they were not supported.

It is not difficult to assess the causes of the afternoon's confused and unsuccessful operation. There is the obvious one that 'Charles' had never been rehearsed, a *sine qua non* in any combined operation where the actors are drawn from two nationalities. Such an exercise would have revealed the poor signal communications and perhaps ensured that the various W/T channels, British and Free French,

[21] It appears that de Gaulle had decided to re-embark the marines because of the news about the French cruisers, and at practically the moment he received the cancellation order from the Admiral. Spears to Ismay, 30 Sept., PREM 3/276.

[22] This was not known until several days after 'Menace', at Freetown, when the reconstruction of movements established beyond doubt that the transports had anchored 7½ miles from Rufisque, not 2 miles, as *Westernland*'s message of 5.25 p.m. on the 23rd had reported. De Gaulle and Spears found this hard to believe, as they were 'on the tail of the sloops & the firing we heard was not more than 2 miles off. On thinking it over this error may be due to our having stopped then gone on again.' 'Dakar Diary', 1 Oct. On the same occasion Cunningham surprised Spears by saying that, according to information from his liaison officers in the sloops, no marines had actually landed, whereas the day after 'Charles' Spears had informed the Joint Commanders that the marines had landed, that the natives had helped to haul up their boats, and that a landing on a considerable scale could have been effected without serious loss, if the operation had not been called off. French Admiralty records agree with the liaison officers.

[23] *Two Men Who Saved France*, p. 200. Colonel Watson, too, suggests that had the marines landed, they would have met little opposition. Watson's letter to the author, 10 Jan. 1974. A year later the officer commanding the Senegalese company fled to Nigeria, where 'he quite firmly maintained that the resistance put up was merely token, that he and the Senegalese had no intention of continuing it, and were stunned with surprise when the Marines withdrew'. Wingate, *Not in the Limelight*, p. 168.

could work without mutual interference. There had been no time at Freetown, besides which there was felt to be a need for secrecy. The failure in signal communications with de Gaulle produced chaotic conditions. The crucial consideration, however, was the thick weather, since, with good visibility, the landing would have proceeded under the protection of the two British destroyers and with speedy reinforcements from the transports. What is more, clear weather would have made it impossible for the Vichy cruisers to reach the vicinity of Rufisque. Irwin afterwards formed the opinion that even if 'Charles' had proceeded according to plan, it would have failed. Any attempt to land in force would have been resolutely opposed, and the Free French troops were not organized or embarked for a landing against such opposition. And given the poor visibility and the threat from the French cruisers, it would have been extremely hazardous to have ordered British troopships to close the shore.[24] We must also bear in mind that 'Charles' was not intended to be pressed home in the face of resolute opposition, but was to be de Gaulle's last attempt at a peaceful approach before the British intervention, in Situation 'Nasty', with unrestricted bombardment and an opposed landing by the total force at their disposal.

The first day's operations had ended in complete failure. All the Allied hopes were shattered. After the attitude of the cruisers in the events of 19–20 September, it did not seem reasonable to anticipate serious French resistance. One wonders why the expedition's commanders did not exercise their prerogative to call off the operation, for it had never been the British intention—nor was it de Gaulle's policy—to become involved in another bloody battle on the pattern of Mers-el-Kébir. Yet the Dakar authorities had made it plain that force would be met by force, nor was there any reason to doubt their word. The offensive spirit of the Vichy French forces had clearly surprised the Allied command, although their air force had done little. (This exasperated the crews, especially in view of the reconnaissance activity of the *Ark Royal* aircraft.)

Cunningham was very angry at the way the first day's operations had turned out and he was, for the moment, terribly depressed. He had, of course, been under great stress all day, a state aggravated by the breakdown in W/T communications. Matters were different in the *Westernland*, where Spears was 'not discouraged and down' and de Gaulle's morale was good. But for a moment the latter thought of chucking the whole business. 'He is inclined to think of Syria

---

[24] Irwin's Report, Ch. III, p. 3.

now, but I say to him he can't play the butterfly & fly off now. This job must be seen thro' somehow.'[25] This was not to be the last time that Spears had to remind the General of where his duty lay. De Gaulle quickly recovered. The calm and dignified manner in which he accepted the reverse at Rufisque was an example to all. His confidence was scarcely diminished by the events of the day. At 5.28 a.m. on the 24th he signalled the War Office: 'Although morale is unexpectedly high we still feel that the reduction of fort and destruction of ships will lead to collapse of resistance in spite of probable land reinforcement which we now must expect. . . . A message received by us from the Prime Minister [see below] encourages us in our determination to occupy Dakar come what may.'

The attitude of the officers and men in the *Ark Royal* was probably typical of the British component in Force M. Writes an old Ark Royal who served in the operation: 'The Ark Royals were angered and confused by the events of this most unsatisfactory day. They could not understand why their old allies should have opposed them so bitterly. One of the officers was discussing the matter with a Free French Colonel [twenty Free French flying personnel under the command of Colonel de Marnier had been embarked at Freetown], "*Je ne comprends pas*", he said. The Frenchman shrugged his shoulders, "*Il ne faut pas tâcher de comprendre*".' The attitude of the Free French in the *Ark Royal* was not perhaps what we would have expected. 'If feeling amongst the Free French on board the *Ark* was typical, we need not have been so squeamish of setting Frenchmen against Frenchmen. Furious at their reception on the previous day, they were longing for action. "If only the fifteen hundred men of the Foreign Legion had been put on shore," they said. "To the gallows with the Admiral!" cried one. Another, patting a 500-lb. bomb which was being wheeled to one of the Skuas, exclaimed, "*Aha! Voilà un joli petit déjeuner pour l'Amiral*".'[26]

The decision to withdraw the troopships and resume operations the next day was signalled to the Admiralty at 4.36 p.m. (received at 7.19 p.m.). During the evening the Joint Commanders considered, and dismissed as impracticable, a British landing at Rufisque that night. At 9.05 they received a personal message from the Prime Minister: 'Having begun we must go on to the end. Stop at nothing.' This message encouraged the Force Commanders to go on. It

[25] 'Dakar Diary', 23 Sept.
[26] Rear-Admiral Sir William Jameson, *Ark Royal, 1939–1941* (London, 1957), pp. 215–16.

crossed a signal from them (8.31 p.m.) that they had decided to issue an ultimatum expiring after dawn on the 24th, and should they fail to obtain acceptance, they would 'proceed with systematic reduction of the defences before landing troops'. The ultimatum was delivered at 11.45 p.m., after de Gaulle had agreed that the situation was indeed now 'Nasty' and that the ultimatum should be issued. It was broadcast in French and English and transmitted to the Dakar radio station. Addressed to the Governor-General, it ran:

General de Gaulle informs us, the Commanders of the British Naval and Military Forces, that you have prevented him from landing his troops for the re-victualling of Dakar. Your attitude gives us every reason to believe that Dakar may at any moment be handed over by you to the common enemy. In view of the importance of this town and this base in connection with the development of the war, and also in view of the fact that the seizing of Dakar by the enemy would cause the population to be oppressed, the Allies regard it as their duty to take such immediate steps as are necessary to prevent this eventuality. Desiring that Frenchmen should not fight against Frenchmen in a pitched battle, General de Gaulle has withdrawn his Forces.[27] Our forces are approaching. It is for you now to speak: you will not be allowed to hand over the French and native people who wish to remain free to the slavery to which Germany and Italy would subject them. Yours is the entire responsibility for what may happen.

We have the honour to inform you that, if by 0600, the 24th September, you have not given your decision to General de Gaulle, the very powerful forces at our disposal will open fire. Once fire has begun it will continue until the fortifications of Dakar are entirely destroyed, and the place occupied by troops who will be ready to fulfil their duty. Only a proclamation that our conditions are accepted could interrupt the carrying out of this programme. Our troops would not land if you decided to join your compatriots in the liberation of your country and not to remain tied to the enemy who holds France at his mercy. There is no compromise possible...

At 1 a.m., before receiving a reply, Cunningham altered to the northward to close Dakar.

The ultimatum reached Boisson at 1 a.m. He was shocked. That Dakar might be handed over to the Germans was, for him, nonsense. There was no German military presence anywhere in French West Africa. Moreover, the fact of an ultimatum made him furious. He would not succumb to pressure. The commanding officers of the

[27] This sentence was inserted at de Gaulle's request. The intention was that he was to keep out of sight until the defences had been shattered or his support was needed to prevent failure.

three Services, who met at a council of war summoned by Boisson, matched his indignation. The sentence in the ultimatum that caused the most violent anger was: 'Your attitude gives us every reason to believe that Dakar may at any moment be handed over by you to the common enemy.' The council of war did not question the principle of defence to the end, but the first thought, of sending a short and rude answer ('*Merde!*'), gave way to a dignified, if curt, reply. This was signalled by Boisson at 4 a.m. (via the *Richelieu*): 'France has entrusted Dakar to me. I shall defend Dakar to the bitter end.'

There was nothing for it but to proceed with the plan for Situation 'Nasty'. Unrestricted naval and air bombardment must overwhelm the forts and the *Richelieu*, preliminary to a British landing. The Free French would have no role in this phase of 'Menace' unless their help was essential to avoid failure.

Chapter Seven

The Second Day of the
Operation: Situation 'Nasty'

Operation Menace carries on its weary and unprofitable course. . . .
Fortune has sunk one French submarine which tried to attack the
battle-fleet and has rescued the crew. But this cannot lead us anywhere, and only risks losses we cannot afford. I find it all terribly
depressing; but some things Winston will *never* learn and one is that
ships cannot fight forts profitably.

Diary of Acting Captain L. H. Bell
(Naval Assistant to VCNS), 24 September 1940

(Charts 6, 7)

(1) The Two Bombardments

BY 7 a.m. on 24 September the battleships and cruisers
(*Australia, Devonshire*) had resumed their bombarding positions to seaward of Dakar. Had the visibility conditions of the
first day persisted, it was Cunningham's intention to confine his
action to air bombardment of the defences. The fog was less dense
than on the previous day: visibility in the early morning had
increased to 9,000 yards and improved steadily during the day,
reaching 15,000 to 20,000 yards at times, but it was still poor. By
7.25, when the ships were within 16,000 yards of the forts, nothing
could be seen. This ruled out the planned long-range bombardment, nullified the Admiral's hope that the ship bombardment
could be simultaneous with the air attack, and forced him to move
his ships still closer to the forts, with the consequent danger, before
the targets were visible. The *Barham* was to shell Gorée, the
Resolution, the Cape Manuel fort, and both were to deal with the
Richelieu. The cruisers were to take on the warships north-east of
Gorée.

The morning attack began with an air bombardment, striking
forces of six aircraft flying off at 6.25, 7, and 8. First, Skuas flew in

above the fog, formed in line astern, and made a level bombing attack, with 500-lb. SAP (semi-armour-piercing) bombs, on ships in the harbour, including the *Richelieu*. There was no fighter opposition and AA fire was light, but poor visibility hampered the attackers and only two near misses on the *Richelieu* and one near miss on the *Fantasque* were claimed. Six Swordfish then bombed Fort Manuel, claiming eight hits. But the battery had suffered no damage; there was one near miss. Finally, six Swordfish of No. 810 Squadron, armed with four 250-lb. SAP bombs, made a high dive-bombing attack on the *Richelieu* at 9, with the bombs released at about 4,000 feet. There were no hits, only several near misses. One cannot imagine that the 250-lb. SAP bombs of the British aircraft would have had much effect on a battleship so heavily armoured (belt, 9 to 16 inches, deck, 8 inches). 'We might as well have dropped bricks!' the commanding officer of the squadron, Lieutenant-Commander M. Johnstone, ruefully remarked. I imagine the aim was to do very temporary damage only to the ship by breaking up control facilities —bridges, aerials, boats, etc. By the time of the third attack the AA fire was hot and French fighters were up, and between them they accounted for three Swordfish and three Skuas, shot down or forced to alight on the water.[1] At 3 p.m. a torpedo striking force of nine Swordfish, escorted by three Skuas, attacked the two cruisers in the bay. Eight torpedoes were launched, achieving no hits, although two hits were claimed on a cruiser with a possible third on a destroyer. Two aircraft were shot down by AA fire, for a total of eight losses for the day. This left 18 Skuas and 19 Swordfish serviceable out of the 51 aircraft in the *Ark Royal*; 8 had been lost and 6 were unserviceable.

Meanwhile, at 8.05, the destroyer *Fortune* detected a submarine within the anti-submarine screen. It was the *Ajax*, which was on the point of making a torpedo attack on the battleships. The *Fortune* dropped a single depth charge, which forced the badly damaged *Ajax* to the surface at 8.31, displaying a white flag. The *Fortune* took the crew off and sank the submarine.[2]

---

[1] The French sloop *Gazelle* was able to recover the air-gunner's notebook, with frequencies, etc., from a Swordfish that had been forced to land in Hann Bay. The French were able during the rest of the battle to confuse the air with jamming and bogus traffic, etc., and get an idea of the number of RN aircraft in the air from call signs, etc. Mordal, *La Bataille de Dakar*, p. 203, as modified by Commander N. R. Corbet-Milward's letter to the author, 20 Nov. 1974, the latter based on correspondence with a Fleet Air Arm Observer at Dakar, Commander J. R. Lang.

[2] Very important information was taken from the *Ajax* before she sank. A document revealed that the French Admiralty had ordered French ships to use only a given code,

When the air attacks of the morning were completed, the warships approached. It was hoped that the bombing would either have destroyed the forts or shaken the morale of the defenders to such an extent that they would not open fire. Vain hopes. The shore batteries opened fire on the fleet at 9.35, and a minute later the *Barham* and *Resolution* opened up on the *Richelieu* at a range of between 13,600 and 15,000 yards. Four minutes later the *Devonshire* and *Australia* were in action, firing on ships in the roadstead from as close as 10,000 yards. At 9.40 the *Richelieu* opened fire with her No. 2 15-inch turret. Defective shell caused one gun to burst in the first salvo and disabled a second gun. The turret was, however, ready to resume firing with the two remaining guns at 10.07. Her 6-inch guns continued to fire. None of the French ships suffered a direct hit during the gunnery duel between the big ships, despite the approximately 100 15-inch shells which swept the harbour from end to end. This was miraculous in view of the limited space in which the French ships could manœuvre. Even more miraculous, as Mordal says, was the absence of collisions despite the zigzagging in the midst of shell splashes and of the 54 cargo vessels dispersed throughout the bay. The British fire was also directed at Cape Manuel, when the *Resolution* shifted target. The battery, situated on a crest, was difficult to hit. Some shells passed over it and fell in the town, causing casualties. The battleships ceased fire at 10.10, when the targets were obscured by smoke, and the cruisers at 10.24, the fleet retiring to the south out of range. A signal of 11.55 from a disconsolate Cunningham reported that they had carried out a bombardment of the *Richelieu* and the fort at 10,000 yards in poor visibility, but that neither was silenced. 'Resistance continues determined.'

The morning's attack had little to show for the heavy expenditure of bombs and shells. *Ark Royal* aircraft reported a 15-inch hit on the *Richelieu* and another on Fort Manuel, and a cruiser set on fire in Hann Bay. French sources confirm only that a shell fragment pierced the hull of the *Richelieu* above the water line. There were

which it was expressly stated could be read by the Germans and Italians. This information was not known until after the operation (28 September). Spears telegraphed Ismay on the 29th, pointing out that it meant that all Allied movements signalled by Vichy ships to each other were read by the enemy, and that any Vichy pretence to independence was proven to be nonsense. 'Not only can its ships not leave French harbours without leave but they may not communicate with each other without every movement being examined and controlled by Axis powers.' 'Dakar Diary' and Spears Mission War Diary, 28 Sept.

extenuating factors for the British performance, apart from the fog, which made range-taking almost impossible (this was before the advent of naval radar-controlled guns): the smokescreen laid by the French destroyer *Hardi*, steaming from north to south, to the eastward of the anchorage and Gorée, which combined with the fog effectively to conceal all targets by 10.10; the failure of the *Resolution*'s director training gear at about 9.45; the *Barham* since her recommissioning had done no bombardment practice (see above, p. 59n.); the two battleships were served by spotting aircraft unaccustomed to working with them, owing to damage to the *Resolution*'s aircraft and the departure of the *Cumberland*, which was carrying the *Barham*'s observer; neither battleship had carried out concentration of fire practice; and the cruisers' fire on the French cruisers inside the boom was rendered still more difficult by the latter taking shelter among the merchant ships in the anchorage.

The British ships had sustained no serious damage, despite the accurate fire of the *Richelieu*'s big guns and the Gorée and Cape Manuel forts. The fire of the *Richelieu*'s 6-inch guns was very accurate for line and would have achieved hits but for its large spread (400 to 500 yards).

The lull which followed enabled the men in the flagship to eat another bully beef sandwich and the officers to feast on cold mutton and hot lime juice. The heat in the wardroom was even more oppressive than on the previous day. Within moments of entering, everyone's shirt was sticking to him with sweat.

Towards 1 o'clock Cunningham's ships began to move, turning parallel to the coast and at 1.05 opening fire. The *Barham*'s target was the *Richelieu*, at 17,000 yards, the *Resolution*'s was Gorée, at 16,000 yards. (The *Devonshire*'s was to have been Cape Manuel, and the *Australia*'s, the cruisers inside the boom. Owing to the misinterpretation of a signal, however, the cruisers took no part in the second bombardment.) The second bombardment, though more intense than the first one, was no more successful against either shore defences or warships. The *Richelieu* and the Gorée and Cape Manuel batteries opened fire on the battleships at about 1.12. The fog and the effective French smokescreen set up by the *Hardi* (by 1.11 targets were becoming difficult to see) again reduced the accuracy of the British fire, as did the constant zigzagging of the cruisers and the aggressiveness of the Dakar aircraft.

There was little to show for the day's actions. Neither the air attacks nor the ship bombardment, which had expended nearly 400

Right: Admiral Thierry d'Argenlieu

Below: The *Richelieu* hit in Dakar harbour, 25 September 1940

Bottom: A French cargo vessel, the *Tacoma*, ablaze in Dakar harbour

Boat being lowered from H.M.S. *Foresight* to take General Spears and General de Gaulle from S.S. *Westernland* to a conference with Admiral Sir John Cunningham on H.M.S. *Barham*

Wounded man being brought alongside transport after a British plane crashed at sea, due to lack of fuel, during operations

rounds of 15-inch ammunition, had succeeded in inflicting damage worth mentioning on the *Richelieu*, the cruisers, or the larger shore batteries, while causing further casualties in the town. The fire of the shore batteries was very accurate, and the *Richelieu* fired her two-gun salvoes 'fairly accurately'. During the afternoon action the *Resolution* was straddled several times by 5·4-inch or 6-inch shells, and in a seven-minute period the *Barham* sustained four hits, three by heavy shells, none of them doing serious damage.[3]

Morale was high on the French side. 'This time confidence had swept away anxiety. Soon it was to yield to enthusiasm. Each time they crossed each other's path, our ships started saluting each other noisily. Applauding each other with endless hurrahs. What was happening? It was hardly credible. For the past 36 hours they had been fighting a powerful squadron and they had not yet been annihilated.'[4]

The weather was hot throughout the operations even for that part of the world; but combat conditions were especially wretched for the British ships that day. A Gunnery Lieutenant in the *Barham* records:

I was the Turret officer of 'B' turret. Humidity conditions were quite appalling and I soon abandoned any idea of the crew wearing anti-flash gear. In fact we wore overalls and nothing underneath. In the magazines men were passing out, being dragged out into the handing room, having a bucket of water thrown over them and then going back in to have another bash. Between bombardment runs we withdrew to seaward and gunhouse crews were allowed on top of the turrets. Completely

[3] One shell came from starboard, plunging through the deck just abaft 'B' turret and out through the port screen. No one was killed. A Gunnery Lieutenant in the *Barham* recalls: 'The effect of this was to make a mess in the space through which it had passed and it killed one rat! Several of us were looking at the rather superficial damage, when we suddenly realised that had "B" not been trained on the beam, the gunhouse would have taken a direct hit on the side!' Commander A. J. Cobham's letter to the author, 8 Jan. 1974. When a 9-inch shell from Gorée landed close to the *Barham* and blew the Admiral's barge overboard, sending a hail of shell splinters aboard, one landed between the feet of Second Lieutenant Irwin's Cockney batman as he sat smoking. He gazed at it for a moment as it sizzled on the deck, then, slowly getting to his feet, he kicked it over the side with the nonchalant observation: 'It makes a bit of a change, don't it?'

[4] Mordal, *La Bataille de Dakar*, p. 210. A message from Pétain to Boisson in the forenoon (intercepted by the British) must have bolstered the morale of the defenders. It read: 'France follows with emotion and confidence your resistance to the partisan treachery and the British aggression. Under your high authority Dakar is giving an example of courage and fidelity. The entire mother country is proud of your attitude and of the resolution of the forces under your command. I congratulate you and assure you of my entire confidence.'

disregarding the Captain, Admiral and General on the bridge above, we all stripped off our overalls and in our birthday suits faced the breeze holding the overalls over our heads to dry out. I should have said that first on stripping we would wring out the overalls, getting a good mugful out of each![5]

The enemy 'will to resist appeared unimpaired', Cunningham noted. The continuance of operations in the face of such a stubborn defence, which was even more effective than on the first day, seemed to be of doubtful value to the British Commanders. They considered a British landing before the shore batteries had been silenced as impracticable, particularly since they had not located the positions of several 5·4-inch batteries, whose fire had proved effective against the destroyers and would be more so against transports. Enemy air action had increased considerably. One of the day's surprises was the determined and aggressive performance of the French Air Force. Their bombers had made four high-level attacks on the cruisers, destroyers, and the *Ark Royal* between approximately 10.30 and 12.30, dropping about fifty bombs, though without scoring a hit. But their fighters blunted the British air attacks on ships in the harbour and were making reconnaissance and spotting increasingly hazardous. The almost complete lack of success by the Swordfish and Skuas, especially on the 24th, was unexpected and disappointing to Cunningham.

In these circumstances the Force Commanders decided to consult de Gaulle. A discouraged Cunningham withdrew to the southward at 1.26, enemy shells bursting all around his ships as they steamed away, shaping course to close the *Westernland*. He got off a pessimistic signal to the Admiralty at 2.17 p.m., reporting that the afternoon bombardment had been 'without apparent result from this or air bombardment carried out earlier. Reduction of defences and neutralization of French battleship *Richelieu* and French cruisers present an impossible project for available forces in prevailing visibility and a most difficult operation for any force in any weather while morale of defences remains as high as at present. Air action against our fleet increasing.'

The *Westernland* had had a quiet day. De Gaulle broadcast several new appeals (at 11, 12, and 2), beseeching Dakar to 'get rid of unworthy leaders' and join his cause. 'We come as brothers.' And so forth and so on. No new note was struck and there was no response. At 2 o'clock one of the little Free French sloops, the

[5] Commander A. J. Cobham's letter to the author, 8 Jan. 1974.

Commandant Duboc, her flag at half mast, came alongside the *Westernland*. She carried out a funeral service, committing her dead from the Rufisque operation (three seamen) to the deep as de Gaulle, Spears, and their staffs stood at the salute, deeply moved. 'It was infinitely pathetic, as if the gallant little craft came close to us for comfort.'[6]

(2) To Try or Not to Try Again?

Towards 4 p.m. that afternoon of 24 September Cunningham brought the *Barham* close to the *Westernland*. Presently the Admiral invited de Gaulle on board for a conference and sent a boat for him and Spears. They came on board the flagship at 4.15. De Gaulle wore 'a light ill-fitting khaki uniform, unadorned by medals or badges of rank, soaked with sweat, and wearing that unbecoming French military sun helmet'. The ship's company of the *Barham* was no more prepossessing, all being unshaven and rather dirty. But they stood in perfect discipline as the two Generals came aboard.

The conference took place on the admiral's bridge. De Gaulle found the British in a grim mood; but there were no recriminations. 'The atmosphere,' Spears observed, 'was rather depressing and everybody showed signs of wear and fatigue.' De Gaulle was magnificent. Always an attractive figure in adversity, his dignity in face of all the disappointments greatly impressed the British Commanders. Throughout the conference he blamed only himself, assuming full responsibility for having pulled back at Rufisque and for so gravely underestimating the strength of the defences and the morale of the defenders. Irwin recorded that de Gaulle's bearing at the conference was 'remarkable for its brave acceptance of a great disappointment and immediate readiness to offer constructive proposals. Both Vice-Admiral Cunningham and I felt the greatest admiration for a man with such quiet courage and with so cool and clear a brain.'[7]

De Gaulle and Spears learnt for the first time what had happened in the actions that day and the preceding afternoon.

[6] 'Dakar Dairy', 24 Sept. This is a good example of Spears's imaginative sympathy.
[7] Irwin's Report, Ch. III, p. 3. Cunningham in his Report (Pt. V, App. 1, p. 4) wrote that de Gaulle's attitude that afternoon, 'when he was naturally suffering from the terrible disappointment which his reception undoubtedly gave him was that of a great man'.

On board the British battleship the atmosphere was gloomy and strained [writes de Gaulle]. They were sorry, certainly, not to have succeeded. But the dominant feeling was that of surprise. The British, being practical people, could not understand how and why the authorities, naval forces and troops at Dakar expended such energy upon fighting against their compatriots and against their Allies at a time when France lay beneath the invader's boot. As for me, I had from that moment given up being astonished at it. What had happened showed me, once for all, that the Vichy rulers would never fail to misuse, against the interests of France, the courage and discipline of those who were in subjection to them.[8]

It was clear enough that the Force Commanders felt that the job was beyond their strength and would have liked to chuck it. The Admiral's reading of the situation was that, given 'the attitude of the place and of the squadron supporting it', bombardment would solve nothing. He spoke of the insoluble problem of battleships versus land batteries. He and Irwin were anxious to know the effect of the bombardment on the morale of the people in Dakar. De Gaulle thought it certainly must have antagonized them. Irwin asserted that a landing under existing conditions, with the Vichy warships free to come out, would be a desperate enterprise. It 'would mean a great risk for each boat and each soldier'. De Gaulle agreed with the British assessment that a British landing was not a feasible operation. From a military point of view it would, he held, be a mere adventure to attempt a landing. He was much shaken by the failure of the bombardments to neutralize the shore batteries and ships, by the doubtful attitude of the Senegalese, and by the message just received from the Admiralty that the battle cruiser *Strasbourg* had sailed from Toulon. He was, nevertheless, prepared in the event of a British landing needing his support to give it regardless of consequences; but he would much prefer not to land his troops even following a successful landing.

De Gaulle was, however, very much opposed to a complete breaking off of the action, as in view of the ultimatum this could be taken as nothing less than an acknowledgement of complete and absolute failure. It would be 'too much of a knock to just slink away and have nothing but a commercial blockade like before'. He suggested as a face-saving device that Dakar be informed that the bombardment had ceased at his request—that he wanted to prevent the shedding of further French blood. But he urged that they should, at least,

---

[8] De Gaulle, *War Memoirs*, i. 131.

prevent Dakar warships from going south. He was told this was not feasible, but the British Commanders liked his suggestion that he and his force should proceed to Bathurst. There he could exercise his troops after their long confinement and have time to consider the situation and gather intelligence prior to a possible advance upon Dakar by way of Kaolack and Thiès. 'In any case, and whatever happens,' de Gaulle proclaimed, 'Free France will continue.' And so ended, at 6 p.m., this melancholy inquest on the operation. 'It had,' remarks General Spears, 'some of the elements of an old Irish wake at which the participants try to pretend the corpse is not dead.'[9]

De Gaulle was always one to face up to facts. '*Les choses étant ce qu' elles sont*' was one of his favourite expressions. On returning to the *Westernland*, he immediately gathered his staff. They expected to hear a critique of events, but the General merely announced: '*Messieurs, l'affaire de Dakar est terminée.*' He then asked them to gather for the next morning all the information they had on Duala and Brazzaville, so that he could decide, in default of Dakar, which would be the least bad choice for the capital of Free France. This order given, he saluted the officers and returned to his cabin without giving them an opportunity to ask any questions.

Soon afterwards de Gaulle unburdened himself to Spears in the blackness of the Captain's bridge. He appeared to have second thoughts about persisting with his West African dream. They must, he said, face up to the fact that there had been a complete failure.

He said to carry out small operations w^d have no effect now & be v. difficult in Senegal where the pro Vichy leaders w^d now have it all their own way. His conclusion is the only way to save himself from the accusation

[9] Spears also contributes this fascinating bit of local colour: 'During the whole of this gloomy exchange of views, from which no light emerged, I had been watching the admiral, whose attention was focused with growing strain and anxiety on the wooden gratings of the bridge, into the deep cavities of which General de Gaulle, who never ceased smoking, kept throwing a constant stream of burning cigarette ends. Down they came like incandescent meteorites with an appropriate escort of match ends. No battleship deck, at least in the British navy, can ever have been treated with such contumely, and the outraged admiral, forgetting Dakar for a moment, propelled an empty pompom shell case towards de Gaulle for him to use as an ashtray. The Frenchman, hardly perceiving it, yet conscious of it as might a sportsman on the edge of a wood awaiting pheasants be aware of the flight of a jay, threw a cigarette end in its direction and missed. Whereupon another shell case was pushed towards him until he was surrounded by them as if he himself had been a pompom firing in a heavy engagement, while the distracted admiral watched the cigarette ends in flight with the hypnotised attention of a Wimbledon fan following a champion's service.' *Two Men Who Saved France*, pp. 207–8.

of fighting Fr men is to go & fight where he can. After parading his men at Duala etc. he w^d take them to Egypt & fight the Italians there. . . . He can't get recruits [in Egypt] save perhaps from Syria. He will cease to exist. Here he can easily increase & consolidate his position & . . . go on threatening & undermining the Vichy position in Senegal. Here he has an embryo empire. To go to Egypt means he is like Boulanger, throwing up the sponge.[10]

After de Gaulle had left, the British Commanders, too, had second thoughts. They decided that if the weather were at all favourable the next day, they would make one more effort to test the defences. Were the bombardment successful, British troops would be landed at Rufisque. Fresh information, which suggested that the damage to French ships may have been more extensive than had been thought, prompted the change of plan. At 6.30 a crew recovered by the *Barham* from a crashed Swordfish had reported that a cruiser was beached and burning east of Rufisque, another was burning in Gorée Bay, and two destroyers were beached in Hann Bay. (The beached 'cruiser' was the super-destroyer *Audacieux*; there was no substance in the rest of the report.) Also figuring in the decision was the slight damage the fleet had suffered and the Prime Minister's message of the previous evening, 'Stop at nothing.'

The Commanders' change of heart was registered in a signal to the Admiralty written at 7.36 p.m. (They did not consult de Gaulle, and it was not until 11.14 p.m. that they informed the astonished General of their intention.) It summarized the results of the conference with de Gaulle in the *Barham*—'any landing operation in face of existing defence is not at present practicable'—and suggested as the only reasonable alternatives: 'immediate withdrawal' or 'systematic bombardment . . . in the hope that resistance may collapse: in our view a very unlikely contingency.' They endorsed de Gaulle's proposal for going to Bathurst with his force. 'We are of the opinion that his proposals offer a good means of discontinuing an operation which on present results holds little prospect of military success commensurate with the probable damage to Naval Forces.' But, the Admiral concluded, if the weather improved sufficiently, they would make a new effort the next day to neutralize ships and forts. 'Should inadequate result be obtained we recommend adoption of De Gaulle's proposals.'

This telegram, which was not dispatched until 1.47 a.m. on the

---

[10] 'Dakar Diary', 24 Sept. General Boulanger was France's would-be man-on-horseback in the 1880s, who pulled back at the critical moment.

25th, arrived at 5.10 that morning. In the meantime, a meeting of the Defence Committee (Operations) of the War Cabinet (Churchill in the chair, Chiefs of Staff, Service ministers, Ismay) at 9.30 in the evening of the 24th had considered the telegrams of 11.55 a.m. and 2.17 p.m. (above, pp. 133, 136). The situation was obviously not promising. But whatever hesitation there may have been in the Defence Committee, the Prime Minister was as stubborn as ever and insisted on going on. He was rather cross and critical, and annoyed at the meagre information sent by the Commanders to explain the still more meagre results of the bombardment at close range. Cunningham's 11.55 a.m. signal had made it appear that the whole fleet had closed to 10,000 yards, when actually it had been only the two cruisers. After discussion, it was agreed to send a telegram to the Joint Commanders asking them for further information.[11] The Prime Minister thereupon sent a long and querulous personal signal to the Commanders at 12.05 a.m. on the 25th, asking for a full account of the position.

We asked you particularly to be full and clear in your accounts. Why have you not sent two or three hundred words to let us know your difficulties and how you propose to meet them?

We do not understand conditions under which bombardment proceeded for some hours at 10,000 yards range without grave damage to ships or forts unless visibility was so bad as to make targets invisible. Also, if visibility bad, why is it not possible to force a landing at beaches near Rufisque in spite of fire from Goree Island?

Without this fuller information we can only ask why you do not land in force by night or in the fog or both on beaches near Rufisque and take Rufisque for a start, observing that enemy cannot be heartwhole and force at Rufisque is comprised largely of native troops. . . .

More ammunition is being sent from Gibraltar, but evidently supplies will not stand many days' firing like yesterday. Neither is there unlimited time, as not only the French but German submarines will probably arrive in six or seven days.

Pray act as you think best, but meanwhile give reasoned answer to these points. Matter must be pushed to conclusion without delay.

Clearly, the Defence Committee, or the Prime Minister, anyway, and the Force Commanders had quite differing views on the resoluteness of the Dakar defenders. Such interjections from Whitehall to the Commander of a force who was conducting a delicate operation could not have been regarded by Admiral Cunningham

[11] DO (40), 31st Meeting, CAB 69/1, Litchfield diary, 24 Sept.

as helpful. His staff were infuriated at Churchill's complaint that they had not sent 'two or three hundred words', being, as Captain Walter says, 'hardly in the mood for composing a further powerful instalment and encyphering it!'

The Commanders replied to the Prime Minister's signal in detail in a message of 3.44 a.m. (25 September). It summarized the actions on both days, noted that the only damage believed inflicted was on one super-destroyer and one submarine, 'leaving defence particularly cruisers and Fantasques virtually unimpaired', and confirmed their 1.47 a.m. message of the 25th that they would continue the operation in the morning and would land if that were practicable. The signal, which was not dispatched until 8.35 a.m., was received in the Admiralty at 10.34 a.m. By that time the drama had been played out.

Chapter Eight

The Third Day of the Operation: Failure and Withdrawal

We went to Dakar
with General de Gaulle
We sailed round in circles
and did bugger all.

Song composed by NCOs and men of the 2nd Battalion,
Royal Marines, after the conclusion of 'Menace'

(Chart 1)

(1) Abandonment of the Operation

THE weather was perfect on the morning of 25 September. The sun shone, the sky was clear, and the visibility was maximum. And so at 6 a.m. the battleships moved northward to take up their bombarding positions at 9 a.m., with the cruisers three miles to the east. The bombardment targets were the same as on the 24th: *Barham v. Richelieu, Resolution v.* Gorée, *Devonshire v.* Cape Manuel, *Australia v.* the cruisers in the anchorage.

But first, at 5.30, the *Ark Royal* had flown off reconnaissance, A/S, and fighter patrols. French fighter planes contributed decisively to the success of their side. They were very active and drove all the aircraft off except for the reconnaissance planes over the Dakar-Thiès area. (This enabled the *Bévéziers* to approach for her attack unreported by reconnaissance planes. See below.) Later they hampered the spotting aircraft of the British ships and shot down *Australia*'s Walrus (8.18 a.m.). Captain Holland had suggested the previous afternoon that he bomb Ouakam at dawn on the 25th with nine Swordfish, because French fighters were making it 'hazardous' for the TSRs to operate in the Dakar area. This was approved by the Commanders at 11.28 p.m. on the 24th, though with Gorée added. Owing to heavy W/T traffic with the *Westernland*, the signal did not reach the *Ark Royal* until 2 a.m. on the 25th. Holland considered it was too late to arrange for action before daylight, and he would not send his old and slow machines on such a mission in daylight, with surprise forfeited. Accordingly, he reported at 2.42 a.m.: 'Too late now, suicidal unless before or at dawn.'[1]

At 8.58 the *Richelieu* opened fire on the *Barham* with two-gun 15-inch salvoes, when the range had fallen to 23,000 yards. At 9.02 the shore batteries opened fire. At 9.01 the signal to turn to bombarding course (a 70° turn to starboard together) for the start of the day's engagement was hauled down in the *Barham*. At 9.02, when the battleships had just begun to turn, the unexpected happened.

The sole remaining French submarine at Dakar, the *Bévéziers*, on patrol 8 miles from Cape Manuel, had been awaiting her opportunity. Her Commander saw 'Blue 7' ('turn to bombarding course') hoisted in the *Barham*. (He knew the British manoeuvring flag signals from having worked with British forces before the fall of France.) He waited until the signal was hauled down before firing a salvo of torpedoes at the turning point of the battleships. The range was about 2,700 yards. A fan of four yellow-headed torpedoes was clearly visible speeding towards the battleships. The *Barham* just managed to avoid them by combing tracks, but the *Resolution* was less fortunate, one torpedo hitting her port side amidships while under full helm. Two passed under the ship. A great column of dirty water rose up alongside the stricken battleship, and she turned with a 12½° list to port and steamed away. The hit caused immediate and serious flooding of her port boiler-room, with consequent loss of motive power, and fire broke out in several compartments. To avoid strain on her bulkheads until the extent of the damage was determined, she reduced to 12 knots. The destroyers *Forester* and *Inglefield* laid down a protective smokescreen at the Admiral's order. The fact that the *Resolution* was listing heavily under helm turning on to the firing course probably saved her. As for the *Bévéziers*, she got away, undamaged by depth charges from the destroyer *Foresight*, which mistakenly reported a kill.[2]

---

[1] Cunningham found this very surprising, since dawn was not until about 5.30, and 2½ hours should have been sufficient to prepare the small striking force for objectives less than 30 miles away. Even if there were a delay, there was no certainty that there would not be ample cloud cover at dawn to make possible a surprise attack. Cunningham's Report, Pt. V, App. IV, p. 4.

[2] The exploit won Lieutenant-Commander Pierre Lancelot promotion to commander. He afterwards served under John Cunningham after the French Navy had re-entered the war and Cunningham was Allied C-in-C, Mediterranean. For his services in the naval operations covering the Allied North African landings in 1943 as commander of the super-destroyer *Terrible*, Lancelot was awarded a British decoration. He introduced himself to Cunningham as 'the fellow who torpedoed the *Resolution*'.

At 9.05 the *Barham* opened fire on the *Richelieu* at 21,000 yards. The *Devonshire* fired at Fort Manuel, and the *Australia* at the cruisers inside the boom. Again a smokescreen frustrated the British gunners. The *Richelieu* was hit by a 15-inch shell from the *Barham* at 9.15, but the damage was slight. No damage was done to the Cape Manuel battery by the *Devonshire*, and Gorée was unscathed by three isolated shells that fell near by. In contrast, the British ships came under heavy and accurate fire. The *Richelieu*, which was firing her two available 15-inch guns and her secondary armament, frequently straddled the *Barham* with heavy shells, hitting her once with a 15-inch shell and the *Australia* twice with 6-inch shells. Both ships suffered only minor damage. The *Georges Leygues* and *Montcalm* fired on the British cruisers. The Gorée and Cape Manuel batteries were fairly quiet, being out of range of the *Barham*.

At 9.12 the *Barham* turned to southward to cover the *Resolution*, and at 9.21 she ceased fire, and with the two cruisers withdrew southward. At 9.32, with the British warships beyond range (nearly 30,000 yards), the action was over.

The hit on the *Resolution* had been the last straw. Not only were the 15-inch guns available now reduced by half, but it was plain to all that further serious damage would be incurred in putting the French ships and shore batteries out of action. The morning had shown that the defences of Dakar were working more effectively than ever, and the French air patrols were stronger. Nor did it seem at all likely that Dakar could ever be captured with the small landing force available. By noon the Force Commanders had decided to abandon the attempt, and all forces began their withdrawal southward to Freetown.[3] Cunningham notified the Admiralty of the decision in a signal of 11.52 a.m. 'After three attempts in widely different gunnery conditions result obviously negative and defences including cruisers and destroyers operating under cover of battery remain

---

The Admiral asked how he had been able to get that hit on her, and, given the answer, replied, 'Good shot!' as he pinned the decoration on Lancelot. The story of 'Blue 7' is on Colonel Watson's authority, but there is, as he admits (*Échec à Dakar*, p. 204n.), some question about its accuracy. The Historical Section of the French Admiralty told him that Lancelot did not mention 'Blue 7' in his report and that they do not think that he could have left his periscope above water long enough to see it.

[3] Though not before de Gaulle had made a last appeal at 11 o'clock. 'The men of Vichy . . . are leading Dakar on the path to destruction. Before this destruction starts, General de Gaulle beseeches once more with all his heart the Frenchmen of Dakar to impose their will and to unite with him without further delay in order to drive out the bad chiefs and take up again the good fight for the liberation of France.'

intact. This together with evidence of fire control by listening device probably moored mine make entry of transport even by night impracticable to effect landing of troops.[4] Regret must now recommend adopting De Gaulle's proposal. Meanwhile continuing withdrawal of whole Force to Southward.'

Cunningham afterwards spelled out the reasons for the decision to withdraw. After covering the retirement of the *Resolution*, he weighed these points: (1) the chance of capturing Dakar was 'remote', since it depended for success upon the low morale of the defence, and the chance of this was slight. (2) A naval action to destroy the *Richelieu* and the two cruisers without disproportionate damage to the *Barham, Devonshire*, and *Australia* appeared improbable given the poor shooting of the *Barham* ('attributable to fighter interference with spotting aircraft and newly-commissioned state of ship'), combined with the accuracy of French fire, their use of smokescreens, and the 8-inch cruisers' lack of protection against even 5·4-inch projectiles. (3) The presence of at least one other submarine (*Bévéziers*) in the neighbourhood. (4) Air opposition was growing. (5) The inability to confirm the possibility that the defenders' ammunition might be nearing exhaustion. (6) 'The effect on our war effort as a whole of the loss or serious damage of a second capital ship for comparatively inconsiderable result which now seemed probable.' (7) The loss of 'general world prestige' which a withdrawal would bring. After considering these points, Cunningham had decided to withdraw.[5]

Before Cunningham's 11.52 a.m. message could be passed (2.52 p.m.), he had received instructions to break off immediately, unless the situation had materially altered. We must return to London. The Defence Committee (Operations), when it met at 10 that morning, the Prime Minister in the chair, had before them the 1.47 a.m. telegram of the 25th from the Commanders stating their

---

[4] Towards 9 the fleet had in closing passed two circular buoys at 23,000 yards from the *Richelieu*. They were assumed to contain a sound-locating device. The Historical Section of the French Navy has affirmed that no such thing as an acoustical device existed, and that the coastal batteries were firing over open sights, that is, directly at the target. Watson, *Échec à Dakar*, p. 230.

[5] Cunningham's Report, Pt. V, p. 17. Irwin's Report (Ch. IV, p. 3) emphasized a factor alluded to in the Admiral's signal of 11.52 a.m. 'The presence of active Cruisers and Destroyers operating under cover of the forts convinced me more than any other factor of the impossibility of effecting a successful landing and a subsequent land advance on Dakar. Until these ships were eliminated, I did not then, nor do I now, doubt that it would have been madness to have attempted landing at Rufisque or elsewhere within the outer harbour.'

intention of having one more go at the defences, and their 3.44 a.m. of the 25th in reply to Churchill's 12.05 a.m. of the 25th asking for more information. The Prime Minister saw the alternatives open to them as a case of a Hobson's choice. They could abandon the operation, which would be a 'bitter blow' to their prestige, or continue the bombardment in the hope that the French resistance might break and a landing might be effected. But 'there were clearly grave risks' in the latter alternative. The CIGS, Sir John Dill, said that a landing in the face of the existing opposition at Dakar was not a sound operation, since it had always been recognized that the strength of the military forces taking part in 'Menace' was based on the assumption that resistance would not be heavy. Pound agreed that a landing and an advance on the town would be 'a most hazardous Operation. If it was now considered that we could not take Dakar, the alternative was to clear out and take our losses.' A blockade of Dakar (de Gaulle's proposal) was out of the question. It was agreed that no pressure should be put upon the Commanders to take any action that was against their judgement of the situation.[6]

At 11.30 a.m. the Prime Minister put the situation before the War Cabinet. During the meeting a Cunningham telegram of 9.36 a.m. arrived, reporting the torpedoing of the *Resolution*, that the damage appeared to be serious, and that she was withdrawing. The fresh intelligence deepened the First Sea Lord's pessimism and it altered Churchill's outlook. He would, he said, have advised the Commanders to go forward with their proposal to effect a landing if this should prove possible, but now the withdrawal of the *Resolution* increased the risk of the operation. The alternative was to order the operation to be brought to an end. The arguments for the former course were formidable: landing troops would incur the risk of having them cut off, or of operations of indefinite length; keeping the fleet off Dakar would expose the ships to the risk of submarine attack; and there was a Tangier report that German and Italian aircraft were flying south-east, possibly *en route* to Dakar; there would be delay in reinforcing the fleet in the Mediterranean; and the *Ark Royal* would be unable to return to England to pick up her new planes. 'A continuance of the "Menace" operation would undoubtedly commit us to a great effort and great risks.' Abandonment 'would undoubtedly mean that we should suffer a serious rebuff and would give a setback to the deterioration which was taking place in

[6] DO (40), 32nd Meeting, CAB 69/1.

the Vichy Government's position.'[7] As for de Gaulle, the Prime Minister continued, if the operation were abandoned, there was no point in his going to Bathurst, where he could not protect his force. He should proceed instead to Duala, where they could provide a naval force to safeguard him. (This was what the Chiefs of Staff had recommended on 15 September. See above, p. 84.)

In the sober discussion that followed, the Lord Privy Seal (Attlee), Foreign (Halifax), War (Eden), and Colonial (Lloyd) Secretaries, and the Minister without Portfolio (Greenwood) agreed that they had misjudged the state of morale at Dakar and that they should call off the operation and cut their losses. The First Lord declared that he had opposed the operation from the beginning, yet would have advised continuing with it but for the damage to the *Resolution*. Her withdrawal had altered the situation, and he agreed that the operation should be abandoned.

Whereupon the Prime Minister withdrew to draft a telegram to the Commanders that reflected the views of the War Cabinet and that would prevent misinterpretation of the last sentence in his telegram of 12.05 a.m. (25th): 'Matter must be pushed to conclusion without undue delay.' He returned with a draft, which was approved with one or two amendments and dispatched to Cunningham at 1.27 p.m. that afternoon (25th): 'On all the information now before us, including damage to *Resolution*, we have decided that the enterprise against Dakar should be abandoned, the obvious evil consequences being faced. Unless something has happened which we do not know which makes you wish to attempt landing in force, you should forthwith break off. You should inform us most immediate whether you concur, but, unless the position has entirely changed in our favour, you should not actually begin landing till you receive our reply.' This was followed a minute later by the Prime Minister's telegram that, on the assumption that 'Menace' was abandoned, British naval forces would try to cover Duala, but could not safeguard de Gaulle's forces if he went to Bathurst.[8] The

---

[7] A Churchill message to Roosevelt on the 25th singled out the damage to the ships and the 'undue commitment' if troops were landed in force as the operative factors. Churchill, *Their Finest Hour*, p. 435.

[8] WM (40) 258, CAB 65/15. At 1.40 p.m. a Somerville telegram of 10.24 a.m. arrived at the Admiralty urging the liquidation of 'Menace' as quickly as possible in view of the vulnerability of Gibraltar to air attack (the French had made a retaliatory bombing of Gibraltar: see below), coupled with the difficulty of maintaining a sufficient naval force in the western Mediterranean to deal with both the French and the Italians.

Joint Commanders lost no time in signalling (2.30 p.m.): 'Concur in breaking off.'[9]

(2) To Freetown and Beyond

The battered fleet made for Freetown, the transports in the van. It was an undignified retreat, with two French bombers harassing the fleet by attacking its reconnaissance Swordfish on the 27th. During the night of the 25th–26th, the *Resolution* had succeeded in reducing her list to 11° and appeared to be getting the fires under control. But she was still in serious difficulty, and the *Barham* deemed it wise to take the helpless '*Reso*' in tow at about 9.45 a.m. on the 26th, and at a speed of 6 to 7 knots the two old warriors limped towards Freetown. With a wound which was discovered to be a hole 'big enough to take a double-decker bus', her upper deck only a few feet above the water on the port side, and a real prospect of having to take to the rafts ever present, 'there was', writes Admiral Eddison, 'a certain morbid fascination in watching the attendant barracuda fish circling the ship throughout our very slow progress back to harbour. We knew them by repute to be carnivorous and to have exceedingly nasty habits where shipwrecked mariners are concerned. I think this threat was more pressing to many of us at that time than the much more serious one of further submarine attack, not necessarily from the French.'[10] And always the Admiral dreaded the appearance of submarines. A submarine, the *Sidi-Ferruch* from Konakry, which attempted to intercept the retiring forces in the late afternoon of the 25th, was caught on the surface by

[9] Fourteen months after 'Menace', it was learned from an American Army officer who had been in Dakar in January–February 1941 that at the moment the action was broken off Boisson was writing out a message of surrender, because ammunition was running out for the ships and the shore batteries. Watson, *Échec à Dakar*, p. 222. The late Commander M. G. Saunders claimed (in his research notes, without citing his authority) that Boisson told Cunningham, when they met towards the end of the war, that he had been on the point of chucking in the sponge when the British were making their final attack, because he had only a few rounds of ammunition left. I find the story highly improbable. French writers do not even mention it, and there is no reference to it anywhere in the British records.

De Gaulle never forgave Boisson for his central role in repulsing the attack. He had his revenge for this defiance. In 1942, when the Allies arrived in North Africa, without de Gaulle, Boisson, who was the Governor, received them, at Darlan's orders, with open arms. Subsequently, when de Gaulle came to power in North Africa, he had Boisson clapped into prison over the strong protests of Churchill and Roosevelt. All that they could accomplish was to have him transferred to a more comfortable cell and given a wheelchair.

[10] Admiral T. L. Eddison's letter to the author, 10 Jan. 1974.

an *Ark Royal* reconnaissance aircraft and forced by A/S bombs to submerge before coming within 10 miles of the ships.

In Dakar the celebration of the 'victory' started on the morning of the 26th, when it was clear that the British had finally broken off the engagement. 'Everybody wrote heroic reports' and posed in front of the cameramen of a French newsreel service who had arrived from France by air. In contrast the return journey of the Allied expedition was a funereal procession. A number of the subalterns were infuriated when the expedition was abandoned—'not because we wanted to die,' writes one of them, a 2nd Lieutenant of marines in the 2nd Battalion, 'but because we thought that Dakar could have been taken by a simple application of the strategy of indirect approach. Some of us thereupon concocted our own operation order for a landing at Rufisque, where I proposed to seize a train and drive in it into Dakar. We formed up to "Nick" Williams [Commanding 2nd Battalion, RM] on deck and he then told us that our collective action amounted to "mutiny". We felt, however, that his anger was in part due to his own frustration.'[11] Perhaps; but Williams, like most of the senior officers, agreed with the decision to abandon the operation, believing that heavy casualties would have been suffered by the British troops and the Free French, as well as the French at Dakar, had they forced a landing. This did not mean that anybody was happy with the outcome. There was considerable disappointment that they did not 'have a go'—that, as one marine officer has put it, 'the dogs had not even been allowed to see the rabbit, not knowing that it was in reality a tiger'. There was also widespread criticism of the planning and execution of the operation. 'Operation Menace. I call it Operation Muddle.' This, from a disgusted *Ark Royal* pilot, summed up the dominant mood in the fleet. Nor was morale improved by the continuing terrific heat during the day, which was still worse at night when, owing to the black-out, everything was closed—no air, no fans.

It would, however, be easy to exaggerate the effect the Dakar failure had on the morale of those who took part in it, more especially in the Navy. In September 1940 officers and ships' companies were still almost entirely regulars, who had become inured to setbacks which had started in Norway earlier in the year. The officers in particular had not expected too much of the operation. They were aware of bad security from the outset, inadequate intelligence and planning, which was brought out as the operation proceeded,

[11] John Biggs-Davison's letter to the author, 11 Apr. 1974.

disagreement and indecision among Commanders, based on differing national and Service standpoints, and poor liaison once the operation had started.

De Gaulle's downcast and irresolute mood was captured by Spears:

G[l] de G is considerably shaken & this worries me. To begin with, he proposed making straight for Konakri & I cheered (having urged refusal to accept defeat). . . . de G then sent for the paper giving the strength of the garrison at Konakri & it was undoubtedly v. strong. He then suggested going to Freetown to —— [?] his people & consult with emissaries. This certainly wiser, but he s[d] have thought of it before. It makes a bad impression, suggests going off at $\frac{1}{2}$ cock & irresolution.

He keeps harking back to taking his troops to Egypt & is so hypnotised by the fear of being accused of attacking Fr men that it is entirely vitiating his judgement. I told him he knew the risk before he started & must not give London the impression of vacillation. He answers that he never envisaged a pitched battle which is true, but that is only half the truth. He is brave, but is more of a gambler than a resolute man it turns out. For the moment he cannot see his way.[12]

De Gaulle picked up the Egyptian theme again the next day, arguing 'endlessly' about fighting the Italians in Egypt in order to efface the impression of Dakar. 'I told him flat,' Spears records, 'we don't want another Boulanger.'[13] De Gaulle had put the Egyptian aberration out of his mind by 1 October, apparently having been convinced by Spears's argument that if Equatorial Africa felt itself abandoned, it would probably revert to Vichy and he himself would be no more than the commander of a small force in Egypt, no longer the leader of Free France.

The whole of the expedition, less the battleships and screening destroyers, arrived at Freetown on 27 September, the *Barham* and *Resolution* at about 6 a.m. on the 29th. The officers and men were very glad. They crowded the dance halls and bars, swam, and rode motor bicycles fast along the shore. But they were on the edge of malarial swamps, and a very high proportion became afflicted.[14]

[12] 'Dakar Diary', 25 Sept. Spears held himself partly to blame. 'I am sad to think of this flat failure & that I pressed for the expedition. I imagine what will be said concerning my Teleg[s] from Freetown urging action.' Ibid.

[13] Ibid., 26 Sept.

[14] Not all the marines and ship's companies could be quartered on shore. This resulted in at least one interesting vignette. H.M. ships, as they use fresh water for washing purposes, always have a fresh-water problem, and by the time they reached Freetown things were getting difficult. However, the facilities at the port were, at the time, not sufficient for a large number of ships. On the second morning in, during the

De Gaulle became still more miserable now, as, holed up in his small, hot cabin in the *Westernland*, he learned through radio broadcasts and the telegraphed reports that Spears kept bringing him that his prestige had taken a catastrophic drop in Britain and the United States. It was he, it was insisted on many sides, who had thought of this absurd plan, who had insisted on going ahead with it despite the Vichy reinforcements, and whose Free French followers had through indiscretions tipped Vichy as to what was afoot.[15] De Gaulle was, naturally, upset by these attacks. A sense of humiliating failure overwhelmed him. He never forgot those days, which were 'cruel' for him. 'I went through what a man must feel when an earthquake shakes his house brutally and he receives on his head the rain of tiles falling from the roof. In London a tempest of anger, in Washington a hurricane of sarcasms were let loose against me. For the American Press and many English newspapers it was immediately a matter of course that the failure of the attempt was due to de Gaulle.'[16]

Within a few days, however, de Gaulle was his old confident self, and even cheerful. Gone were the dejection, the doubts, and the hesitation of the first days after the withdrawal and in Freetown. He seemed to be quite unperturbed by the fiasco and almost laughed it off as a chance of war. Dakar was but another setback. His duty was still to free France, whatever the obstacles. He was comforted by the steadfastness of his troops and by telegrams from London and Equatorial Africa which revealed no defections (though few recruits were coming forward) and that Churchill was standing by him. The Prime Minister declared in the House of Commons (28 September) that 'all that had happened had only strengthened His Majesty's Government in the confidence they extended to General de Gaulle'. British officers in contact with de Gaulle at this time found his

---

breakfast hour, there was a heavy rainstorm. With most commendable thoughtfulness the Captain of the *Barham* piped 'Hands to bath on the upper deck'. Some 900 or 1,000 officers and men stripped off with nothing but bars of soap and had a really cool, refreshing shower bath! The tough men of the Foreign Legion, 'almost frantic with frustration and months on board ship', were allowed to land. To everybody's surprise, they did not burn down the port, though they returned to their ships much the worse for wear and liquor.

[15] President Roosevelt, never enamoured of the Dakar operation, believed that de Gaulle had put his own interests above those of the French and the Allies. 'Roosevelt never lost the distrust of De Gaulle's judgment and discretion which he formed then, and this distrust was a major factor in French–American relations right up to the President's death in 1945.' Robert Murphy, *Diplomat among Warriors* (London, 1964), p. 103.

[16] *War Memoirs*, i. 133.

determination to win through very appealing; he became almost a personal hero to many of them.

De Gaulle agreed with Spears on the importance of early action and was anxious to take such action. But where? De Gaulle's first idea (24 September, see above, p. 139) had been to go to Bathurst, thence advance on Kaolack and from there to Dakar. His first thought after 'Menace' had been called off was to go direct to Konakry, land his troops there with British naval support, rally French Guinea, and march on Bamako with a view to an eventual overland operation against Dakar. Irwin's forces were to disembark at Freetown and be ready to support him, if necessary. In response to de Gaulle's telegram of 7.09 p.m. on the 25th putting forward this project, the Chiefs of Staff, on 26 September, strongly recommended against it: it was 'not a sound military proposition and is unlikely to achieve any useful results'. The last thing they wanted was a repetition of 'Menace'. Konakry was now a defended port, and as a result of the Dakar operation surprise was not possible. 'As it is essential to avoid another shooting match such as occurred at Dakar, a landing at Konakri is undesirable unless de Gaulle were assured of a welcome.' But opposition would be almost certain. Even if de Gaulle were welcomed at Konakry, he would be faced with insuperable problems in moving his troops 400 miles by rail (MT by road) to Kankan, thence 230 miles by road to Bamako, and approximately another 600 miles by rail to Dakar. The road was unlikely to be passable at that time of year, and there would be an almost insoluble petrol and maintenance problem. Moreover, the Dakar authorities would doubtless move reinforcements to Bamako and forestall de Gaulle, and their aircraft could operate against Konakry and de Gaulle's line of advance.

The Service Chiefs also opposed the project on broad strategic grounds. It was impracticable to afford de Gaulle naval cover at Konakry, since the naval force was required for more important commitments. They needed to re-establish control of the Western exit to the Mediterranean by reconstituting Force H at Gibraltar as quickly as possible. As for Force A (Irwin's troops), it was not organized for extended land operations of the sort required by de Gaulle's plan, but it might be needed shortly for Operations 'Alloy' and 'Shrapnel' (to capture the Azores and Cape Verde Islands, respectively). 'The reason which led us to undertake Operation "Menace" was the belief that there was a fair chance of de Gaulle being welcomed in French West Africa or at least establishing himself there with little or no opposition. Since it is now evident that this belief was unfounded, our efforts should be to restore the status quo as soon as possible and avoid further hostilities with the French in North West Africa, including further bombing of Gibraltar' (on which see the following chapter). The Chiefs recommended that de Gaulle and his force go to Duala, where the situation was favourable and from where he should be able to consolidate his position throughout French Equatorial Africa and exercise a favourable influence on the Belgian Congo.[17]

But already, within hours of making his Konakry proposal, de Gaulle had given it up as too risky. His computation of forces available at Konakry convinced him that he would have to face the possibility of very strong opposition if he attempted a forced landing. He could not bear the thought of engaging his forces against Frenchmen, and he worried about the effect this would have on public opinion in France and among his own supporters. 'The opinion of the troops on board,' Spears telegraphed to London, 'undoubtedly is that they are infuriated at having been fired at and would not in the least mind tackling those Fr men who have caused them losses. But it cannot be denied that General de Gaulle is entitled to fear the accusation of provoking civil war.'[18] De Gaulle now wanted to go to Freetown, where he could land his troops—they had not been ashore since England—and obtain information from his emissaries. An operation against Konakry was possible from there.

The War Cabinet, too, was not sure of their mind. Their first thought was that British naval forces should attempt to cover de Gaulle at Duala, in the recently rallied French Cameroons, but could not safeguard him at Bathurst. Churchill's signal of 1.28 p.m. on the 25th so notified Cunningham. Churchill realized that it would be a blow to the General's prestige if he were to show up at Duala; from this point of view, the Konakry proposal was to be preferred. On the other hand, this argument was made for a Duala landing at the War Cabinet of 26 September (noon): that the failure of 'Menace' would probably weaken the Gaullist position in Equatorial Africa,

---

[17] COS (40) 781, 'Operations in West Africa', 27 Sept. (though the paper was written on the 26th), CAB 80/19. The Service Chiefs had closely followed the arguments and the recommendations of the Joint Planners, who in turn had embellished the report of their Strategic Planning Section. Respectively, JP (40) 489 and JP (40) 488 (S) Draft, both of 26 Sept., CAB 84/19. A comparison of all three papers is instructive as to how the whole planning system worked.

[18] Spears to Ismay, 8.57 p.m., 25 Sept., Spears Mission War Diary.

unless de Gaulle took action to strengthen that position. The meeting, however, deferred a decision on the destination of de Gaulle's force and the disposition of Force M until they had more information from de Gaulle and the British Commanders.[19] But he was, initially, to go to Freetown with his force. On the 28th Churchill accepted the Chiefs of Staff Konakry/Duala recommendations of the 27th.

On the same day, the 28th, after his arrival in Freetown, de Gaulle definitely abandoned the Konakry project and now favoured the idea of going to Duala, escorted by a British naval force. He would use Duala as a base for extending the Free French influence in the West African colonies—specifically, to capture Libreville and the Gabon Colony, which formed a Vichy enclave in Free French Equatorial Africa. The French Governor in Libreville was a stubborn Vichy supporter and was backed by an equally stubborn air force commander and by the Bishop of Gabon. The War Cabinet on 1 October took note that de Gaulle was proceeding to Duala, but they expected to be consulted before he undertook any further operation.

The *Barham* returned to the Mediterranean, where she was urgently needed, after repairs at Gibraltar. The *Resolution* went to Gibraltar for temporary repairs. Other ships of Force M formed an escort for the Free French forces when they left Freetown on 3 October for Duala. On 8 October de Gaulle landed his contingent in Duala, where he was gratified by the 'extreme' enthusiasm of the welcome. On 12 October he informed Churchill that he had decided to liquidate the Gabon enclave as a preliminary step to the establishment of a Saharan theatre of operations on the Chad-Libyan border, 'ready for the day when the evolution of events would permit a French column to seize the Fezzan and debouche from there upon the Mediterranean. . . . The distant objective for everyone was French North Africa'. He would start in a week.

Wishing to avoid further antagonizing Vichy, the British Government instructed Cunningham not to participate in the Libreville operation, but to give it indirect assistance. 'At this moment,' the Prime Minister telegraphed the Admiral on 25 October, 'there is a tremendous trial for mastery going on between Petain and Laval and we do not want to compromise this by local action at Libreville . . . French reinforcements should be made to turn back, if possible without active fighting. An ostentatious patrol by *Devonshire* and

[19] WM (40) 259, CAB 65/15.

Delhi off Libreville should be instituted forthwith. This may act as a good deterrent.'[20]

De Gaulle proceeded with his own resources. A combined operation—a naval force under d'Argenlieu,[21] two Free French columns advancing overland in a pincer movement, and a Free French assault force landed from the sea—moved on Libreville. The defence consisted of but a few native troops and a few small naval craft. The town was entered on 10 November, thereby rounding off the conquest of Equatorial Africa and, after a fashion, winning some compensation for the repulse at Dakar.[22] De Gaulle, who had been visiting the other territories in Equatorial Africa and receiving enthusiastic welcomes, arrived at Libreville on 15 November. Two days later he left 'Free French Africa', now organized as a Confederation of Free French Equatorial African states, for England, encouraged with 'the thought of the ardour which the national cause was exciting among those who were free to serve it'. The future of Free France was secure.

I conclude with the account of a little-known operation off Libreville of the comic-opera variety. It provides a rather lighthearted tail-piece to 'Menace'. It was known that there were French naval units in Libreville, particularly submarines, and with the recent experience of Dakar still fresh in memories, resistance was expected. The operation started at dawn with a shore bombardment by the Free French warships, and French troops were successfully landed along the coast. Meanwhile the Walrus seaplane from the *Devonshire*, on patrol in a spectator capacity, spotted a submarine (the *Poncelot*) coming out of Libreville on the surface. Enthusiasm got the better of the pilot and he conducted a dive-bombing attack on the submarine, which promptly submerged. The aggrieved submarine spotted a vintage British sloop inoffensively watching the proceedings from outside the touchline, and fired a torpedo at it which hit the sloop amidships, merely denting the side, where it failed to explode. The submarine surfaced to watch the sloop sink, but

[20] Annex to COS (40) 359th Meeting, 25 Oct., CAB 79/7. The First Sea Lord had approved the telegram. There is evidence that Churchill had wished to involve the Navy directly at Libreville, but was shaken by bitter Admiralty opposition to this course. Bell diary, 22 Oct.

[21] Since we shall not be meeting this delightful person again, let me say that he became an admiral, but returned to the monastery after the war, emerging on special occasions as an admiral once more!

[22] The winning of the whole of French Equatorial Africa was a not insignificant accomplishment in view of the later development of the trans-African air transport route from Takoradi on the Gold Coast to the Middle East.

too late appreciated its error. The incensed sloop immediately set off in pursuit of the submarine at its flat out speed of 17 knots, while the submarine made off on the surface at 18 knots. The forward single 4-inch gun of the sloop meanwhile was blazing away enthusiastically, and whether by luck or good judgement achieved a direct hit on the conning tower of the submarine, which so discouraged the submarine that it stopped. The sloop went alongside and cheerfully signalled the flagship that it had captured a French submarine. This did not have the intended result in the flagship, as the Admiral was immensely embarrassed by this success off the West coast of Africa in an operation in which he was expressly required to dissociate himself! The submarine conveniently scuttled itself, much to the chagrin of the sloop, and the crew were turned over to the Free French. 'Rather naturally a heavy blanket of silence fell over this particular operation, our only success of the series.'[23]

[23] Major R. P. Owen's memorandum for the author, 9 Jan. 1974, from which the whole incident is derived.

Chapter Nine

Post-mortem and Repercussions

> It would be difficult to find, in the whole history of war, a more deplorable fiasco than this.
>
> Admiral Sir Herbert Richmond,
> *Statesmen and Sea Power* (1946)

> If 'Menace' had had its fair share of luck, it might have resulted in one of the most spectacular and fruitful operations of World War II and might well have changed the course of that war to the advantage of the Allies.
>
> Colonel John A. Watson, *Échec à Dakar* (1968)

> It must be clear that in the event the weaknesses of the plan proved decisive and this expedition must be added to the many in the past which have failed because military requirements have been subordinated to political ends and because the lessons of the past continue to be ignored.
>
> Major-General N. M. S. Irwin, in his Report,
> 7 October 1940

(Chart 1)

(1) Results, Causes, Lessons

FRENCH casualties were surprisingly small, considering the duration of the bombardments and their intensity at times. The dead totalled 166: 92 Europeans (82 Navy, 2 Army, 8 civilians) and 74 natives (12 Army, 2 Navy, 60 civilians); the wounded, 340: 107 Europeans (81 Navy, 6 Army, 2 Air Force, and 18 civilians) and 233 natives (53 Army, 1 Navy, 179 civilians). On the other side, losses were light: 3 Free French killed and 5 wounded, and about 36 British killed or wounded. During the three days when Dakar was subjected to the guns of 20 British warships, the damage to military installations and guns, as well as to ships, was negligible.[1]

[1] Seven years later, when Irwin was C-in-C, West Africa, and visited Dakar as the guest of the C-in-C, French West Africa, he was asked at a dinner party by the wife of a battalion commander who had been in the town during the bombardment—she had a twinkle in her eye: 'Why did you keep on shelling my vegetable garden, couldn't

In *matériel*, French losses were the submarines *Ajax* and *Persée* and the cargo vessel *Tacoma*. One ship, the super-destroyer *Audacieux*, was seriously damaged and needed two years to repair. Slightly damaged were the *Richelieu*, the cargo vessels *Korsholm* and *Tamara*, and the steamer *Porthos*. Although the *Richelieu* had suffered little damage from the one 15-inch hit, the damage from the torpedo on 8 July took a year to repair. She joined the Allies in November 1942, was refitted in the United States, and then saw service in the Mediterranean with the Home Fleet, and finally, in April 1944, in the Far Eastern Fleet against the Japanese. A French fighter plane was lost and a seaplane damaged.[2]

The Allied naval force suffered no losses, but the *Devonshire* was the only one of the battleships and cruisers present which did not sustain damage from enemy action. The *Resolution* and the *Cumberland* were seriously damaged. The former underwent temporary repairs at Freetown, returned to England six months later, and was then sent to Philadelphia in the United States for refit. It was a full year before she was ready for active service. The *Cumberland* was out of action for thirteen days. In addition, the cruiser *Fiji* was incapacitated for six months. (See above, p. 62.) The battleship *Barham*, cruisers *Australia* and *Dragon*, and the destroyers *Foresight* and *Inglefield* were slightly damaged, their fighting power scarcely impaired. (The *Barham*'s days were, however, numbered. She was sunk, with enormous losses, on 25 November 1941.) Aircraft losses were severe. On 21 September the *Ark Royal* had 30 Swordfish and 21 Skuas. On 27 September she had only 16 of each type: 19 aircraft had been put out of action, of which 12 had been brought down.

Why had this ill-starred enterprise ended in almost total failure? We can dismiss at once Churchill's belief that the arrival of

---

you hit anything else?' The answer came, not from the General, but from the commander of the shore battery on Cape Manuel, which had been one of the major targets for the fleet. With a similar twinkle, he told Irwin that the only damage inflicted by the three days' shooting was one cornerstone chipped off a barrack building a hundred yards from the nearest gun! Major A. S. Irwin, 'Defeat before Dakar', n.d., Irwin MSS., IRW 1/2. This incident, which is not reproduced in the published version of the same article (*Royal United Service Institution Journal*, cv (Aug. 1960), 344–60), is an embellishment of General Irwin's own version of the episode in his ' "Dakar" 23rd September 1940', n.d., Irwin MSS., IRW 1/4.

[2] Cunningham's estimate, 'after considering all evidence', was two submarines sunk, one severely damaged by gunfire, two super-destroyers and one class unknown burnt out and beached, and two probable 15-inch hits on the *Richelieu*. Cunningham to Admiralty, 1.06 p.m., 26 Sept.

'reinforcements, good gunners and bitter-minded Vichy officials' sealed the fate of 'Menace'. (He ascribed the failure also to over-confidence in reports of conditions from men on the spot.) At the time he declared: 'There was no doubt that the arrival of the French cruisers had changed the whole complexion of the situation. They had almost certainly brought to Dakar determined officers, who had been put on shore to stiffen the forces there.'[3] There were neither reinforcements of troops nor officials, bitter-minded or otherwise, in the ships of Force Y—only 120 gunlayers, who re-placed the sailors from the *Richelieu* at the Cape Manuel batteries and manned the Bel-Air battery. Despite Admiral Muselier's asser-tion, the cruisers carried no shells for the *Richelieu*.[4] For de Gaulle the failure was mainly due to the sudden arrival of Force Y. It 'produced a complete change in the situation. The French naval vessels afforded a powerful defence of the port and the batteries had been taken over by the naval personnel.'[5] Relative to the shore batteries, the *Richelieu*, the submarines, the cruisers, and the super-destroyers had played a comparatively minor role. If the *matériel* and personnel additions to Dakar's defences were slight, what of the argument that the arrival of Force Y galvanized the morale of the defenders? To a degree, yes: it must have encouraged the authorities in their determination to resist the British and Free French. But Mers-el-Kébir and the subsequent attack on the *Richelieu* had already stiffened the will of Dakar's defenders to resist British pressure and armed force. Even French writers make the mistake of exaggerating the significance of the arrival of Force Y, Kammerer, for instance, asserting that 'the operation against Dakar was condemned to defeat through the sudden dispatch of reinforce-ments for French West Africa'.[6]

We must give the French full credit for a gallant and effective defence. The defending forces threw in every variety of weapon they possessed with considerable *élan*. Apart from shore batteries and naval gunfire, torpedo attacks were launched from submarines with effect; fighter aircraft shot down British spotter aircraft and attacked the naval task force. Although the disparity of forces was too great to

[3] WM (40) 258, 25 Sept., CAB 65/15. And to President Roosevelt the same day: 'Vichy got in before us and animated defence with partisans and gunnery experts.' *Their Finest Hour*, p. 435.

[4] Muselier, *De Gaulle contre le Gaullism*, p. 80.

[5] Report of an interview with de Gaulle by an unidentified high Foreign Office official, 28 Nov., FO 371/24345. On the gunners, see above, p. 108.

[6] Albert Kammerer, *La Passion de la flotte française* (Paris, 1950), p. 252.

permit Admiral Lacroix to attempt a sortie and fight in the open sea, the French ships had a less disadvantageous position than Gensoul's squadron at Mers-el-Kébir, since all except the *Richelieu* were able to manœuvre. The fire of the 9·4-inch guns of the shore batteries and the 15-inch of the *Richelieu* was accurate, even if, of some 1,200 shells fired during the three days of the action by the French ships and shore batteries, there were no more than thirteen hits. The fire of the *Richelieu*'s 6-inch guns, good so far as direction was concerned, showed a wide spread. The fire of the cruisers fell generally quite short. The aircraft fought with tenacity. The remarkable liaison established between the three Services and their Chiefs contributed greatly to the success of the defence.

The French had done it all by themselves, for, as we have seen, the British charge of German pressure at Dakar, or that Germans had assisted in the defence of Dakar, was a myth. Thus, on 26 September the GOC, West Africa (Achimota), reported that five Germans had arrived in Dakar on 23 September 'presumably to help organize resistance'.[7] On 28 September the Air Section of the Spears Mission informed the Air Ministry that the 'efficient and determined' air opposition 'indicate probable control of Wakam [Ouakam] aerodrome by Germans and possibly German pilots flying French aircraft'.[8] It is worth repeating that the German presence in Dakar was miniscule at the time of the operation.[9]

So far we have been considering the French pluses. What went wrong on the side of the British and Free French? For one thing, co-operation between Allies in a joint operation, always difficult, was compounded by the physical separation of the British Commanders and de Gaulle. It was Cunningham's judgement that 'the

---

[7] ADM 199/817.

[8] 'Dakar Diary', 28 Sept. At about this time the BBC asserted that the stubborn defence of Dakar was the result of its direction by German officers.

[9] See above, pp. 8–9. A German 'economic' mission of three 'distinguished economists' (one of them a *Wehrmacht* Colonel) left by air for Dakar on 24 September. It was to have been followed by a second plane carrying the staff of the mission. The real purpose of the mission, in the opinion of the Vichy Foreign Office, was 'to plant in West Africa a German control commission, a net of observers for the Reich'. F. Charles-Roux, *Cinq Mois tragiques aux affaires étrangères (21 Mai–1er Novembre 1940)* (Paris, 1949), p. 333. The Foreign Office thwarted the German scheme by telegraphing General Noguès to forbid the continuation of the first plane when it landed at Casablanca on the 25th. The French stood firm. They had no intention of weakening the moral strength of their position and the good faith of their denials to the British of a German presence in West Africa by permitting an 'inconsiderate and inopportune visit of German officers and civil servants' there. The Germans were forced to recall the mission. Ibid., pp. 334–6.

reluctance, perhaps natural of General de Gaulle temporarily to establish his Headquarters on board H.M.S. *Barham* undoubtedly led to confusion and greatly magnified the already formidable difficulties of communication'.[10] Language and personality difficulties worsened the problem. Spears, Watson, and others in the Spears Mission had no language problems with their French colleagues in the *Westernland*, due to the perfection of their knowledge of the French language and the French people. But this did not apply generally in the relations between the British and Free French. De Gaulle was, of course, the personality problem. Most of the British who had worked with the General in the operation were, despite their admiration for him, glad to be rid of him at Duala. I offer this story to illustrate the difficulties of working with the Free French. It is told by Cunningham's Staff Officer (Operations).

After transferring back to *Neptune*, we anchored off Duala while the two Free French minesweeping sloops proceeded up river and secured to a jetty in the town. Here an operation against Libreville was planned to be entirely carried out by Free French with assistance from us with the planning only. I was sent to persuade the sloops that it might be a good idea to go to sea before the operation to check their minesweeping gear. I found no officer on board the senior ship except an officer from the other sloop who was locked in one of the cabins with a woman. We finally established contact with them on a Wednesday when we learnt that they were unable to go to sea on Thursday because that was a Saint's day. Friday was also ruled out, as they would be recovering from celebrations. Saturday and Sunday were impossible, as they never went to sea at week-ends. Monday was another Saint's day with Tuesday needed for recovery, but on Wednesday they were prepared to go to sea.[11]

'War without allies is bad enough—with allies it is hell!' I am in full agreement with this aphorism of Marshal of the Royal Air Force Sir John Slessor.

'Pitting ships against forts is always hopeless, if the forts mean business.' This was Admiral Sir William James's first reaction to the failure of the operation.[12] And it had been axiomatic in the Royal

[10] Cunningham's Report, Pt. V, App. I, p. 3. Colonel Watson would make an exception. With reference to the Rufisque operation, he points out that when communications with the flagship were interrupted, de Gaulle was able to take certain justifiable initiatives which a subordinate would not have dared to take in his place. *Échec à Dakar*, p. 231.

[11] Commander T. C. Crease's letter to the author, 22 Nov. 1973.

[12] Letter of 25 Sept., James (then C-in-C, Portsmouth), *The Portsmouth Letters* (London, 1946), p. 84.

Navy since Nelson's day, if not earlier, and had supposedly been confirmed at the Dardanelles in 1915. Indeed, it was recognized in the planning that naval guns are not usually capable of knocking out shore batteries, which was why reliance was placed on agents' reports that the crews of the guns at Dakar would quickly rally to de Gaulle. The thick fog, which was contrary to all meteorological forecasts, of course played a significant role in the first two days. It deprived the expedition of what might have been a tremendous psychological effect on the first day, hampered all movement at sea and in the air, and was a powerful factor in the inaccurate shooting of Force M. The fog compelled the ships to close to within a few thousand yards of the 9·4-inch batteries of the forts, which put the ships at a disadvantage.[13] Had visibility conditions permitted a range of 23,000 yards or so, that is, at the maximum range of the battleships, which may have been just outside the range of the big coastal guns, and with proper spotting by aircraft less vulnerable than the old Swordfish, the battleships could have destroyed the 9·4-inch batteries, despite the inherent advantage of forts over guns.[14] (Of the range of the big coastal guns we can only be sure that it was somewhere between roughly 22,000 and 26,000 yards.) It would, however, have taken a long time, lots of ammunition, and appalling damage to Dakar. We must remember, too, that the battleships had also to cope with the *Richelieu*, whose 15-inch guns outranged the heavy guns of the elderly *Barham* and *Resolution*: their turrets had not been modernized to give extra elevation. (The range of the British 15-inch was 23,400 yards at maximum elevation

---

[13] General Irwin in his Report cited as a weakness of the plan 'the continued adherence to the hope, in spite of all historical examples, that ships can reduce forts'. Churchill reacted strongly. It would, he said, be a mistake to assume 'that ships can in no circumstances engage forts with success. This might well be true in the fog conditions which so unexpectedly and unnaturally descended upon Dakar; but it would not necessarily be true of the case where the ships' guns could engage the forts at ranges to which the forts could not reply, or where the gunners in the forts were frightened, inefficient, or friendly to the attacking force.' Churchill's minute to Sir John Dill (CIGS) and Sir James Grigg (Permanent Under-Secretary of State at the War Office), 21 Oct., *Their Finest Hour*, p. 605.

[14] As regards the role of the Fleet Air Arm, 'Reconnaissance beforehand was difficult,' Irwin remarked in his Camberley lecture. 'It had to be done by naval aircraft with naval observers, and they were really having to do a form of military reconnaissance which they were not accustomed to and were not trained for.' Cunningham, on the other hand, had kind words for air co-operation generally. During the operation the *Ark Royal* aircraft 'supplied invaluable reconnaissance information. Striking Forces attacked the objectives in the manner and with the spirit expected of the Fleet Air Arm until prevented from doing so by increasing fighter opposition.' Cunningham's Report, Pt. V, App. IV, p. 1.

of 20 degrees, the *Richelieu*, 35,100 yards at 35 degrees elevation.) Immobile as the *Richelieu* was, moreover, with the protection of the breakwater and able to fire at least two of her 15-inch, she was in a sense a powerful fort. Neutralizing her would have been a tougher nut to crack, but it could have been done, once Gorée and Cape Manuel had been disposed of. Later war experience proved that when conditions were right, warships could reduce forts or strong coastal defences.

The chaotic communications were a serious drag on the operation, notably in the afternoon of the first day. One difficulty was that communications were clogged almost from the beginning. As summed up by Spears, with reference to 'Charles'. 'The radio telephones went out of order [R/T failed owing to jamming], the wireless seized under the enormous pressure of messages, and visual signalling did not work for the obvious reason that we were all lost in invisibility.'[15] The restricted use of V/S put a greater burden on W/T (the Fleet Wave, which was manned in the flagship). Add the stream of demanding signals from Whitehall and Chequers, which cluttered up the air.

[15] *Two Men Who Saved France*, p. 197. Cunningham's Report, Pt. V, App. III, deals fully with the communications facet of the operation. Irwin's Report has less to say on the subject, though there is a valuable enclosure in the shape of a report from his Signals Officer, Lieutenant-Colonel E. C. L. Bearcroft, RM. The copy of the enclosure in the Irwin MSS. (IRW 1/2) is far more legible than the one in WO 106/2858. Spears's reference to R/T needs to be explained. When the *Westernland* left Liverpool (31 August), Lieutenant P. Julitte, the Officer in Charge of Signals, Free French Forces, was informed of the British signalling arrangements to be applied during the different phases of 'Menace', and he was instructed to organize Free French signals accordingly (in consultation with Commandant d'Argenlieu). He realized at once that no special radio liaison was provided for the *Westernland*, which would have to share radio communications with six or seven other ships, all British. This would cause overcrowding and delays, especially since the signallers on the flagship would be Royal Navy personnel and those on the *Westernland*, Foreign Legionaries, not familiar with British material and not accustomed to naval practice, and vice versa. Julitte spoke to de Gaulle and attended the conference on signals which was held at Freetown on the flagship. It was agreed that a special and exclusive liaison would be established between de Gaulle and Cunningham—this was radio telephony (extremely rare at the time)—and that the Signal Corps, which settled in both ships, the *Barham* and *Westernland*, would run it. Unfortunately, when the Signal Corps started working, the apparatus designed to ensure secrecy of conversation (it would be called a 'scrambler' today) jammed all the flagship's radio communications, and the Flag-Lieutenant in the *Barham* had the radio telephony stopped. The naval operators in the flagship, thinking that the *Westernland* was being looked after separately, paid little attention to her signals and concentrated on the other ships, which were given priority no doubt because they were engaged in a battle. Hence, an important reason for the muddle and confusion. Lieutenant-Colonel P. Julitte's letter to Colonel Watson, 30 Apr. 1968 (copy in the author's possession) and the latter's gloss in a letter to the author, 22 Nov. 1974.

Clogging was not the only problem. The transmission of intelligence from Free French ships first to the *Westernland* and then after considerable delay, if at all, to the *Barham*, 'rendered valueless,' said Cunningham, 'much that was potentially useful had it been received in time.' Again, inefficiency in communications was practically guaranteed by the fact that the Force A signals staff, which had been got together hurriedly at the eleventh hour, consisted of officers and men detailed for the job without preliminary organization or training. Many of the men were quite unskilled in their trades, having only just emerged from the training depot. None of them had ever worked with the Navy before or had had any experience of signalling at sea. Also, 'the inclusion of Free French Ships and Troops,' wrote the Admiral, 'introduced a whole series of problems concerning cyphers, codes, personal and W/T organization (including Tuning) which had to be settled at a very early stage, mainly by compromise.'

An effort had been made when the expedition was in Freetown to go over the communications plans and instructions with the officers and men principally concerned. Given the fact, however, that the Force was assembled in Freetown for only four days, during two of which most of the warships, including the *Devonshire*, were chasing the French cruisers, it was not possible to hold any comprehensive tests or rehearse communications.

There were serious weaknesses in the planning. The operational orders were hemmed in by restrictions on the use of force that conflicted with the attainment of the objectives. This stemmed from the failure clearly to define the objectives of the operation. If peaceful persuasion failed, how far should force be used? Sir Ronald Wingate puts it well: 'Planning had been muddled. An operation intended to be a peaceful take-over, had been regarded only vaguely as a possible military operation involving casualties, and had not been carried to its logical conclusion because of the danger of causing serious losses to the British fleet.'[16] De Gaulle's extreme reluctance to spill French blood was a complicating factor. Cunningham held no brief for it. 'Firmly fixed in his mind is, however, his aversion to Frenchmen shedding the blood of other Frenchmen and until this idea is eliminated from the Command and from most of the Free French Naval Officers and Ratings it is difficult to foresee any substantial measure of success attending their operations against Vichy French territory in Africa.'[17] Most of de Gaulle's followers

[16] Wingate, *Not in the Limelight*, p. 169.   [17] Report, Pt. V, App. 1, p. 4.

apparently did not share his compunctions. An incident reported by Spears is illustrative. 'The attitude of these Frenchmen is very curious. When a French plane flew over Freetown on Saturday [28 September] by far the best shooting was done by the French sloops who very nearly brought it down, and all the French troops cheered wildly.'[18]

Allied resources were inadequate for a decisive result on a defended coast, the troops at the disposal of the Commanders being severely limited by the commitments elsewhere. They were enough to do the job only if the resistance had been of a token nature or half-hearted. This brings us to the crux of the matter.

When everything has been said, about the arrival of Force Y, the fog, the difficulties of communications, and the rest, one factor stands out as the supremely important one. Two conditions had from the beginning been regarded as essential for success—that the garrison should be suffering from low morale and with little stomach for a fight, and that there should be considerable local support for de Gaulle. On the basis of reports from his agents and a large dose of wishful thinking, de Gaulle believed that the French at Dakar would receive him peaceably or, at worst, after a few face-saving shots. The British accepted this estimate without any serious question. The hostility of the authorities and the garrison, and their willingness to fight hard, came as a shock to de Gaulle and the British Commanders. The gamble on the favourable conditions existing at Dakar was made on shaky and insufficient evidence, hence was an unjustifiable gamble. This was generally recognized in the post-mortems. Lord Halifax summed this up in pithy terms: 'First, reliance on misleading information as to the measure of support likely to be forthcoming for General de Gaulle at Dakar and as to the will and power of the local authorities to resist attack; secondly, an under-estimate of the vigour and resource likely to be shown by the Vichy Government in reinforcing and organising that resistance. We were disagreeably surprised on both points.'[19] Two sides of the same coin. General Spears drew the correct lesson: 'A further mistake was to base a serious military operation on unverified and unverifiable political assumptions. The only political assumption it is ever safe to make is that all the doubtful factors will operate against you until you have clearly established your

---

[18] Spears to Ismay, 30 Sept., PREM 3/276. And see above, p. 128.
[19] WP (40) 392, 'Policy towards Vichy Government', 27 Sept., CAB 66/12.

Admiral Sir Dudley North at his official residence, The Mount, Gibraltar, with Admiral Esteva (left) and Admiral Ollive, 1940

Admiral Sir Dudley North with General Sir Clive Liddell, the Governor of Gibraltar, and the latter's Chief of Staff at Gibraltar, 1940

Left: Admiral Sir Dudley Pound in his office at the Admiralty *c.* 1941

Below: A. V. Alexander, First Lord of the Admiralty, at his desk in 1941

superiority, or given the impression of having done so.'[20] Operation 'Menace' is a classic example of wishful thinking, which is thinking directed more by personal wishes than by objective or rational factors. Always a part of man's makeup, it flourishes with special vigour in wartime on the part of both decision-makers and commanders.

Intelligence was woefully inadequate in other respects. Dakar's defences included many more guns, and heavier ones, than the attackers suspected, and many more defenders. Irwin was especially critical of this deficiency. 'The absence of good information about a place in which we had service officers for 8 or 9 months requires little but adverse comment.'[21] The importance of gaining information about the beaches was not understood. 'In the past naval intelligence had not interested itself in this subject. It was the business of ships to avoid the coast, not beach upon it. Now the slope of a beach, the surf on the beach and the exits from a beach were matters of vital importance, and no landing attack could be launched without knowledge of them.'[22] As it developed, the landing conditions on the discarded beaches to the westward of Dakar (see above, p. 44) turned out to be ideal. Had these been used, surprise and success might well have been achieved. And, of course, intelligence failed over the presence of Germans in Dakar.

What about the Force Commanders? That the enterprise failed was in no way due to any inadequacies of Admiral Cunningham or General Irwin. As General Spears observed, 'The Dakar Expedition is one of those military operations where all concerned did their duty, but which gave no opportunity either for brilliance in leadership or for heroic adventure'. I very much doubt that Nelson and Wellington could have done any better than Cunningham and Irwin. There was little criticism in London of their conduct of the operations, it being realized that they had done the best that was possible in the exceptionally difficult circumstances. Churchill did not blame them. He stated his guiding principle in these matters a month after the operation: that 'any error towards the enemy, and any evidence of a sincere desire to engage, must always be generously

[20] *Two Men Who Saved France*, p. 211. Irwin, in a covering letter to his Report, phrased the same point this way: a weak factor in the military plan was 'reliance on too sure an assessment of an unassessable factor—i.e. Morale, resulting in much obvious "wishful thinking".'

[21] Irwin's Report, Ch. IV, p. 1.

[22] Maund, *Assault from the Sea*, p. 73.

judged'.[23] The two Commanders were continuously employed in important posts until the end of the war. John Cunningham succeeded Andrew Cunningham as C-in-C, Mediterranean, in October 1943 and as First Sea Lord in 1946. He became an Admiral of the Fleet in 1948. After returning to the United Kingdom and further training of troops, Irwin moved to India in 1942, where he first commanded a corps and then the Eastern Army. He retired as a Lieutenant-General.

We cannot leave the Commanders without noting that 'Menace' would probably have turned out differently had Churchill accepted the independent requests of the Force Commanders to postpone the whole operation by a month at least, and two weeks at worst, i.e. to mid-October or the end of September. (With the subsequent delays, the date would have been moved into mid- or late October.) This course, if adopted, would have given them more information and time to study Poulter's report before sailing, and would probably have resulted in the strengthening of Force A. It would also have enabled them to complete the training of the force for an opposed landing, should that become necessary, and, finally, they would have had better weather conditions. Irwin made these points at the time, adding: 'Having failed to carry out the operation as originally described by P.M. at the earliest moment, it would have been better, as the event proved, to have waited as recommended by Cmds.'[24] But Churchill, with his eye on the desperate needs at home and in the Middle East, to say nothing of the security factor, would not listen to the Commanders. (See above, pp. 51–2.)

When Irwin visited Dakar in 1947, he had conversations with a

---

[23] Churchill's minute on Irwin's Report, 21 Oct. He did go on to express puzzlement, if not criticism, that Irwin should have wished to persist in the operation, given his strong feelings beforehand about the difficulties and shortcomings, and especially after the arrival of Force Y at Dakar, which had 'so formidably aggravated' the 'defects and dangers' of the operation. I find it difficult to reconcile Churchill's principle and Cunningham's advancement with this passage from a letter that the Admiral wrote to Admiral North on 15 January 1946: 'They grilled me pretty thoroughly when I got back, &, as you know, W.C. has never & will never forgive me for my part in it.' The extract is in a memorandum by Admiral Sir Herbert Richmond of 21 Feb. 1946 (North had loaned him Cunningham's letter), Richmond MSS., RIC 7/4. Cunningham had a premonition that he would be in for a rough time on his return to England. At a meeting in the flagship after returning to Freetown, he was understandably depressed and made the remark to one of his Captains that he expected it would mean a bowler hat for him. Captain R. R. Stewart's letter to the author, 3 Dec. 1974.
[24] 'Notes by Major-General N. M. S. Irwin on the "Dakar Operation",' Irwin MSS., IRW 1/2.

number of Frenchmen who had been there in the fateful days of September 1940.

The general opinion seemed to suggest two main reasons for failure. The first, our decision to broadcast in advance our intentions, instead of carrying out surprise landings at dawn on the beaches, where, it is said, we would have been heartily welcomed by the troops and the bulk of the population, in spite of any resistance decreed by the Governor or Military Commander. This was in the nature of a tactical error. The second was a psychological error in raising the curtain with a broadcast by General de Gaulle. In the traditional respect for seniority ingrained in the French Military and Civil system, an instant reaction must inevitably occur, as indeed it did, in the hearts of the more senior officers ashore against subordination to an officer so junior as a 'General de Brigade', the rank held by General de Gaulle.[25]

Irwin found 'much apparent justification for these reasons for failure'. I have serious reservations about the validity of these 'errors'; but Irwin, I feel, is correct in singling out two extremely important extenuating factors. One was the British feeling that no premature action must be taken during that period of uncertainty in France which could push a sensitive France into the German camp, especially when there was faith in France's ability to arise from her stricken state and stand once more beside Britain in the fight against Germany and Hitlerism. The other was that, given Britain's own desperate situation, the prospect, or at least hope, of achieving her ends by peaceful means, that is, through the agency of de Gaulle, was compelling.

Although the first Allied combined operation of the war had been a failure, and to criticize failure is the easiest of all exercises, out of the failure came many of the lessons which in the following years would make possible the successful combined operations that were to play a major role in winning the war. Since no landings had taken place, no lessons were learned about landings as such, although there was valuable experience in close co-operation between the Naval and Military Staffs in drawing up extremely detailed operation orders and in organizing the administrative problems of supply.

Security arrangements were tightened, following the recommendations in a joint report by the EPS and the Inter-Service Security Board. They recommended, *inter alia*, that leave not be granted after troops had reached the port of embarkation, without reference to Movement Control, and that a special security officer be

[25] Irwin, ' "Dakar", 23rd September 1940.'

attached to the staff of Movement Control at the two main ports, Liverpool and Glasgow, to prepare a plan for, and to ensure the enforcement of, adequate security measures.[26] These recommendations appear to have been accepted.

The keen disappointment of the Joint Commanders at the inadequacy of military and naval information about Dakar, and the incorrect intelligence on internal conditions and the attitude of the people and the defenders of Dakar, was eventually reflected in methods to remedy this weakness. It needed one more experience, Operation 'Jubilee', the Dieppe Raid of August 1942, to drive home this lesson of Dakar. British Intelligence greatly underestimated the strength of the Dieppe garrison; beach intelligence was also poor. Admiral of the Fleet Lord Mountbatten of Burma asserts that 'the successful landing in Normandy [1944] was won on the beaches of Dieppe'.[27] I would have this read: '. . . at Dakar and on the beaches of Dieppe.' Another larger result of Dakar, reinforced by the experience of Dieppe, was the realization that the means used must be sufficient to obtain a quick result.

There was a plethora of lessons as regards communications. One was the recognition by the Commanders of the great differences in method and skill between the signal personnel of the two Services, 'V/S, for example,' said Irwin, 'not being understood in the Army, and W/T largely giving place to R/T. The exact opposite is the case in the Navy.' He recommended the establishment of a combined signal staff. Cunningham's proposal was similar—that a Navy and Army Communications Staff, or a Nucleus Staff at any rate, should be kept permanently trained and ready for combined operations.[28]

General Irwin found the planning organization deficient in an important respect. The Commanders would have been helped greatly had they taken over a skeletal staff which had examined all the factors relevant to the operation. 'To take over plans from people who do not have to take any part in carrying it out is always unsatisfactory; and against human nature at least without careful scrutiny. A planning staff which would become the operational staff would at least present a commander with a reasonable organisation on which

[26] JP (40) 465 (E), 'Operation "Menace"—Security Arrangements', 21 Sept., CAB 84/19.

[27] Mountbatten of Burma, 'Operation Jubilee: the Place of the Dieppe Raid in History', *RUSI Journal*, cxix (Mar. 1974), 29, 30.

[28] Irwin's Report, Ch. IV, p. 2, and his Camberley lecture, Cunningham's Report, Pt. V, App. III, p. 7.

to build.'[29] Steps in this direction were taken in the following year.

Irwin was critical of how 'the military commander is liable to be flitted round the sea on sudden naval occasions and divorced from his troops'. Dakar showed the importance of a special Headquarters ship, with the necessary communications system. In his Report Irwin wrote, 'Seldom have I felt so impotent as during this expedition when I was separated from my forces and tied to any Naval operations which might become necessary at shortest notice.' He referred to the occasion when he was 'heading northwards at 25 knots while my forces were proceeding south at 12 knots, and on another I was returning at 5 knots to the advanced Base while the transports preceded me at 12 knots. The solution to this problem must lie in a special H.Q. Ship . . .' Also, the sudden departure seaward of the warship that housed the military headquarters, the *Devonshire*, when Cunningham went off to intercept the French cruisers on the 19th, had led to a hurried transfer of Irwin and his headquarters to the troopship *Karanja* in the middle of the work of preparation. There was more to Irwin's argument. He believed 'emphatically' that 'the Joint Commanders of a combined operation must NOT be in a bombarding ship. The Commanders must be kept separate from the local Naval operations.' This again pointed to the building of a special combined HQ ship from which command of an operation could be exercised.[30] The need for a Headquarters ship had been a contentious question which had been under discussion for several years. Ultimately, and largely as a result of 'Menace', such a ship came into being. (This lesson, well learned by the British at Dakar, had to be relearned by the Americans in the invasion of North Africa.)

Irwin closed his Report with 'the strongest recommendation that the office of Director of Combined Operations should be itself or should contain the permanent nucleus of a Combined Operation H.Q.' 'The last recommendation,' observes Brigadier Fergusson, 'was to give rise to a lot of what sailors call tooth-sucking.' Or, as the Combined Operations History (1956) expressed it: 'If for no other reason, Dakar is important since it forced, at an early stage of the war, the recognition of a need which later became more generally understood.'

Finally, there is a most important material development that came out of 'Menace'. At a meeting of the Directors of Plans

[29] Irwin's Camberley lecture, Report, Ch. IV, p. 2.
[30] Ibid., pp. 2–4.

summoned by the Prime Minister after the Dakar expedition (see below, p. 189) it was made clear that no such operation could succeed without supporting armour, but that no vessels capable of carrying tanks, transporting them over a long sea journey, and landing them directly on an enemy shore, were in existence. The Prime Minister stated that this was a problem that would constantly recur and no offensive would be possible until it was solved. The Admiralty were directed to produce these ships as a matter of urgency. As a result of Churchill's directive there came into being the LST ('landing ship tank'), which was larger and more seaworthy than the LCT ('landing craft tank'), then under development. The first one to be commissioned was the *Misoa* in the summer of 1941. The LST has been hailed as 'the biggest of all material contributions to the successful landings in the Mediterranean and on the Normandy coast, as well as to the spectacular performance of the Americans in the Pacific'.[31] The LST and its successors of various designs were to influence future amphibious warfare in a similar way to which the armoured tank had already changed many aspects of land warfare.

(2) Repercussions

The diary of Vichy's Foreign Minister gives a vivid picture of the Government's reaction to Dakar. Thus, on 23 September: 'If Dakar falls, North Africa will soon be invaded by the Germans. This means a campaign in Africa, and certainly the occupation of Marseilles and Toulon. The whole structure of the armistice will collapse. It is to bring this about that a Frenchman makes the English fire on his fellow-countrymen. I am prostrated: but Dakar will and must hold out.'[32] An enraged Darlan had sent three submarines from Casablanca to Dakar after the fighting began, also bombers from Morocco. He would have gone much further. In the evening of 23 September the French asked the German and Italian Armistice Commissions for permission to dispatch from Toulon the battle cruiser *Strasbourg*, two 10,000-ton cruisers, a 7,600-ton cruiser, and a number of destroyers. They also asked for the free disposition of the aircraft in Africa, that is, to enable them to send air reinforcements to Dakar. (The French Air Force had been exempted from the disarmament clauses of the armistices.) Although

[31] Fergusson, *The Watery Maze: the Story of Combined Operations*, p. 68.
[32] *The Private Diaries of Paul Baudouin*, pp. 246–7.

Raeder and the German Naval War Staff supported the French request, 'now that', as the latter put it, 'the French have shown a bona fide desire to defend their colonies',[33] the Axis Governments rejected it during the night of 23rd–24th. At midday on the 24th the Germans modified their position: the French air units could be released, but the ban on the sailing of the ships was maintained. The Italians agreed to the German position some hours later.[34]

Dakar convinced the German Naval War Staff that the loyalty of the French armed forces could be relied on. They believed that a French victory would strengthen Germany's military-geographical position, and it was therefore a matter of regret when Hitler reacted negatively to the French proposal for the release of additional naval forces. The following extract from a memorandum composed in the SKL on 25 September, when the issue at Dakar was still in doubt, shows how keen Raeder was on taking advantage of the situation:

It can be assumed that the attack on Dakar represents only the beginning of a far-reaching British political plan in Africa, which might even have Roosevelt's connivance. . . . According to a report from Portugal, the British military experts have repeatedly declared the occupation of French Morocco to be essential to the further conduct of the war, not only on strategic grounds, but also economically for securing supplies to Britain. Moreover, British control of Morocco and North Africa would make it very difficult for Italy to remain in the war for any length of time, if indeed it did not altogether eliminate her.[35]

They regarded the moment as propitious for persuading Vichy to take up arms with the Germans against Britain in Northwest Africa.

Raeder took these ideas up with Hitler at a private conference on 26 September. He urged the importance of co-operating with France in the protection of Northwest Africa by stationing a German air force in Casablanca, and he would encourage the French, who had about 25,000 troops in the Dakar area, to attack the neighbouring British territory, where there were only six to eight battalions. The idea was to occupy Freetown and thus deliver a blow to British supply lines. The thrust of Raeder's presentation was the need to give priority to the defeat of Britain by means of a vigorous prosecu-

---

[33] Assmann, *Die Bemühungen der Seekriegsleitung um ein deutsche-französisches Zusammengehen*, citing a War Diary reference (KTB Skl. Teil A, Sept. 1940, pp. 322–3).

[34] *Documents on German Foreign Policy, 1918–1945*, Ser. D, xi. 160, 165.

[35] Assmann, *op. cit.*, citing the same KTB (War Diary) reference, pp. 331–2.

tion of the war at sea from Atlantic ports, and for a policy of reconciliation with France in order to secure her collaboration in the use of French West African bases and in establishing Axis command of the Mediterranean. Hitler approved these ideas in principle and expressed his intention to discuss the problem in the very near future with Mussolini and possibly with Franco. But it was quite obvious that he was not prepared to encourage the French to fight alongside German troops. This would have infuriated an already frustrated Mussolini, who had yet to reap very substantial gains from France as a result of his brief and undistinguished part in the war. The Italians wanted to see the French armed forces in the Mediterranean defeated, so that Italy could ensure the occupation of Tunis and Corsica as a *fait accompli*. In any case, Hitler's mind was set on other objectives than those espoused by Raeder and the Naval War Staff.

Hitler failed to exploit French indignation over Dakar and their resolve actively to defend their empire against the British and Free French. Dakar had been grist for Laval's mill. For a time, in late September and early October, the Vichy Government became more pro-German as Laval, then Vice-Premier, redoubled his efforts to put France in the German camp. On 11 October Pétain declared in a major policy speech that the new France 'must liberate itself from traditional friendships and intimacies'. If Germany knew how to 'rise above her victory, we will know how to rise above our defeat'. But Hitler's abortive attempt at Hendaye on 23 October to obtain Franco's active participation in the war at the expense of French Morocco, and his ambivalent attitude towards Pétain at their celebrated meeting at Montoire, near Tours, on the following day had the effect of antagonizing rather than encouraging the Vichy collaborators. Raeder's more practical concepts were never put to the test, since Hitler had decided to keep France subdued; the idea of working with her was 'out'. A new Franco-German relationship failed to develop, except in Africa, directed against the Anglo-Gaullists, and the French were allowed to activate more weapons, including tanks, in Africa. But we are straying from our main theme.

Vichy's reaction to the events at Dakar had been, all things considered, mild. War was not declared; the War Cabinet had judged the situation correctly. Roosevelt's warning (see below) may have influenced the French. On 26 September the Admiralty informed Cunningham that war with Vichy was unlikely. However, the excitement of the military and Laval and his supporters forced Vichy to take reprisals for the British attack, as they had after Mers-el-Kébir. Darlan secured the unanimous agreement of the Government for two retaliatory air attacks, which were made from Morocco on Gibraltar harbour and dockyards. The first, by 40 aircraft on 24 September, dropped 150 bombs; the second, on the 25th, by over 100 aircraft, dropped some 300 bombs. AA fire was ineffective on the first day because of a curtain of cloud over the Rock, but on the second day it brought down three aircraft. The attacks appear to have been halfhearted in execution, despite the near absence of British fighter aircraft, which were heavily concentrated at home during the Battle of Britain. Many of the bombs fell in the water or on barren parts of the Rock, and casualties and damage of consequence were light. The A/S trawler *Stella Sirius* was sunk and there was considerable damage to buildings, but only slight damage to dockyard equipment. There were two near misses on the *Renown*. Since the denial to the British of the use of Gibraltar harbour and dockyard would have posed awkward problems, they were considerably relieved to learn on the 27th, via Lyons Radio, that the French Admiralty had announced the suspension of the reprisal raids on Gibraltar, now that the attack on Dakar had ceased. I should also note the feeble French naval demonstration in the early hours of the 25th, when four destroyers from Casablanca entered the Straits of Gibraltar and one of them opened fire on British destroyers on patrol at the eastern entrance.

Dakar allowed the French to rid themselves of the inferiority complex that had seized many of them after the events of May 1940. To have successfully resisted the first navy of the world raised the confidence of the Vichy régime, which exulted over 'the great naval victory of Dakar', and it boosted the morale of the French Navy and the French nation at large. It also intensified anti-British feeling in certain French naval circles, still smarting from Mers-el-Kébir. The French Admiralty let the British know, through their Naval Attaché in Madrid, 26 September, that their Navy would retaliate against any further attack. 'The attack on Dakar was answered by bombardment of Gibraltar. We will continue to answer in the same way every new attack and we can make Mediterranean untenable for English, unless H.M. Government will formally engage (*a*) To suspend all attacks, (*b*) To renounce all propaganda for Civil War, (*c*) Not to impede sea navigation [corrupt group] applicable to feeding.' The British were, the Naval Attaché added, 'playing into hands of Laval, who is now completely German.'[36]

The anti-British and collaborationist forces in Vichy had stiff competition from the pro-British faction, who wished to improve relations with Britain. This group included the Minister of Finance, Bouthillier, the Foreign Minister, Baudouin, and nearly the whole of the Foreign Office. These men saw no future for their country except through a British victory. The prospect of serious food shortages in the coming winter, caused by the British blockade, was another factor in their desire to improve relations with London. For them the lifting of the British blockade, so that the colonies could feed France and France remain in contact with her colonies, and the 'dissidence' issue were the prime desiderata of normal relations. In the tug of war in Vichy the pro-British forces gradually won the upper hand during the autumn. Meanwhile, Vichy's foreign policy *vis-à-vis* Britain struck an uncertain note. For their part the British were ready to let bygones be bygones, so long as Vichy kept the Germans and Italians out of the French Empire and did not require the British Government to abandon their support of the Free French movement. These were the essential conditions of a *modus vivendi*. At the same time the British reserved their rights of blockade.

On 25 September Baudouin let Hoare know, through the French Ambassador in Madrid, de la Baume, that he regarded Dakar as a wholly inexcusable aggression. 'From the standpoint of general politics, there has been a definite improvement in Franco-British relations during the past weeks. . . . I cannot understand what advantage England hopes to gain by upsetting this state of affairs. It can be said of her aggression that it was worse than a crime—it was a blunder.' But two days later the French Ambassador gave Hoare a conciliatory message from Baudouin. If the French Government were not to be driven entirely into German hands, Britain must permit supplies from the French colonies to reach non-occupied France. The French would guarantee that these supplies would not get into German hands, and if the Germans attempted to seize the supplies, the French Government would move to Morocco

---

[36] Naval Attaché, Madrid (Hillgarth), to DNI, 27 Sept., ADM 199/817. (c) called for allowing the passage of food supplies to the unoccupied zone of France. There was no British reply. There is a useful 'Summary of Anglo-Vichy relations since Dakar', a Foreign Office résumé of the more important exchanges via Madrid, 6 Nov. 1940, FO 371/24303. And see Sir Llewellyn Woodward, *History of the Second World War. British Foreign Policy in the Second World War* (3 vols., London, 1970–1), i. 411ff.

and France would again be united with Britain against Germany.

Before the abortive attempt on Dakar, it had seemed to Lord Halifax that French opinion had been moving steadily in their direction. Dakar might halt this development, and yet it might work out well if it stimulated French self-confidence. It was Britain's task to transform this feeling into anti-German sentiments.[37] The Admiralty were in full agreement with the Foreign Office views that the whole policy towards the Vichy Government should be reviewed and that they should lose no opportunity of reaching a tolerable agreement with Vichy. An important memorandum of 30 September stated their case, which was based on the proposition that 'the strategical situation in the Mediterranean and the demands on our naval forces should be governing considerations'.

The policy pursued so far has imposed very considerable commitments on the Navy, which it has only been possible to meet by weakening our forces in the important theatres of the war, i.e., (1) Home Waters, (2) Mediterranean, (3) trade protection.

The Admiralty view with considerable concern a continuation of a policy that will bring our Navy into conflict with the ships of the Vichy Government. Our naval strength is already inadequate for fighting Germany and Italy, and the Admiralty consider that our policy towards the Vichy Government should be largely governed by the need to keep the calls upon our naval forces (other than for operations against Germany and Italy) down to the minimum.

Stress was laid on the vulnerability of Gibraltar to French air action. 'If Gibraltar is made untenable, our whole strategical position in the Western Mediterranean is lost, and not only should we be unable to carry on operations against Italy in this area, but our control of the bottleneck through which supplies must go to Italy and unoccupied France would be gone.' The conclusion was that the Dakar incident had made it even more necessary than before to reach a *modus vivendi* with the French on the subject of their colonies and with regard to economic questions.[38]

At a full-dress debate in the War Cabinet on 1 October on the future course of relations with Vichy, Halifax pressed for reaching a *modus vivendi* with the Vichy Government. There was agreement on the principle of initiating talks with Vichy, the broad lines of which

[37] WM (40) 259, 26 Sept., CAB 65/15, 'Policy towards Vichy Government', WP (40) 392, 27 Sept., CAB 66/12.
[38] WP (40) 396, 'Policy towards the Vichy Government', CAB 66/12.

were discussed and determined largely by the Prime Minister's views.[39] The result was conveyed in a firm reply to de la Baume through Hoare on 3 October. The British would retaliate at once against French colonial ports and territories, if the French made any further attack, and they would continue to support the Free French. Subject to these conditions, they were willing to discuss these questions: How to ensure that Vichy-controlled colonies did not fall under Axis influence; trade between the French colonies and unoccupied France; and how to ensure that French warships did not under any circumstances fall into German or Italian hands.[40]

The French reply on 14 October, again through Madrid, was that they had no desire to become an aggressor against Britain, but would reply to attacks on their ships or territory. They warned that British recognition of the Gaullist movement or support of its attempts to detach French colonies from the authority of the French Government would make a reconciliation impossible. They 'earnestly' wished for an 'economic *modus vivendi*' as regards trade with their colonies. The War Cabinet found the reply disappointing, but the important thing is that exchanges of views via Madrid continued, preserving a link between London and Vichy for the day when collaboration against the common foe became possible.

It is paradoxical, as Mordal brings out, that Dakar not only did not aggravate Anglo-French relations, after the first days, but that it contributed to their amelioration. A *détente* of a sort set in during October. French commercial traffic through the Straits of Gibraltar with a light escort, which had been inaugurated on 7 September and had proceeded without incident, had been suspended during the hostilities at Dakar. It was resumed on 27 September. War Cabinet policy was that French merchant ships passing through the Straits were not to be interfered with if escorted (which was nearly always the case, besides which the ships invariably kept in Spanish territorial waters), but if unescorted they were subject to normal contraband control measures. On 18 November, however, the War Cabinet instructed the Admiralty to intercept escorted French convoys attempting to pass the Straits. Few warships could be spared for this work and few ships were intercepted. French traffic

[39] WM (40) 263, CAB 65/15.

[40] De Gaulle, sent a copy of the telegram, protested against the item about trade. '. . . there is no doubt that these arrangements would entail a strengthening, at any rate temporarily, of the influence of Vichy on the colonies, which at the moment is dwindling.' De Gaulle's telegram to Churchill, 3 Oct., de Gaulle, *War Memoirs*, i., Pt. 2, p. 42.

in the Mediterranean was not interfered with. The blockade of the French West African colonies practically broke down, since ships were not available to make it effective.

Churchill did not see eye to eye with the Admiralty on the blockade issue, particularly as regards West Africa. He would stop the trade between French West African ports and French Mediterranean ports, whereas the Admiralty thought that the trade with West Africa was not important enough to stop, if it involved the risk of a French bombardment of Gibraltar. Churchill was prepared to face that threat. If the French retaliated by bombing Gibraltar, they should bombard Casablanca and Vichy itself. But he did not think matters would go to such extremes.[41] Churchill's opposition to relaxing the blockade of French territories was an irritant to the Admiralty. It was for them another example of Churchill's anti-Vichy 'pin pricks', which swallowed, or threatened to swallow, so much naval force when they ought to be concentrating on fighting Germany and Italy. Another of these pin pricks occurred when, on 11 October, the French cruiser *Primauguet* was sighted south of Casablanca proceeding to the south, escorting an ammunition vessel. The Admiralty intended doing nothing, but the Prime Minister prevailed on them to take steps to try and turn the ship back. The attempt was apparently unsuccessful. Captain Bell's diary on 12 October has this eloquent bit: 'VCNS seems in good form after his [two-day] spell on leave but is absorbed in our attitude to Vichy France & trying to stop the Prime Minister being absurd & goading Vichy into war with us.'

*   *   *

In the perspective of history the failure at Dakar proved to be no more than a setback, yet it was a blow to the prestige of Great Britain almost everywhere at a time when the world was wondering whether she could stand alone against the German tyranny. The British Ambassador in Madrid summed up the Franco Government's reaction to the fiasco in these words: '. . . it has seemed to show once again our incapacity for carrying through any military plan.'[42] Of far greater concern to Britain was the reaction in Washington.

[41] The contrasting views of Churchill and the Admiralty are spelled out in Churchill's minute to the Chiefs of Staff, 28 Sept., annex to COS (40) 788, 'Operations in West Africa', 27 Sept., CAB 80/19, WM (40) 267, 7 Oct., WM (40) 272, 10 Oct., and WM (40) 273, 18 Oct., CAB 65/9.

[42] Hoare to Halifax, 26 Sept., Hoare (Viscount Templewood), *Ambassador on Special Mission*, p. 86. 'On the other hand,' he had added, 'I have been making the most of the

The British had kept President Roosevelt *au courant*, notifying him on 22 September of the coming operation and the projected strategy, and keeping him abreast of developments as events unfolded. When the British Ambassador, the Marquess of Lothian, read Churchill's telegram to the President in the evening of the 22nd, Roosevelt was 'delighted and repeatedly said "splendid". At the end he said he was "happy" about it.' At Lothian's suggestion, Roosevelt promised to tell Vichy that a declaration of war on Britain would be derogatory to Franco-American relations and would mean the loss to Vichy of French possessions in the Pacific and West Indies.[43] The 'Former Naval Person' in his turn was delighted. 'I was encouraged by your reception of information conveyed by Lord Lothian about Dakar. It would be against our joint interests if strong German submarine and aircraft bases were established there. . . . what really matters now is that you should put it across the French Government that a war declaration would be very bad indeed for them in all that concerns United States. If Vichy declares war, that is the same thing as Germany, and Vichy possessions in the Western Hemisphere must be considered potentially German possessions.'[44]

The President, who had been following every Vichy move in Africa with extreme suspicion, went some way towards meeting his promise to Lothian. When the French Ambassador, Henry-Haye, complained to the American Under Secretary of State that 'there was no justification whatever for this [Dakar] attack', the latter replied that only a British victory would lead to a restoration of an independent France, 'and that if such an anomalous situation were presented as the Vichy Government declaring war upon Great Britain and thus becoming the ally of Germany against her own recent ally, Great Britain, the Ambassador could well imagine what the impact upon American public opinion would be'. The Ambassador did not believe his Government would go that far. The Under

---

argument that the incident shows our desire to avoid intervention except where it is the obvious will of the population. The latter argument goes some way to reassure the Spaniards that we are not contemplating any intervention in Morocco.' Two days earlier, Hoare had on instructions formally reassured the Spanish Foreign Minister, Colonel Beigbeder, that the Dakar operation was 'not intended to be followed by a similar *coup* in Morocco . . . none of His Majesty's Government's actions at Dakar is in the slightest degree inimical to Spain . . .' FO 371/24511.

[43] Lothian to Foreign Office, 22 Sept., FO 371/24332.

[44] Churchill, *Their Finest Hour*, p. 432. The message was dispatched by the Foreign Office early on the 24th.

Secretary then rubbed in the fact that German control of Dakar would not be to the interest of either country, the United States or France, and that a German victory over Britain would mean just that. He surprised the Ambassador by asking him whether there had not been a German military mission and other German emissaries in Dakar in recent weeks. This the Ambassador denied.[45]

The failure at Dakar chilled pro-British feelings in the United States, though only temporarily. Their Military Attaché in London regarded Dakar as 'probably another one of Churchill's military inspirations, like Antwerp [1914]'. It 'appears to have been as great a mistake as the attempt upon Norway'.[46] A *New York Times* correspondent spoke (27 September) of the 'depression, bewilderment, and disappointment' of Britain's well-wishers in the United States. His newspaper editorialized on the preceding day: 'From first to last the Dakar adventure appears to have been a major blunder. It would be folly for the British or their friends to minimize the probable effects of this defeat.' American radio commentators in the evening of the 25th attacked 'not the plan—whatever it was—to seize Dakar, but the apparent inadequacy of the means taken to carry it out'. The *New York Times* struck the same note in its leader of the 26th: 'A wise commander never begins a battle unless he has the strength and the determination to carry it through to the end.' As a side effect of Dakar, the leaks of information attributed to the Free French strengthened Roosevelt and his military advisers in their mistrust of de Gaulle's judgement and discretion, and when the United States entered the war, resulted in the refusal to allow the Free French to have any knowledge of future operational plans.

The reaction in Australia was one of distress, their Prime Minister, Menzies, telegraphing Churchill (29 September) that he found it 'difficult to understand why attempt was made unless overwhelming chances of success. To make what appears at this distance to be a half-hearted attack is to incur a damaging loss of prestige.' Churchill replied sharply (2 October) that 'if it is to be laid down that no attempt is to be made which has not "overwhelming chances of success", you will find that a complete defensive would be imposed upon us. In dealing with unknown factors like the degree

[45] Memorandum of conversation by Sumner Welles, 24 Sept., *Foreign Relations of the United States, 1940* (5 vols., Washington, D.C., 1955–61), ii. 591.
[46] 25 Sept., 2 Oct., Leutze (ed.), *The London Observer: the Journal of General Raymond E. Lee, 1940–1941*, pp. 71, 76.

of French resistance it is impossible to avoid uncertainty and hazard.' He also took umbrage over the reproach of making 'a half-hearted attack'. 'I hoped that you had not sustained the impression from these last five months of struggle that we were "a half-hearted Government" or that I am half-hearted in the endeavours it is my duty to make.' Menzies was disturbed (4 October) that Churchill should have thought his telegram to be 'carping or discouraging'. He confessed to having expressed himself 'somewhat crudely' but failed to see how his telegram could have been construed as charging the British Government with half-heartedness.[47] The storm blew over quickly, but it had given the Government fresh evidence of how disturbed even Commonwealth opinion was by the Dakar setback.

At home the reception of the news of the repulse was no better than it was abroad. The DDOD(H) was furious. 'Another British defeat, no more no less. An operation badly conceived, badly executed, which might have been a very different story. Again the Old Man ran it all and never asked the advice of the Staff.'[48] The last sentence needs to be qualified (see below, p. 190), but, as with Norway in the spring, undoubtedly reflected a widespread feeling at the Admiralty. The Naval Assistant to the VCNS took a broader, though equally critical, view: 'A bad blunder which has caused us losses in men and damage to ships that we can ill afford, and has lowered our prestige by our failure to do what we intended, and probably antagonised most Frenchmen, even those who were slowly coming over to our cause. . . . Probably relations will now settle down to a kind of sulky distrust of each other without active hostilities, but the Germans and Italians are likely to get the use of North African ports in fact if not in name.' On the following day: '. . . one cannot disguise the fact that we have failed in an operation whose only excuse would have been its success. I hope Winston will learn from this, otherwise we shall have gained no good at all from MENACE.'[49] These were no doubt representative Admiralty opinions. And not only at the Admiralty. These views reflected the general feeling in the defence establishment as a whole.

The official explanation for home consumption did its best to conceal the realities. A statement issued by the Ministry of Information late on the 25th and which appeared in the press the following

[47] Churchill, *Their Finest Hour*, pp. 645-7.
[48] Edwards diary, 25 Sept., REDW 1/2.
[49] Bell diary, 25, 26 Sept.

day stressed these points: de Gaulle 'had good reason to believe from the information which reached him that a large proportion of Senegal supported the Free French movement and would welcome his arrival'; the Government was all the more ready to support the General in the operation because of information that 'German influence was spreading to Dakar'; there was no interference with the passage through the Straits of the Vichy cruisers because it was not British policy to interfere with French warships which were not proceeding to German-controlled ports, and they were permitted to proceed when they pursued a southerly course (!). The operations themselves were sketched. '. . . when it became plain that only a major operation of war could secure the fall of Dakar it was decided to discontinue hostilities, as it had never been the intention of H.M. Government to enter into serious warlike operations against those Frenchmen who felt it their duty to obey the command of the Vichy Government.' The Free French explanation of what had gone wrong, which appeared in the press on the 27th, had its share of half-truths and inaccurate statements. Thus, 'General de Gaulle knew that the great majority of the population were resolved to rally to the Free French cause. But there had been so much German infiltration that this succeeded in frustrating their object, so that General de Gaulle found himself faced with a situation in which he would be forced to resort to bloodshed. . . . It is now known that under German pressure the Dakar authorities opened fire on the troops who were attempting a peaceful landing . . .' Of course, the Free French believed all this to have been the case. Although the official accounts in the press were cleverly worded, they could not disguise the fact that the operation had been a total failure.

The British reception of the news of the repulse at Dakar was what one would have expected. The American Ambassador's summation was accurate: 'The Dakar situation is a bitter pill for the entire Cabinet and, from my observation, for the entire country. The newspapers have been most critical. It is the first real break in the Churchill popularity and there is a definite feeling that they have not a Prime Minister but a Generalissimo.'[50] For Harold Nicolson Dakar was 'about as bad a show as it could be. It will ruin de Gaulle's prestige and will affect Winston's. The effect on France and America will be deplorable. I am deeply depressed.

---

[50] Joseph P. Kennedy's telegram to Secretary of State Cordell Hull, 27 Sept., *Foreign Relations of the United States, 1940*, iii. 48.

Why is it that we are never successful? This is worse than Norway.'[51]

Faulty war direction was charged on many sides. To the Liberal *Manchester Guardian* (27 September) 'the mystery is how so great a mistake came to be made'. Apparently, de Gaulle had been 'gravely misinformed' about the true situation in Dakar, and the Government was to blame for the intelligence failure that permitted the escape of the French cruisers. The Liberal *News Chronicle* (27 September) called for 'an immediate and public inquiry into the deplorable fiasco'. It was 'too reminiscent' of Norway, and its effect on British prestige would be as disastrous. Further to the left, the *New Statesman* (28 September) declared that there was 'much explaining to do about Dakar', especially as regards the 'great mystery' of the passage of the French warships through the Straits. The Labourite *Daily Herald* (27 September) raised questions. 'With stakes so high, the gamble was sheer folly. Why was it undertaken? Because of bad information, or bad judgment?' The popular *Daily Mirror* (27 September) gave no quarter. Its leader, entitled 'Major Blunder', asked whether they were 'still in the stage of gross miscalculation, of muddled dash and hasty withdrawal, of wishful thinking and of half-measures? So the fiasco of Dakar suggests. . . . Narvik was quite a distinguished naval exploit compared with Dakar! Dakar has claims to rank with the lowest depths of imbecility to which we have yet sunk.' The Conservative press was not much kinder. To *The Times* (30 September) it appeared that there had been 'an error of judgment in launching the venture in view of the reports that the Vichy Government had consolidated its position in Senegal and that there was a primary mistake in permitting the French naval squadron to sail to Dakar'. The *Daily Telegraph* (27 September) called Dakar 'a severe disappointment' and a 'lost golden opportunity'. The *Daily Mail* (26 September) spoke of 'a fiasco which will discourage our friends and give joy to our enemies. . . . If there was no good prospect of success why was this expedition ever sent? To have begun it and to have ended it in such a fashion is far worse than never to have undertaken it at all.' The *Sunday Times* (29 September) deemed it 'a most unfortunate episode' and 'a bitter disappointment'. It was not critical of the Government, but it raised questions about the passage of the French cruisers. The *Observer* (29 September) wrote of the 'uneasy feeling'

[51] Diary, 27 Sept., Nigel Nicolson (ed.), *Harold Nicolson: Diaries and Letters, 1939–1945* (London, 1967), pp. 118–19.

[in Parliament] that somewhere a mistake or, at least, a bad miscalculation was made.'

(3) The Churchill Connection

Churchill did not make his statement to Parliament until 8 October, ostensibly because he wanted to have all the facts, but probably, too, because the delay would give Parliament and the public time to get over the worst of their disappointment. Although the expedition was, he said, primarily a Free French enterprise, he refused to lay the blame for its repulse upon de Gaulle. The General was 'right in believing that the majority of Frenchmen in Dakar was favourable to the Free French movement', and their 'opinion of him has been enhanced by everything we have seen of his conduct in circumstances of peculiar and perplexing difficulty. His Majesty's Government have no intention whatever of abandoning the cause of General de Gaulle . . .' What had wrecked the prospects of success was the arrival at Dakar of the French ships, 'which carried with them a number of Vichy partisans, evidently of a most bitter type. These partisans were sent to overawe the population, to grip the defences and to see to the efficient manning of the powerful shore batteries.' He attributed the arrival of the squadron at Dakar to 'a series of accidents, and some errors which have been the subject of disciplinary action or are now subject to formal inquiry . . .' As a result, neither the First Sea Lord nor the War Cabinet was aware of the approach of the ships to the Straits until it was too late to interdict their passage. The efforts to stop the ships at Casablanca or, as a last resort, to prevent them entering Dakar, had failed. He assured the Commons that 'the mischievous arrival of these ships, and the men they carried, at Dakar arose in no way from any infirmity of purpose on the part of the Government; it was one of those mischances which often arise in war and especially in war at sea.' He sketched the fighting at Dakar and summed up the damage to warships: two French destroyers set on fire, a cruiser heavily hit, and the *Richelieu* suffering further damage. On the British side, a battleship and a large cruiser suffered damage which would 'require considerable attention when convenient'. He urged that they not 'allow a failure of this kind to weaken or hamper our efforts to take positive action and regain the initiative', and he concluded with a blast at the press which revealed his native pugnacity: '. . . criticism which is well meant and well informed and searching is often helpful, but there is a tone in certain organs of the Press, happily not numerous, a tone not only upon the Dakar episode but in other and more important issues, that is so vicious and malignant that it would be almost indecent if applied to the enemy.'[52]

What was the mood of the Commons? The *Manchester Guardian*'s Political Correspondent saw it this way (9 October): that the House was 'ready to pass the sponge of oblivion over Dakar', but it did not like the story of the blunder that allowed the French squadron to pass Gibraltar. '. . . the only point that evoked any approving cheers was Mr. Churchill's advice that we must not let what has happened divert us from regaining the initiative.' The *Spectator*'s Parliamentary Correspondent (11 October) thought that 'it would be foolish to minimise the shock which the Dakar incident has imparted to all members. The Narvik episode came back to the minds of many.' As for Conservative press opinion of the Prime Minister's speech, *The Times* (9 October) found nothing to criticize in it; the *Daily Mail* (9 October) absolved the Government of responsibility for the 'first-class blunder' made in allowing the French ships to pass the Straits; the *Daily Telegraph* (9 October) praised Churchill for drawing 'the right moral when he insisted that the failure should teach us to redouble our efforts to seize an initiative'; the *Spectator* (11 October) found Churchill 'something less than illuminating' on the subject of the passage of the French ships through the Straits; and the *Economist* (12 October) called for the removal of those responsible for the bungling of the expedition. The rest of the press was less charitable as regards the central prosecution of the war. Thus, the *Daily Mirror* (9 October): 'As to Dakar, Mr. Churchill describes the affair as "a series of accidents": a new name for one big blunder.' The *Daily Herald* and *Manchester Guardian* (9 October) queried the efficiency of the Intelligence Service; the *New Statesman* (12 October) adopted the position of the *Spectator* (above); and the *News Chronicle* (9 October) found that their criticisms were proven justified by the speech.

Churchill had agreed with Halifax that they 'should be careful of embarking upon new adventures with inadequate preparations. But nothing was easier or more fatal than to relapse into a policy of mere negativism.'[53] When a report arrived from Madrid early on 25 Octo-

---

[52] Parliamentary Debates (Hansard), 5th ser., Commons, Vol. 365, cols. 298–301. Halifax made a simultaneous and similar statement in the Lords.

[53] WM (40) 259, 26 Sept., CAB 65/15.

ber that Darlan and Laval were pressing hard for an agreement with the Germans for the transfer of the French Fleet and French bases to them, Churchill quickly went into action. '. . . if the Fleet and Naval bases were transferred to Germany, our navy would be faced with the most serious problems, and the situation would become an anxious one.'[54] Measures to meet the emergency included personal messages from President Roosevelt and King George VI to Pétain to resist the German demands. Churchill had taken a much bolder step on the 24th, sending an extraordinary minute to the Chiefs of Staff:

> I see rumours in the papers that they may cede the use of their bases or some of them to Germany and Italy. If anything like this were to come from Vichy immediate action would have to be taken. Let the Joint Planning Committee set to work at once upon a plan to capture Dakar as an important and purely British operation. . . . I should think myself that a landing by fifty or sixty tanks out of range of the guns of the fortress would very quickly bring about a decision. It must be recognized as quite intolerable that Dakar should become a strong German U-boat base. Time is very precious, and the sooner a plan is made the better. We can go into ways and means after.[55]

The closing words are typical of Churchill at his worst. What was the use of making a plan unless you 'go into ways and means' *first*? He was carried away by his magnificent offensive spirit beyond the bounds of ordinary common sense.

Churchill was like a giant tied with the bonds of insufficient resources, which the Service Chiefs and the Joint Planners were determined to conserve until they could take the offensive against really vital targets. Inevitably, a ding-dong contest ensued, with the Prime Minister pitted against the Chiefs and the planners. The EPS produced their appreciation for the Directors of Plans on 26 October. They emphatically rejected the possibility of capturing Dakar either by a direct assault (through beach landings on the Cape Verde Peninsula or by direct entry into the port itself) or a landward attack (advance over land after landing the force outside the defences). A direct assault was no longer practicable owing to the strengthened French air force at Dakar and the possibility of quick reinforcement from Morocco, the British inability to provide adequate air support for the attacking forces from existing airfields at Bathurst and Freetown or from aircraft carriers, and

[54] WM (40) 277, 25 Oct., CAB 65/9.
[55] JP (40) 577 (E), 'Operations in West Africa', CAB 84/21.

the strength of the fixed defences. The alternative of reducing the coast defences by ships' gunfire offered little chance of success because of the strength of the defences, the small results obtained in the recent operation, the scale of air attack that could be brought to bear against the ships, and 'the evidence of history' (forts *v.* ships). The attack from landward was no more practicable because of the lack of suitable bases, their inability to rely upon being able to land on a beach, and the impossibility of developing sufficient air support to neutralise the French air defence. Overall limitations were the state of morale and general alertness at Dakar, which had improved since 'Menace'.[56]

The Joint Planners were in 'full agreement' with the EPS report.[57] They spent much time at this long meeting on the 27th 'thinking of how to "put" our rejection of P.M.'s idea to him'.[58] The Chiefs of Staff expressed general agreement with the conclusions in the EPS report, recognizing that it was impracticable to neutralize the formidable defences of the fortress or to attempt a landing in the sheltered bay under the fire of the coast defence guns. Similarly, the alternatives of a landing at St. Louis or Bathurst were out of the question. On the other hand, 'it might be feasible to land on certain beaches on the Dakar Peninsula which were un-protected by coast defence guns and on which a landing might not be expected. Such a method of attack would be largely dependent upon the weather conditions . . .' While admitting this proposal was a 'forlorn hope', they instructed the Joint Planning Staff to prepare an outline as soon as possible.[59] The conclusion reported by the Joint Planners on the 29th was that beaches undefended by coast-defence guns existed only on the north shore of the Peninsula east of Kambéréné, and on the south shore east of Rufisque, and that landings on these beaches were possible only in ideal weather conditions. Such conditions were rare. 'It thus appears to us that it is not reasonable to despatch a force 4,000 miles with the full knowledge that its only chance of success rests on climatic conditions which, in the words of the beach report, "are subject to Atlantic swell to such an extent that a single calm day cannot be

[56] JP (40) 579 (E), 'Capture of Dakar', CAB 84/21.
[57] JP (40) 583, 'Operations in West Africa', 27 Oct., CAB 84/21. The Ds of P at this date were Captain C. S. Daniel (Admiralty), Air Commodore C. E. H. Medhurst (Air Ministry), and Colonel K. G. McLean (War Office).
[58] Litchfield diary, 27 Oct.
[59] COS (40) 18th Meeting (O), 27 Oct., CAB 79/55, JP (40) 587 (E), 'Operations in West Africa', 27 Oct., CAB 84/21.

relied upon". The success of such a venture must also depend upon surprise, which, after Operation "Menace" we think is most unlikely to be achieved.'[60] In a meeting that afternoon the Chiefs of Staff 'reluctantly agreed' with these conclusions.[61] The 'reluctance' may have been to save appearances, since the Service Chiefs were very much opposed to a continuing diversion of effort when they were so hard pressed in the Middle East.

That same evening the Prime Minister chaired a two-hour meeting of the Directors of Plans at 'the Barn', parts of a deep underground tube station (what is now Green Park station on the Piccadilly Line) that he occasionally used as an alternative head-quarters. Captain Daniel gave the Prime Minister a full account of the JP examination of the Dakar problem, and stated that their conclusion was that the capture of Dakar, 'except possibly as part of a major campaign in Africa, was not at present a practicable Military proposition'. Churchill then spoke. The chief problem they were up against, he emphasized, was that of getting tanks ashore in a heavy swell. (See above, pp. 171–2.) There were no facilities whatever for doing this at the time. The flavour of Churchill's remarks is better captured in Captain Litchfield's diary (29 October) than in the dry official minutes. 'Long tirade about Dakar—inability of B. Empire to capture, etc.—lack of imagination in Services before war—no plans—no special material, etc. But he was nice withal—just wanted them to see his pt. of view. . . . P.M. agreed [Dakar] not militarily practicable with present resources & technical material. Instructed Ds of P. [actually, the D of P, Admiralty] to harness "best engineering brains in country" onto problem of finding way of landing tanks on beach in 10 ft. of water.'[62]

Churchill was like a dog with a bone, but he seldom, if ever, actually overruled the Chiefs of Staff, though he sometimes wore them down by argument. In this instance, he had in the end given way and accepted the views of the Service Chiefs and the planners. Some time not long after Churchill had finally been persuaded to give up his cherished plans for a 'Second Dakar', he invited the three Directors of Plans to dine and sleep a night at Chequers.

The dinner was massive and everyone enjoyed it. Then, over the brandy and port, Winston grew serious. 'I have sent for you officers,' he

[60] JP (40) 593, 'Capture of Dakar', CAB 84/21.
[61] COS (40) 365th Meeting, CAB 79/7.
[62] The minutes of the meeting are in JP (40) 119th Meeting, CAB 84/2.

said, 'because I well know that you were responsible for the opposition to my views on Dakar. I have accepted your advice. But I want you to know why I was so unwilling to do so. You must understand that I am the Prime Minister of Britain, and you have been telling me that Britain is not capable of capturing a second-rate French colonial port with all the great forces we now have at our command. This is not a situation I can willingly accept; and this is why I refused to accept it for so long. I am fully aware of how much trouble and vexation I have caused you. I regard you as Masters of Negation!'[63]

It is usually said that Churchill's political aims tended to cloud his military judgement and that his interventions, though often beneficial, could be disastrous, as in the case of Dakar. It would be foolish to deny that he was the enthusiastic chief sponsor of 'Menace'. It was his pet scheme, his boundless drive and energy had breathed life into it, and he contributed importantly to shaping its strategy. In the process he often disregarded what Sir John Slessor calls 'the squalid realities such as forces available, the probable reactions of the enemy and other practical considerations'. The operation was undertaken on Churchill's insistence against all professional advice. The Directors of Plans were dead against the operation, the Chiefs of Staff were at best lukewarm, and the Admiralty had never had their hearts in it. But this is not to say that Churchill ran the operation once the decision had been made to proceed with 'Menace'. The Chiefs of Staff had the last word on strategy, and the Commanders were given a free hand; if anything, he leaned over backwards to ensure that the professionals would have the last word. The one exception lies in his insistence on an earlier date for the operation. Captain Litchfield, in a diary entry of 26 September, got it exactly right: 'In Map Room with P.M. at 7.30 this morning. The old man looks a bit shaken by DAKAR, which was very much his pet scheme and, like the Dardanelles, has proved a costly fiasco. Not that he has actually overridden professional advice: but rather that he has been the driving force behind the operation, & his the conception.' And a bold conception it was, reminiscent of his Dardanelles strategy in 1915. Like

[63] Captain Litchfield's account of the 'beano' at Chequers, which was told to him by Admiral Daniel immediately afterwards. Daniel 'evidently felt rather emotionally about it'. Litchfield cannot vouch for the words but only for the sense. Admiral Daniel has written to the author (29 July 1973) that the ideas of the JP 'didn't go with much of a swing. It led to some heavy pushing—but we stuck to our views, and were never very popular again.'

it, it failed, so far as the operation proper is concerned through no fault of his.

The fiasco left Vichy in undisputed control of French West Africa. The one success that could be claimed for Admiral Cunningham's ships is that they turned back the four cruisers that had hoped to reinforce the authority of Vichy in the French Equatorial colonies, and de Gaulle was able to consolidate his authority throughout French Equatorial Africa. The decision to risk so many valuable ships on this enterprise at a time when they were so urgently needed elsewhere indicates the importance that the War Cabinet, the Prime Minister in particular, attached to Dakar. In German hands it would have been of the utmost value to the U-boat campaign and the surface raiders. Yet Hitler never seriously contemplated seizing the base, although this step was advocated by Admiral Raeder. In the hands of Frenchmen loyal to the Vichy Government, Dakar played no appreciable part in the war. Had 'Menace' succeeded, it would have provided the Allies with a most useful staging point and a much needed additional base for convoy protection and general naval and air operations. But Dakar remained firmly under the control of Vichy, where it was as safe from German intrusion as it proved to be from British, up to the time of the Allied landings in North Africa in November 1942, when the port with its garrison and ships joined the Allied cause.

Was 'Menace', therefore, necessary? Strictly speaking, *no*. But if, as in the case of Oran, we view the matter in its *contemporary context*, there was ample justification for the operation. There were solid grounds for the belief that the Germans contemplated the seizure, or at least the effective control, of Dakar. And nothing in the performance of the Vichy Government since the Armistice gave the British reason to expect that Vichy would, or could, keep the Germans at bay. Quite apart from German designs on Dakar, we have to remember the important strategical advantages to the British if they had use of that base. In addition, they would have secured the gold[64] and valuable raw material, prestige, and an access of strength to the Free French movement which might have brought North Africa in. It can, on the other hand, be argued that these gains would have been largely offset by the Germans. They had made it clear to the French delegation at Wiesbaden that, if

[64] See above, p. 7. The German Government pressured Vichy into bringing the gold back to France between December 1940 and May 1942; the Reichsbank took it over for 'safekeeping'.

de Gaulle had been installed in Dakar, they would have invaded North Africa almost immediately. And, asks Mordal, 'Who could possibly have prevented them from doing so? What turn would the battle of the Mediterranean, the defence of Malta, of Suez, and the Allied landings of 1942 have then taken?' Finally, there was an unexpected and lucky plus in the utter failure of the operation. Vichy's spirited resistance at Mers-el-Kébir in July and successful defence of Dakar in September convinced the Germans that they could trust the French to defend Dakar and the rest of the colonial empire against the British. There was no need for the Germans to occupy Morocco and French West Africa, and they could safely allow the French to maintain their sizeable colonial army and to strengthen their air force, which were eventually to be turned against the Germans in Tunisia and Italy—and in France herself in the final battles.

* * *

Commander Crease remembers Admiral Cunningham remarking during 'Menace' that the Prime Minister and the Admiralty were determined to have someone at Gibraltar's 'balls for a necktie'. Churchill's remarks in the Commons on 8 October concerning the passage of the French ships through the Straits appeared to bear out that prognosis—that the Prime Minister was attempting to shuffle the bad business off on other shoulders, though he alone was widely believed to be responsible. This brings us to the highly controversial story of Admiral Sir Dudley North. We last met him on 11 September, when he had allowed Force Y to pass through the Straits of Gibraltar, certain that he had acted 'in accordance with Admiralty wishes'. He was soon to be rudely disabused of this conviction, at the same time experiencing a trauma from which he was never to recover.

Part Two

The Story of Dudley North:

WAS JUSTICE DONE?

Admiral Sir Dudley B. N. North, who died yesterday at the age of 79, is best remembered as the officer whose treatment in the Second World War provided a close parallel to that meted out to the unfortunate Admiral Byng in the eighteenth century. Both were made the scapegoats for disasters which resulted from mismanagement in London.

Obituary, *The Times*, 16 May 1961

It ought to make an interesting study for students of Naval History in the future & perhaps I had better be content with my memorial taking the form of the young Naval officers of future Staff Courses saying 'What a damned shame'.

Admiral Sir Dudley North to Rear-Admiral Lord Mountbatten of Burma, 11 November 1947

Chapter Ten

Genesis of the Affair

Their Lordships in their letter [15 October 1940] state that I have forfeited their confidence owing to my failure 'in an emergency to take all prudent precautions, without waiting for Admiralty instructions.' This, in effect, accuses me of a default, whereas, I submit, at the most I can only be charged with an error in judgment.

Admiral Sir Dudley North to the Admiralty,
27 October 1940

. . . had they [the French ships] proceeded to the northward Admiral North would have been in no position to intercept them owing to his failure to order *Renown* to proceed to sea. I should call this failure 'Omission to perform one's duty' rather than 'Error of Judgment'.

Admiral of the Fleet Sir Dudley Pound, minute,
12 November 1940

I can recall no situation during the war when I had so little doubt that we were doing the right thing. We may be blamed for not requesting instructions, but I personally never do this unless I am in doubt as to what action I should take. In this case I had no doubt at all, and as my views were shared by both you and the Governor, I felt that we were acting in accordance with the wishes of the Government in allowing these ships to pass.

Admiral of the Fleet Sir James Somerville,
shortly before his death in 1949, in a
letter to Admiral Sir Dudley North

(1) North's Removal

IN the official history of the Royal Navy in World War II Captain Roskill writes that 'there is evidence that Ministers had lost confidence in the Admiralty's representative at Gibraltar after the attack on the French Fleet in Oran in the previous July, and this may have affected the later decision to relieve him'.[1] Roskill was unable, for certain practical reasons,[2] to specify the evidence when

[1] *History of the Second World War. The War at Sea* (3 vols. in 4, London, 1954–61), i. 314.

[2] See Duff Hart-Davis, 'Navy's "filthy job" at last cleared up', *Sunday Telegraph*, 9 Dec. 1973.

he wrote, but we know that it was North's message to the Admiralty on 4 July, the day after the Oran operation, and the Admiralty's reaction to it. North had spelled out the views which prevailed at Gibraltar before the operation, explaining how repugnant the use of force against the French had been to himself, Somerville, Vice-Admiral Wells, and the Captains and staff officers concerned. The First Sea Lord, Pound, and even more so the First Lord, Alexander, were infuriated. The Admiralty reply (17 July) was a strongly worded 'bottle' (reprimand). The contents of North's letter showed a 'most dangerous lack of appreciation of the manner in which it is intended to conduct the war', and surprise was expressed that 'comment of the kind received should be made'. Alexander went so far as to propose (15 July) that North be superseded as FOCNA. 'I feel at the critical stage we have reached in our national affairs, it is of the highest importance that I may be able to rely on the Board of Admiralty's orders when finally given very firmly carried out without question.' Pound did not think there was a strong enough case for supersession.[3]

One may speculate that North's letter was intended, as Marshal of the Royal Air Force Sir John Slessor has suggested, 'to stimulate at least more careful consideration in Whitehall before the repetition of anything like [Operation] "Catapult".' And Authority may have over-reacted. Nonetheless, the letter was not the height of wisdom or tact. Admiral of the Fleet Lord Chatfield afterwards called the letter 'stupid. He could have sent a personal one to the First Sea Lord.' It seriously damaged the Admiralty's confidence in North's judgement and outlook. Alexander went so far as to say many years later: 'His principal fault was in connection with Oran. He would probably have been recalled then but for the plea by Sir Dudley Pound that he should be given a further chance.'[4]

[3] On the whole incident see *From the Dardanelles to Oran*, pp. 269–70. The documents are in ADM 1/19177, 19178. See also ADM 205/11.

[4] Lord Alexander of Hillsborough (as he then was) to Harold Macmillan, 27 May 1957, Alexander MSS., AVAR 5/17/14. The First Lord was still smarting over the letter when North came to see him in January 1941. He ought never to have written such a letter, he was told—that it was not his business to decide who were the King's enemies. In another version, to the Secretary of the Admiralty (9 Aug. 1953): 'Admiral North was wrong about Oran. It was the decision of the Prime Minister, myself & the Defence Committee to get the French to sail their Fleet or to destroy it that marked the turning point in mid 1940. The world began to understand we meant business. In June 1940 Maisky [the Soviet Ambassador] came to see me twice & both times asked "How long can you possibly hold out?" He never asked that question again! It was the kind of case where the decision of the Executive was imperative, & one which must be immediately accepted & operated by the Crown's servants.' AVAR 5/16/9(a).

Even before North's letter, however, there were misgivings at the Admiralty over his ability to do the job at Gibraltar with the added importance that the Western basin of the Mediterranean was assuming after Italy's entrance into the war on 10 June. North was a sound, universally popular, but in no way brilliant officer. During the 1914–18 War he served as a lieutenant, then commander, in the battle cruiser *New Zealand* up to December 1916, taking part in the three principal North Sea actions of the Heligoland Bight, the Dogger Bank, and Jutland. He was promoted to captain in 1919. He had done well in first-class appointments (1926–34), as Flag-Captain of the battleship *Revenge*, Atlantic Fleet flagship, Flag-Captain and Chief of Staff in the Reserve Fleet, Director of the Operations Division, Naval Staff, and, his first flag appointment, Chief of Staff to Admiral Sir John Kelly, C-in-C, Home Fleet. Yet North was widely regarded in the Service as the epitome of the courtier sailor (of whom, incidentally, he was the last, in that the monarch still retained sufficient influence to further the careers of his favourite officers), because he had served in the battle cruiser *Renown* in the Prince of Wales's world tours of 1920–2, as the Senior Equerry to H.R.H., and again in the battle cruiser *Repulse* in the 1925 tour, and had been Rear-Admiral Commanding H.M. Yachts at Portsmouth (1934-9). His stocky, robust figure was covered with 'gongs'; he gave some the impression of being a bit of a snob. Reckoning that North had been too long in the Royal Yachts, Pound had no intention of sending him to sea after the war broke out. But he had to find an appointment for him, especially in view of the King's interest. Flag Officer Commanding the North Atlantic Station (FOCNA, or alternatively, ACNA, Admiral Commanding North Atlantic Station), and Admiral Superintendent, Gibraltar, really a shore appointment at Gibraltar, was, Pound considered, well within North's ability at a time when the station had not assumed its later crucial importance, and there the 59-year-old North had gone in November 1939. He was promoted to Admiral in May 1940. The Principal Private Secretary to the First Lord remembers that 'in the top levels of the Naval Staff there had grown up a strong feeling, which the First Lord shared, that North was not the man for a key post in those desperate times. In other circumstances he might well have been perfectly adequate and I dare say it can be more or less proved that he did nothing wrong. I have, however, a distinct recollection that people at the top in the Admiralty were becoming fed up, to use a colloquialism, with the readiness with which he appeared to find reasons for inaction or delay.'⁵

By themselves, the post-Oran message and the general feeling that North was perhaps not the best man for the Gibraltar command would not have led to his supersession. It needed a catalyst, and this was provided by the French squadron. Pound's Secretary has emphasized 'how fortunate North was to retain his appointment after the letter he wrote to the Board criticising the Oran operation. Dudley [Pound] was hopping mad about it. When North did nothing about the passage of the French warships through the Straits there was no question in Dudley's mind whether he should remain.'⁶

*   *   *

On 24 September 1940 Admiral Sir James Somerville wrote to his wife: 'These blasted French adventures fill me with the deepest gloom. They're always too precipitate. . . . one of the BBC bulletins said that the failure of de Gaulle to be received at Dakar was due to the arrival of six French warships. I suppose they'll try & put the blame on me if Dakar is a blob as it looks like being at present.' On the 27th: 'Well I suppose they'll try & find a scapegoat & from certain signals asking me where I was at certain times it looks rather as if they might be on my track.'⁷ Their Lordships were also on the track of Admiral North.

On 27 September North received an Immediate telegram from the Admiralty asking when he had received the Naval Attaché, Madrid's telegram regarding the passage of the French warships, and what action, if any, he had taken on it. North replied on the same day that he had received the signal at 12.08 a.m., 11 September, and had passed it to the forces at sea at 2.15 a.m.; *Hotspur*'s sighting report had been received at 5.12 a.m. and passed to the Admiralty in an Immediate signal at 6.17 a.m.; the patrolling ships were ordered to take no action beyond reporting; and the French ships passed Europa Point in the Straits at 8.30 [8.45] a.m. and were shadowed

---

⁵ Sir Clifford Jarrett's letter to the author, 9 Sept. 1973. In 1950, when he was Naval Assistant to the First Sea Lord (Fraser), Vice-Admiral Sir Peter Gretton was detailed to carry out an examination of the records of the North Affair, with reference to Pound's alleged loss of confidence in North. 'I got the firm impression that Pound lost confidence in North quite early on in his time at Gibraltar and thought that he was not imbued enough with the offensive spirit.' Admiral Gretton's letter to the author, 29 Sept. 1973. See further, addendum on p. 225, below.

⁶ Vice-Admiral Sir Ronald Brockman's letter to the author, 28 Sept. 1973. See above, pp. 69–77, for the events of 11 September 1940 and their background.

⁷ Somerville MSS., SMVL 3/22.

by aircraft until their arrival at Casablanca.[8] In the late morning of 2 October, as Admiral North was sipping his morning tea, perfectly relaxed and at peace with the world, he was handed an Admiralty telegram of 2.33 a.m. which revealed that the hunt was really on. (But 'so clear was my conscience,' North wrote later, 'that I was not in the least worried by these enquiries.') 'Admiralty message 0241/12th July paragraph (c) made it clear that we should take action against French warships proceeding to enemy controlled ports. . . . A report in writing is to be forwarded as to why no action was taken to order H.M.S. *Renown* to sea on receipt of either Naval Attaché's 1809/10th September or H.M.S. *Hotspur*'s reporting signal in case these ships proceeded northward.'

North's reply of 6 October must be reproduced in full, since it triggered the decision to recall him. It will facilitate an understanding of the respective cases if I juxtapose North's arguments and the pertinent sections of the First Sea Lord's minute of 8 October, which criticized North's letter seriatim.

His job was to stop them if they did go North.

Be pleased to lay before Their Lordships this report, which is forwarded in compliance with Admiralty message 0233 of 2nd October, 1940.

2. The reason why no action was taken on this occasion was because my Intelligence did not lead me to believe that these ships could be going to Northern ports. On the contrary, it pointed the other way, and as I knew Their Lordships had at least as much information as I had, and probably more, concerning our relations with the Vichy Government, I had

---

[8] Some time afterwards North wrote of his reply: 'Looking back on it now, it might have been better if I had added that Force H had been brought to one hour's notice for steam in case the Admiralty decided to exercise the right reserved [in its 12 July signal, on which see below] to take action against French ships. . . . Actually I paid scant attention to the enquiry. I had little time for anything except the conduct of affairs in my command.' North, 'Circumstances attending my removal from my command,' n.d. (late 1943 or early 1944?), Part I of a lengthy paper entitled 'Gibraltar', Somerville MSS., SMVL 7/25. Part II consists of most of the relevant 'Signals and Correspondence' of July–December 1940, and Part III is a 'Commentary' on Parts I and II. A somewhat different version of the 'Commentary' is to be found in the North MSS., NRTH 1/4. My quotations from the 'Commentary' are from the version in the Somerville MSS., with an exception or two which will be noted. All the North, Somerville, and Admiralty signals and correspondence through 1940, and including the Admiralty minutes, will be found in ADM 1/19180–19187. Somerville's reports and correspondence are also in SMVL 7/4, 26. Only a few of the more significant documents will be given a precise reference.

every confidence that Their Lordships would have informed me if they considered that they might be going North, and would have instructed me to exercise the right reserved in paragraph (c) of Admiralty message 0241 of 12th July, 1940.

3. Since receiving Admiralty message 0241 of 12th July, 1940, I had received no information which led me to think that relations with the Vichy Government had changed for the worse. I had reason to believe from my local Intelligence that the attitude of the French Navy was becoming less hostile, and this was confirmed when I received Naval Attaché, Madrid's 1842 of 5th September, to the Director of Naval Intelligence. This reported a distinct improvement in the attitude of the French Navy, and indicated that Admiral Darlan himself desired contact to be maintained with the British Naval Attaché at Madrid. On receiving Naval Attaché, Madrid's 1809 of 10th September, it appeared to me that this improvement in attitude was bearing fruit and that some of the Naval forces in Toulon intended to break away to French Colonial ports. This opinion was strengthened by the following facts:

This was no guarantee that they were not going North. N.A. Madrid's 1809/10 said 'Destination not known'.

(a) Formal notice had been given of the time of their passage through the Straits.

(b) That they made no attempt at concealment, and burnt all lights at night.

(c) That they reported their names at once when asked.

A.T. 1724/28 said a 'detached squadron'— there was nothing about it being an independent command as stated by FOCNA. Because movements of Force H have generally been ordered by the Admiralty there is no reason why FOCNA should not take action in [an] emergency.

4. As regards the actual ordering of H.M.S. RENOWN to sea, Admiralty messages 1724 and 1738, both of 28th June, 1940, make it clear that Force 'H' constitutes a detached squadron under the independent command of Vice Admiral Sir James Somerville, charged with certain special duties to be carried out subject to any instructions which might be given by the Admiralty. H.M.S. RENOWN's movements have, therefore, always been ordered by the

Admiralty or by the Flag Officer Commanding, Force 'H', and in no instance by me.

Here he contradicts his argument at C [para. 4] and says that under certain circumstances he would have ordered *Renown* to sea. All this argument about 'independent command' therefore falls to the ground. *I can't condone the attitude of an officer who takes the line that because there has been time for the Admiralty to give orders and they have not done so therefore he does nothing.*

At the same time, in any emergency of which the Admiralty had no previous knowledge, I should not have hesitated to order H.M.S. RENOWN to sea, had it been desirable, but this cannot be considered as being the case on this occasion as presumably Naval Attaché, Madrid's 1809 of 10th September was passed to the Admiralty direct and so I considered that there had been time for Their Lordships to order whatever action, if any, they might consider necessary. Actually, Flag Officer Commanding, Force 'H', brought his ships to one hour's notice, and awaited instructions from Their Lordships as to action to be taken.

The aerial reconnaissance need not have stopped them going North.

5. I arranged for aerial reconnaissance, as reported in my 0711 of 11th September, 1940. This confirmed that the ships were not proceeding to the North.

6. If Their Lordships consider that I should have ordered H.M.S. RENOWN to sea, I regret that I did not do so, but I submit that, with the information at my disposal, there was no reason for me to take such action.[9]

North showed Somerville the Admiralty letter of 2 October and his reply when the *Renown* came back to Gibraltar on 7 October. Somerville was surprised that it was North, not himself, who was cast as the scapegoat, and he was 'furious', because ordering Force H to sea when the French squadron passed through the Straits was *his* responsibility. Always fearless in speaking his mine to higher authority, a 'damned angry' Somerville wrote to thd Admiralty that day, backing North and accepting full responsibility for not proceeding to sea.

Rightly or wrongly, we were both of the opinion that, in view of what appeared to be the ample warning Their Lordships had received of the intended movement and notification of the presence of these vessels approaching the Straits, it was not desired to interfere with this movement or to provoke any sort of incident.

If, however, the action taken is considered to have been incorrect, I wish to accept full responsibility, since at the time in question I acted in

[9] ADM 1/19180.

the full belief that responsibility for any action to be taken by Force H rested with me.

On 25 October a personal letter dated 15 October arrived from the Admiralty in reply to Somerville's 7 October. It exonerated him on the grounds that, as he had not received the Madrid signal until 8 a.m. on 11 September, he had been unable to take action on it in time to intercept the French ships, whereas North had received the signal at 12.08 a.m. and had taken no action at all, 'though it was his duty as Senior Officer to see that the necessary action was being taken'. They noted that Somerville had taken action on receipt of *Hotspur*'s signal at about 5.12 a.m. to bring the *Renown* to short notice for sea. The reply did nothing to mollify Somerville, who was by now 'absolutely furious'. He protested to the Admiralty (25 October): 'I note . . . that I am exonerated on the grounds that I did not receive sufficient warning of the impending movement to take action in time to intercept the ships in question. I wish to be quite frank about this matter and to state that even if I had received sufficient notice to enable *Renown* and the one or two destroyers available to proceed to sea, I should have refrained from doing so for the reasons set forth in my Report of Proceedings, No. 60/8 of 17th September, 1940.'[10] He received a curt acknowledgement on 31 October.

On the same day that Somerville had learned of his exoneration (25 October) the Admiralty reply to North's 6 October, dated 15 October and marked 'secret and personal', was delivered at The Mount, North's beautiful official residence on the Rock, by the 'safe hand' of a young Flight Lieutenant. Again, the importance of this document requires that it be reproduced. But first I must sketch the Admiralty's reaction to North's message.

The First Sea Lord's counter-arguments have been reproduced above. The same minute went on:

---

[10] The more important reasons given there were, first, that he had considered Casablanca as the probable destination of the French ships, and 'it was not the policy of H.M. Government to interfere with the movements of French warships to French controlled ports'. Also, he had assumed that the Admiralty were fully aware of this movement of the French ships and would therefore have sent him any instructions, had any intercepting action been required of him. In the same report Somerville said that he had 'considered proceeding to sea to the Westward in *Renown* but decided that, owing to the lack of destroyer escort, this was inadvisable; further, it seemed unlikely that *Renown* could make sufficient ground to the West to avoid being sighted by the French Force.' 'Report of Proceedings of Force "H" for the Period 11th September, 1940, to 14th September, 1940,' Somerville MSS., SMVL 7/4.

The general tenour of this letter gives one a most unfavourable impression as it depends on [an] attitude of mind that is always waiting for orders instead of wishing to take the initiative and forestall any orders from the Admiralty. What he ought to have done was to order *Renown* to sea and at the same time inform the Admiralty what he had done. If the Admiralty did not like what he had done they could recall him. Under the circumstances Admiral North no longer retains my confidence. Flag officers are of no value if they do not possess initiative and accept responsibility.

There are two alternatives.

(*a*) To relieve Admiral North in due course.

(*b*) To order him to haul his Flag down and proceed home at the first suitable opportunity.

I am in favour of (*b*) . . .

The First Lord 'entirely concurred' in Pound's comments and approved his (b) recommendation. In the end, however, the First Sea Lord deemed it wiser to relieve North rather than to order him to haul down his flag. In the discussion on what to include in the letter to North, the Secretary of the Admiralty, Sir Archibald Carter, 'much preferred' that it limit itself to saying that 'it should, in Their Lordships' opinion, have been plain to you that this was an occasion demanding every precaution, whether instructions had been sent from the Admiralty or not.' He reasoned that 'this would provide the minimum of surface for purposes of future controversy'. Alexander went a step further. He had no objection to informing North simply that Their Lordships were not satisfied with his explanation and instructing him to haul down his flag. But Pound wanted the Admiralty case to be stated, and this was what was decided upon.[11] And therein lay the seed of all the subsequent controversy. The text of the Admiralty's 15 October, which was largely Pound's phraseology, follows:

Their Lordships have received and considered your letter, X.224/465 of the 6th October, in which you have stated your reasons for omitting to order H.M.S. RENOWN to sea when you received the Naval Attaché, Madrid's message 1809/10 September that French Cruisers had left Toulon and would pass through the Straits or when you received H.M.S. HOTSPUR'S signal reporting them.

The message from the Naval Attaché, Madrid, had stated that the destination of these ships was not known. It could not be certain that they were not proceeding North and it was necessary to stop them if they did. Later aerial reconnaissance which showed that they were not proceeding

[11] Minutes of 9–14 Oct., ADM 1/19180.

to the North would not have prevented their doing so. That Force H was a detached squadron (Admiralty Message 1724/28 June) and that the movements of the force had in general been ordered by the Admiralty does not affect the issue.

The Naval Attaché's signal was received by Gibraltar at 0008, 11th September, but was only received by Senior Officer Force H at 0800/11th September.

HOTSPUR'S report of the approach of the French ships was received at 0512/11th September, and it was presumably on this information that Senior Officer, Force H at 0530/11th September ordered RENOWN to come to one hour's notice for steam.

Senior Officer, Force H in his report states that he considers the responsibility for intercepting these ships was his, but however much this may be the case the fact remains that the earliest information he received of the passage of these ships was at about 0512; which left insufficient time for RENOWN to proceed to sea and intercept them.

Their Lordships are of opinion that on receipt of the Naval Attaché's signal at 0008, it was your duty to ensure that action was taken which would enable these ships to be intercepted, either on receipt of instructions from the Admiralty or without such instructions if the situation developed in such a manner as to need it.

Their Lordships cannot retain full confidence in an officer who fails in an emergency to take all prudent precautions without waiting for Admiralty instructions. They have accordingly decided that you should be relieved of your present command at the first convenient opportunity.[12]

The Admiralty never added to, or elaborated on, this letter—not for Admiral North's consumption, that is.

Churchill's statement in the Commons on 8 October (above, p. 185) had been the first indication to North that an attempt might be made to fix the blame for the Dakar fiasco on him. But now the axe had fallen. North was 'astonished at this amazing decision', as were all his staff officers and senior officers in his command, as well as Somerville, Sir Samuel Hoare, and the Governor of Gibraltar, Sir Clive Liddell. None of them could understand the reasons for the Admiralty's decision, unless it was a case of Authority, meaning Churchill in particular, trying to pass the blame for Dakar to North. Somerville, to whom North had telephoned the news of his dismissal, hustled over to The Mount. 'Something stinks here, Dudley. . . . They are blaming you for what happened at Dakar.' Liddell off his own bat sent a strongly worded telegram to the CIGS (28 October): he could not 'conceive how by any

[12] ADM 1/19180.

stretch of imagination he can be convicted of failure to take prudent precautions. The impression created here is that the Dakar operation was planned on inaccurate information ending in a fiasco and that the Home authorities are endeavouring to pass the blame on to a local commander in no way responsible for that failure.' North's removal would 'create a distrust and want of confidence in the conduct of the war which must affect adversely the morale of this fortress'.

North did not propose to roll over and play dead. He at once signalled the Admiralty, protesting at his relief from his command 'for an alleged failure to perform my duty', and asking them to suspend action on him until he had an opportunity to reply to certain statements in their letter. This was granted. The thrust of his letter of 27 October (Somerville had helped to draft it) was that his orders at the time were to avoid incidents with the French, and therefore he had expected that, had the Admiralty decided to change their policy (message of 12 July, which stressed the undesirability of maintaining the tension between the two navies) by denying the passage of the Straits to French warships, they would have informed him. The Admiralty refused to reopen the question. They acknowledged his letter (31 October), in which he had stated his 'further reasons for omitting to order H.M.S. *Renown* to sea,' but said there was nothing in the letter which would cause them to modify the opinion expressed in theirs 15 October. Back came North with a stinger (7 November). He took umbrage over the word 'omitting'. There was no question about his omitting to perform his duty, since

I did carefully consider the whole question and came to the definite decision that it was not desirable to send the force to sea.

This decision was based upon what I had every reason to believe was the intended policy of H.M. Government.

Omission to perform one's duty is a serious charge and in this case I submit it is quite unjustified and not in accordance with fact and I therefore ask that it should be withdrawn and a more appropriate reason be substituted for relieving me of my command.

The First Sea Lord minuted (12 November) that any alteration of wording at that stage 'might be construed as a sign of weakness in the Admiralty case. Moreover, as I see it, the situation is quite clear.' And that was that. The Admiralty reply to North (14 November) regretted their inability to alter the opinion expressed in their letter of 31 October.

On 21 November North submitted that he 'be given an opportunity in due course to vindicate myself before whatever Board or
Tribunal Their Lordships may see fit to appoint.' When he heard
that Admiral of the Fleet the Earl of Cork and Orrery, accompanied
by Vice-Admiral D'Oyly Lyon, was to arrive in Gibraltar to conduct
an inquiry into Somerville's conduct in a recent action against the
Italian Fleet, he signalled the Admiralty (2 December) requesting
that the inquiry he had asked for be held after the Somerville
inquiry, 'as a sufficiently senior officer and local witnesses will be
available.' Again a curt no from Whitehall (4 December): 'After
fullest consideration Their Lordships reached a decision in your
case and informed you accordingly and re-affirmed that decision after
an appeal from you. In these circumstances, no object is seen in
reopening the question . . .'

North formally renewed his request on 8 December, 'unless a
grave miscarriage of justice is to be perpetrated.' The attached
memorandum reviewed the events of 11 September and their
immediate background, and the correspondence between him and
the Admiralty from the end of September, and concluded with an
eloquent summing up:

I submit that any impartial survey of all the circumstances attending
this incident must inevitably lead to the conclusion that had the departure
of these ships from the Mediterranean been regarded as a matter of prime
importance there was ample time in which special instructions could have
been issued to deal with the matter.

It must also appear obvious to any reasonable person that when it was
subsequently appreciated that the arrival of these ships at Dakar had or
might have exercised an adverse effect on the intended operation there,
blame was laid on me, strangely enough, not for failing to stop the ships
from proceeding to the South, but for not having taken steps to prevent
them from proceeding to the North.

The fact of my being relieved must inevitably arouse considerable
comment and it may well be thought that blame is attributable to me for
the failure at Dakar and that I am the officer against whom disciplinary
action has been taken as mentioned by the Prime Minister. I feel therefore that it is in the public interest that the true facts should be brought
to light.

I consider that an impartial tribunal could not fail to establish the fact
that my action on this occasion could by no stretch of the imagination
have affected the outcome of what has been universally described as an
ill-judged adventure.

It was for this reason that I asked for an enquiry into this incident.

This request has been refused. I find myself in the position of a Flag Officer who, whilst endeavouring to serve the interests of his country to the best of his ability, and to put into force what he conceived, and what a brother Flag Officer conceived to be the policy of H.M. Government, is now discredited, owing to an alleged failure to implement an ambiguous instruction, which had no connection with the issue involved.[13]

Again the Admiralty saw no reason to review their decision, since North had, in their belief, presented no new facts or interpretations,[14] and they so informed him (24 December). Vice-Admiral Sir Frederick Edward-Collins was appointed to relieve North. Ironically, he was an indifferent flag officer, who owed his advancement to Pound, with whom he had served five times, including being Pound's rather ineffective COS in the Mediterranean, 1936–8. He went up in Pound's train and did the latter's reputation no good.

On 31 December North hauled down his flag at Gibraltar and almost at once asked for an inquiry. It was without result. Four days later he sailed for home. Soon after his return, in mid-January, he had most unsatisfactory interviews with the First Sea Lord and the First Lord. Pound had known North for years, yet, according to North's account of their brief meeting, he was unsympathetic, impatient, even rude. He was 'furiously angry' and 'very contemptuous in his manner'. He accused North of having waited weakly for orders instead of acting on his own initiative and ordering the *Renown* to be in a position to intercept the French Force, and he brushed aside North's attempt to explain the situation as he had viewed it. Pound concluded with the 'insulting remark', 'You and the Governor of Gibraltar filled your heads with all sorts of silly ideas about the French,' and by saying that he had recommended to the First Lord that a court martial or inquiry not be granted. North, who had held his temper in check throughout (a charge of insubordination would have utterly destroyed what chances might still exist for his further employment), charitably attributed Pound's attitude to poor health. He was in 'a very exhausted and nervous condition, with an utterly washed-out appearance, his eyes looking like dark holes in his white face.' (Afterwards, however, unable to contain himself, he inveighed against the First Sea Lord to his friends, adding, 'His name isn't even Dudley!' It was, to be sure, not his first Christian name!)

[13] 'Passage of Three French Cruisers and Three French Destroyers from Toulon through the Straits of Gibraltar on 11th September 1940,' ADM 1/19187.

[14] Except for the intimation that he was being made a scapegoat for Dakar. 'Dignity and prudence alike suggest that this should be ignored,' minuted the new Secretary of the Admiralty, H. V. Markham. And it was ignored in the reply.

North's interview with Alexander, which followed immediately, went better, in that the First Lord was affable and apparently sympathetic. But the result was nil. He turned all North's complaints down by saying that it was all a naval matter, and he was not competent to give a judgement on it, and he told the Admiral what he already knew—that Pound had advised him not to grant an inquiry or a court martial. North's impression of his interviews was that 'these two men did not wish to be reminded of this unfortunate incident [Dakar]. I had been disgraced, and the nation had accepted the fact that the failure at Dakar was all my fault, and there was I coming along and wanting to raise the whole matter again, just as if there wasn't a war on.'[15]

Soon after the interviews, on 20 January 1941, North wrote to the Admiralty, rebutting the charges made by the First Sea Lord, alluding to his 'insulting remark', asserting that it was 'perfectly obvious that because the Admiralty failed it was decided to blame the man on the spot', and concluding: 'My professional reputation unblemished during 46 years of service has been impugned and I have received the severest punishment a flag officer could receive during war time. Either the Admiralty should withdraw their accusation that I failed in my duty, or else I should be permitted to appear before a properly constituted Board of Enquiry to vindicate my action.' The Admiralty reply (28 January) was a cold douche. Having given the case a 'very full and careful consideration', they had no intention of reversing their decision. They took 'strong exception to the tone' of North's letter. North submitted a qualified apology (3 February): 'In view of the fact that I have been accused of a definite offence, adjudged guilty *without trial*, and very heavily punished,—it is hardly surprising when presenting the hard facts of my case on paper, that the phraseology should appear stronger than is customary in official correspondence.'

So much for the narrative of the circumstances attending North's removal. We must now examine more closely the arguments of the two sides and also determine who bore the principal responsibility for the decision to relieve the Admiral. Some repetition of material is unavoidable.

---

[15] North's account is to be found, among other places, in his 'Commentary'. Admiral Brockman was not in the First Sea Lord's room during the first interview, but he remembers the occasion well. 'ISL was hopping mad. North must have been a very vain man if he imagined he was going to be received with sweetness and light. He was tough as old boots and it was certainly characteristic of him that he should deal hardly with an Admiral whom he considered had failed.' Brockman's letter to the author, 3 Nov. 1973.

(2) The Admiralty v. North: the Respective Cases

Vitiating the whole of the exchanges between the Admiralty and North was North's (and Somerville's) assumption that London had all the information (the Tangier and Madrid signals) that had reached Gibraltar and had received it at the same time or sooner. It was not until his interview with the First Sea Lord that North learned that an officer at the Admiralty had received the Madrid message but had not taken action. North drew the logical conclusion: 'Whilst in fact the news of the proposed or actual passage of these ships did not come to the notice of the First Sea Lord until after they had passed, there was no reason why I should have assumed this to be the case . . .'[16] It was not until after the war, in 1947, that North learned the whole story of the blunders connected with the arrival of the Tangier and Madrid signals in London. (See below, p. 231n.) The public did not learn about the serious negligence in Whitehall until the publication of Churchill's *Their Finest Hour* in 1949. The position of the Admiralty, which was not communicated to North, was that the Admiral had no right to assume that they had received the signals.

Moving on to the principal points at issue, did North have any knowledge of Operation 'Menace'? If the answer is no, it would help to explain why Gibraltar was not expecting a French naval move through the Straits to Dakar. Actually, the Admiralty never raised this point, but North's defenders did. Thus, Monks, in *That Day at Gibraltar*, declares (p. 7): 'Somerville and North knew little about "Menace".' Neither the Flag Officer North Atlantic nor anyone else on the Rock had been officially informed of the impending assault on Dakar. 'The Admiral was *not* in the Dakar circle,' says Churchill. Yet he was far from ignorant of 'Menace'. To Admiral Sir Herbert Richmond North wrote (27 October 1945): 'There is one remark in your paper [the Oran/Dakar section in his *Statesmen and Sea Power* (1946)?] which I think it might be better to omit . . . "Nor had he been informed that an expedition to Dakar was about to be undertaken." I knew,—from various facts—but they had not

[16] 'Commentary', North MSS. In discussing the events of 11 September with Captain Hillgarth several years later, North stated 'very definitely that to him the vital point was that the Immediate signal [from Hillgarth] was *addressed to the Admiralty* and only repeated to him. In British naval parlance that meant that the responsibility for any consequent action was that of the addressee and not of any other authority to whom it might have been repeated. On the morning of 11th North and Somerville (who had been acquainted by North) were waiting almost in agony for the orders that did not come.' Captain Hillgarth's letter to the author, 28 Oct. 1973.

troubled to inform me officially.'[17] North and Somerville did know, however indirectly and unofficially (he knew of it 'casually', North once said), what was afoot—that they had large forces at sea bound for Dakar. Therefore, they might reasonably have been expected to be suspicious of an attempt by a French squadron to leave the Mediterranean. This does not excuse the Admiralty for not having taken 'prudent precautions' of their own. It was, after all, likely that, with substantial French naval forces in the Mediterranean, in one way or another North and Somerville would become involved in the consequences of 'Menace', and therefore the Admiralty should have informed North of the impending operation. 'Not having full confidence in North,' observed Lord Chatfield in May 1957, 'it was all the more essential still to keep personal touch.'

Should North have assumed command of Force H, as the Admiralty letter of 15 October implied he should have done? There was a full Admiral at Gibraltar as Flag Officer North Atlantic, and a Vice-Admiral in command of Force H, which had been constituted on 28 June (signal 1724/28). It was defined as a 'detached Squadron', based on Gibraltar, whose tasks, 'subject to any instructions which may be given by the Admiralty', were '(a) To prevent units of the Italian Fleet from breaking out of the Mediterranean. (b) To carry out offensive operations against the Italian Fleet and Italian coasts.' A later signal the same day (1738/28) instructed the SO Force H 'to inform Admiralty in advance of your intentions regarding operations against the Italian coast', and laid down that the 13th Destroyer Flotilla (under North) was to be at Somerville's disposal for any operations where he required more destroyers; when Force H was in harbour, its destroyers were to assist in the patrol of the Straits as required by FOCNA.

These signals left the relative responsibilities of the two Admirals and their relationship anything but clear, particularly with regard to an attempt by French warships to pass through the Straits. Though senior to Somerville, North was never ordered by the Admiralty to take Force H under his command, and both Admirals acted on the assumption that the squadron was under the direct operational control of the Admiralty. And well they might, since operational orders were signalled straight to the Flag Officer Force H.

Captain Roskill describes the chain of command as 'ill-defined' and 'operationally dangerous'. North and Somerville were well

[17] Richmond MSS., RIC 7/4. We have still more positive evidence that Somerville knew about 'Menace' on 11 September. See below, p. 217n.

aware of this, but, as Roskill says, they 'seem to have been satisfied that they could best discharge their responsibilities by working very closely together, and that their precise constitutional positions could well be left unclarified'.[18] The two Admirals were different in important respects. Somerville was clear-sighted, often brilliant, and often unorthodox. His officers and men were singularly devoted to 'Uncle James', even if he sometimes drove them wild with his impatience over slackness of any sort. More to the point, North and he were close friends, who worked together in perfect harmony. They were together every afternoon when it was possible, walking up to the top of the Rock for exercise and to talk things over privately.

To come to the specific point at issue, North contended that Force H was an independent command and that if the Admiralty wished to take any action, they would issue orders directly to him, as they always had done.[19] The Admiralty position was that the detached nature of Force H and the fact that its movements had generally been ordered by them had no bearing on the matter. As the Senior Officer, it was North's duty to take charge in an emergency and use any ships that were available to him. That, said the

[18] *The War at Sea*, i. 310. 'In the light of after events it may seem that Admiral North would have been wise to ask the Admiralty whether Somerville was or was not under his orders. But it is doubtful whether, even had he done so, the Admiralty would have given a clear answer quickly, because when it was later admitted in London that the position of Force H was "not left quite as clear as it might have been", and that "it seems true to say that it was an independent force", the redefinition of its position to the satisfaction of the Admiralty proved difficult.' Ibid., p. 311. The delineation of responsibilities between Flag Officer Force H and FOCNA was not made clear until 30 December 1940, after discussions that extended over nearly three months. The fresh Admiralty statement read: 'F.O.C.N.A. is responsible for preventing passage of the Straits of Gibraltar by all enemy vessels and by vessels of other nations as may be ordered by the Admiralty from time to time. Whilst Force H is based at Gibraltar F.O.C.N.A. is to call upon S.O. Force H for such assistance as may be necessary. . . . S.O. Force H remains responsible for the administration of Force H and for its tactical employment during operations, whether acting under the strategical control of Admiralty or C.-in-C., Mediterranean, or in compliance with the requests of F.O.C.N.A.' ADM 1/19182.

[19] North long afterwards introduced this argument: 'Of course the whole unfortunate incident goes to prove once more that, if you operate a force by wireless from the Admiralty, some of the time, you must continue to operate it so, all the time. You can't control a force from a distance one minute by WT, & the next minute complain because the fellow on the spot hasn't acted.' North in a private letter to Rear-Admiral Lord Mountbatten in India, 11 Nov. 1947. This raises the sticky question of the degree of operational control that should be exercised from Whitehall. In this particular instance, it was only prudent that the Admiralty exercise close operational control over Force H, since Mediterranean operations required the most intricate 'knitting' between the Admiralty, Force H, and the C-in-C, Mediterranean.

Third Sea Lord and Controller, was 'the custom of the Navy'.[20] North had declared in his 6 October message that 'in an emergency of which the Admiralty had no previous knowledge', he would not have hesitated to act. A qualified statement, but it weakened his case, as the First Sea Lord was quick to observe.[21] Elsewhere North admitted his overall responsibility for local events at Gibraltar, and Somerville gave evidence that he did not believe his was a completely independent command answerable only to the Admiralty: 'At 1200 [11 September], taking into consideration all the circumstances, I approved Flag Officer H's request that Force H should revert to 2 hours' notice for steam.'[22]

The Admiralty accused North of having done nothing on receipt of the warning message from Madrid: he neither immediately alerted the ships under his own local command, nor alerted Flag Officer Force H, nor took such steps as to insure that dispositions could be made to intercept the French ships if the Admiralty ordered such action to be taken. He had instead waited for instructions from the Admiralty. North argued (as in his letter of 20 January 1941) that it was not true that he had done nothing. 'Although I was sure that the French force was going South to Casablanca (as it did), *Renown* was at 1 hour's notice from 0545 and could have proceeded to sea at 0700 which allowed ample time to intercept the French ships which did not pass the Straits until 1¾ hours later.[23] There was no need to send *Renown* to sea when she

[20] Admiral of the Fleet Lord Fraser of North Cape, in the House of Lords, 26 July 1954.

[21] North phrased the argument this way in a newspaper interview long afterwards (The *Observer*, 6 June 1954): 'The Admiralty finally decided that I should have sent the Fleet out, which I considered was their show entirely and nothing to do with me at all. If it had been an emergency I would have ordered Admiral Somerville to go out. But if it had been an emergency he would have gone out anyway.'

[22] 'Circumstances attending my removal from my Command.' The Admiralty acknowledged in 1957 that there was 'some unclearness in the Admiralty Directive about Force H and that it was not helped by the Admiralty's practice of issuing direct instructions to Flag Officer, Force H.' But they regarded North's 'approval' (1020/11, above) as 'significant'. 'In any case the Admiralty have always reserved the right to issue orders direct to any of H.M. Ships if they consider they have a better picture of events than the Flag Officer in command. This has never been interpreted by Flag Officers as justifying inaction on their part, especially at times when events are moving rapidly. Present Admiralty opinion is that the Admiralty was right.' The five Admirals of the Fleet who called on the First Lord in May 1953 to press for an inquiry (see below) admitted: 'The decision Admiral North had to make (namely, whether to interfere with the French squadron or not) was one for which he as S.N.O. was responsible . . .' *The Times*, 8 June 1954.

[23] The *Renown* would have required a half hour to leave the mole and another half hour to clear Gibraltar Bay and get into the Straits.

was in a position to intercept whilst remaining in harbour. The sole reason why this force was not intercepted was a failure at the Admiralty.' The Admiralty riposted with the charge that North had received the Madrid signal at 12.08 a.m. on the 11th, whereas Somerville, who (according to his own report) did not see it until 8 a.m. and whose earliest information of the French ships was at about 5.12 a.m. (*Hotspur*'s sighting report), had taken swift action to bring the *Renown* to one hour's notice for steam.[24] To this North could only reply that he had indeed taken action—that Somerville's decision had been made after consultation with him. North, in his official residence, The Mount, and Somerville in the *Renown* were connected by private telephone to the office of North's Chief of Staff in 'The Tower'; they could talk direct with each other, and often did at all hours. After the receipt of *Hotspur*'s sighting message at 5.12, North had had a telephone discussion on the whole matter with Somerville, as a result of which Somerville brought Force H to one hour's notice for steam. Again the Admiralty were not impressed. It was *Somerville*, not he, who had taken action, and, moreover, the *Renown* and the destroyer *Vidette* were never ready to go to sea that night. They were never at less than one hour's notice for full speed. To Somerville's assertion (25 October) that even if he had received sufficient warning of the impending move-ment of the French ships, he would not have sent his ships to sea (see above, p. 202), Pound countered: 'The fact however is that because he would not have done what he ought to have done, it does not excuse Admiral North for not doing anything.'[25]

Had North indeed taken all 'prudent precautions'? Putting aside

[24] North claimed that the Madrid message was sent over to the *Renown* and, though it may not actually have reached Somerville until 8 a.m., the contents were known to him and his staff early in the morning, owing to the signal made to vessels on patrol (2.15 a.m.), as well as in the telephone conversation informing him of *Hotspur*'s sighting report. 'Extracts from a letter from Admiral Dudley North', n.d. (1945?), Richmond MSS., RIC 7/4. This does not appear in North's messages to the Admiralty. At any rate, the 2.15 signal was *not* repeated either to the Admiralty or to Somerville. The latter's own account (report of 17 September) makes it quite clear that *Hotspur*'s signal was the first he had heard about the French ships since the Tangier report, received on the previous evening. As a matter of fact, North never affirmed that he personally had anything to do with the making of the signal at 2.15. Declares an Admiralty memorandum of 1957, 'It would have been a very natural action by the F.O.C.N.A.'s Staff Officer Intelligence, to whom the Naval Attaché's signal was addressed, to relay the information to ships at sea who might encounter the French force. There is no evidence available to Admiralty to support the picture of Admiral North awake and thinking at 0215 but even if there were, any thought that emerged was misdirected, since he did nothing to put himself in a position to execute Admiralty orders should they arrive.'

[25] Minute, 29 Oct., ADM 1/19185.

the question of the confused chain of command, there were, in his view, only two alternatives open to him on the morning of 11 September *in the absence of Admiralty instructions.* One was to let the French ships pass, which is what he did. The other was to prevent the ships from passing by intercepting them and, if necessary, using force to stop them. This would, in his judgement, have been an *imprudent* 'precaution', because, had there been an engagement, which was 'more than probable', the combined forces of the Gibraltar command and Force H would not have been up to the job. The *Renown* and the six destroyers available[26] would not have stood a chance against the three modern cruisers and three super-destroyers under Admiral Bourragué, who would have received powerful air support from Casablanca. North had no aircraft, except a few old 'London' flying boats.[27] (The Admiralty had nothing of the sort in mind. See below for what they expected North to do.) Moreover, North believed, to have taken action against the French force would have been to act in flat contravention of his instructions. What were they? Here we come to the crux of the matter from North's point of view.

On 4 July a lengthy Admiralty signal had laid down guidelines for H.M. ships *vis-à-vis* French warships. They were (*inter alia*): to be prepared for attack but were not to fire the first shot; to avoid contact with equal or superior forces; if a 'definitely inferior' French force were met, to persuade it (using force in the last resort) to proceed to a British port. On 6 July North asked for a clarification, as he was uncertain what action he should take if French warships attempted to pass through the Straits. The existing instructions to the Straits Patrol were to permit the passage of French warships

---

[26] Force H had lost five of its six destroyers (8th Destroyer Flotilla) to Force M on 6 September. The remaining boat was not operational on the 11th. Available was the 13th Destroyer Flotilla, which was under North's command: three World War I boats and three comparatively modern boats (one of each was non-operational; a fourth modern boat had gone with Force M).

[27] In his 'Commentary' he noted that the guns from the fortress at Gibraltar would have been of little assistance, since the French ships would probably have kept close to the southern and Spanish shore of the Straits, which would have been out of range of the batteries. 'The loss of one capital ship at a time when we were very short, with the large and modern Italian Navy having just entered the lists against us, would have been a disaster of the first magnitude for which I, acting against my existing orders, would have been wholly responsible.' Further complications, he said, would probably have been caused through the almost inevitable violation of Spanish territorial waters by the British force during the action. Spain was 'exceedingly truculent', and it would not have needed much to push Franco from non-belligerency into a military alliance with the Axis. This would have made Gibraltar untenable.

unless they committed a hostile act, but these instructions did not agree with those the Governor of Gibraltar had from the War Office. The Admiralty replied on 7 July that the orders of the 4th applied, and that the forts at Gibraltar were, if possible, to assist in the execution of these instructions. The War Office would be asked to amend their orders. On 12 July the Admiralty sent North revised instructions (approved by the Prime Minister), whose important paragraphs follow:

(*b*) The further maintenance of the present state of tension between French Navy and ourselves is very undesirable and might even lead to war with that country.

(*c*) H.M. Government have consequently reviewed our policy regarding the French Navy and have decided to take no further action in regard to the French ships in French Colonial or North African ports. We shall of course however reserve the right to take action in regard to French warships proceeding to enemy controlled ports [i.e. in the occupied zone of France].[28]

North assumed that the last of these rather muddled sets of instructions superseded the previous ones. He read them to mean that he was enjoined not to take action against French warships if they were not sailing to ports under enemy control, and, moreover, that *any special measures that might become necessary in the event of the French ships sailing to enemy controlled ports would be initiated by the Admiralty*. Or, as he put it in his letter of 20 January 1941: the 12 July telegram could mean only one thing to him: 'that unless orders were received from H.M. Government to take action against French ships the primary consideration was the avoidance of incidents. I acted accordingly.'[29] In such a situation the most that he felt that he could do would be to be alert, ready for *whatever action London decided on*. This he had done by bringing the one big ship available, the *Renown*, to readiness for rapid action. Somerville had read the situation the same way. North did not consider that H.M. Government 'reserving the right to take action' constituted

---

[28] Admiralty message 0241 of 12 July, ADM 1/19180.

[29] He mentioned this to the First Lord at their interview in January 1941. 'He agreed that there was something to say on my side, but asked, if the meaning was not clear to me, why did I not ask what it meant. I told him that it was clear to me; that it meant that incidents with the French were to be avoided, and that Government instructions would be issued if operations against French ships were to be undertaken. . . . There was no reason whatsoever for me to order Admiral Somerville to sea (against his inclination) in the absence of such instructions.' North, 'Commentary'.

executive orders for him to engage the French ships in the absence of Admiralty or Government instructions.

The 'predominant impression' in North's mind early in September, derived from the 12 July instructions, was that (as he wrote to the Admiralty on 8 December)

the Government policy was to avoid any incidents which might tend to restore the tension between the French and ourselves. Of what may have passed between H.M. Government and Vichy I have small knowledge, as little information on political progress was sent to me but, from my local intelligence, it was abundantly clear that relations with the French Navy were improving, although perhaps slowly. Information brought from time to time by individuals from Morocco pointed to this improvement in attitude, and this was also further confirmed by a message from the Consul General at Tangier on 31st August in which he informed me that Admiral Ollive, the French Admiral in command at Casablanca, was shewing distinct signs of changing his views. This, the Consul General regarded as significant as the Admiral was known to be fundamentally anti-British.[30]

The 'local intelligence' that most impressed him, and which he regarded as the 'fruit' of the Government's policy of avoiding incidents, was a Naval Attaché, Madrid report of 5 September. The French Naval Attaché in Madrid had recently returned from a visit to Vichy, where he found that the officers and men of the French Navy were much less hostile to Britain, and that the general French feeling was hope in the British and the intention to resume hostilities when possible. Admiral Darlan had instructed him to keep in close, but discreet, touch with the British Naval Attaché, and to tell him that the spirit of resistance was increasing in France. Somerville was of exactly the same mind as North concerning the significance of the 12 July instructions, as note this extract from a letter of 12 September to his wife: 'I really did think I'd finished with those bloody Frenchmen. . . . I came to short notice for steam but as the policy was not to create any more incidents I did not put to sea.'

The friendlier mood in the French Navy was the direct cause of North's downfall. When he got word of the French ships from Toulon, he thought they intended to break away to French colonial ports. As he explained in his 8 December memorandum: 'In view of what had so recently transpired it appeared clear to me that this force was taking advantage of an opportunity to leave Toulon for Casablanca in order to escape from the German and Italian control

[30] ADM 1/19187.

liable to occur at the former port.[31] The fact that no instructions of any sort with regard to the interception of these ships had been received by me from the Admiralty after the Consul General Tangier's message, confirmed this conclusion, and I decided that no action should be taken to interfere with their passage through the Straits.' The thought had also occurred to North that the movement of the French ships may have been effected with the 'connivance' of the British Government, which would account to some extent for the absence of orders to him on how to meet the situation.[32]

Why did North not take precautions against a possible French movement to the northward? He believed that the French ships were proceeding to the south, which, as he interpreted the 12 July instructions, was permissible. To the Admiralty charge (15 October) that it could not be certain that the ships were not proceeding north, and it was necessary to be able to stop them if they did, North's reply was:

> If so, why did not the Admiralty who knew of their approach before I did, issue instructions to that effect? . . . The Admiralty had at least seven hours to make up their minds as to whether they wished the French force to be intercepted or not. . . . Is it seriously contended that, having no orders by 0700, I ought to have ordered Force H to sea against the opinion of Admiral Somerville, with orders to instruct the French force that it might go South but was not to go North? This would, to my mind, have been entirely contrary to the Government instructions to avoid incidents.[33]

The First Sea Lord swept aside as not 'really relevant' North's

[31] Somerville had the same idea. In his report of 17 September he had written of the events of 11 September: 'It seemed to me most improbable that the Force would proceed to a Bay [of Biscay] Port and that Casablanca was the probable destination. So far as I was aware, it was not the policy of H.M. Government to interfere with the movements of French warships to French controlled ports. The possibility of this movement being connected with Operation "Menace" was considered but in view of the report from the Naval Attaché at Madrid, 1842 dated 5th September, 1940 [above], it appeared to me that quite possibly the French wished to remove these ships in order to prevent their seizure by the Germans in retaliation for any action taken by us at Dakar.'

[32] Years later, North amplified this argument. 'Altogether, this significant silence on the part of the Government, combined with what little information I had on the general situation, led me to believe that, as a considerable section of the French people were bound to be in favour of the Dakar operation, and possibly (in spite of Mers El Kebir) a few of the French Navy, this movement was according to plan, and the French cruisers were in fact escaping from Toulon to join up with us. This opinion was shared by Vice Admiral Somerville with whom I was in constant consultation.' North to Churchill, 4 Mar. 1948. All the North-Churchill correspondence is in the North MSS., NRTH 2/2.

[33] 'Commentary', North MSS.

arguments about the emphasis in the 12 July message on the undesirability of maintaining the tension with the French Navy; about
the growing friendliness of the French Navy; and that, had the
Admiralty decided to deny the passage of the Straits to French
warships, which would represent a complete change of policy, they
would have sent him definite instructions to that effect. Pound
stressed North's 'failure to take the necessary action to prevent these
ships going North'. And what was the 'necessary action'? North
should have made arrangements to have the French ships followed—
i.e. by sending Force H to sea—to ascertain their probable destination, and had he done so, they could have been dealt with on further
instructions from the Admiralty.

But the French force had *not* gone to the northward, North
countered. That signified nothing to the First Sea Lord. 'Admiral
North's instructions were that the French ships were to be prevented
from proceeding to German occupied ports, and there was no
guarantee that the forces proceeding through the Straits were not
proceeding to the northward. In point of fact these ships proceeded
to the southward but had they proceeded to the northward Admiral
North would have been in no position to intercept them owing to
his failure to order *Renown* to proceed to sea. I should call this
failure "Omission to perform one's duty" rather than "Error of
Judgment".'[34] Although the Admiralty stressed North's obligation
to ensure that the French did not go to the northward, Dakar was
not absent from their calculations. 'Had Admiral North obeyed his
instructions and taken action to prevent these ships proceeding to a
Northern port, the Admiralty would have been in a position to have
given orders to prevent them reaching Dakar.'[35]

Then there was North's defence that the Admiralty had not given
him instructions as regards the interception of the ships, which
under the 12 July instructions he had every right to expect. Here
we come to the quintessence of the Admiralty's case against North,
and it brings us full circle. In Pound's words:

This is the fundamental difference in Admiral North's conception of
what a Flag Officer should do and what the Admiralty consider he should
do. Having received the instructions in A.M.0214/12th July, it was
Admiral North's duty as Senior Officer to take the necessary action to
carry out these instructions and not assume that any further instructions

---

[34] Minute, 12 Nov., ADM 1/19186. See above, p. 205.
[35] Pound, 'Points which Admiral North Has Made', minute of 23 Jan. 1941, ADM
1/19187.

would be received from the Admiralty. In this case it was certainly not necessary for the Admiralty to issue any supplementary instructions as they would assume that Admiral North would have already taken steps to act on the instructions he already had. In effect what Admiral North did was to take no action on receipt of N.A. Madrid 1809/10 which was received by him at 0008/11, that is on the morning of the day the ships actually passed through the Straits.

RENOWN was brought to one hour's notice at 0530/11 by F.O. Force H. This was a half measure which could be of no use unless the force was ordered to sea.

Admiral North, however, takes the line that the ships having been brought to one hour's notice, it was up to the Admiralty to order them to sea. This is exactly why the Admiralty lost confidence in Admiral North in that he failed to take effective action and waited instructions from the Admiralty.[36]

In other words, Admiral North had not shown the kind of awareness that the Admiralty demanded of Flag Officers.

(3) Responsibilities

One gets the impression in studying the records that neither side heard very well—that it was a case of the deaf talking to the deaf. Admiral North was incapable of understanding why, in the opinion of Authority, he had failed. He never understood how risky an assumption it was to make that the French ships were unlikely to go to the north, but were proceeding to Casablanca or Dakar. For all he knew they were *en route* to Brest to join up with the Germans. (It is the weakness in Roskill's argument that he does not allude to this important point.) It was even riskier to assume that a strong French naval squadron proceeding to the south was on a peaceful mission, in the light of 'Menace', of whose existence and objectives he was aware. The Admiralty were entitled to think that, in spite of unclear orders and signals going astray, their man on the spot should, without waiting for orders, have taken greater precautions to meet any possible emergency in connection with the French squadron—that it was a serious error of judgement (or an 'omission to perform his duty', as they would have it) to allow a large Vichy force, *destination unknown*, to pass Gibraltar with only a *bon voyage*

---

[36] Ibid. 'The First Sea Lord said to me that any officer who waited for Admiralty instructions before taking the initiative was not fit to be in command of an important place like Gibraltar.' Admiral of the Fleet Lord Fraser of North Cape, in the Lords, 26 July 1954.

signal. North had plenty of time to get the *Renown* and the six destroyers under way so as to be ready for anything, especially as he knew they had large forces at sea bound for Dakar, and the Admiralty might wake up at any moment.

At the same time, the Admiralty did not recognize that North had sufficient and genuine grounds for misunderstanding, which should have tempered their judgement. North had every right to assume that the Tangier and Madrid signals had been received at the Admiralty—how could he have been aware of the breakdown in the Admiralty machinery at that vital moment?—and his interpretation of the 12 July instructions was a reasonable one. The chain of command *was* indefinite, as the Admiralty had so far controlled Force H direct, and the extent to which North could intervene was left vague. To an unprejudiced mind, it appears that the five Admirals of the Fleet (see below) had it exactly right in their memorandum of 1953: North's fault was at the most ' "an error of judgement, a misinterpretation of Admiralty orders," but was *not* "neglect of duty".'

The wording of the Admiralty letter of 15 October might suggest that North's removal was a Board decision: 'Their Lordships cannot retain full confidence in an officer who,' etc. On the other hand, the First Lord told North when they met in January 1941 (and in a letter to the Secretary, Sir John Lang, on 9 August 1953) that he had been condemned by the Naval Staff. This would mean the First Sea Lord and Chief of Naval Staff (Pound), the VCNS (Phillips), and the three ACNS, Vice-Admiral Sir Geoffrey Blake (Foreign) and Rear-Admirals H. R. Moore (Trade) and A. J. Power (Home). The formal parlance about 'Their Lordships', and the First Lord's statement, disguise the fact that three men were responsible for the action taken against North: the First Sea Lord, the First Lord, and the Permanent Secretary (Sir Archibald Carter). There is no record that the case was decided by the full Board. The only addressees and minutes on the documents that led to the Admiralty letter of 15 October are those of Pound, Alexander, and Carter.[37] Since, however, in the Letters Patent any two members ('Lords Commissioners') can constitute a legal Board meeting, there was nothing unusual, still less improper, in Pound dealing with

[37] Admiral Moore informs me (letter of 6 Sept. 1974) that he was not consulted on the matter. Nor, apparently, was Phillips, unless informally by the First Sea Lord. The Naval Assistant to the VCNS writes: 'I am pretty sure that no papers on this subject passed through his office, or that he ever expressed an opinion in writing on it.' Captain L. H. Bell's letter to the author, 17 Sept. 1974.

North's case himself with the First Lord and the Secretary. They were the only Board members really concerned with the decision.

North's defenders, and North himself, in 1940 and subsequently, wrote off Alexander as the prime mover. After the war, with Pound dead, Churchill silent, and Alexander, in the Lords, opposing an inquiry, he became a wicked person indeed in the eyes of North and his friends. We must pause to examine Alexander closely, since he was to remain a central figure in the North Affair until its ultimate resolution in 1957. The 'Wooden Battleship' (as he was known) was a man of medium height, but broad in the shoulder and deep in the chest, with a square jaw to match. His most striking feature was an unusually broad mouth, sometimes set in a firm, tight line, but often parted in a good-humoured smile. In personal contact he could appear gruff and even forbidding, as when he told his Principal Private Secretary at their first private meeting, 'They tell me you are some good. You had [expletive deleted] better be or you won't last long with me.' Behind the occasional growls, however, was a man of innate kindness and humanity, with a great gift for friendship, conviviality, and conciliation. As wartime First Lord, Alexander displayed an extraordinary physical and mental stamina, putting in a normal work-day of 15 hours, with little time out for rest and relaxation. He had a good quick intelligence, could talk on any subject, and was a fluent and forceful speaker in Parliamentary debates, with a great capacity to 'think on his feet'. His real grasp of naval matters went back to his time as First Lord in 1929–31 (MacDonald's second Labour Government). For some years up to May 1940, when he returned to the Admiralty, he had been the Chief Opposition spokesman on naval affairs. His gift for getting on with people, his understanding of naval affairs and abiding admiration and affection for the Royal Navy, and, not least, his recognition that the direction of naval operations was not his responsibility, account for the excellent relations which he was able to maintain with senior naval officers, notably the two wartime First Sea Lords, Pound and A. B. Cunningham.

In the Navy Alexander had the reputation of being a 'rubber stamp' and a 'cipher', who did what he was told by Churchill and Pound. It is true that he stood in such awe of the Prime Minister and had such respect for the First Sea Lord that it would never have occurred to him to cross either one, let alone both, on any matter they deemed of importance. The First Lord was responsible for the personal selection of admirals for the higher appointments, though, naturally, he acted on the advice of the First Sea Lord, who was also the Chief of Naval Staff. No matter what his responsibilities, Alexander was hardly the person to have taken the initiative in the North case, even if it was he, not Pound or Churchill, who had in a moment of extreme anger urged the Admiral's removal after his post-Oran letter. Churchill was sympathetic to the idea, but Pound had vetoed it. The ultimate decision to remove North, however, did not originate with Alexander, though he supported it without reservations. His Secretary confirms this: 'A. V. Alexander was by nature very fair in his judgments and certainly not given to harsh verdicts when people had done their best in difficult circumstances; but, to the best of my recollection, he went along spontaneously with the view that Dudley North had to be replaced in the interests of the vigorous prosecution of the war.'[38] Admiralty minutes show the First Lord 'agreeing' and 'concurring' with Pound's hard-line policy, but not offering much comment.[39]

Sir Archibald Carter, who had succeeded one of the great Permanent Secretaries of the Admiralty, Sir Oswyn Murray, in 1936, was a friendly person and a man of balanced judgement and understanding, and good at grasping the essentials of a problem. But he never succeeded in getting himself quite accepted in the Admiralty. Murray was a 'tough act' to follow. More important, though, was Carter's non-Admiralty background. He had come there from the India Office, presumably because there was no one sufficiently outstanding at the time on the Admiralty civil staff to warrant promotion to so exalted a Civil Service rank. Also, Carter did not like serving in the Admiralty and expressed his delight when he was relieved at the beginning of December 1940. In the result he

[38] Sir Clifford Jarrett's letter to the author, 9 Sept. 1973.

[39] Alexander, in the opinion of his Parliamentary Private Secretary, was 'almost entirely in the hands of the Chief of the Naval Staff, Admiral Pound'. 'Interview with Lord Winster', n.d. (early 1945), North MSS., NRTH 1/9. On the same occasion Winster told North that he 'had not felt at all happy' about the decision to relieve him, and had warned the First Lord that 'he did not like the look of it. However, Pound seems to have been adamant on the subject and A.V.A. dug his toes in and refused to consider my protest giving as one explanation (and this is a most extraordinary one that cannot be quoted publicly because he admitted it to Lord Winster very confidentially) that if he gave in and admitted that a mistake had been made he felt that it would lay himself open to the accusation that he had yielded to Court pressure!' I would not query this 'most extraordinary explanation'—it was in keeping with the First Lord's staunch Socialist principles—but it is my judgement that this was at most a secondary consideration. Lord Winster, by the way, was R. T. H. Fletcher in 1940, a onetime lieutenant-commander, RN, who had turned politician. When he first joined Alexander as PPS (he served in that capacity from May 1940 till December 1941), they were very close.

seldom exerted the influence on Admiralty policy one would expect of a Secretary of the Admiralty.

Carter had approved—more accurately, *accepted*—the decision to remove North, for he had gone along with the First Sea Lord and the First Lord despite his serious doubts. 'If,' he declared in a minute to the First Lord (10 October), 'Admiral Sir Dudley North has lost the confidence of the First Sea Lord and yourself, that, of course, ends the matter so far as the tenure of his appointment is concerned.' But he obviously thought the Admiralty case was shaky, for, he continued, he was 'anxious to avoid a reasoned reply [to North's 6 October] since, simply as a matter of argument, *I don't feel too confident that Sir Dudley North hasn't the best of it.* He is a person of influence who may well start a controversy, and we don't want to make the mistake of providing him with a letter from the Admiralty in which the argument fails to convince others.' Pound challenged the words I have italicized in a minute to the Secretary on the same day: 'Admiral North has not the best of it. Admiral North claims that Admiral Somerville's squadron was an Independent Command. So far as I can see there is nothing in A.T. 1724/28 to endorse this but it is possible that he bases the statement on A.T. 1738/28. . . . The real point at issue seems to be whether an officer has any right to assume that a signal must have been received by the Admiralty just because it is addressed to the Admiralty.' Carter's response the next day, while conceding something to the First Sea Lord, must have given him small comfort. Among the points that the Secretary made were these:

My doubts about entering into argument with Admiral Sir Dudley North, at all events at this stage, were mainly based on the consideration that it was an occasion when it was only to be expected that instructions would come from the Admiralty. However, it is no doubt true, as you said this morning, that the situation was such that it was essential to take every step to be ready for any action that might prove necessary.

I think the contingency of a signal not reaching the Admiralty cannot perhaps be entirely dismissed from the mind of a Flag Officer, but it does seem rather a remote contingency unless there was some reason to suspect that communication had been interrupted.

I do not feel that the position of Force H was left quite as clear as it might have been. It seems true to say that it was an independent force but that nevertheless it would have been entirely proper for the Flag Officer Commanding North Atlantic to issue instructions to it if an emergency made this necessary.[40]

40 ADM 1/19180.

A month later, Carter was still expressing doubts. He had 'never been at all happy about the controversy with Admiral North as to the reasons for relieving him of his command.'[41]

The principal responsibility for the disgrace of North lies with a tough and unyielding First Sea Lord who had little patience with senior officers who, in his judgement, had failed, as through not demonstrating initiative. He had 'a thing' about initiative, and though his own over-detailed orders tended to cramp it in others, he always appreciated this quality when it was displayed. The Admiralty records make Pound's dominant role clear beyond any shadow of a doubt.

Heckstall-Smith suggests that Pound's dislike for North may help to explain his decision. This dislike, he goes on, was due to the tremendous differences in character and temperament between the two men—Pound, a 'stern disciplinarian dedicated to duty', etc., and North, 'witty, humorous and . . . a good companion'. Heckstall-Smith admits that Pound had a Service reputation for being just and fair. 'In normal circumstances, he would never have allowed his personal likes and dislikes to interfere with his judgement. But by the autumn of 1940, Pound was already seriously ill and the burden of his office was becoming too heavy for him.'[42] (The opening sentence of North's record of his interview with Pound reads: 'My first impression was that of a man in a very exhausted and nervous condition.') Although the two men were on good terms, I concede that Pound may have had a personal antipathy towards North—the dour professional *v.* the companionable courtier, and there was possibly a predisposition to prejudge North if anything went wrong in his parish. But I attribute no great significance to these considerations in the context of the events of the summer of 1940. As for the health factor, barring periods when a terribly overworked First Sea Lord gave evidence of strain and exhaustion, Pound did not reveal serious signs of physical and mental decline before 1943.

Although many very experienced officers in a good position to form an opinion are convinced that the Prime Minister was closely

---

[41] Minute, 11 Nov., ADM 1/19186. Carter's successor, on 3 December 1940, Markham, was an entirely different cup of tea. He had spent his whole Civil Service career in the Admiralty and had long been regarded as a man of quick perception and balanced judgement. His self-confidence and his performance bred a general confidence in the new Secretary of the Admiralty and restored the influence which Murray had had. And that influence was thrown behind the Pound-Alexander policy of refusing an inquiry or court martial to North.

[42] *The Fleet that Faced Both Ways*, pp. 172–3.

involved, there is no evidence that Pound was influenced by pressure from him, or indeed that there was any.

Everyone whose recollection might help has been questioned [reads an Admiralty memorandum of 1957], and there is no evidence that there was pressure from outside the Admiralty at this time to have Admiral North removed. Lord Bridges [Secretary to the Cabinet, 1938–46] and Sir Eric Seal (then P.S. [Principal Private Secretary] to the Prime Minister) both say that the Prime Minister was very angry over the whole affair, i.e. the escape from the Mediterranean of the French ships, especially the part played by Admiral North, but there is no evidence whether the Prime Minister discussed the matter at all with the First Lord and/or First Sea Lord or if he did so what object he may have had in mind.

The Prime Minister had no high opinion of North. 'It is evident that Admiral Dudley North has not got the root of the matter in him, and I should be very glad to see you replace him by a more resolute and clear-sighted Officer.'[43] This had been his reaction (20 July) to Alexander's proposal that North be replaced. Churchill had not insisted on the point and thereafter apparently did not very much concern himself with North's fate, beyond, as Minister of Defence, concurring without hesitation in the decision of the Admiralty to remove him.[44]

[43] ADM 1/19177.

[44] Neither the wartime Churchill Papers in the custody of Mr. Martin Gilbert, nor the Premier (PREM) 3 files at the Public Record Office, which constitute the bulk of Churchill's wartime papers, contain anything on his involvement in the decision to remove North. Sir John Slessor, for one, is not impressed by the absence of any written evidence in the Churchill Papers. 'A hunt for a personal scapegoat,' he says, 'is not a very glamorous business; and I myself have attended enough "midnight follies" of the kind which must have kept poor old Dudley [Pound] up half the night time and again, to know that the old boy was very capable of getting a point across (and keeping it up) without committing himself to paper.' Slessor's letter to the author, 31 Oct. 1974. The charge cannot be summarily dismissed; but, given the absence of positive proof, I prefer to give Churchill the benefit of the doubt.

ADDENDA

To p. 73n. Churchill, regarding the punishment inflicted on Bevan as 'minor and altogether inadequate' for 'a gross case of neglect of duty in a Staff Officer', 'strongly pressed' on the First Lord that Bevan at the least be placed on half-pay. Withstanding Churchill's pressure, Alexander consulted the Naval Staff and Naval Law, then informed an irate Prime Minister that 'they advised against this punishment being inflicted as being contrary to Naval Justice and to civil practice.' Minutes of 19–27 Oct., PREM 3/71.

To p. 198, n.5. These misgivings at the Admiralty stemmed in part from 'the rather defeatist attitude of mind he adopted in July '40 when the question was raised of the feasibility of defence of the Rock against hostile action from Spain. You will recall that the First Lord commented particularly on this aspect.' Acting Captain Ronald Brockman's minute to Pound, 22 Jan. 1941, ADM 205/11.

Chapter Eleven

North's Campaign for
Vindication (1945–57)

I have been wrongly accused, adjudged guilty *without trial* and removed from my command. My conscience, however, is so clear that I have never been mentally distressed by what has been done to me. Very angry indeed and angry that such a thing is possible in a Service which prides itself on fair play to all.

Admiral Sir Dudley North to
Admiral Sir Herbert Richmond, n.d. (early 1945?)

As a race we are very reluctant to dig up every skeleton before it has been buried for at least a hundred years! no matter how unfair such a practice is to the living.

Admiral Sir John Cunningham to
Admiral Sir Dudley North, 15 January 1946

Is it wise to depart from that cardinal principle, that justice not only must be done but must be seen to be done.

Lord Ailwyn, in the House of Lords, 15 June 1954

The past cannot be completely thrown overboard; punishment carried out cannot be cancelled, but honour can be restored. The name of Mr. Harold Macmillan will not speedily be forgotten by the Royal Navy.

Admiral of the Fleet Lord Chatfield, in a letter to
The Times, 25 May 1957

(1) The Affair Simmers

WHILE the war was on, North made no public fuss, though some of his friends advised him to get questions asked in the House of Commons. He refused, as he had no desire to raise his personal troubles publicly with the nation engaged in a desperate war; it could only harm the war effort. 'Not prepared to be an agitator in wartime, although discredited by Their Lordships and punished without trial', North did nothing to re-establish his unblemished professional reputation, beyond occasionally reminding the Admiralty of his grievance and sending *pièces justicatives* to various brother officers.[1] He made no attempt to conceal the fact that he had been 'slung out', so did not mind if this material were shown to others. 'Scapegoats,' he wrote to Captain Layman early in 1945, 'should be of Admiral's rank when selected and [this] no doubt appears in the Politicians' "How to get out of a hole handbook".' He received scores of supporting letters from naval officers of all ranks and from other individuals of high repute. 'In every wardroom,' writes Noel Monks with more than a touch of hyperbole, 'there was a feeling that by denying Admiral North an Inquiry or Court Martial, the Admiralty was depriving an officer of his traditional right. What happened to North, could happen to them.' Among senior officers who were furious at his treatment and attributed it to the need to find a scapegoat for Dakar were, besides his personal and deeply loyal friend James Somerville, Admirals Sir William James, Sir Herbert Richmond (then retired, pursuing his interest in naval history), Sir Andrew Cunningham (C-in-C, Mediterranean), and Sir Bertram Ramsay (Flag Officer Commanding Dover). Ramsay, for example, wrote: 'I think that you have been disgracefully treated and that what you did and did not do is exactly what any normal sensible person would have done in your place.'[2]

North spent over a year on the active list unemployed (to his surprise, as he had expected another appointment). No appointment having arisen for which he was regarded as suitable, the Admiralty transferred him to the retired list on 15 February 1942.[3] But not before he had reminded them (5 January) that he had never been given any 'substantial reason' for his removal. '. . . it will be necessary for me, in due season, to take such suitable & dignified steps as are necessary, to place my part in a correct light . . .' A postcard acknowledgement was all he got for his pains.

North joined the 1st Battalion of the Dorset Home Guard, rising from sergeant to major and Second-in-Command in a year's time. In 1943 he was recalled to an insignificant shore command at Great Yarmouth with the rank of Rear-Admiral. From there he wrote to

[1] The North-Admiralty correspondence and Admiralty minutes of 1941–3 are in ADM 1/19188–19190.

[2] Letter of 13 June 1941, North MSS., NRTH 2/7.

[3] There was unintentional irony in the Admiralty letter of 20 December 1941 notifying him of their intention—a reference to Their Lordships' 'high appreciation of the eminent services' he had rendered the Navy during his 'long and distinguished career'!

the Admiralty (29 October 1943) that he found himself 'still at a loss' to understand why he had been relieved, and again he asked for an inquiry. If they were not prepared to afford him this opportunity to clear his name, he asked at least for an answer to the question: 'In view of the terms of Admiralty message 0233 of 2nd October, 1940, is it Their Lordships' considered opinion that the passage in Admiralty message 0241 of 12th July, 1940, reserving the right to H.M. Government to take action in regard to French warships proceeding to enemy controlled ports, placed on Admiral Commanding North Atlantic the duty to send forces under his command to intercept French warships, which, from his intelligence were considered to be, and in fact were, Southbound?' And again he received short shrift from the Admiralty (19 November): they were 'unable to find any reason to alter the fully considered decision' conveyed to him in response to his memorandum of 8 December 1940. As for his query, he was referred to the Admiralty letter of 15 October 1940, in particular paragraphs 2, 6, 7 (above, pp. 203–4). They had nothing to add.[4] 'It may be thought,' North observed in his 'Commentary', 'that raising this matter again after all this time is "flogging a dead horse". This horse to my mind is far from dead, no more dead than was that of Dreyfus or that of General Gough of the 5th Army during the last war: these two obtained justice after a considerable lapse of time.'[5]

When the war ended, North retired to his home near Beaminster in Dorset. King George VI had from the beginning shown himself in wholehearted sympathy with the Admiral, who he thought had been treated most unfairly. But the King was powerless in such

[4] The First Sea Lord was now Sir Andrew Cunningham. (Pound had died a few weeks earlier.) The Secretary, Sir Henry Markham's, minute on North's letter (12 Nov.) observed that his question 'shews that, wittingly or unwittingly, he avoids discussing the real reason for his supersession. The destination of the ships is irrelevant. The case against Sir Dudley North is that he did not take adequate precaution to ensure that those ships could be intercepted wherever they were going and that he waited on the Admiralty instead of acting on his own responsibility. Paradoxically enough his case would, I believe, have been stronger if no precautionary steps at all had been taken; in fact, Force "H" was brought to one hour's notice.' Markham found no grounds on which it was possible to advise the Board to reconsider their decision not to grant the request for an inquiry. 'The moment chosen by Sir Dudley North to raise this matter again cannot but be deplored.' ADM 1/19190.

[5] General Sir Hubert Gough, commanding the 5th Army on the Western Front in 1918, was summarily dismissed from his command after the German breakthrough in March, at the behest of the Prime Minister, Lloyd George, and the CIGS, Sir Henry Wilson, over the protests of General Haig, the C-in-C. An inquiry was denied to Gough. It was not until 1937, when he was created a GCB, that the injustice done to him was officially recognized.

matters, above all in those difficult days of 1940 and 1941. In 1946, as a mark of his confidence in the Admiral, he requested that his old friend be appointed Flag Officer Commanding H.M. Yachts. North held the appointment only until May 1947 for reasons of economy. He then reverted once more to the retired list. In June he was made a GCVO in the King's birthday honours list. At all times, during the war and afterwards, North was 'scrupulously careful' never to ask the King to intervene on his behalf, having no desire to sow any discord between him and his ministers.

The war over, North was prepared to break his silence and get his case before the public. Churchill, now Leader of the Opposition, remained silent. Clement Attlee was the Prime Minister of a Labour Government, but Alexander was still the First Lord. He was succeeded in October 1946 by G. H. (soon to become Viscount) Hall (–1951), assuming the post of Minister of Defence in December 1946 (–February 1950). The First Sea Lord was Admiral of the Fleet Viscount Cunningham of Hyndhope, who was followed in 1946 by Admiral Sir John Cunningham, with the latter giving way in 1948 to Admiral of the Fleet Lord Fraser of North Cape. Markham, who had died, was succeeded by Sir John Lang in January 1947. North could not have expected much sympathy from a Government in which Alexander was a member, despite the presence of the two Cunninghams in succession at the Admiralty. Moreover, the politicians and sailors were too engrossed in postwar problems to give much thought to North's troubles.

North preferred not to raise the matter himself and was therefore grateful when Admiral Richmond consulted him on the story of Oran and Dakar, which he proposed to treat in an appendix to his *Statesmen and Sea Power*. 'If some-one gets hold of the fact that an Admiral has been shamefully treated, & writes it up sensationally in the Press, there may be a first class row. Well, it won't be of my raising, & that is all the better. So—off you go Sir, and if the fur does fly, I don't think it will be mine.' 'I only hope that some critic will take notice of your comments and that Albert Victor [Alexander] will be called upon to explain his departure from the ordinary standards of English justice.'[6]

Richmond's brief treatment of the North Affair in his book (pp. 361–2), which was published in September 1946, was only the second public mention. 'On more occasions than one in British history a Government which has blundered in its conduct of an

---

[6] North to Richmond, 27 Oct., 14 Nov. 1945, Richmond MSS., RIC 7/4.

operation has sought shelter from attack by throwing the blame upon its commander.' Richmond cited the example of the Duke of Newcastle *vis-à-vis* Mediterranean operations in 1741, and again in 1755, when Newcastle 'procured the judicial murder of Admiral Byng in order to stave off the criticism of the country. . . . So, in 1940, when, after the failure of Dakar . . . the blame was thrown on the admiral at Gibraltar . . .' Richmond threw the entire blame on the Admiralty and the Government for not giving the Admiral any clear instructions as to how he should act, and 'to crown all, following an evil precedent of the previous war, the admiral was refused the trial by court martial to which naval officers in the past had always been regarded as entitled . . .'

The first public mention of the affair had been made a few months earlier, in May 1946, by Admiral Sir William James, who, in his *Portsmouth Letters* (p. 100 of this collection of wartime letters) expressed the opinion that North had been 'the victim of a grave injustice'. James was an old friend and *Britannia* term-mate. The book and the fact that he was told by James that Churchill had a copy encouraged North to write to Churchill, who as Minister of Defence in 1940 'must have borne some of the responsibility'.

> Many of my brother Officers have asked when I intended to get this obvious wrong righted, and now that Admiral James has brought the matter to light in his book,—which has a very wide circulation,—the affair is being much discussed and the time has, I think, come for me to see what can be done.
>
> And so Mr. Churchill I start with you. Several years after the First World War, Mr. Lloyd George made a public 'amende honourable' to General Gough; I ask you in all sincerity whether you might not follow his good example in my case.[7]

He received no reply or even an acknowledgement, but afterwards, when they met (see below), he learned that Churchill had not answered because he was not in full possession of all the facts: times of dispatch and receipt of the relevant messages, etc.

On 4 February 1947 the two men met at the Founders' Day dinner of the Royal Navy Club of 1765 and 1785, which was honouring Churchill. The First Sea Lord, Sir John Cunningham, took North up after dinner and introduced him to Churchill, saying, to North's embarrassment, 'He says he's the ram in the Dakar thicket.' Churchill was at first nonplussed, and said, 'Who?', and

[7] North to Churchill, 28 Aug. 1946.

then, 'Oh, you're the fellow who let those cruisers through the Straits.' He was, however, quite amiable and after some conversation asked for the timings of the principal signals on 11 September 1940. North sent him the information on 4 March, imbedding it in a long letter which laid out his entire case and explained his silence during the war. 'But now I do ask for vindication. The damage of the premature termination of my career as a full Admiral can never be restored to me, but somehow or other, my professional reputation must be cleared.' All he got back was an acknowledgement on 29 March. 'No reply from Winston,' wrote North to Rear-Admiral Lord Mountbatten (16 August). 'I don't think he knows what to say!'[8] As 1947 neared its end, North was thinking of abandoning the struggle—'it is such ancient history now,' and he was getting nowhere in his campaign for vindication.

On 19 April 1948 North wrote to Churchill concerning his war volumes to ensure that nothing was said which would so damage his reputation as to cause him to take legal proceedings. 'If he says anything not in accordance with fact, I enter the arena!' He would write at once to *The Times*. This time Churchill replied (7 June), saying that his treatment of Dakar would not concern itself with the North Affair. 'It is no part of my task to apportion credit or blame to individual officers unless I myself initiated action reflecting on their conduct. The Dakar operations are no exception to this rule and I shall be careful to avoid reference to contentious details or entering into questions which lie solely within the jurisdiction of the Admiralty.' In consequence there was no mention of North's removal in *Their Finest Hour* (1949).[9]

[8] It was at this time that North learned from Mountbatten the full story of the Admiralty's unawareness of the movements of the French ships until after they had passed through the Straits. This information invalidated North's contention that he had expected instructions from the Admiralty on 11 September, but not his 'main claim' that his instructions were ambiguous. He now understood the Admiralty's inaction, but this 'in no way altered my opinion that I was absolutely right in what I did'. Mountbatten to North, 16 Sept., North to Mountbatten, 11 Nov. 1947.

[9] There is evidence, however, that Churchill had at first planned to deal with the North Affair in this volume. Sometime in 1948, I suspect *before* Churchill's letter of 7 June, Captain G. R. G. Allen, who had just begun to assist Churchill with the naval facets of his wartime volumes, came to see him, at his request, at Hyde Park Gate. Churchill was in bed, recovering from a hernia operation, and was surrounded by papers, including some of his own drafts of the early war operations, among them an account of the North Affair. He asked Allen to study the matter and give him his view. Allen researched the case at the Admiralty and by writing to North for his version. He also discovered that Rear-Admiral H. G. Thursfield, a retired officer, who was Editor of *Brassey's Naval Annual* and Naval Correspondent of *The Times*, intended to launch a pro-North campaign if Churchill implied in his book that he was a party to the dismissal

In October 1948 Rear-Admiral Thursfield went ahead and published a strong article in the *National Review* which for the first time publicly laid out most of the details of what had happened at Gibraltar. Thursfield charged that North had been made the scapegoat for the lack of success at Dakar.

A number of salutary naval traditions, some of which had endured for centuries, went by the board . . . during the late war; one of them, it seems, was the principle that an officer accused of having failed in his duty 'by negligence or default' was entitled to demand a trial by court martial.

. . . it is now time that the stigma that has lain for eight years on the reputation of a gallant and deserving officer should be removed. It is to be hoped that Mr. Churchill's version of the incident in his forthcoming volume will go far towards securing that result.[10]

The article attracted some discussion in the press and in the Service clubs.

On 3 September 1949 North made a formal request to the Board of Admiralty that the 'injustice' to him should be remedied. The reply was that they were not prepared to alter their fully considered decisions. In May 1950, referring to this letter, North wrote again: 'I have consequently now no other alternative but to take such steps as are open to those who are condemned and punished—unheard.' He sought legal advice on whether a case for a Petition of Right existed; the answer was negative. He still refused to enter the lists in person.

The nearly dead embers of the affair were stoked in the spring of 1953. There was a new régime in Whitehall. Churchill had succeeded Attlee in October 1951. The First Lord of the Admiralty (1951–6) was J. P. L. Thomas, and the First Sea Lord (1951–5), Admiral Sir Rhoderick McGrigor (promoted to Admiral of the Fleet in 1953). Sir John Lang was still the Secretary.

'Jim' Thomas had been Financial Secretary to the Admiralty in the last two years of the war. He was a tall (about 6 ft. 2 in.), handsome ('boldly cut features and a fresh complexion'), and charm-

---

of North. Allen warned Churchill of this, pointing out that the decision had been made by the First Sea Lord, and that it would be unwise for him to declare himself as a party to it. Allen prepared a draft in which he referred to North's dismissal, but without mentioning the Prime Minister. 'He agreed in general with my draft, but I was rather surprised to see on re-reading this chapter now that there is no mention of North's dismissal. He must have cut this out *deliberately*, there can be no doubt about this, probably wisely.' Captain Allen's letter to the author, 31 Dec. 1973.

10 ' "Pour Encourager les Autres". A Naval Episode of 1940', cxxxi. 343–53.

ing bachelor, an amusing and enjoyable companion who much appreciated his comforts and the good things of life. He was a connoisseur of food and wine who was said to possess 'hollow legs', each of which could accommodate a bottle of whiskey between dinner and bedtime without any noticeable effect upon him except a slight slurring of his speech. He was an intelligent conversationalist with a fund of anecdotes who could talk about history, art, music, or furniture with equal ease, but perhaps without much depth. As First Lord he did not have many original ideas or even really understand all the implications of the matters under discussion. On the other hand, from the point of view of the Royal Navy, at least those elements (always in a decided majority) who regarded the best First Lord as one who interfered least with the Naval Staff and did what he was told, Thomas was an excellent First Lord! He would listen carefully at briefings and when he had hoisted in the arguments, would stick to his brief through thick and thin. His Naval Secretary thinks that 'he went through several fairly rough times with W.S.C. because of this admirable loyalty to his department. All in all he was a good parliamentary work-horse, but not in the top class.'[11] Concerning the North case, Thomas took the view, which was held by many others at the Admiralty, including his Naval Secretary, that it was much ado about very little and that it was much best to let sleeping dogs lie. Moreover, he felt that 'lobbying' by retired flag officers and Admirals of the Fleet (see below) was quite improper.

Admiral McGrigor was very short and slim, but fit and wiry and of boundless energy. He was known affectionately throughout the Service as 'The Wee-Mac'. Though a kindly and homely man, it was difficult to penetrate the armour of his reserve or to know what he was thinking. The only person in his confidence was his Secretary (Captain B. G. Teale). A man of intense religious belief (he was a staunch Scottish Presbyterian) and great integrity, McGrigor found it difficult to understand or to tolerate any departure in others from his own personal standards. When C-in-C, Plymouth, he surprised the Commander of the Cadet Training Cruiser by making him recast an entire half-year's programme for the ship, because he had timed some arrivals and departures at deserted anchorages for the Sabbath Day. Admiral Onslow says: 'He was *absolutely straight* in all his dealings, guile of any sort being quite foreign to his nature.' 'Roddy' McGrigor played the North Affair very close to the chest,

11 Admiral Sir Richard Onslow's letter to the author, 11 Dec. 1973.

but his views seem to have been roughly the same as the First Lord's.

Sir John Lang's appearance—fresh complexion and a full head of well-trimmed dark hair—belied his years. (He was in his 57th year in 1953.) He was the first man who rose from being a second division clerk in the Admiralty to become its Permanent Secretary. He owed his promotion to A. V. Alexander, whose Socialist principles rebelled against the established order that so exalted a rank required a university background. Lang had proved himself remarkably efficient during the war with his organization and running of the War Registry, and so when the time came for Alexander to follow his theories about promotion from the ranks, Lang was the obvious choice. And he was a triumphant success. This tight-lipped and canny Scot was a modest, hardworking, extremely efficient, unflappable civil servant. He never spoke without a long pause to consider his words, and even then his speech remained slow and deliberate, delivered with a touch of his Scots accent. He never let his hair down, certainly never to any serving officer, but he was inspired by intense loyalty to the Navy. One would expect that he would have had a great influence on the First Lord and First Sea Lord in the North Affair through the esteem in which he was held as well as by his clear marshalling of precedents and facts. His memory was remarkable and he could quote precedent back to the time of Samuel Pepys. Lang's views on the North case were in harmony with those of Thomas and McGrigor. In his own words: 'The Admiralty in the 50s—First Lord, First Sea Lord and Secretary—would be bound to view with much doubt a suggestion that years after the event an officer who had lost the confidence of the professional head of the Navy should be given a "vote of confidence" unless the evidence was overwhelming (which it was not). Such a "vote of confidence" would imply distrust of the then First Sea Lord. And the Admiralty maintained this attitude even against five Admirals of the Fleet who chose to back North in his campaign.'[12]

In the spring of 1953 North enlisted the help of Admiral of the Fleet Lord Chatfield, the onetime First Sea Lord and Cabinet Minister, and a sailor of especially high repute in political circles. Chatfield communicated with other high-ranking naval officers. Five of the most distinguished senior officers, an impressive group indeed, all Admirals of the Fleet and three of them former First

[12] Sir John Lang's letter to the author, 9 Dec. 1973.

Sea Lords, joined forces to take up North's case. They were, in addition to Chatfield, Lord Cork and Orrery, Lord Cunningham of Hyndhope, Sir John Cunningham, and Sir Algernon Willis. On 30 April they sought an interview with the First Lord, accompanying their request with a short but forceful memorandum. It stated that they were 'most loath' to raise the case in Parliament, both out of loyalty to the Admiralty and because a controversy in Parliament 'might arouse very undesirable public reaction'. They preferred to come and see the First Lord, not to plead North's case, but respectfully to ask him to set up without delay a confidential inquiry by 'a few senior Naval Officers with unprejudiced minds'. North and others should be heard and a report made to the Board. If it cleared North's reputation, partly or wholly, it should be publicly announced. 'Meanwhile, we have requested Admiral Sir Dudley North to stay his hand.' The memorandum made these further points:

> That there has long been, and still exists, a considerable opinion in the Service that Admiral North was unjustly punished; or, if he deserved censure, that his punishment was harsh and excessive. This view indeed has been publicly expressed in writing by Senior Naval Officers, and remains unanswered, which we feel is very harmful to the Service.
>
> The refusal despite his many applications, official and private, to grant him a Court Martial in accordance with Service custom, or another form of inquiry, is not understood in the Service. If it is said the Admiralty have an unanswerable case, then an inquiry would endorse it. From this arises, we believe, a suspicion that the Admiralty case is not unanswerable. This also is harmful to the Service.

The essence of the Admiralty's case and North's was presented, and the conclusion here was that (as already mentioned) North's fault was at most ' "an error of judgement, a misinterpretation of Admiralty orders", but was *not* "neglect of duty".'[13]

On 16 May four of the five Admirals of the Fleet—Cork was ill—paid an unprecedented visit to the First Lord to press their case in person. The only people from the Admiralty present at this two-hour meeting were, it appears, the First Lord, the First Sea Lord, and the Secretary. Thomas's Naval Secretary had, at his request, given him a verbal summary before the meeting of what his generation of naval officers thought of the whole lamentable affair.

This was [to quote Admiral Onslow] that the move by Dudley North to enlist the support of the Admirals of the Fleet was *wholly improper*, and that *their* agreement to bring pressure to bear on his behalf was *equally so*.

[13] The text was reproduced in *The Times*, 8 June 1954. See below, p. 241.

Dudley North had been relieved of the Gibraltar command on the grounds that the Board of Admiralty had *lost confidence in him*. Nobody had ever implied any criticism of either his honour or his courage. 'Loss of confidence' can be brought about by many things, particularly when dealing with people like W.S.C. and Dudley Pound. 'Inquiries' would have been endless if every commander relieved because of loss of confidence had appealed to the senior members of his own Service to form a lobby on his behalf. Most of them took it with dignity: Wavell and Auchinleck, to quote but two. The current feeling in the top and middle ranks of the Service was 'Why can't the old chap let sleeping dogs lie? After all, everybody would have forgotten about it by now, if he had kept his mouth shut.'[14]

Chatfield opened the proceedings by expounding the memorandum paragraph by paragraph. His three colleagues then spoke in support. It was made clear that their main concern was the honour and good name of the Royal Navy. The First Lord promised to look into the matter and let them know the result. Having gained the impression at the interview that its object had been achieved, Chatfield wrote to North (28 May) telling him, 'There is to be an Inquiry and you will be called before it with others.' North read the letter with shaking hands. 'It seemed too good to be true,' as Monks relates. 'He knew, in his heart, that if there were an inquiry, then there could only be vindication for himself, and for the Service.' Alas for his fond hopes, there was to be no inquiry.

On 14 September, four months after the deputation had called on him, Thomas sent for Chatfield and informed him bluntly, 'I have decided not to grant Admiral North an inquiry'. The Admiral argued for an hour, but he got nowhere. Among the First Lord's arguments were that to reopen the case might lead to the reopening of others in other Services, which Chatfield refused to accept, and that North had lost the confidence of the Admiralty *before* 11 September. This was the first time the latter point had been admitted, and Chatfield found it strange that this had never been

[14] Admiral Onslow's letter to the author, 6 Dec. 1973. One of the Principals in the Military Branch at the Admiralty (1945–50), who had a great deal to do with North's 'complaints', writes in similar terms of the slightly earlier period: 'North's behaviour was very adversely contrasted by almost everybody at the Admiralty with that of such people as Wavell, Auchinleck and Ritchie, who had also had to leave their commands without a chance to vindicate themselves, because the success of the war effort depended on having people at the top who inspired confidence without question.' G. C. B. Dodd's letter to the author, 7 Oct. 1973. The references are to General Sir Archibald Wavell, C-in-C, Middle East, 1939–41, his successor, 1941–2, Sir Claude Auchinleck, and Lieutenant-General Sir Neil Ritchie, Commander, 8th Army, Libya, 1941.

communicated to North. Chatfield's main point was that a private inquiry would do no harm if it supported the Admiralty's belief that North had been relieved for good reason. '*If no inquiry is held as requested and advised by five senior officers, then Admiral North will be free to take personal action which may be bringing to public knowledge the whole facts of the case and will do the Navy much harm.*' Thomas confirmed his rejection of an inquiry in a letter to Chatfield the next day which made the point that the question of confidence in an officer was not appropriate for examination by a board of inquiry. 'Both in peace and war (and especially in war) the Admiralty must be free at their own judgement to relieve an officer whom they have come to regard as unfitted for his appointment.' He offered to see the five Admirals of the Fleet again. They decided it would be a waste of time, and instead had the last word in a joint letter of 14 October which emphasized two things: the main object in asking for an inquiry had been to avoid the harm to the Navy by the threatened discussion in Parliament and press; and the Admiralty letter of 15 October 1940 gave as the reason for North's relief that he had 'failed to take action'. This was a charge of neglect of duty, which gave the Admiral the 'customary right to defend himself, which has been denied him'.[15]

What had happened in the corridors of power between 16 May and 14 September? The amiable Thomas was not the sort who would on his own responsibility have rejected the advice of such an enormously experienced and distinguished body as the five Admirals of the Fleet. Nor was McGrigor likely to have spurned their recommendations. Intervention by the politicians was the decisive factor. On 24 June the First Lord minuted the Prime Minister, telling him that he was under pressure to hold an inquiry. Churchill thought (31 July) that such a precedent might open a great many doors and that, anyhow, Alexander of Hillsborough (A. V. Alexander had received a viscountcy in 1950) should be consulted. The Secretary consulted Alexander (4 August), whose views were expressed in a letter of 9 August which has already been referred to in other contexts. He came down strongly against an inquiry.

In War, the decision of the Executive must be obeyed loyally.

There should be the right of a Court Martial if requested by an officer who is *charged* with an *offence* or actual *dereliction of duty*.

[15] Monks, *That Day at Gibraltar*, pp. 132–5, quoting from the North MSS.

But where an incident or incidents build up into a feeling that a new Commander is required in a particular Station it is quite impossible to admit that a decision in such a case is subject either to Court Martial or Court of Inquiry procedure.[16]

Alexander's opinion overcame any hesitations that Thomas may have had. The First Lord minuted the Prime Minister (1 September) telling him of Alexander's views and saying that he would see the spokesman of the senior naval officers who had represented North's case to him and would explain that no inquiry would take place. Churchill minuted (5 September) that he was certain this was the correct decision.

And so 1953 ended, with Admiral North seemingly as far from clearing his name as he was 13 years earlier. And his health was now bad, as he had suffered a stroke (not directly attributable to the affair) and was thereafter a semi-invalid. He decided for the time being to hold his hand: 'a campaign of publicity would be unlikely to achieve much success when opposed by such all-powerful and ruthless forces.' But in 1954 a *cause ignorée* became a *cause célèbre* which rekindled North's hopes.

(2) The Affair Comes to a Boil

The publication of the first volume of Captain Roskill's official *The War at Sea* on 20 May 1954 marked the beginning of the last phase of the North Affair. Roskill, who had no axe to grind and whose account had in August 1953 been found by the Admiralty 'quite acceptable' to them, claimed that North's action in 1940 was a correct one and that his dismissal was unjust. Roskill's treatment of the episode was well publicized in the press and heartened the old Admiral. 'Through the pages of the book that deal with this operation there is a thread of events that show I was right. . . . I shall never rest till this slur on my loyalty and conduct is removed. Now is the time for the Admiralty to show some respect for my long service by giving me the opportunity of clearing my name.'[17] North was overwhelmed with letters and calls. Admiral James supported him with a strong letter in *The Times* (25 May) which declared that all North's friends rejoiced that the official history of the war at sea had 'publicly cleared [North] of any responsibility for the failure of the expedition. . . . Service Ministries quite

---

[16] Alexander MSS., AVAR 5/16/9(a).
[17] As reported in the *Sunday Dispatch*, 23 May.

properly feel an honourable obligation to protect the reputation of their predecessors, but in this case the commendable intention has gone too far because, so long as the official historians gave a dispassionate account, the whole unpleasant story was bound to become public sooner or later.' Viscount Templewood (the former Sir Samuel Hoare) contributed an article to the *Sunday Dispatch* (30 May) inveighing against the judgement of 1940, which, 'given hurriedly at a moment of great crisis, was unfair to a gallant admiral.'

On 23 May North informed the Press Association that Roskill's account exonerated him and that he was considering steps which might clear his name, including the possibility of having questions asked in Parliament. On 31 May his solicitors, Messrs. Charles Russell and Company, issued a 'brief statement of facts' to show how, despite the Admiral's persistent attempts to clear his name, he had 'at every stage been refused a hearing'. The statement revealed the deputation of the Admirals of the Fleet in May 1953. Inevitably, Parliament took notice of the affair.

The first Parliamentary discussion of the question took place in the House of Commons on 2 June when the First Lord engaged in lively exchanges with the Labour MPs R. R. Stokes and James Callaghan, the latter a onetime lower-deck sailor in the Royal Navy and Parliamentary and Financial Secretary to the Admiralty (1950–1). Stokes asked whether, in view of the statements in Roskill's history, the First Lord would now grant North a public inquiry or a court martial. The Admiral, replied Thomas, had been given the opportunity to explain his conduct, and the main facts were not in dispute. He had been relieved because he no longer had the confidence of the Admiralty, and no court martial or board of inquiry could then or now have affected that loss of confidence. The Opposition broke into shocked exclamations when Thomas stated that the 'primary object' of the five Admirals of the Fleet in seeking an inquiry was that 'this might avoid unwelcome publicity for the Navy and discussion in Parliament'. 'I told them,' said the First Lord, 'that I could not yield on the issue of lack of confidence in Admiral North and that I was prepared to face the publicity.' Further questioning led Thomas into a somewhat jumbled discussion of the signals North had received on 11 September (corrected by an Admiralty spokesman in the Commons on 16 June in reply to a question from Stokes) and their bearing on the passage of the French ships. The flurry ended with Stokes explosively castigating the First Lord's explanation of the signals as 'quite preposterous', and giving notice that he was 'coming back to this matter very often'.[18]

The refusal of an inquiry only caused North to reaffirm his determination to fight to clear his name through an inquiry or court martial. Press support encouraged him to persist. 'Justice Deferred' was the title of a leader in *The Times* on 3 June. 'It has long been common knowledge, in circles far wider than those of the service concerned, that an impressive weight of professional opinion supports Admiral North's complaint that he has been made a scapegoat. . . . Unless he is given an inquiry, the Admiralty—and the Government which control it—will be widely held guilty of one of those exhibitions of official obstinacy which are never in the public interest and which never, in the long run of history, succeed in keeping dark the truth.' The *Sunday Times* (6 June) took a similar line. 'The Admiralty would appear to be ill-advised in steadfastly refusing any impartial review of the case . . . The widespread suspicion that the Admiral was a scapegoat may be completely unjustified, but it is there, and its existence is not calculated to improve relations between the serving sailor and his superiors in Whitehall.'

On 6 June The *Observer* published an interview with North that caused a splash. It went over the events of 11 September from the perspective of the Admirals at Gibraltar and refuted the Prime Minister's statement in the House that the whole situation had been transformed in a most unfavourable manner by the arrival of the French ships which carried with them a number of the most bitter Vichy partisans. 'They had no one of that sort on board at all,' as he had learned through the French Admiralty. He believed that in deciding to blame him for the French passage of the Straits, the Admiralty were influenced by his post-Oran letter, which 'created a terrible disturbance at the Admiralty', and which he thought was the beginning of the mistrust of him held by 'a small number of

---

[18] Parliamentary Debates (Hansard), 5th ser., Commons, Vol. 528, cols. 1284-7. Callaghan had a good deal more to say through a pair of articles in the Labour newspaper the *Daily Herald* (14, 15 June). They were a tidy summary of North's case, while admitting a weakness in that case: 'How did he know it [the French force] was bound for African ports and not for German-controlled ports? If it was bound for the latter, then under the directive of July 12 to which he was working he should have been alert to take action.' (*And* to have *taken* action, the Admiralty would have added.) 'It is time the Admiralty made out its case against Admiral North in greater detail. Unless it does so, it will be regarded as having sat in judgment and convicted a man to whom it had given the impossible task of carrying out orders that were confusing—and maybe contradictory—and having him made a scapegoat when its plans failed.'

people at the Admiralty.' 'The passage of the French ships was a difficult thing to blame directly on me,' the Admiral continued, 'because the person in command of the ships at Gibraltar and the person they signalled to was Admiral Somerville. He was in command of Force H. They simply settled on me because they remembered I had been a nuisance before for having objected to their action at Oran and for saying that I thought it was a mistake.' Over the incident at Gibraltar, he had been made 'a scapegoat for the Admiralty'. It is not difficult to see why the interview caused the Prime Minister 'such annoyance' (in the First Lord's words) and raised the First Lord's hackles. It practically guaranteed that the Admiralty would attempt to 'tough it out'.

The five Admirals of the Fleet kept the pot in a boil by publishing in the press on 8 June the memorandum they had submitted to the First Lord a year before. The decision to publish was provoked by the First Lord's statement about the purpose of their visit. Thomas was annoyed. 'The five Admirals seem infuriated with my reply about them in the House of Commons, though my answer was practically word for word based on what Chatfield told me in their second memorandum [above, p. 237], which they did not publish.'

The next scene in the developing scenario took place in the House of Lords on 15 June. Viscount Elibank, a Liberal peer who had been in close touch with North and had adopted his cause, asked the Government if, in the light of the findings in the Official History, they would state the reasons why North was relieved of his command, why his request for an inquiry or court martial was refused, and whether they would now afford him 'an opportunity of publicly clearing his name of an unjust stigma before a tribunal appointed by the Admiralty'. The Lord President of the Council, the Marquess of Salisbury, rose to defend the Admiralty and the Government. (It was the First Lord's hope that 'Bobbety Salisbury may be able to settle things finally in the Lords'.) He asserted that North 'was not relieved on the grounds that he allowed the French ships to pass through the Straits, nor is there any question of him having been made a scapegoat for Dakar. He was relieved because the Admiralty had lost confidence in him. . . . [Confidence] had already been shaken at an earlier date.' North's request for a court martial or a board of inquiry was refused because, whatever its report, it would not have affected the loss of confidence, and that remained true. Elibank asked whether it was not 'astounding—indeed incredible' that anybody who had read Roskill's account and the memorandum of the Admirals of the Fleet could still believe that North was not 'as a matter of fair play and justice entitled to a court of inquiry in public'. To which Salisbury retorted that the Official Historian's conclusions were his own 'and must not be regarded as Holy Writ'. The debate degenerated at times into sharp exchanges between Elibank and Salisbury. Elibank was supported by the Conservative Lords Ailwyn and Cork and Orrery, and the Labour peer Winster. Only Alexander supported Salisbury. 'There should,' he said, 'not be a new precedent established regarding a change of officer in those circumstances; and if an inquiry of this sort were now to be granted I do not know how many more requests of a similar kind the Government might receive.' He warned against the danger in another war of 'creating a precedent in this case which would be exceedingly dangerous'.[19]

Salisbury had not 'settled things finally in the Lords'. The agitation was only beginning. *The Times* (18 June) in another blistering leader claimed that 'nothing said in either House of Parliament by the official apologists . . . has checked the increasingly anxious suspicion of laymen that an individual has been unfairly treated. . . . the defence put up against an inquiry does not hold water.'

On 23 June in the Commons the indefatigable Stokes tried to justify North's assumption that the Admiralty knew what was happening, and since they had sent him no instructions, that he was justified in assuming his instructions of 12 July remained in effect. The First Lord in reply went to the heart of the Admiralty's case: 'Even if he assumed that the instructions remained as they were on 12th July, he still should have made his ships ready for action in case of an order by the Admiralty, in view of the fact that he did not know whether the ships were going to enemy-occupied ports or not.' He added: 'There is absolutely no slur in any way or any stain upon Admiral North's honour.' Stokes also made the point that it was hardly likely that the Admirals of the Fleet would have intervened 'unless they thought that Admiral North had a case of real standing'. Thomas repeated what he had said on 2 June about the main reason for the deputation. He was prepared to stand his ground. And it was strong ground. That the *main* object—not the *only* object—of the Admirals of the Fleet was indeed to avoid publicity rather than to plead North's case was plainly set out in

[19] Parliamentary Debates (Hansard), 5th ser., Lords, clxxxvii, cols. 1121–30.

both their published memorandum and Chatfield's letter of 14 October. Perhaps the most startling speech on 23 June was by Captain Ryder, a retired naval officer and a Conservative, who declared that North's removal had been a wise decision, and that officers in all Services supported the Admiralty in their decision not to hold an inquiry![20]

Stokes was back in action on 30 June. He was at his gadfly best, firing broadsides at the Admiralty over North's signals on the morning of 11 September. His thrust was that North was not inactive, that he and Somerville had been 'in continuous consultation ever since the morning of 9th September, and knew exactly what was going on, and knew what one another was doing.' The First Lord went over the case against North. His statement that North did not pass on the Madrid signal until 8 a.m., which was only a half-truth (see above, p. 213n.), brought the retort from Stokes: 'That is not true, it is a lie.' To shouts of 'withdraw', Stokes replied, amidst laughter: 'I withdraw that it is a lie, but it is completely untrue!'[21]

On a motion by Lord Winster, the circumstances under which North was ordered to haul down his flag and the reasons for the denial of an inquiry were aired in a dramatic 3½-hour debate in the Lords on 26 July. North's case was argued with eloquence by Winster, Elibank, Ailwyn, and Chorley (Labour); the Government's, by the Conservative peers Teynham (one of Somerville's Captains in Force H) and Salisbury, and the Labour peers Alexander of Hillsborough and Pakenham. Admiral of the Fleet Lord Fraser of North Cape (the Third Sea Lord and Controller in 1940), an Independent peer, spoke on *both* sides, making more sense than anybody. The debate, which had a number of acerbic exchanges,[22] went over much ground already covered, though in greater detail.

It was not disputed by either side that the Admiralty's loss of confidence in an officer was sufficient justification for relieving him of a post without a board of inquiry. These points were made by

[20] Ibid., Commons, Vol. 529, cols. 424–7.

[21] Ibid., cols. 1330–3.

[22] As when, in reference to Salisbury's remark about the Official History on 15 June, Winster commented: 'The noble Marquess has provided us with a new definition of history: history is history when the noble Marquess, Lord Salisbury, agrees with it; when he does not agree with it, it is merely an opinion.' Salisbury retorted: 'Is the noble Lord arguing that because a thing is in black and white, it is necessarily true or correct or accurate, or represents a true and balanced point [of view]?'

supporters of the motion: (1) Somerville, not North, was responsible for the operation of Force H, and directly to the Admiralty. The answer: whatever ambiguity existed at the time about the position of Force H, it had always been clear that the Senior Naval Officer on the spot, North in this case, had always had the duty to take charge of all forces available to deal with any emergency. (2) The instructions of 12 July were not clear. The answer: North obviously did not think so at the time, since he asked for no clarification. (3) North had no obligations to take steps to prepare any ships unless he received definite instructions from the Admiralty. The answer: though North had received the Madrid message soon after midnight, and had no reason to suppose that instructions would not arrive, he took no initiative. 'Sir Dudley Pound took the view that any officer who waited for instructions before taking action was not worthy to occupy the important position of Flag Officer, Gibraltar, in the times which then existed' (Salisbury). (4) An inquiry would not be a departure from precedent. It was the established practice in the eighteenth century to allow naval officers charged with offences connected with their duties to vindicate themselves before a court martial. As recently as 1914 Troubridge was summoned home for a court martial on the escape of the *Goeben*. The answer, presented by Alexander, was one he had used previously, 'that if we had made a precedent of that nature in the case of Admiral North, many other officers might have demanded inquiries about other charges in other Services'. Salisbury referred to the age-old rule, supported by Parliament, that the Admiralty had the right to take such action as they thought proper, without inquiry. Besides, what value could an inquiry have in the absence of 'vital witnesses' (Pound, Phillips, and Somerville), and what would be its *raison d'être*? 'It is not for the present Board of Admiralty either to justify or to condemn the views on confidence held by their predecessors fourteen years ago.'

This interesting and at times moving debate of course settled nothing. The Government would not agree to an inquiry or court martial, and the motion was withdrawn. North's supporters had accomplished this much, however, said Winster: 'that at long last, after fourteen years, Admiral North has had his case publicly stated in detail. It is now for the public and all concerned to make up their minds whether or not they think the case that an injustice has been committed and an inquiry should be held is made out.'[23]

[23] Parliamentary Debates (Hansard), 5th ser., Lords, clxxxix, cols. 50–119.

The impression given by North's supporters in the debates was that most naval officers were outraged by the treatment that had been accorded to North in 1940 and subsequently. We have no poll, scientific or otherwise, to guide us to the truth, but we do know that the Service was *not* of one mind on the question. Many naval officers had little sympathy with North, accepted the Admiralty case, and were bored with the whole business. One such was the first wartime DNI, Admiral J. H. Godfrey, who comforted the First Lord in two letters after the debates had ended. 'I have,' he wrote, 'always felt that the North agitation is a great pity, and that the very distinguished officers who exacerbated it were doing him and the service an injury. I have read the House of Lords debate in Hansard and think Salisbury put the case very well. . . . What a lot of harm it has done, especially to North, but let's hope it has now blown over.'[24] It was generally recognized by the supporters of the Admiralty that a measure of injustice had been done to the Admiral, but he was regarded as an officer of average ability, and some officers felt that he should have accepted the fact that in the heat of war injustices are bound to be done to individuals, and that no very useful purpose was served in dragging them up and possibly washing dirty navy linen in public.

Nor was public opinion as wrought up over the affair as one or two speakers in the Lords debate of 26 July seemed to think. Alexander said he had had no letters on the subject. Press interest steadily waned after the first days of June, with scant attention paid to the debates in both the news and leader sections. There appeared to be no danger, despite the fears expressed by Lord Ailwyn on 26 July, that the North case might degenerate into a *cause célèbre* like the Dreyfus case. Ludovic Kennedy got it right when he noted in the middle of July: 'The emotionalism surrounding this *cause célèbre* has now somewhat died out,' only I would delete 'somewhat'.

North himself was disappointed in the Lords debate of 26 July, and particularly in the 'somewhat strange statements made by [Alexander] . . . that it was this letter of mine which I had apologised for, and which I had entirely forgotten, which remained against me for all the time that I served at Gibraltar.'[25] The declining interest of the press doubtless was another discouraging factor. North turned down literary agents and publishers after the Parliamentary

[24] Godfrey to Thomas, 2 Aug., Godfrey MSS.
[25] An undated memorandum, 'Admiral Sir Dudley North', in the North MSS. (NRTH 1/9), obviously written soon after the debates.

debates; they wanted him to write his story. The Admiral was not interested. As he told Noel Monks, 'Seventy-three is not the best age for a man to take up writing.' And so the year 1954 ended with the impasse unbroken and North's spirits at a new low.

(3) Vindication—of a Sort

Churchill's leaving office in April 1955—Sir Anthony Eden succeeded him—and Admiral of the Fleet (as he was to become in 1956) Earl Mountbatten of Burma's relief of McGrigor as First Sea Lord at the same time aroused North's hopes, even if Thomas was still First Lord. He had for some time pinned his hopes on Mountbatten getting to the top and championing his cause from a position of strength.

Mountbatten had first met North when he was a young naval cadet in 1913 on board HMS *New Zealand*. They were shipmates in the *Renown* on the Prince of Wales's tours to Australia and New Zealand in 1920 and to India and the Far East in 1921–2. They got to know each other 'extremely well', Lord Mountbatten has written, 'so much so that we had always regarded each other as personal friends.' Mountbatten had from the beginning felt that North's removal was no mere wartime 'sacking' after 'loss of confidence', but that he had been made a scapegoat for the failure of Dakar. The two Admirals corresponded from time to time and saw each other on occasion. Though fully sympathetic with the old Admiral—more than once he referred in their correspondence to the 'grave injustice' that had been done him—Mountbatten's advice to him had been not to press for an inquiry, as he did not think this would be in his, or the Navy's, best interests. In short, he ought to let sleeping dogs lie. North saw things differently, and now, in 1955, Mountbatten's elevation gave him reason for hope. He sent a timid feeler to the First Sea Lord on 12 June 1955 in the guise of a congratulatory message on his GCB. He wondered if Churchill's departure would not enable the petition of the Admirals of the Fleet to be taken notice of.

Mountbatten was in a quandary. His feelings of that time are summarized in this statement of 1957:

In the interests of the Service I would in the early days have liked to have seen an enquiry; but I have felt more and more as the years passed that an enquiry would only stir up mud all round and damage the best interests of the Service.

Moreover, two years ago I discovered for the first time that the then First Sea Lord, Admiral of the Fleet Sir Dudley Pound, had expressed lack of confidence in Admiral North on more than one occasion in the few months previous to this incident; and it became clear to me that he had sacked Admiral North as an ordinary 'loss of confidence' matter, so common in war.

He sought the advice of the Secretary, Lang, as to how he should reply to North's letter. 'I thought this was all settled and that he had been turned down firmly both by the Admiralty and in the House. [There had been no votes taken in Parliament.] . . . I should like to be kind to the old Admiral . . .' Mountbatten and Lang were in agreement on what needed to be said. The reply to North (16 June) read: 'From feelers I have put out, I do not think that Winston or no Winston makes any difference to your case; the Government are determined not to reopen it. I am sorry to be blunt about this, but I know that you would wish me to be honest rather than raise undue hopes.'[26] Monks termed this letter 'perhaps [North's] greatest disappointment in all the years he has been fighting for justice'.

The fact is that, with the very best intentions in the world, Mountbatten could not have moved in the face of the attitude of the Government—and of the Admiralty, where opinion had undergone no change since 1953–4. The VCNS in 1954–7 has written: 'There was a little sympathy for Admiral North, but not a great deal in the Admiralty either at the time of his dismissal or when the matter was reopened again in the 1950s.'[27]

The smouldering affair burst into flame for the last time with the publication late in April 1957 of Noel Monks's strongly partisan *That Day at Gibraltar*. The author, a journalist with the *Daily Mail*, had had access to the North papers and profited also from correspondence and interviews with the Admiral.[28] The book gave the

[26] Whether before or after consulting the Secretary, but apparently before writing to North, Mountbatten 'sounded out the First Lord, Jim Thomas, who said Winston was pathological on the subject and he was not prepared to go back to him unless new circumstances arose. In fact the previous "Government Decision" was upheld by the First Lord.' Mountbatten to Marshal of the Royal Air Force Sir John Slessor, 5 Dec. 1972, Slessor MSS.

[27] Admiral Sir William Davis's letter to the author, 14 Jan. 1974.

[28] The Admiralty were aware of the forthcoming publication early in the year, and that North had allowed the author to see all his correspondence. But they saw no object in trying to stop publication through an injunctive action. It would only be 'a wonderful advertisement for the book'. Both the First Sea Lord and the Secretary of the Admiralty expected it would be no more than a 'nine days' wonder', anyway.

impression of having been thrown together, and it was no more than a nine-days' wonder. But it did the job. The press began to stir, and voices were again raised for a hearing to remove the 'unjustified slur' on North's reputation.

The last act of the drama opened with two new principal characters. Harold Macmillan had succeeded Eden as Prime Minister in January 1957, at which time the Earl of Selkirk became First Lord. Mountbatten remained as First Sea Lord.

Monks's book triggered action in the House of Commons. On 6 May the Liberal Party leader, Grimond, tabled a motion calling for a Government inquiry into the circumstances of North's removal from his command. It was supported by the Liberal Whip, two Conservative Members, and two Labour Members, and attracted seven more signatories, Conservative and Labour, in the following days. Grimond queried the Government on 9 and 13 May: would they allow time to debate the all-party motion? *The Times* came out on the 13th with a plea for an inquiry. 'Until the facts are established, those who oppose inquiry will be accused of withholding disagreeable truth. Sooner or later history will establish the facts.'

The Admiralty (through the First Sea Lord) recommended to the Prime Minister that he refuse an inquiry into the events of 1940. It could serve no useful purpose, especially since there was no dispute on the essential fact. North was relieved because he no longer held the confidence of the Admiralty. In time of war there could be no disputing the relief of an officer without question, or, if necessary, without giving a reason. A covering letter noted: 'On the other hand, because of North's age and infirmity, the First Lord would have no objection to letting him down as lightly as possible, provided that this would not involve giving way on the Government statements made in 1954.' On 14 May the Prime Minister announced in the Commons that he needed more time to read with care the huge dossier of relevant papers, and he promised to make a statement the following week.

Macmillan was to make his statement on 23 May. In the interval the First Sea Lord had two changes of heart. He was 'considerably shaken' when Admiral of the Fleet Lord Cunningham, whom he had met at Greenwich, told him that in his considered opinion an inquiry should be granted, if North insisted on it. Cunningham was, as Mountbatten viewed the matter, 'probably the most ruthless officer in the Service and would have been the last person I would normally have thought of for wishing to have an inquiry into a routine sacking.' The fact that the onetime C-in-C, Mediterranean, and First Sea Lord, with all his contemporary knowledge, thought a case could be made out of unfair treatment of North caused Mountbatten to waver. But in the end he recommended to the First Lord against an inquiry. The matter, he believed, had been dealt with so well by Salisbury, Alexander, and Fraser in the Lords on 26 July 1954 that there was nothing more to be said.

But Lord Mountbatten has told me he had 'always been pretty miserable about this case', and that he continued to explore ways to achieve an honourable settlement of the affair. He and the First Lord spent about ten hours reading every word that they could find on the subject: the relevant pages in Hansard, all the files and correspondence, all the signals, and the logs of the *Renown*. They then went to the Prime Minister and gave him all these materials; he spent a whole weekend reading up the case.

> Bit by bit [Lord Mountbatten says] we three established to our own satisfaction beyond all doubt what had actually occurred. None of us felt that an enquiry would bring any new facts to light. We were then left with a question of principle, of how the Board of Admiralty of the day dealt with the matter. It had all happened seventeen years ago when I was a young Captain and the remainder of the present Board were mostly two and a half or three stripers! And so I hit on the idea of asking the Prime Minister to call in the five Admirals of the Fleet who were contemporaries of North and who had raised his case with the First Lord previously. The First Lord supported this idea and to my great joy the Prime Minister accepted it.

What Mountbatten apparently hoped for was that the Admirals of the Fleet would assist the Prime Minister in working out an acceptable statement—acceptable to them, to the Service, and to North.

The conference took place in the Cabinet Room at No. 10 on 21 May. Present were Macmillan, Selkirk, Mountbatten, and four of the Admirals of the Fleet. Chatfield, who was on the sick list, sent a letter to the Prime Minister stating his views. It is one of the most cogent documents in the whole sorry affair, making the crucial point that the 1940 Board had gone wrong in making a written accusation and not giving North the opportunity to defend himself. The letter reads in part:

> North could have been relieved at any moment, if the Admiralty

thought they had a *better Admiral* for the Gibraltar Command; quite apart from the 'Cruiser' occurrence. That was within the Admiralty right. But in using that right, the Board must *not make a charge* against the Admiral of a serious nature. . . . By making a charge, they gave the Admiral the historic right, not only of an Admiral, but of any British Sailor, to defend himself against it. . . .

The fact, as the First Sea Lord knew, that the incident for which North was dismissed from his Command occurred from 75 per cent Admiralty and Whitehall default, should have made the First Lord (Alexander) doubly or trebly careful to do no injustice. In particular, the Admiralty should have taken publicly their 'share of the "muddle".' They threw all the blame on North and failed to disclose the Admiralty's blame. . . .

Instead of acting as they did, it would have been wiser to inform North they had decided to relieve him by Admiral X in say three months. North could have been given another post of less importance. No charge ought to have been made against him.

It was not the removal from his Command, but the words of disgrace attached to the dismissal which North resented, and, I think, had the right to resent.

The letter, which Macmillan read out, was the basis on which he discussed the situation with the Admirals of the Fleet. They expressed their agreement with Chatfield's views. The Prime Minister explained the difficulties of holding an inquiry: Pound was dead, the memories of the other principals would be uncertain, the morale of the Navy would be weakened by the recriminations which an inquiry would involve, and an inquiry could add nothing to the facts. In these circumstances he thought that the affair could be disposed of with justice to all concerned, and with proper regard to the morale of the Navy, if he stated in the Commons that North could not be accused of any specific misconduct, but that the Board of Admiralty had been entirely justified in replacing him, if they believed that he was less qualified than other officers for that appointment. Macmillan then read out the draft of his proposed statement.

The Admirals of the Fleet were in accord that an inquiry could serve no useful purpose and would do harm, and that the Prime Minister's statement would remove all North's sense of grievance and dispose of the matter with complete justice to all concerned. There was, however, one discordant note. 'Ginger' Cork and Orrery was very outspoken: 'Prime Minister, this won't do. You're letting the Admiralty off. The Admiralty behaved disgracefully. We want the world to know how the First Sea Lord and the Board of Admiralty behaved at the time.' Macmillan would not accept the idea of a public rebuke of the Admiralty. A compromise was reached: the Prime Minister would insert words into his statement making it clear that in the stress of the situation the signals from the Admiralty were not as clear as they should have been. The Admirals of the Fleet who were present authorized the Prime Minister to say that they agreed with his statement, and they would themselves write to Admiral North and assure him that his professional honour was now completely vindicated. In the event, the Prime Minister merely thanked them in the Commons for their assistance. It had been a long, frank, and full discussion, and it broke the impasse.[29]

Macmillan had been staggered to find that the Admirals of the Fleet believed that Churchill had behaved disgracefully. He had to decide how to handle the matter without blaming Churchill, who was, of course, alive at the time. The problem was how to find a formula which would take the blame from North without shoving it on to Churchill or the Admiralty. This was not easy, but it was the sort of thing that Macmillan enormously enjoyed doing. No one else at the time could have handled the whole sticky affair in such a statesmanlike manner.

The Prime Minister's neatly balanced speech in the Commons on 23 May attempted to put the affair 'in its proper perspective' (as he told Alexander the next day). The more substantive sections follow:

> In the circumstances of that period, the authorities concerned formed the view that they needed a different naval commander at Gibraltar. I must insist upon the constitutional rights of the Admiralty ... to choose officers in whom they have confidence at moments of supreme crisis. Any other system would be dangerous in peace and fatal in war.
>
> A careful examination of the records has led me to the conclusion that, so far as concerned the passing of the French ships through the Straits of Gibraltar, Admiral North cannot be accused of any dereliction of duty. He obeyed his orders as he interpreted them and some blame must rest on the fact that they were not drawn with complete clarity. [A classic understatement!] Nevertheless, in those dangerous days the Admiralty felt that they required at Gibraltar an officer who would not content himself with strict adherence to his orders, but who would be likely to show a greater degree of resource and initiative in an emergency. ...
>
> In my view, a general distinction must be drawn between two things. On the one hand are definite charges of negligence and the like or reflecting

[29] The details of the meeting are in Mountbatten to Slessor, 6 Nov. 1972 (Slessor MSS.), a Mountbatten interview with Mr. Richard Hough, 28 June 1973, and his correspondence with the author.

on an officer's honour. Any charge of this kind against Admiral Sir
Dudley North could not, in my view, be sustained . . . On the other hand,
the Board of Admiralty have the right and duty to decide on broad grounds
whether an officer possesses the qualities necessary for a particular
command. . . .

I am satisfied that Admiral North was not the victim of Service or
political prejudice. [And so was Churchill exonerated in a few deft
words.] He has nothing with which to reproach himself. He had forty-
four years long, distinguished, and devoted service in the Royal Navy,
and there is no question of his professional integrity being impugned.

In these circumstances, I do not see that anything is to be gained by an
inquiry regarding facts that are well documented and undisputed.[30]

'This is all pretty typical Macmillanese,' a distinguished officer
commented years afterwards, when studying the affair. 'He's more
concerned to whitewash WSC and the Admiralty than to do
justice to DN.' Perhaps so, but the Prime Minister was in the
exceedingly difficult position of giving as much satisfaction as he
could to all three parties without offending any one.

The Prime Minister's gracious *amende honorable* was well
received in the House, the Service, and the press. Four of the five
Admirals of the Fleet contacted by *The Times*, which was unaware
that they had helped to shape the statement, expressed satisfaction
with it: it vindicated North's honour, and there was no point now
in holding an inquiry. (Cork and Orrery could not be reached.)[31]

The press almost unanimously hailed the statement as an honourable ending of the affair: a wrong had been righted and justice at
last done to North and his name after 17 years. *The Times* (24 May)
made this shrewd assessment:

Qualifications introduced by Mr. Macmillan into his balanced judgment were, no doubt, inevitable. Face has to be saved wherever Very

[30] Parliamentary Debates (Hansard), 5th ser., Commons, Vol. 570, cols. 1401-4.
[31] *The Times*, 24 May. We know that Cork did not entirely agree with Macmillan's
statement, feeling that the Board of Admiralty of the time ought to have received a
rebuke. But he did not think this worth pursuing. A letter from Chatfield in *The Times*
of 25 May sang the Prime Minister's praises. 'All will hope that the last word has now
been said about the case of Admiral Sir Dudley North; but I feel the Royal Navy would
wish its gratitude to be expressed to the Prime Minister for the remarkable action he
took in solving it.' Admiral of the Fleet Willis sent a line of congratulations to Mountbatten (23 May) for 'moving the Board to deal with the North case in what I believe is
the most sensible manner. The tragedy is that TLs wouldn't do this, which we As of F
pressed them strongly to do in 1953 after we were refused an enquiry. . . . I consider the
PM has done a fine thing and so have you & Selkirk. God bless you.' Mountbatten's
inquiries of a dozen Admirals, retired and serving, showed that 'without exception' the
Navy was happy with the statement.

Important Persons are concerned and this consideration also explains why an inquiry was deemed imprudent. But, as the Admirals who are best qualified to pilot a course through the tricky waters of Service opinion have expressed themselves as well satisfied, it is reasonable to agree the matter has now been taken as far as it can be.

. . . he has cleared—and generously cleared—an officer of the worst accusations. All the greater is the pity that the matter should have had to wait so long and that no one before Mr. Macmillan was prepared to clear it up.

Only the *Daily Mirror* (25 May) among the London newspapers thought the statement a pretty lukewarm and inadequate one. '*The Mirror is NOT satisfied. There is nothing here to cheer about.*' In a reference to *The Times*' leader of the 24th, it asked, 'What is more important—justice or saving Very Important Faces?' Monks's book proved that North was 'entitled to a full inquiry. He has been fobbed off with a one-man inquiry conducted by Mr. Macmillan. *THIS IS NOT JUSTICE. IT IS JUSTICE WITH STRINGS.*'

Another dissenter, for quite different reasons, was Alexander, who was resentful of the reflection on his own, and Churchill's, administration. After Lord Selkirk's reading of Macmillan's statement in the Lords (23 May), he rose to take exception to certain phrases, which were 'somewhat weaker' than the case which was so adequately stated by Salisbury in July 1954. 'But I gather that it is felt that some little concession has to be made to Admiral North to set his mind at rest on things, and therefore these words have been included in the statement. . . . I think the decision taken at the time in regard to Admiral North was completely justified.'[32]

The sourest note of all—and the only comic relief in the whole affair—was struck abroad. The newspaper of the Soviet Navy saw 'Menace' and the North Affair as, not surprisingly, a capitalist and imperialist plot.

The English bourgeoisie decided to extract every possible advantage from the defeat of France. They cast envious eyes on the rich French colonies in Africa. . . . But haste was necessary. Across the ocean American businessmen were turning their greedy eyes [in this direction]. They also

[32] Parliamentary Debates (Hansard), 5th ser., Lords, cciii, col. 1178. Alexander let the Prime Minister know how he felt (27 May). 'I am glad you remained firm against the demand for an enquiry, but I do not, however, agree that, as the statement goes on to say, that he had "nothing with which to reproach himself". If that had been so he would not have been superseded. . . . As I feared, the Press regards the Government's change of attitude as a complete justification . . . and by implication that Pound, Winston and myself were wrong.' Alexander MSS., AVAR 5/17/14.

were not averse to taking part in a division of the colonial inheritance of their French brothers who had fallen on misfortune. Such schemes could not, however, suit the taste of the monopolists supporting Pétain, or the group of French bourgeoisie whose interests were voiced by General de Gaulle. . . . De Gaulle noticed without surprise how American and English monopolists were putting their feet inside the French colonial door. In these circumstances he decided to attempt to seize power in the important port of West Africa, Dakar, which was under the jurisdiction of Vichy.

Though 'disturbed by the fact that his plans had been found out', Churchill had agreed to an Anglo-Gaullist expedition. The North facet of 'Menace' was then described, drawing on Churchill's *Their Finest Hour*. ' "This chain of circumstances decided the fate of the Franco-British expedition to Dakar," writes Churchill. Such a wealth of "circumstances" . . . could hardly be accidental. They all testify to the fact that it was not in Churchill's plan to allow de Gaulle an opportunity to seize Dakar and settle down in the French colonies.' Monks's *That Day at Gibraltar*

clearly hinted that persons considerably higher in rank than the ill-used Admiral were responsible for the ease with which the Vichy ships passed through the Straits. A series of English military leaders demanded an investigation, wanting to prevent the blame for a conspiracy of the higher politicians from falling on the general staff. But English ruling circles showed no desire to reconsider their decision in the North Affair. They do not look favourably on the prospect of bringing to light the machinations of English diplomacy directed against the interests of France—Britain's partner in the intervention against Egypt [1956]. In their opinion, this could only hinder the strengthening of so-called 'Atlantic solidarity'. However, whatever tricks these circles resort to will not succeed in hiding the very ignoble role of the English imperialists, who had put a spoke in the wheel of their Ally [*sic*] in their most difficult period. The 'North Affair' is another indication of the real value of 'friendship' between imperialists, who always keep a stone up their sleeves to hurl at their competitors.[33]

North informed *The Times* on 23 May that he was prepared to let the matter rest, but he had some doubts the more he reflected on the statement.[34] On BBC-TV the next day this exchange took place:

[33] 'Behind the Scenes of the "Admiral North Affair",' *Sovietskii Flot*, 9 June 1957.
[34] He told the *Daily Mirror* the same evening: 'I am a very tired man. There is nothing that I can do. There is some satisfaction in hearing that I was not guilty of any dereliction of duty. But the fact remains that someone in the Admiralty said, "North must go. North must go". That person was not prepared to give a reason. He left it to the

BBC Interviewer: What is your reaction to the Prime Minister's statement?

Admiral North: Very satisfactory as far as the Prime Minister can be at present.

Interviewer: Do you think the Prime Minister has vindicated you?

Admiral North: As far as he can he has vindicated me in every way.

By early July North was not at all sure that he had been vindicated. Lord Mountbatten informs me that he wrote to North at the beginning of July to say how glad he was that his name had been vindicated at last and that he felt this was a satisfactory end to the affair. He was surprised to receive this reply from North on 5 July:

I certainly think that the Prime Minister went a long way in his statement to put things right, but not quite far enough, to clear my name entirely.

The Admirals of the Fleet certainly did very well, but whether you can call it a satisfactory end to the affair is rather another matter.

The whole country knows quite well now, that I was relieved for no reason at all, and that while one man remains alive, things must remain as they are. . . .

I am undecided at present as to what I am going to do.

The point is of course that the Admiralty had no justification for presuming me to be frightened of the French, and they were not entitled to relieve me suddenly from my post. . . .

The Admiral did nothing further. The end of his life was clouded and saddened by the very cruel end to his career. He died in May 1961, never really feeling that he had been vindicated. A man of great pride and loyalty, he just could not understand what had gone wrong in the Service he loved. 'Not understanding,' says Lord Mountbatten, 'he always felt he had been made the victim of circumstances.'

Prime Minister many years later to try to explain it.' To the *News Chronicle*: 'I am naturally disappointed that they are not going to hold an inquiry. I think they ought to have done something about it but we must leave it as it is.' And to the *Daily Express*: 'There is no doubt about it. I was thrown out of my job, and it ought to be put right.'

Chapter Twelve

Reflections

We will deny justice to none, nor delay it.

Magna Carta (1215)

Consider what you think justice requires, and decide accordingly.
But never give your reasons; for your judgement will probably be
right, but your reasons will certainly be wrong.

William Murray, Earl of Mansfield (1705–1793)

There is a point beyond which even justice becomes unjust.

Sophocles, *Electra* (*c*. 450 B.C.)

(1) Was Justice Done?

NOBODY should quarrel with the right of the Admiralty to
relieve anyone in high command, if they are not satisfied with
his performance and no longer have confidence in him. The
Admiralty had always claimed and exercised prerogative right (derived
no doubt from the Crown by the Lord High Admiral, whose
powers were assumed by the Board of Admiralty in the eighteenth
century) to remove officers from their command without inquiry,
trial, or reasons stated. Parliament had expressly preserved such
powers for all the Services. In any case, once an officer, *for whatever
reason*, has forfeited the confidence of his superiors, it is better for
him, as well as for the Service and the war effort, that he be moved
to some other appointment, if a suitable one is available. In contrast,
Somerville was not relieved because, despite the events of 11 September, he continued to enjoy the confidence of Pound and Alexander. *The mistake of the Admiralty was to couple the statement about
North's relief with a definite charge of dereliction of duty*. It was on
this ground that North was entitled to a court martial or a court of
inquiry, which is traditional in the Royal Navy.

Jo Grimond, the Liberal leader, uttered these words of common
sense in Parliament on 13 May 1957: 'As an ex-director of personnel myself, I believe that it is always wiser, when one wants
to get rid of someone, not to give reasons. Here, part of the trouble

was that the reasons were set out, and once one begins to set out reasons one opens oneself to counter arguments and disputes. I suggest that anyone who has to make awkward decisions of this kind should simply make them and, if possible, leave it at that.'[1] This may be cynical, yet it surely would have made good sense in October 1940.

Where the Admiralty made their second great mistake was in the *manner* of North's removal. Compared with the quiet fading out of many other Service commanders, it was unduly harsh. It would have been easy, confidence in North having been lost, to replace him quietly after a proper interval and without making him appear, as Service opinion and later public opinion generally regarded it, as a scapegoat. After all, North was a full Admiral, in a post equivalent to a Commander-in-Chief, and he had not been accused of anything that would have subjected his conduct on 11 September to a court of inquiry or a court martial.

Why had the wartime Admiralty refused every request of North's for an inquiry into the reasons why he was relieved from his command? The Deputy Secretary of the Admiralty, Sir J. Sidney Barnes, may have let the cat out of the bag at the time of North's request of 21 November 1940. 'After making enquiries, I am satisfied that it is a long established practice that when the Board have reached a decision and promulgated it, and, as in this case, have re-affirmed that decision after an appeal, they will not grant any further enquiry which would necessarily re-open the question, and might conceivably record a decision different from that already reached. To grant such an enquiry might obviously suggest that the Board had acted too hastily in the first place.' The First Sea Lord and First Lord found nothing objectionable in this minute, which smacks of *Realpolitik*.[2] I shall return to the alleged 'long established practice' in a moment. We must look elsewhere than the Deputy Secretary's minute for the underlying cause of the Admiralty's reluctance to grant North a hearing. The Admiral was not only the victim of a confused situation, but also of the high pressure under which the responsible naval authorities were working. There was no time to examine the rights and wrongs of what had taken place.

Well, then, what about the postwar period? Not even the five Admirals of the Fleet could get the Admiralty to admit that North was entitled to any sort of hearing. They wriggled and wriggled on the specious ground of lack of precedent, and, more plausibly, on

---

[1] Parliamentary Debates (Hansard), 5th ser., Commons, Vol. 570, col. 110.
[2] Minutes of 3 Dec., ADM 1/19180.

the grounds of the length of time since the incident had occurred and the fact that two of the principal officers concerned, Pound and Somerville, to say nothing of the VCNS, Phillips, were dead. One can easily dismiss all this as one of the five Admirals of the Fleet did: 'It is a curious thing but the Admiralty will never admit it can be wrong.' This is a simplistic answer. The Admiralty, to be sure, did not have a leg to stand on as regards precedent.

A board of inquiry is convened by the Admiralty when they need to be better informed of the facts and circumstances of an incident. For example, after Admiral Troubridge had failed to bring the *Goeben* and *Breslau* to action on 7 August 1914, he was ordered to return to England so that a court of inquiry could investigate his actions. It was held at Portsmouth on 22 September and reported on the following day in a sense unfavourable to Troubridge. Troubridge was tried by court martial on 5 November 1914 on a charge under Section 3 of the Naval Discipline Act and was honourably acquitted. Again, during an operation off Cape Spartivento on 27 November 1940, Admiral Somerville abandoned the chase of an Italian force when it appeared to him that a headlong pursuit might bring him near the enemy coast and endanger the Alexandria-bound convoy that he was escorting. A board of inquiry was set up at Gibraltar even before Force H had reached Gibraltar. Somerville's reasons for breaking off the action were accepted by the board as satisfactory. No further action was taken against him. In these cases the Admiralty needed the facts to be sifted and clarified. Neither Admiral asked for an inquiry, but the Admiralty were not reluctant to order one or, in the one instance, a court martial. One can go back to the eighteenth century for older precedents. Thus, Byng, when sent home, was granted a court martial.

Ah well, the Admiralty and Government spokesmen replied, the relevant facts in the North case were, unlike the Troubridge and Somerville cases, known, and it was only necessary to ask the Admiral for an explanation of his conduct. There was no need to set up a court of inquiry to clarify the facts: Admiral North had not taken action to prevent the French ships proceeding to enemy controlled ports, should they have turned to the northward after passing through the Straits of Gibraltar. The First Sea Lord decided, on the facts, to replace North. This he was entitled to do; but he was not required to arrange a board of inquiry or to bring North to trial by court martial, if this was contrary to the public interest in wartime. The facts were, then, as absolutely clear to the postwar Boards of Admiralty as they had been to the Alexander–Pound Board in 1940 and after. The difficulty here is that the facts were *not* clear, certainly not as they pertained to 'that day at Gibraltar'. In particular, the Admiralty instructions of 12 July were ambiguous. It was indeed this problem of clarity that lay at the bottom of all that had gone wrong on 11 September. An inquiry or court martial would have revealed the completely different premises under which the Admiralty and the Admirals at Gibraltar were operating at that time. More convincing are the arguments about the passage of time and the absence of key witnesses. An inquiry under these circumstances might well have been unjust to the 1940 Board, and especially to Pound.

Then there was the factor of morale in the Navy upon which postwar authorities dwelt, and properly so. An inquiry would have led to the slinging of much mud and to mutual recrimination, for we must bear in mind that the Royal Navy was far from being unanimously behind North. And there was the argument that there were other instances of officers being relieved who had not had their cause taken up. 'If an Admiral gets away with it,' declared an Admiralty statement in 1957, 'there are Generals who have at least as good a case to try on.' Finally, there was the fear that an inquiry might impair the executive right to relieve officers in whom confidence had been lost.

But should not the dispensation of justice to Admiral North, at whatever cost, have been the overriding concern of the Government and the Admiralty? Is not justice 'the crowning glory of the virtues', as Cicero tells us? Yes, *but* . . . Cicero in the same essay (*De Officiis*, 78 B.C.) says: 'The fundamentals of justice are that no one shall suffer wrong, and that the public good be served.' It was not possible in the North Affair to square the two parts of this maxim. The public good, it seems to me, would not have been served by an inquiry or court martial in the postwar years any more than it would in the wartime years, though for different reasons. Again, as the nineteenth century American philosopher and essayist Ralph Waldo Emerson tells us, 'One man's justice is another's unjustice', 'another' in this case meaning Dudley Pound, who could not have put forward his views after 1943. Nor must we forget that an inquiry or court martial, in whatever period, would not necessarily have vindicated Admiral North completely. North was *not* blameless, and the Admiralty *did* have a case. The more I wrestle with the whole problem, the more I am convinced that Macmillan's statement on 23

May 1957 was Solomon-like in its wisdom, restoring North's honour while at the same time not unduly denigrating the Admiralty.

What I am unable to condone, any more than could a great many officers of that time, was the 17-year delay. The Admiralty and the Government behaved very shabbily in delaying so long before making some amends to North. The Admiral may not have been the greatest brain in the Service, but that should not have affected considerations of fair play.[3] This brings us to the Churchill connection once more.

(2) Was North Made a Scapegoat?

In his interview with the First Lord in January 1941, North claimed that his relief was caused by the failure of the Dakar operation, and that had it been a success, he would have heard no more about the events of 11 September. Otherwise, how could one explain the delay of 16 days in the dispatch of the Admiralty signal of inquiry on 27 September (above, p. 198)? At other times North made much of Pound's friendly letter to him of 22 September, which contained no mention at all of the French ships. The implication was that Pound's loss of confidence in him came *after the failure at Dakar*. North offered the Prime Minister's statement of 8 October in the Commons (see above, p. 185) as further proof that, because the Admiralty had failed, it had been decided to blame the man on the spot.

Alexander's explanation of the first point was that the Naval Staff were very hard worked, which had precluded them from dealing with the North case more quickly. Or as Pound put it afterwards:

[3] Monks in several places in his book says that North's sacking deprived him of the probable opportunity of becoming First Sea Lord. This is nonsense. Although a competent officer, he had never held an operational command as a Flag Officer and would therefore not have been eligible for consideration to be appointed First Sea Lord. He was not First Sea Lord material and would never have gone to the top. Monks's statement was derived from a letter that Mountbatten had written to North on 26 February 1941, in which we find: 'I saw H.M. the King at the investiture yesterday. . . . I had the temerity to tell H.M. that everyone in the Service had always regarded you as a certainty for "First Lord and Principal", and the King seemed to be far from unsympathetic to this idea.' *That Day at Gibraltar*, p. 74. There is no such appointment, and the reference was undoubtedly meant to read: 'First and Principal', which was the Navy's way of referring to 'First and Principal [i.e. Senior] Naval Aide-de-Camp', a position in the King's household which might well have been held by an Admiral who had commanded the Royal yachts. Lord Mountbatten confirms that my interpretation is the correct one. He suggests that Monks did not understand and inserted the word 'Lord' on his own. Letter to the author, 18 Sept. 1974. I have been unable to trace the original of Mountbatten's letter. It is not in the North MSS., as one would expect, and Lord Mountbatten did not retain a copy. Indeed, only one of his letters to North is in the North MSS.

'It was perfectly obvious on the day that the French cruisers passed through the Straits that Admiral North had not carried out his instructions but while operation MENACE was in progress the Naval Staff were too fully occupied to deal with a question which was in no way urgent.'[4] I detect nothing implausible, false, or evasive in this explanation; it rings true.

North's second point had an even simpler explanation. Pound's letter was only a belated answer to one from North written in July and confined itself to the points raised in that letter.

As for the third point, the First Sea Lord answered it this way. The Prime Minister had stated on 8 October: 'By a series of accidents, and some errors which have been made the subject of disciplinary action or are now subject to formal inquiry, neither the First Sea Lord nor the Cabinet were informed of the approach of these ships to the Straits of Gibraltar until it was too late to stop them passing through...' 'There is,' commented Pound, 'nothing in the statement to give the impression that the failure to prevent these ships reaching Dakar was due to Admiral North having failed to take action. . . . It is his failure to carry out his instructions to prevent the ships going North, had they shown any signs of doing so, for which Admiral North was blamed, not for failing to prevent the ships reaching Dakar.'[5] That, combined with previous incidents, made Pound and Alexander unwilling to retain North in the Gibraltar command. Again I find no reason to question the *bona fides* of the First Sea Lord. Too much has been made of Churchill's remarks in the Commons: he was doing little more than giving public expression to his annoyance over the foul-up at Gibraltar. And as Alexander informed the Secretary of the Admiralty (9 August 1953), 'When, however, the French cruisers escaped, whilst the Prime Minister was justly incensed he was not alone, & my recollection is that Sir Dudley Pound & Tom Phillips thought on a purely naval basis of the handling of the situation.'[6]

[4] Pound, 'Points which Admiral North Has Made'. There is nothing in the Admiralty records to bridge the gap between 11 September 1940, when the Admiralty first knew what had happened, and 27 September. Declared an Admiralty memorandum of 1957: 'The conditions prevailing in London obviously affected the urgency with which the post-mortem was pursued. The Battle of Britain was at its height; daily meetings on anti-invasion preparations, at the highest levels; the preoccupation of the Naval Staff with Operation MENACE and current operations in the Mediterranean, not to mention the preliminaries in the exchange of Lend-Lease destroyers from the United States—and the day to day business of the war,—all took precedence.'

[5] 'Points which Admiral North Has Made.'

[6] Alexander MSS., AVAR 5/16/9(a).

Legend is always stronger than fact, and the scapegoat theory, which figured prominently in the Parliamentary debates of 1954, has never received the decent interment that it deserves. But, then, legends never do! North's supporters in the Service (and North himself) in 1940 and in all the years that followed had no doubt that North had been deliberately picked on as a scapegoat for the sins of Churchill and the Admiralty, and that the chief culprit was the former. Among the early proponents of this *idée fixe* were Admiral Sir Bertram Ramsay and Admiral of the Fleet Lord Cunningham. To the latter, 'It has always been the same with WC. The blame has never been his—he has always thrust [it] on to some wretched soldier or sailor.'[7] Lord Mountbatten never 'met any senior naval officers who doubted that Winston was responsible for making North the scapegoat for his ludicrous fiasco at Dakar (*Menace*), and these officers greatly resented Winston's unfair treatment of North which held him to blame. The fact that A. V. Alexander (as First Lord) and Dudley Pound (as First Sea Lord) were made to bear the brunt of this treatment only makes the case worse.'[8] So diverse a group as Slessor, Captain H. F. Layman (*Hotspur*), and James Callaghan, who have all studied the case, accept the scapegoat theory and the primary responsibility of Churchill. Slessor, for example, says that 'there is no doubt that . . . the less admirable side of his nature got the upper hand—he was adamant to find a scape-goat and was himself responsible for the glaring injustices to North.'[9]

Almost as pervasive is the companion theory that Churchill vetoed an inquiry in the fifties, when he was again Prime Minister. Thus, in the letter to Slessor quoted above, Lord Mountbatten says that 'it was most probably Winston's known views that caused the Admiralty to refuse the request of the five Admirals of the Fleet for an enquiry'. North was certain that the veto of an inquiry was Churchill's 'last act' before he left office in 1955. To Vice-Admiral Sir Aubrey Mansergh it was 'quite clear' that the 'unbelievable stubbornness' of the Admiralty in refusing to accede to this request 'must have arisen solely out of loyalty to Churchill'.[10]

[7] Letter to North, 22 Nov. 1940, North MSS., NRTH 2/3.
[8] Mountbatten to Marshal of the Royal Air Force Sir John Slessor, 5 Dec. 1972.
[9] Slessor, 'Operation "Menace": the Attack on Dakar'.
[10] Mansergh's letter to Captain Layman, 30 June 1961, Layman MSS. Mansergh also believed (as have many other officers) that 'Pound (and of course Alexander) was completely dominated in this affair by W.S.C. Great man though Winston was, he had the failings of his qualities, especially (as his books show) he always *had* to be right. He *couldn't* admit that he had misjudged the whole Dakar project and, when it miscarried . . . North had to go.' Ibid. Here and there were people, like Lord Altrincham, who

What are the facts, in so far as we know them? First, that, as pointed out above (pp. 224-5), it was *Pound*, not Churchill, who was responsible for the removal of North from his command. There was, so far as we know, no pressure from Churchill, who appears to have played no more than a supporting role. The situation is more complicated when we come to Churchill's second tenure at No. 10 Downing Street. He *was* consulted by the First Lord in 1953, and he *did* express the opinion that an inquiry would be undesirable. (See above, pp. 237-8.) But I would emphasize that the Board of Admiralty itself was opposed to an inquiry, so that the Prime Minister's views were hardly a decisive factor. They did no more than strengthen the Admiralty in their stubborn refusal to grant an inquiry. Sir John Lang, who, remember, was the Secretary of the Admiralty from January 1947 (-1961) and was 'privy to any policy matter, operational or otherwise, in which the Admiralty was concerned,' writes: 'Winston was Winston and was not likely to welcome any public development after the war which might show his war-time actions to be questionable. But I have no recollection at all of his either being consulted by the Admiralty or of his issuing a *diktat* to the First Lord [on the question of reopening the North case].'[11] Lang adds that Thomas 'would have stood up to Winston over something in which he was personally concerned but he was fundamentally not a strong personality and if Winston as the P.M. during the war had taken a line with Thomas about some war-time incident, Thomas would have found it difficult to oppose the war-time P.M. unless the Admty record available to him were compelling (though he might have suspected Winston's bona fides).' But, as I have suggested, there was no need for Churchill to take a line with the First Lord. Finally, there is the testimony of Sir Jock Colville, who was Churchill's Assistant Private Secretary in 1940-1 and Joint Principal Private Secretary in 1951-5; 'I don't really remember anything about Churchill's reactions to the Admiral North Affair, either in the War or subsequently. Had there been any violent reaction, or had the matter been brought very seriously to his notice, I should probably have remembered it; for when he had something much on his mind it was difficult not to be aware of the fact. No doubt he was kept informed, but I expect that there were

---

attributed Churchill's blocking of an inquiry to his 'blind and fanatical devotion' to Pound.

[11] Lang's letter to the author, 9 Dec. 1973. Churchill's minutes in 1953 apparently do not come under Lang's definition of 'consultation'.

still more urgent matters on which he had to concentrate.'[12] Having said this much, however, I happily concede that the last word on Churchill's role in 1953–4 must await the opening of the Churchill Papers at Churchill College and, *in toto*, the Cabinet and Admiralty records at the Public Record Office—under the Thirty-Year Rule, in 1984–5.

But I must add that it is a thousand pities that, when Prime Minister again, Churchill did not issue something similar to Macmillan's statement which closed the case in 1957. The postwar Admiralty would not make any mitigating statement for North. This could only have been done by the Prime Minister in Parliament. Even Churchill's critics admit that he was capable of being generous and kind, but he would not raise a finger to help North. I can empathise with Lord Chorley, who declared in the House of Lords on 26 July 1954: 'I feel it particularly disturbing that the Prime Minister, whose magnanimity is one of the finest personal traits in that great man's character, should have failed, on this occasion, to show that magnanimity.' Why? We can only speculate. Was it loyalty to Dudley Pound? Or was it, as Sir John Lang suggests, a distaste for showing up his wartime actions as 'questionable'? Or perhaps a personal dislike for an officer who continued to raise such a fuss, in contrast to General Auchinleck and other wartime commanders who had accepted their removal with quiet dignity? Since humans regularly act from a complex set of often contradictory motives, I would hazard the guess that all these factors, and possibly others, were involved in Churchill's attitude.

The North Affair does not compare in magnitude with the controversies that punctuated the 'Fisher Era' and just after, notably the Fisher-Beresford feud and the Jellicoe-Beatty controversy. Compared with these, the North Affair was, as Admiral Godfrey put it, 'mere chicken feed'. Yet in one vital respect the North case had much greater significance than its twentieth-century predecessors. It contains a valuable object lesson on the relations which should (or should not!) exist between the Government and the highest military authorities in Whitehall, and commanders on lower levels. And it brings out the extraordinary difficulties in attempting to define and to apply the concept of justice. But, then, Socrates and Plato made the point over 2,300 years ago in *The Republic*.

[12] Colville's letter to the author, 22 Oct. 1974.

Index

All officers and titled people are indexed under the highest rank and title attained. Ships are indexed under 'Warships, British' and 'Warships, French'.

cussions (1953), 239–40, 241–4; interview in *The Observer*, 240–1; degree of support in Service and country, 245; disappointed and discouraged, 245–6; hopes aroused by Mountbatten as First Sea Lord, 246; Monks's *That Day at Gibraltar* initiates last phase of Affair, 247–8; resolution of Affair, 248–52, reception in country, 252–3; North's reservations, 254–5; Admiralty mistakes, 256–7; why Admiralty had refused inquiry, 257–9; should not justice have been overriding concern?, 259–60; as possible Senior Naval Aide-de-Camp, 260 n.; Churchill's role in Affair, 262–4; Affair cf. other controversies, 264

Onslow, Adm. Sir Richard George (1904–): on de Gaulle, 32 n., 53, Thomas as First Lord, 233, McGrigor as First Sea Lord, 233, naval opinion on North Affair 235–6
Owen, Maj. Richard Percival (1920–): on briefing in *Devonshire en route* to Dakar, 101, weather conditions at Dakar, 106, comic-opera incident post-'Menace', 156–7

Paget, Lt. (RNVR) Reginald Thomas (1908–): 27; criticizes security leaks, 48
Pakenham, 1st Baron: *see* Longford
Peirse, Air Chief Marshal Sir Richard Edmund Charles (1892–1970): 35 n.
Pétain, Marshal Henri Philippe (1856–1951): 3, 79; sends message to Dakar's defenders, 135 n.; rivalry with Laval, 155; interested in closer relationship with Germany, 174; pressured by Roosevelt, George VI, 187
Phillips, Act. Adm. Sir Tom Spencer Vaughan (1888–1941): 19, 20 n., 35, 60 n.; opposes Churchill's policy towards Vichy, 179; and decision to relieve North, 220, passage of Force Y through Straits, 261
Playfair, Maj.-Gen. Ian Stanley Ord (1894–1972): 17 n.
Pleven, René (1901–): Gaullist 'missionary', 6
Poulter, Capt. John Gustave Leslie (1895–1952): 30, 168; reports Dakar French Army feelings, 41; cross-examined on Dakar's defences, etc., 43–5

Pound, Adm. of the Fleet Sir Alfred Dudley Pickman Rogers (1877–1943): 13 n., 28, 78, 185, 195, 207, 225 n., 228 n., 236, 262, 264; and Operation 'Scipio', 19; not enamoured of 'Menace', 56; finally sees NA Madrid signal, 73; learns of passage of Force Y, 76; orders *Renown* to raise steam for full speed, 76; on interception of Force Y, 78; favours going on with 'Menace', 87; on turning back of Force Y cruisers, 97; pessimistic *re* continuation of 'Menace', 147; and post-'Menace' strategy, 156 n.; appoints North to Gibraltar, 197; infuriated by North's post-Oran message, 196, 198; reactions to North's 6 Oct., 199–201, 202–3; and decision to relieve North, 203, 205, 220–1, 222, 223, 224–5, 258–9, 261, 262 n., 263; interviews North, 207–8; sweeps aside North's arguments, 217–219; A. V. Alexander's attitude towards him; 221–2; portrait, 224; confidence in Somerville, 256; and refusal of North inquiry, 257; friendly letter to North, 260; explains delay in dealing with North (Sept. 1940), 260–1; on Churchill's 8 Oct. statement to Parliament, 261; reaction to passage of Force Y through Straits, 261

Raeder, Adm. of the Fleet (Grossadm.) Erich (1876–1960): wants Dakar as U-boat base, 8, 191; supports French request for reinforcements to Africa, 173; urges importance of co-operating with France, 173–4
Raikes, Adm. Sir Robert Henry Taunton (1885–1953): and nurses in *Westernland*, 68 n., chase of French cruisers, 93
Ramsay, Adm. Sir Bertram Home (1883–1945): supports North, 227; on Churchill's role in Affair, 262
Richmond, Adm. Sir Herbert William (1871–1946): judgement on 'Menace', 158, North Affair, 209; supports North, 227, 229–30
Ritchie, Gen. Sir Neil Methuen (1897–): 236 n.
Roosevelt, Franklin Delano (1882–1945): and 'Menace', 148 n., 152, 174, 180, 181; protests treatment of Boisson, 149 n.; urges Pétain to resist German demands, 187

* Abbreviations: AC, aircraft carrier; B, battleship; BC, battle cruiser; CR, cruiser; SM, submarine; TBD, destroyer

Charts

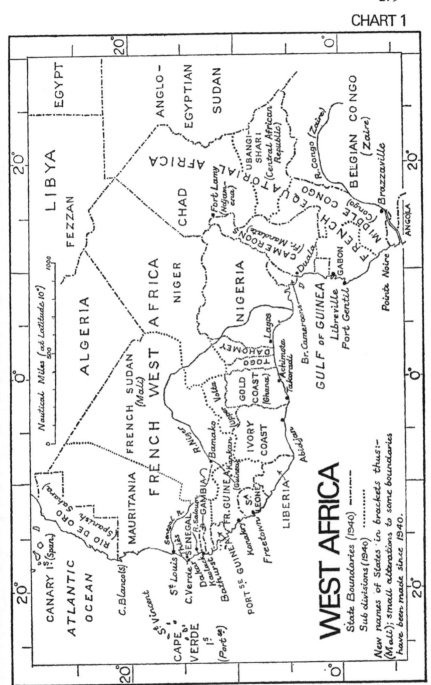

WEST AFRICA

State Boundaries (1940) ———
Sub divisions (1940) ··········

New names of States in brackets thus:-
(Mali); small alterations to some boundaries
have been made since 1940.

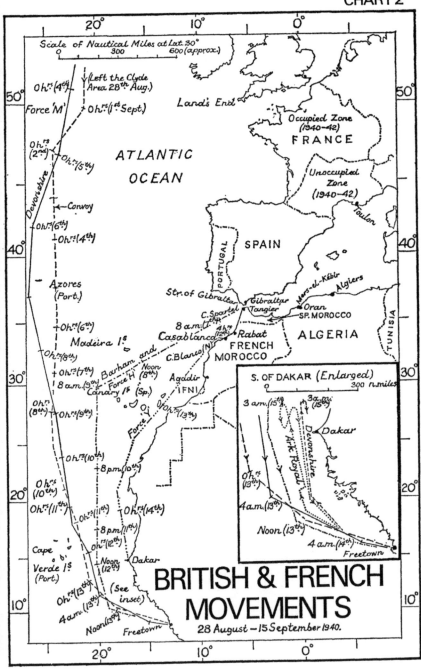

Scale of Nautical Miles at Lat. 30°
0   300   600 (approx.)

0h.ʳˢ (4ᵗʰ) Left the Clyde Area 28ᵗʰ Aug.)
Force 'M' 0h.ʳˢ (1ˢᵗ Sept.)

Land's End

Occupied Zone (1940-42)
FRANCE

ATLANTIC OCEAN

0h.ʳˢ (2ⁿᵈ) 0h.ʳˢ (5ᵗʰ)

Devonshire

Unoccupied Zone (1940-42)

Convoy

Toulon

0h.ʳˢ (6ᵗʰ)
0h.ʳˢ (4ᵗʰ)

SPAIN

PORTUGAL

Azores (Port.)

0h.ʳˢ (6ᵗʰ)

Str. of Gibraltar
C. Spartel
8 a.m.(1ˢᵗ) 4h.ʳˢ (12ᵗʰ)
Casablanca
C. Blanco (N)
FRENCH MOROCCO
Rabat

Gibraltar
Tangier
SP. MOROCCO
Mers-el-Kébir Algiers
Oran
ALGERIA
TUNISIA

0h.ʳˢ (8ᵗʰ)
0h.ʳˢ (7ᵗʰ)
8 a.m.(9ᵗʰ) Barham and Force H
Madeira Iˢ
Canary Iˢ (Sp.)
Noon (8ᵗʰ)
Agadir
IFNI
Force

0h.ʳˢ (13ᵗʰ)

S. OF DAKAR (Enlarged)
0   300 n.miles

3 a.m.(15ᵗʰ) 3 a.m.(15ᵗʰ)
Dakar
Devonshire
Ark Royal

0h.ʳˢ (13ᵗʰ)

4 a.m.(13ᵗʰ)
Noon (13ᵗʰ)
4 a.m.(14ᵗʰ)
Freetown

0h.ʳˢ (8ᵗʰ) 0h.ʳˢ (9ᵗʰ)

0h.ʳˢ (10ᵗʰ)
8 p.m.(10ᵗʰ)

0h.ʳˢ (10ᵗʰ)
0h.ʳˢ (11ᵗʰ)
0h.ʳˢ (11ᵗʰ) 0h.ʳˢ (14ᵗʰ)
8 p.m.(11ᵗʰ)
0h.ʳˢ (12ᵗʰ)

Cape Verde Iˢ (Port.)
Noon (12ᵗʰ)
Dakar
(See inset)

0h.ʳˢ (13ᵗʰ)
4 a.m.(13ᵗʰ)
Noon (13ᵗʰ) Freetown

BRITISH & FRENCH MOVEMENTS
28 August – 15 September 1940.

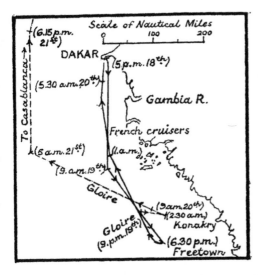

CHART 3

THE
CHASE

19 – 20 September
1940

CHART 4

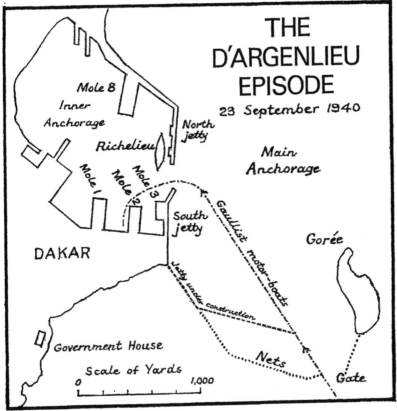

THE
D'ARGENLIEU
EPISODE

23 September 1940

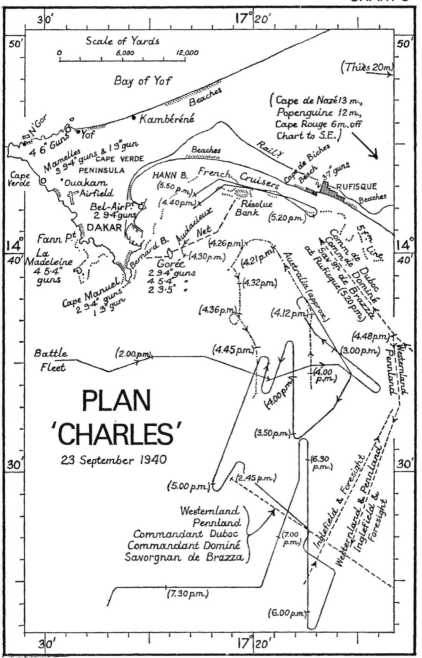

PLAN
'CHARLES'

23 September 1940

Westernland
Pennland
Commandant Duboc
Commandant Dominé
Savorgnan de Brazza

Bay of Yof

(Thiès 20m)

(Cape de Nazé 13 m.,
Popenguine 12 m.,
Cape Rouge 6 m. off
Chart to S.E.)

N'Gor
4 6" Guns
Yof
Kambéréné
Beaches

Mamelles
3 9·4" guns & 13"gun CAPE VERDE
PENINSULA
Ouakam
Airfield
Bel-Air Pt
2 9·4 guns
DAKAR

Cape
Verde

Fann Pt
La Madeleine
4 5·4" guns

Cape Manuel
2 9·4" guns
1 3" gun

HANN B.
(5·50 p.m.)
(4·40 p.m.)

Bernard B.
Audacieux

Gorée
2 9·4 guns
4 5·4" "
2 3·5" "

French Cruisers

Rail'y

Cape de Biches
Beach
2 3·7" guns
RUFISQUE
Beaches

Résolue
Bank
(5·20 p.m.)

Net
(4·26 p.m.)
(4·30 p.m.)
(4·21 p.m.)
(4·32 p.m.)
(4·36 p.m.)
(4·12 p.m.)

5·fin Line
Comm dt Dubos
Comm dt Dominé
at Sav gn de Brazza
at Rufisque (5·20 p.m.)

Australia (approx.)

(4·48 p.m.)
(3·00 p.m.)
(4·00 p.m.)
(4·00 p.m.)
(3·50 p.m.)
(6·30 p.m.)
(2·45 p.m.)
(7·00 p.m.)

Westernland
Pennland

Inglefield & Foresight

Westernland & Pennland
Inglefield &
Foresight

Battle
Fleet
(2·00 p.m.)
(4·45 p.m.)

(5·00 p.m.)

(7·30 p.m.)

(6·00 p.m.)

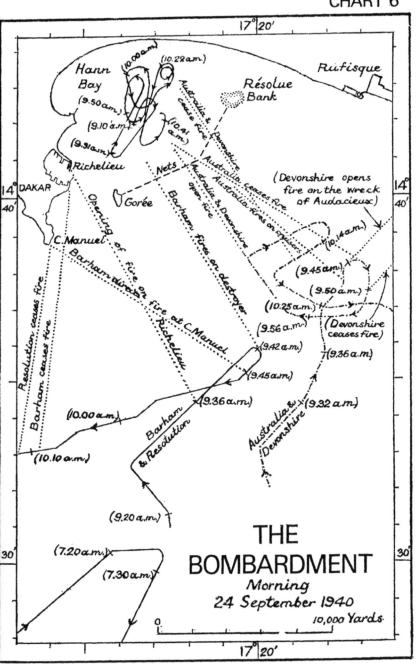

THE
BOMBARDMENT
Morning
24 September 1940
10,000 Yards

CHART 7

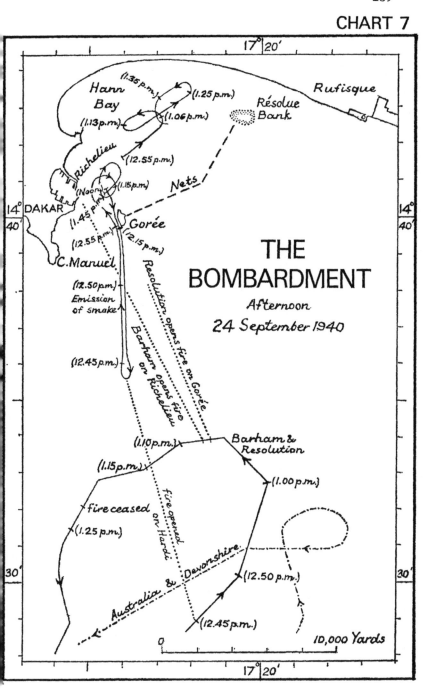

Rufisque

Hann Bay

(1.35 p.m.)
(1.25 p.m.)
(1.13 p.m.)
(1.06 p.m.)

Résolue Bank

Richelieu

(12.55 p.m.)

Nets

(Noon)
(1.15 p.m.)

14° DAKAR
40'

(1.45 p.m.)

Gorée

(12.55 p.m.)
(12.15 p.m.)

C. Manuel

14°
40'

THE
BOMBARDMENT

Afternoon
24 September 1940

(12.50 p.m.)
Emission
of smoke

Resolution opens fire on Gorée

Barham opens fire on Richelieu

(12.45 p.m.)

(1.10 p.m.)

Barham &
Resolution

(1.15 p.m.)

(1.00 p.m.)

fire ceased

fire opened on Hardi

(1.25 p.m.)

(12.50 p.m.)

30'

Australia & Devonshire

30'

(12.45 p.m.)

0

10,000 Yards

17° 20'

17° 20'